"…an intellectually ambitious attempt to synthesize Marxism, feminism, and post-colonialism, and not with the usual sellotaped hyphenations."
—Jenny Turner, *London Review of Books*

"It's time to acknowledge James's path-breaking analysis: from 1972 she reinterpreted the capitalist economy to show that it rests on the usually invisible unwaged caring work of women."
—Peggy Antrobus, feminist, author of *The Global Women's Movement: Origins, Issues and Strategies*

"For clarity and commitment to Haiti's revolutionary legacy…Selma is a sister after my own heart."
—Danny Glover, actor and activist

"The publication of these essays reflects in concentrated form the history of the new society struggling to be born. Their appearance today could not be timelier. As the fruit of the collective experience of the last half-century, they will help to acquaint a whole new generation with not only what it means to think theoretically but, more importantly, the requirement of organization as the means of testing those ideas. In this respect, Selma James embodies in these essays the spirit of the revolutionary tradition at its most relevant."
—Dr. Robert A. Hill, literary executor of the estate of CLR James, University of California, Los Angeles, and director of the Marcus Garvey Papers Project

"In this incisive and necessary collection of essays and talks spanning over five decades, Selma James reminds us that liberation cannot be handed down from above. This is a feminism that truly matters."
—Dr. Alissa Trotz, associate professor of women and gender studies, director of Caribbean studies, University of Toronto

"With her latest book, Selma James reaffirms what has been evident for some time: she is—quite simply—not only one of the most outstanding feminist thinkers of her generation but, as well, an insightful and exceedingly intelligent political analyst."
—Gerald Horne, historian and author, John J⸝ ⸝ ⸝⸝⸝⸝ Moores Chair of History and African American Studies at

T0125931

Common Notions is an imprint that circulates both enduring and timely formulations of autonomy at the heart of movements beyond capitalism. The series traces a constellation of historical, critical, and visionary meditations on the organization of both domination and its refusal. Inspired by various traditions of autonomism in the U.S. and internationally, Common Notions aims to provide tools of militant research in our collective reading of struggles past, present, and to come.

SEX, RACE, AND CLASS

THE PERSPECTIVE OF WINNING

A SELECTION OF WRITINGS, 1952–2011

Selma James

Sex, Race, and Class—The Perspective of Winning: A Selection of Writings, 1952–2011

© Selma James

This edition © PM Press 2012

ISBN: 978-1-60486-454-0
Library of Congress Control Number: 2011927963

Cover by Josh MacPhee (justseeds.org)
Layout by Jonathan Rowland

10 9 8 7 6 5 4 3

PM Press
PO Box 23912
Oakland, CA 94623
www.pmpress.org

Printed on recycled paper by the Employee Owners of Thomson-Shore in Dexter, Michigan.
www.thomsonshore.com

CONTENTS

A GRATEFUL PREFACE

MARCUS REDIKER

Selma James is a treasure, as this volume of riches makes clear. For more than half a century she has played a significant role in a wide variety of radical organizations and movements, many of which are not nearly well enough known. From the Johnson-Forest Tendency and the Facing Reality group of the 1950s, to the Race Today Collective in Brixton, to Global Women's Strike, James has animated and embodied a kind of radicalism that is increasingly relevant in today's world.

Her close association with the great Trinidadian scholar-activist CLR James provides a key to her political approach. One of the main ideas embodied in James's writings is what the late George Rawick, another close comrade of CLR James, called "working-class self-activity": those many and various and often invisible things the working class, broadly defined, does for itself in the quest for emancipation. The emphasis is on action, agency, new meanings and possibilities generated, often unpredictably, from social movement and conflict on the ground. CLR James always emphasized the importance of new forms of struggle that bubble up constantly from below, often alongside and sometimes against established left-wing institutions such as unions and political parties.[1]

If the promise of Tom Paine's *The Rights of Man* (1791) was expanded by Mary Wollstonecraft's *A Vindication of the Rights of Women* (1792) and by the lesser-known

---

1   George Rawick, "Working Class Self-Activity," *Radical America* 3, no. 2 (1969): 23–31. See also David Roediger, ed., *Listening to Revolt: The Selected Writings of George Rawick* (Chicago: Charles H. Kerr Publishing Co., 2010).

but hugely important work of Thomas Spence, *The Rights of Infants* (1796), James has continued in this direction, asking how it came to be that "Women do two-thirds of the world's work, receive 5 percent of world income, and own less than 1 percent of world assets"—and asking, impatiently, how can this sordid reality be changed. She was doing pioneering theoretical and historical analysis of "race-class-gender," with an emphasis on how each constitutes the other, long before this became a popular analytical approach during the 1980s.

James's political theory and her organizing strategies thus come "from below"— that is to say, not from intellectuals or party functionaries who tell working people what they should be doing, but rather from factory workers, housewives, prostitutes, and migrants, as the following pages will show. And those people come not only from London and New York but from places that range from Mexico and Venezuela and Haiti to Kenya and Tanzania. James insists not only on deriving her ideas from interaction with working people of all kinds and all nations, she consistently tests and refines them in the same constituency. From her very first pamphlet, which she discussed with her fellow workers and neighbors, she has always trusted not only the decency of common people, but their ability to think and act. "Every cook can govern," wrote CLR James in 1956. James carried that optimistic message into the woman's world of work, the kitchen, and in so doing deepened and expanded its meaning.[2]

The pamphlet James cowrote with Mariarosa Dalla Costa, *The Power of Women and the Subversion of the Community*, which is excerpted here, is, in my view, a classic of radical literature and one of the most important political documents of the 1970s, contributing as it did to both the working-class movement and the women's movement—indeed, showing activists in both that they shared a common struggle! The "Wages for Housework" campaign carried the message around the world. In this respect as in so many others, James's work has consistently expanded our idea of what the proletariat is, moving beyond the factory gate to the household, the streets, and the prison.

A case in point is her recent work with prisoner Mumia Abu-Jamal, a former Black Panther and one of the world's most eminent political prisoners. When James visited him at the SCI-Greene Supermax Prison in Waynesburg, Pennsylvania, their wide-ranging political discussion turned to what prisoners do for themselves in their struggles against the law. The result was *Jailhouse Lawyers*, a fascinating study of working-class self-activity—how the prison functions as a kind of school and how prisoners educate themselves in order to help each other in their cases. James saw that vital, creative political work was being done in the belly of the beast, and she wanted everyone to know about it. She encouraged Mumia to write the book, which he did. When

---

2   *A New Notion: Two Works by CLR James: "Every Cook Can Govern" and "The Invading Socialist Society"* (Oakland: PM Press, 2010).

you read it, you will have a better understanding of race and class in America, and how a previously little-known movement from below is challenging the powers that be. You will also have a better understanding of what kind of political thinker James is.[3]

Another thing I like about this collection of essays is their practicality: they show not only thought in relation to action, they convey a vivid sense of how a talented organizer actually works. In our rush to glorify theory, we too often forget the craft of practice, the democratic art of working with people amid all the contradictions of their lives. That is something James knows and does extremely well. These essays distill the precious wisdom of the organizer, much of it gained at the Crossroads Women's Centre in London.[4]

In the end, I am delighted that PM Press has published this volume, because it will help James to become better known and to enable her to take her rightful place as one of the key political thinkers and activists of our times. She is, and has long been, a critical contributor to our knowledge commons, where a better future must lie. Indeed, she has been building it for almost six decades, as readers may now happily see for themselves.

---

3   Mumia Abu-Jamal, *Jailhouse Lawyers: Prisoners Defending Prisoners v. the USA* (San Francisco: City Lights, 2009).

4   There are important parallels between James's approach to organizing and one developed by Staughton Lynd called "accompaniment." See Staughton Lynd, "Oral History from Below," *Oral History Review* 21, no. 1 (1993): 1–8; and *From Here to There: The Staughton Lynd Reader* (Oakland: PM Press, 2010).

A WINNING PERSPECTIVE

NINA LÓPEZ

Selma James has made and continues to make a critical contribution to the movement for social justice, starting with the women's and antiracist movements. Some of her early writings have become classics. But since what she has said or written aims to change the world rather than merely to interpret it, most of her work and the perspective it comes from have been neglected or misinterpreted.

But then grassroots organizers rarely receive the acknowledgment they deserve—they are too daring, too threatening of the status quo. As a result many people are deprived of knowing who they are and what they are doing—a piece of living history which may help the rest of us understand where we've come from, where we may want to go and how we may get there.

This collection aims to make James accessible, in her own words, to a wider audience. Arranged in chronological order, it allows us to consider James's perspective and how it has evolved over sixty years—starting in the 1950s when she was a member of an organization led by the Marxist historian CLR James, to today as the point of reference for a growing international network.

James has been breaking new ground since 1952 when, as a twenty-two-year-old mother and factory worker, she wrote the pamphlet *A Woman's Place*. Based on her experience and that of others around her, she described women's lives with uncompromising precision. Twenty years later, as the women's movement erupted, she cowrote *The Power of Women and the Subversion of the Community*, which has become a movement classic and is often taught in Gender and Women's Studies courses. Her pamphlet *Women, the Unions, and Work, or What Is Not to Be Done*, also published in 1972, told some bold truths about women and unions which many at the time were not prepared to hear. Another classic, *Sex, Race, and Class*, soon followed. In *Marx and Feminism*, ten years later, she offered an original reading of Marx from the point of view of women's unwaged work.

These pieces (together with "Wageless of the World," the introduction to the Latin American edition of *Power of Women*) set out a new perspective based on the autonomous struggles of each sector of the working class. She starts with unwaged women—housewives, mothers, carers who produce and reproduce all the workers of the world. Their struggle, and that of other sectors, is not only an independent entity but also an expression of class struggle and an essential component of working-class unity. Her analysis has been praised for its "eloquent distinction between caste and class…an important critique of what came to be known as identity politics."[1]

James coined the word "unwaged," now widely used, and helped to put women's unwaged work on the international agenda. She has made visible the struggle of previously invisible sectors and drawn out the connections among them. *Hookers in the House of the Lord* (1983) is an account of how sex workers, for whom she was a spokeswoman, many of them Black, took sanctuary in a London church for twelve days to protest "police illegality and racism." *Strangers and Sisters* (1985) sums up a conference she coordinated, where immigrant women came together for the first time to speak about their experiences and contributions.

Her writings are organizing tools rather than just accounts or explanations. *Hookers* was intended to be (and became) a blueprint for sex workers in other countries. *The Global Kitchen* (1985), which contains some of James's most perceptive and moving prose, was used by an international women's team to convince the United Nations that unwaged work should be counted. (*An Offer We Couldn't Refuse* (1986) reviews the UN Decade for Women during which this and many other questions were fought out.) *Women's Unwaged Work—The Heart of the Informal Sector* (1991) aimed to push economic experts to back women's case. *The Milk of Human Kindness* (2002), which claimed the contribution of women's biological work, launched a forceful defense of breastfeeding, exposing the economic and political forces that were undermining children's right to this natural food.

Her call for women to mobilize together across international boundaries (Global Women's Strike, 2005) sums up her perspective that society "invest in caring not killing," developed in the course of organizing an anti-imperialist, anti-sexist, anti-racist network in a number of countries, South and North.

---

1   Rosemary Hennessy and Chrys Ingraham, "Introduction: Reclaiming Anticapitalist Feminism," in *Materialist Feminism*, eds. Hennessy and Ingraham (New York: Routledge, 1997), 13.

Many of us who have come into contact with Selma James directly or through her writing credit her with changing our lives: enabling us to be more self-conscious and to make more authentic choices.

But how did she arrive at this new perspective, and how much influence has it had?

I met Selma in London in 1976, protesting outside a conference of socialist economists. She was warm, friendly, funny, full of energy, and indignant that the conference disregarded women's unwaged contribution to the economy. She spoke in words of one syllable and I was surprised that a Third World immigrant woman like myself who at the time could speak little English, could understand her. Everything she said seemed obvious; yet I had never heard it before.

Not long after, I joined her organization, the International Wages for Housework Campaign (referred to as the Campaign), which will be celebrating its fortieth anniversary as this book is launched. Throughout these years, I have worked closely with her.

James was born in 1930 in Brooklyn, New York, in a movement household. Her father, a Jewish immigrant from the Austro-Hungarian Empire, was a truck driver who never went to school. He was an internationalist, an anti-Zionist, an orator who fought to form a Teamsters Union local in Brooklyn, and then had to fight the mafia that took the union over. Her U.S.-born mother had been a factory worker from when she was twelve, and was now a housewife. She was involved in the community in which they lived; like activists of today's Occupy movement, she defended evicted families, fighting to move them from the pavement back into their homes, and to get Home Relief (welfare).

James was trained by that thirties movement—as a six-year-old, she collected tin foil "for bullets" for the 1936–1938 Spanish revolution. At fifteen, she joined the Johnson-Forest Tendency, a political organization led by CLR James, who later became her husband.

Johnson-Forest took to heart what Vladimir Lenin said: that the working class was "shy." In "Striving for Clarity and Influence: the Political Legacy of CLR James," published here for the first time, Selma James tells how they worked hard to ensure that different sectors of this "shy" working class, those at the bottom of the hierarchy, spoke up for themselves. This "third layer," as CLR James called them—Black people, women, factory workers, young people—were being trained to stand up to their own leaders and prevent organizations they had created from turning against them (unfortunately a common experience). Selma James, a third layer person, was encouraged to speak and write—it was a formative experience. Her account of Johnson-Forest reveals and reclaims CLR James as an imaginative anticapitalist organizer who broke with Trotskyism to build the "self-mobilization of the proletariat"—a different person from the intellectual popular among academics.

Selma James and her son Sam Weinstein joined CLR James, who had been forced to leave the United States during McCarthy's repression, in England in 1955; she worked as his secretary from then on.

Moving to Trinidad and Tobago in 1958, they were active in the movement for independence and federation in the Caribbean. She worked on *The Nation*, a biweekly newspaper of the ruling nationalist party. She later said that her time there was a source of learning from which she has continued to draw. "I fell in love with the West Indies. Everything seemed possible. I had to learn that it was a microcosm of global politics and that what we confronted there was the same enormity that we confront everywhere. The United States was in charge as they have been in much of the world."

Back in Britain in 1962, James paid the rent by working as a free-lance audio-typist for the BBC. She was fast and accurate, and was soon transcribing interviews that were needed quickly or had "difficult" accents. Her audiotyping was a school: it was a time of creativity and experimentation at the BBC and all kinds of interviews for documentaries went through her ears. Orson Welles made a lasting impression—she was outraged at the shabby way in which he was treated by the film industry. "He was too anti-racist, they couldn't stand it"—and Francis Bacon—"who taught that our eyes had been corrupted."

She was later to make two films with the BBC. *Our Time Is Coming Now* (1970) with Michael Rabiger, has recently been rediscovered and praised. *All Work and No Pay* (1976) was part of the BBC Open Door series: it had unique pictures of the general strike of women in Iceland the previous year which had received hardly any media coverage.

She was involved in the anti-racist and anti-deportation movement—James was the first organizing secretary of the UK's Campaign Against Racial Discrimination in 1965. But even now, after spending most of her adult life in Britain, she brings to her politics an understanding of the centrality of race that is uniquely of the United States, deepened by her time in the Caribbean and by the antiracist movement in the UK. Some white people in Britain find "race issues" embarrassing, a reality they would rather not face. In the United States, with its legacy of slavery, civil war, and Jim Crow segregation, race is always present, even when unmentioned.

Today, true to her own background, James is a founding member of the International Jewish Anti-Zionist Network. In her speech to the 2010 U.S. Assembly of Jews, she reclaims the Jewish legacy of commitment to movements for social justice.

From 1970, James was active in the women's liberation movement in the UK. She was at the conference that launched it—defending women in prison from the floor, she got a standing ovation. Most feminist spokeswomen were young and middle-class university graduates, while James was neither of those: she was working-class and had refused to go to university ("I was afraid it would ruin my mind"); she was forty and had been engaged in the "woman question" all her life.

In 1972, she founded the Power of Women Collective, which became the International Wages for Housework Campaign to demand that the State pay for caring work. As she explains in the introduction to "Women, the Unions, and Work," this proved controversial. She was attacked and ostracized both by the male Left whose only interest in women was to recruit them to a party or a union, and by feminists for whom the women's movement was a launch pad to a career.

She focused on building a network, starting with four women in four different countries and helped open a women's center in London. In the following years a number of autonomous groups (of women of color, lesbian women, prostitute women, women with disabilities, single mothers) sprang up within the Campaign and across the United States, as well as a group of men who embraced the recognition of caring and other unwaged work, and the need to reclaim the military budget, not only to stop men (and increasingly women) being trained as killers but to support caring workers.

The involvement of these sectors changed everything. From then on the collective experience we have been making as a network of organizations addressing practical situations, has tested, enriched, and constantly updated James's perspective.

The Campaign is not based on horizontalism; its members do not pretend to be "equal." Instead we acknowledge the power differences among us and confront these divisions from the bottom up by consulting across sectors. As James indicates in *Sex, Race, and Class*, in order to come together as a class, each sector must "make its own autonomous power felt," to ensure that its contribution to the movement for change and its specific needs are visible, acknowledged, and acted on. The autonomous Campaign organizations have enabled each sector to make its "specific case" while working with other sectors and taking into account how its own demands may affect the others. In this way, we aim to be mutually accountable, to train each other, to prevent ourselves from scabbing on each other—lured by fool's gold into believing that our sector can win without other sectors and even at their expense; or that negotiation can replace mobilization.

Organizations of domestic workers in Peru and Trinidad and Tobago, rural women in India and Uganda, street vendors and sex workers in the Philippines joined the network. This widened further with the new millennium as the Campaign launched the Global Women's Strike (the Strike), coordinated by James. Rooted in the struggles and demands of grassroots women, the Strike provides a common agenda for women to act together, and for men to act with women in their own interest.

Payday—the network of men working with the Strike and for whom James has been a key point of reference—used the Strike's perspective to campaign for conscientious objectors and others who "refuse to rape or kill" for the military-industrial complex and its imperialist pursuits.

Red Thread in Guyana had brought grassroots women together across race; in a society sometimes violently divided across race lines, this is an extraordinary achievement. Battling to move from income generation to campaigning on shared interests, it found a home in the Strike, and in turn transformed it.

James reminds us constantly that "there are no shortcuts to building the movement." She has spent much of her time training the network and leading in the collective development of organizational principles that enable individual members to find our voices while remaining collective. Much of what was written by Campaign members over the years was helped by James's prodding, through questions, suggestions, drafting, and redrafting. This painstaking work was done nationally and internationally—James never believed that we could win unless we organized internationally, so working across national boundaries by phone (and more occasionally travel) was prioritized despite the cost (before Skype, international calls took most of our funds).

Training has been a two-way learning process. James says: "I trained myself by training others, trying to be useful to them, to understand what they were having trouble with. I still do. It's a big discipline. To explain myself I had to find out what I thought. I can never just sit down and think things through, but as I speak and try to find the right words my thoughts become clearer. I hate imprecision. It's the enemy."

While always updating herself, James is "of a piece"—her earlier writings are not contradicted later in any basic way. The hidden experiences and struggles of the housewife, the mother who faces a double or triple day of unwaged and waged work to support her family—in the South and the North, the countryside and the city—have remained central.

But the conclusions she drew from these experiences were shaped by the developing movements. Third World liberation, civil rights, Indigenous, land rights, antiwar, students, immigrants, women, lesbian/gay/bisexual/trans/queer, sex workers, disabled women and men, pensioners, prisoners—these were community struggles; but the connections had to be drawn out with those at the waged "point of production" from which they have been so artificially cut off. This reconnection with waged workers was based on giving voice to unwaged workers, starting with welfare mothers and young people who rose against both war and work.

James reminds us that until recently most of the world lived in the countryside; only a minority worked for wages, even in the cities. She says:

> We were invited to choose national liberation, peasant and student movements
> over and against the traditional waged working class. I could never turn my back
> on waged workers. My father was a union man; we were a union family. I had been
> a factory worker, and so were my mother and sister; my other sister was an office
> worker, not so different. But I was also a mother and my son a student trying to
> avoid the draft. We needed both sides of the wage divide; we couldn't do without
> either.

Malcolm X had been a jailbird; that's what helped make him a great point of reference. Welfare mothers, many of them Black, had won some money from the State, an income independent of men, recognition for the work of raising children, for children's right to free, non-segregated education. Their impact was huge. The movement was broadening and redefining itself. You needed not be limited to one struggle. You could start anywhere and especially with yourself. Wages for housework was learnt from all these movements, putting the lessons together.

Forty years of collective work have refined and developed her views. She has tried to reflect this in the brief introductions to each piece. Her intro to *Women, the Unions, and Work* acknowledges the impact that committed individuals who rise to the top within unions, and within institutions generally, can have if they survive the pressure and "keep in touch with their members and the movement outside." She is always glad to work with and support such people.

Far from being retired, James's activism has increased as the network she has been building is deeply engaged in today's movement in a number of countries. Her recent articles published in the UK's *Guardian* draw on that activism: her attack on the dismantling of the welfare state, her rejoicing at the new women's movement—from Egypt's Tahrir Square to SlutWalk.

Trained to assume that, no matter how bleak a situation may appear, there is always something that can be done, James presents the truth in ways that are uplifting. She starts with what the movement achieves, despite tragic setbacks, and the new possibilities that appear daily. In her own words: "Information and understanding of how and where we resist and rebel are the basis on which we build our determination to win and our confidence that we will win."

She asked Mumia Abu-Jamal (then a death-row prisoner) to write a book about jailhouse lawyers, which she introduced, to show "what extraordinary lives of resistance some prisoners have created out of desperation, determination and imagination." In her letters and articles on Haiti and Venezuela, she refers to some of the obstacles the revolution faces (from U.S. intervention to the managerial class and the NGOs), but the context is the movement's accomplishments and possibilities. When she spoke to students at the Aristide Foundation for Democracy in Haiti (2011) she was aware of their ambivalence about their future; she acknowledged their revolutionary legacy of ending slavery and defeating dictatorship, before articulating the stark choice they faced: they could use education "to rise out of poverty…or to work to eliminate poverty…for all of us to rise out of poverty together. Not leaving our community behind." In the United States, she reminded students of their history with Women's Studies and Black Studies, while inviting them to confront a racist, imperialist reality.

From CLR James, she learnt that "'high culture' belongs to all of us—we have made everything there is, it's ours by right." She has pursued Mozart, especially the opera where women unite across class to fight rape and male rulers: "He learnt as a child sitting on the laps of baronesses and cooks." She has read and reread Jane Austen, Jean Rhys, and Virginia Woolf's *A Room of One's Own*. She incorporated all this into her politics, often commenting that there was more truth in works of fiction than in political essays. Her *Jean Rhys* excerpt reveals both the divisions of race and the possibility of overcoming them.

James always says that our class power lies in the collective, that no matter how talented and skilled an individual may be, "Genius is not enough." Only together can we strive for "clarity and influence" (CLR James's phrase for what we aspire to as a movement). From the first to the last piece in this collection, the reader will find a determination to be precise.

To do this and to keep herself grounded, she always uses Marx. His *Ethnographic Notebooks* have confirmed her conviction that human society has communistic beginnings and a communistic tendency. She touches on this in "Rediscovering Nyerere's Tanzania" (2007–2009).

A close friend and playwright from the Caribbean once referred to James's writings as "lucid." I would add: just like her politics. What better example of path-breaking lucidity than James's explanation, given in correspondence and interviews, of why our organization has been using the term "grassroots" often in preference to "working-class":

> We use the word "grassroots" to expand the definition of class. First of all, we make clear that women, children, rural and other unwaged people are part of the working class rather than an adjunct to it, and that the methods of struggle they may adopt signal not different classes but different sectors within the same class.

> We find that "grassroots" is a unifying term which can also include higher sectors than those traditionally identified as working class, sectors that may be anti-capitalist because they are in some way discriminated against and exploited and not part of the managerial structure. By acknowledging that the working class is divided by sectors, we offer those from higher sectors who have a case against capital, access to our collective power in exchange for their accountability—an indication of how broad the movement can be. For example, two early members of the IWFHC were corporate wives, one married to the head of Chrysler Europe and the other to a manager in an oil company—as housewives they identified with working class housewives, and saw themselves as unwilling—and unpaid—servants of the multinationals.

The term "grassroots" is a rejection of assumptions common with the Left that some sectors, and therefore some struggles, are more important than others.[2] Some sectors seem to have more power against capital than others, but no sector can win alone. We are all dependent on other sectors making their own struggle, and on the unity that must come from that.

Those hostile to wages for housework have tried to dismiss it as a short-lived women's lib idea dead in the water. In fact, as the span of this collection shows, it is much more than an idea and it is very much alive—as a demand, an organizing perspective and a campaign. Its influence has been greater than they would dare to admit. The recognition of unwaged caring work has entered the national accounts, laws, and constitutions of a number of countries; academic careers have been made and grant money accumulated using variations of James's "women count, count women's work"; grassroots groups have been strengthened by working collectively across national boundaries; women and men on five continents and from many sectors have met, marched, picketed, occupied, to the tune of "Invest in Caring Not Killing" and won specific demands…

James's perspective for winning has sustained many of us during the years of the unbridled and untethered market launched by Thatcher and Reagan. That phase is over. Latin America's shift away from Washington, the recent revolutions in the Arab world and the Global Occupy movement they have inspired are pointing to a new confrontation between capital and an increasingly militant grassroots. When she spoke at Occupy London Stock Exchange (OLSX) in November 2011, she pointed out that "All power to the 99 percent is a most antiracist twenty-first-century statement. To highlight the 99 percent versus the 1 percent is to expose the basic hierarchy in society. It stakes a claim that almost all of us, waged and unwaged, belong together."

As the movement finds new points of reference, and refines and broadens its objectives and actions, there is a hunger for reevaluating what it has produced in past decades. Forty years of building an international network have made James a creative point of reference for organizers from the bottom up. Her articles and speeches are being sought out by a new generation of activists and professionals ready to use their position to help change the world. They will rejoice at this timely collection.[3]

---

2   Of course, no term is ever foolproof, as it can only express power relations at a moment in time, and "grassroots" is now sometimes being used by those who are trying to pass as the movement while doing the State's bidding. Even the Tea Party, bankrolled by the biggest Republican fortunes, claims to be grassroots.

3   While the Global Women's Strike had been discussing an anthology of Selma James's writings for some years, we owe this publication partly to the Feminist Women's Circle in Turkey, who published a shorter and somewhat different selection in Turkish in 2009. Their enthusiasm and seriousness helped us to overcome overwork and look for a publisher in English. Marcus Rediker suggested PM Press.

A WOMAN'S PLACE
(1952)

had been telling CLR James, who founded and led the Johnson-Forest Tendency of which I was a member, about being a housewife and about the women in my working-class neighborhood. He had been enthusiastic about what I told him, since he had never heard anything political about housewives before. Later he asked me to write a pamphlet about it.

After some months, he phoned to ask why I hadn't written it, and I said, "Because I don't know how to write a pamphlet." "The way to do it," he said, "is to take a shoe box and make a slit at the top; then whenever you have an idea jot it down and slip the piece of paper into the shoe box. After a while, you open the box, put all these sentences in order and you have a draft." There was a national meeting of the leadership in a few weeks (very rare because fares were costly and travel time-consuming). That gave me a deadline, which helped me to pin myself down.

I knew that if I stayed home from work to put the draft together, I would end up cleaning the oven or doing some other major piece of housework, so I arranged to spend the day at a friend's. I left home at the same time as I would have if I'd gone to work, dropped my son at the nursery, and arrived at my friend's at 8 a.m., just as she was leaving for work. The house was empty. I had no distractions or excuses. I opened the shoe box, and by six or seven that evening, I had the draft of a pamphlet, just as CLR had said.

In the following weeks, I showed it to my neighbors, who were not "political." They had plenty of comments. Most of them I disagreed with, but I made changes to reflect what they had said, sometimes incorporating comments, mostly responding to them. Even when I rejected what they said, it helped to clarify what I thought and focused me on what had to be addressed. One way and another, my neighbors helped shape the contents.

This became my collective way of working on drafts, typical of the organization that had asked me to write such a pamphlet in the first place.

I didn't know how to conclude the pamphlet. I wanted to make clear that I was for radical change but I didn't want a political commercial. It took months to work out the last page, one that rang true to all I'd said, but at the same time was not the usual: "Come the revolution, all these problems will be solved."

I still use the shoe box method (although I now use notebooks and a computer folder called Shoe Box). It helps ensure that the ideas and perceptions that float in the mind all the time are what you get down to saying when you write or speak, rather than falling back to earlier words which are constantly outdated by rapidly changing times.

When the pamphlet was published, I took it in to work with me and sold a few copies to the women I knew in that factory. And I think I sold a couple to the same neighbors who had commented. We have to remember that this was during the McCarthy witch-hunt when people were worried that something different might be dangerous. But this was about women and the family, and was likely to be "safe" rather than political.

It was entirely new then for the opinions of a working-class woman, especially a housewife, to be published, even by a socialist organization. It was the working class speaking for itself. Urging working-class sectors to speak for ourselves was crucial to the political perspective I was lucky enough to be trained in, and from quite young.

I later learnt that of all the publications Johnson-Forest put out, this was the only one that sold out. It may have sold only a thousand or fifteen hundred, but it did sell out, and I think that may have been because the men were almost as interested as the women in finding out what it had to say about daily life from women's point of view. And nobody ever told me that it wasn't "Marxist" or "politically correct."

Looking back later, I realized that the advice CLR gave me as a person with no writing experience says a lot about him and indicates what a great organizer he was. I suspect he invented the shoe box method on the spot.

One other fact. I had signed the pamphlet with another woman (Filomena Daddario, who named the pamphlet) so we could both speak for it. We didn't use our real names—we could have lost our jobs during McCarthyism (and ultimately I did lose mine). I called myself Marie Brandt because I was Jewish and wanted to make clear that I had nothing against Germans because of Hitler. Some fool at the central office in Detroit took the *d* out, making it Anglo-Saxon. I was upset but never said anything 'til now.

* * *

Today, more than ever before, magazines and newspapers are full of articles about women.

Some just discuss what the society women are doing and who of the upper class is getting married. Others discuss the fact that there is a high divorce rate and try to give some answer to all this. Or they discuss millions of women going into industry or the restlessness of housewives. These articles don't show what this restlessness means and can only try to make women feel that they are better off than they have ever been.

They plead with women to be happy.

None of these articles, none, points out that if women are in any way better off than ever before, that it is women who have made this change themselves. They don't point out that women want a change now and it is they who will make this change.

The method that these writers have in avoiding woman's role in making history is to avoid the daily lives of millions of women, what they do and what they think.

It is the day-to-day lives of women that show what women want and what they do not want.

Many of the writers of these articles are women, but career women who are not a part of the working women and housewives of this country. These writers realize that if they stated the facts, it would be a weapon for women in their struggle for a new life for themselves and their families.

So they don't take up the daily pressures that women face. They don't take up the fact that women, dealing with these pressures in their own way, realize the strength of themselves and of other women. They avoid saying that women, feeling their own strength and doing away with the old relations, are preparing themselves and their husbands for a new and better relationship.

The coauthors of this booklet have seen this in their own lives and in the lives of the women they know. They have written this down as a beginning of the expression of what the average woman feels, thinks, and lives.

The Single Woman

A lot of women work before they get married and find that they are well able to take care of themselves. They are very independent as compared to single girls twenty years ago. They want to get married but they say their marriages will be different. They say they will not let themselves be the household drudges their mothers were. A friend of mine says that she is different from her mother because she wants more from marriage. "She didn't expect it. I'm different. I expect it."

Women want a part in the decisions that have to be made and very often they don't want to struggle along on one paycheck. They prefer to continue work even if just for a while after they are married so that they can at least begin to have some of the things that they want and need.

One of the greatest problems a young single woman has to face, aside from how to support herself, is what her attitude to morals she has been taught is going to be. In the process of working this out, single girls have started a whole new set of morals. Even though many girls have not thought about their actions in this way, they have gone against the whole code of morals that they were taught to live by. Many women have affairs before they are married and are not looked upon as fallen women or bad women. It is not the same as one woman, years ago, going with a man and keeping it within herself. One girl told me that all of her friends had had sex relations with their boyfriends and that they discussed it openly. They feel that they are entitled to this and are willing to go against the school authorities, their parents, and even those men who will not accept them. Whether or not society approves, they do what their friends are doing and insist upon approval by the force of the number who feel and act the same way.

"Hey, You're Scaring Me."

A single woman thinks twice about getting married and giving up the freedom that she has had before marriage. Before, she went out as she pleased and bought clothes as she needed them. She never had the freedom that men have but she was on her own. One young woman of twenty that I work with says that she almost got married twice and she is certainly glad that she didn't. She told me, "I know how well off I am when I hear the married women talk about their husbands. I do what I want to do now." When she hears the married women talk, she says, "Hey, you're scaring me. You'll make me an old maid."

But all women want a home and family. This same girl is always talking about having children and about her boyfriends. Young women nowadays feel that their good times and the closeness that they have with their boyfriends should not end with marriage but should make their marriage into a real experience. It is clear that these girls don't reject men or marriage, but they reject what marriage is today.

The Married Woman

As soon as a woman gets married she finds that she must settle down and accept responsibility, something women have always been trained to do. She realizes that she has the job of making the house that she and her husband live in a place where they can invite their friends and where they can relax after a hard day's work. And even though a woman works, it is assumed from the very beginning that the main responsibility of the house is the woman's and the main job of support is the man's. The husband is to go out and support you and the children. You are to make sure that the house is clean, the children are cared for, meals are cooked, laundry is done, etc. This seems to be the fair way of doing things. But soon you find that the job of staying home and taking care of the house is not as it is painted in the movies. Housework is a never-ending job that is monotonous and repetitious. After a while doing things in the house such as ironing or getting up early to make lunches or breakfast is not something that you want to do. It becomes something that you have to do.

The Children

Some couples try to get away from this division of the work at the beginning. For instance, when a woman works, the man will share the work when they get home. The husband of one woman did more of the housework than she did, before they had children.

But any idea of sharing the work disappears when children come. When there are children the whole setup of a man working outside and a woman working inside is shown for what it is—an inhuman setup. The whole load of children, house, everything, becomes the woman's. As soon as a woman quits work to have children, a man doesn't feel he has to help her with anything. What was a division in their marriage when they first got married is now a split. Instead of the children uniting them, children divide a marriage and stick the woman in the house and glue the man to his job. But very often for a woman who works and looks forward to quitting when she has children, the coming of children makes working out of the home a life sentence. After a month or two, she is back working again.

Few men take an interest in the details of taking care of the baby. They feel it is not their job to diaper and bathe the children. Some men even feel that, though their wives have to stay home with the children, there is no reason for them to stay home with her. So they go out and do as they please, if their wives let them, knowing that their wives are stuck at home constantly taking care of their children. If a man goes out with his friends, a woman usually fights for the right to go out with hers. One woman told me that she was pregnant and that she was sorry since she had a four-month-old baby. She said her husband was glad. She said that he knew that if she was stuck with a child he could go out as he pleased. Fewer and fewer women take this nonsense from their husbands. Women fight tooth and nail against being shouldered with the whole responsibility of the house and the children. They refuse to stay home and be tied to the house while their husbands continue life as though nothing had happened. If women are going to stay home their husbands are going to stay home with them.

The Family Is Divided

Women are trying to break down the division that has been made between the father and the children and between the mother and the father. The privilege that society has given the man, women are not allowing him. It is a privilege that he suffers by as well as she. Men know little about their children, are not close to them, and don't know what giving time and work to a child gives back to you. It is this giving that a woman does that makes her so much closer to her children than a father ever can be. Men feel that supporting a child is all they have to do to get the love of their child and the respect of their wife. They feel that nothing else should be asked of them— but the less that is asked of them the less they get in return.

It is not an easy thing for a woman to get used to being a mother. For one thing you know that you are responsible for this child completely. If your husband stops supporting him then you have to. You have to raise him. No one else will. Whatever kind of person he grows up to be will be mainly your doing. As soon as you have a child you have to make your marriage work. Now it is not only you but another person who didn't ask to be born who will suffer if your marriage goes on the rocks. A lot of marriages that would ordinarily break up are held together by the woman in order to save her child from a broken home.

A woman's whole life revolves around her children. She thinks of them first. She finds that these are the only people in her life who really need her. If she has nothing more, she lives for them. She organizes her work so she can give them the best care. The schedule that she lives on shows that her time is not her own but belongs to her children. She must often go without things so that they will have what they need. She must try to live in a house that is safe enough and roomy enough for them. Sometimes she even has to fight with her husband for something that she feels they need and he is not willing for them to have. She plans her life according to their age.

It is easy for a man to say it is his child but for the real worry when they are sick or misbehave, how they are eating and how much they sleep, these things are on the woman's shoulders. How a child's shoes fit him, where his clothes are kept, even things like this most fathers don't know anything about. This doesn't mean that fathers like it this way. It's just that even if they didn't there is very little that they can do about it. When they go away in the morning, the kids are usually asleep and when they get home at night they are near their bed time. Their whole lives are concerned with making a living, and the problems involved in that. Because they are not around their children enough, they have very little idea about what children need, not only in the way of physical needs, but in terms of discipline and love and security. The division that is made between home and factory creates a division between the father and his children. It is obvious that when the father and mother lead separate lives, the children as well are going to suffer. They are often used by each parent as weapons against the other. The children seldom know where they stand and try as soon as possible to get away from it all. They refuse to be a part of this constant family war and just disassociate themselves from it as soon as they are old enough.

Then the Kids Come Home

The work that is part of having a child destroys much of the pleasure of having them for the one that has to do the work. To be with the children day in and day out, week in and week out, to clean up after them, and to keep them clean, to worry about whether they are going in the street or are catching a cold is not only a terrible strain, but it becomes the only thing that you see in your child—the work and the worry involved. You begin to see in the child only the work and none of the pleasure. You feel that every stage of his growing up means, not just a developing child but more work for you to do. You see a child as a hindrance to your getting your other work done and to your having free time. He seems to be "in your way" rather than part of your life. Just about the time that you think you're finished cleaning the house, the kids come home and the whole routine starts all over again, finger marks on the wall, muddy shoes and scattered toys.

You don't ever realize how much of a barrier the work of raising a child creates until he finally gets into his teens. He is less work to you and you have more time and more of a chance to appreciate him as a person. But then it is too late. He has grown away from you and you can't really see him and know him and appreciate him.

If a woman can't make her husband understand this (and since a man doesn't go through it, it is very hard for him to understand), she must literally force out of him some free time away from the children for herself. This doesn't solve anything but it relieves the tension for a while. Sometimes men don't want their wives to have any freedom at all. They don't trust them or have some old-fashioned idea that they don't need it or shouldn't have it. The only people you can turn to in those situations are your neighbors. Very often, they are the only people who understand, since they are women too and have the same problems. For a small amount of money or for an exchange of care, they may be willing to take care of your child for an afternoon. Even then you are not really free. When you are away you may worry about whether the children are being taken good care of. Sometimes you even feel guilty about having left them at all. No one ever lets you forget that you should be home with your children. You can never really be free of them if you are a mother. Nor can you be free when you are with them. A woman finds out early that what she wanted from having children she cannot have. Her situation, her husband's and the children's, put the children in immediate conflict with her.

When a woman has children, she is tied down to the house and to these same children that are so important to her. You never know what it is to be a housewife until you have children.

The House

Everything a housewife does, she does alone. All the work in the house is for you to do by yourself. The only time you are with other people is when you have visitors or go visiting yourself. People think sometimes that when women go visiting they are just wasting time. But if they didn't go visiting occasionally, they would go mad from boredom and the feeling of not having anyone to talk to. It's so good to get out among people. The work is the same, day in and day out. "Even if you died the house would still be there in the morning." Sometimes you get so bored that you have to do something. One woman used to change the furniture around about every two weeks. Other women buy something new for the house or for themselves. There are a million schemes to break the monotony. The daytime radio serials help to pass the time away but nothing changes the isolation and boredom.

The terrible thing that is always there when you are doing the housework is the feeling that you are never finished. When a man works in a factory, he may work hard and long hours. But at a certain time, he punches out and for that day at least he is finished. Come Friday or Saturday night he is through for one or two days. In the house you are never finished. Not only is there always something to be done, but there is always someone to mess up almost before you are finished. After four or six hours of a thorough housecleaning the kids will come home and in five minutes the house will be a shambles. Or your husband will dirty all the ashtrays there are in the house. Or it will rain right after you wash the windows. You may be able to control your children or get your husband to be more careful, but that doesn't solve much. The way that the house is set up, neither the husband nor the children have any idea how much effort and real hard work and time have gone into cleaning the house. The way that the house is set up you have no control over the hours of work, the kind of work that you will have to do, and how much work you do. These are what women want to control.

The rest of the family is no part of the house. They just live there. You make the home what it is—a place where they can relax. You make it livable. You make it attractive. You make it comfortable. You keep it clean. And you are the only one who can never completely enjoy it. You always have your eye out for what has to be done. And picking up after people seems to be a never-ending job. You can never relax where you spend most of your time, energy and ability.

Most women don't even make the real decisions where the house is concerned. Even though they can use their own judgment on many small things, the really big things are either decided outright by the husband or he makes sure that his pressure is felt. Women feel that they must have a say in the house. They participate in the decisions of the house more than ever today. But they have had to put up a long fight to get this recognition.

"Your Own Boss"

They say a woman is her own boss. That is, no one tells her how fast to work. No one tells her how much to do. And nobody stands over her all day. She can sit down when she wants to and smoke a cigarette or eat when she gets hungry.

A housewife has an entirely different kind of a boss. Her first boss is her husband's work. Everything a woman has to do is dependent on the job her husband has. Whatever her husband makes, that is what the family has to live on. How much clothes she buys, or whether she has to make them, whether clothes go to the laundromat or are washed by hand, whether they live in a crowded apartment or in a house with enough room for the family, whether she has a washing machine or does clothes by hand, all of these things are decided by the kind of job her husband has.

The hours that her husband works determines her whole schedule and how she will live, and when she will do her work. One big problem for a woman is having a husband who works nights. Then there is no schedule. By the time that the housework is done, her husband gets up and the house is messed again. If there are children then there are two schedules to be met. The children have to be kept quiet during the day, which is almost impossible with children.

Whether her husband has a comparatively easy job or a hard one affects her life, too. A man who works very hard is not going to help her with any of the work around the house. He is going to come home a lot grouchier and harder to live with. The woman has to learn to keep her temper a lot more if there is to be any peace. And the children have to be kept in line more, too.

Even where she lives is decided by her husband's work. The part of town that makes going to work the easiest is the part of town that you live in. And if there are no jobs in that town that are in your husband's line of work then you have to forget all your friends and all the ties of family and you go to where he can find work.

The children and the demands of taking care of them is the next decider of how a woman is to spend her life. There is nothing, nothing more demanding than an infant. When they want something, they want it at that moment and not a moment later.

But the most ruthless boss and the one that really keeps a woman going is the work itself. The work does not look on you as being a human being. It is there no matter how you feel or what you want to do. It dominates every spare moment that you have, either in the house or away from it. You are constantly trying to finish work that has no end. You want to do all that you have to do in the least possible time and have free time for yourself. And after you think you are finished you find that there is something else. Sometimes women will give up and let the house go for a few days or a few hours. But they are the ones who are bothered by it. And then they will work twice as hard trying to make up for lost time. You are always doing what you have to do. What you want to do doesn't count for much.

Most women are very responsible. They feel that, as mothers and wives, they want to do the best possible jobs. They want to be proud of their homes and children. There is no other place where they can show what they can do. If a woman is a good manager she has the respect of other women and that is important to any woman.

So there is really no need of a foreman or lead girl at home. It is the way a woman lives and the work that she must do that keeps her toeing the mark. It is this way of life also that teaches her discipline. She learns when to say something and when to keep quiet. She learns to do things on her own. If there is something that has to be done and her husband won't do it, she does it herself. One woman with four children painted the whole outside of her house. She said that she didn't want to wait another five years for her husband to do it.

It Takes Experience

Every time a woman's husband gets a raise she says to herself, now I will catch up. That extra few dollars will change things. But, by the time he gets that raise, prices have jumped to make up for it, or he has been sick and lost a day's pay, or there has been an "extra." And even if things have gone along fairly smoothly, you go and buy the things that you have needed all along but just weren't able to afford before. So you are right back where you started from. Almost all workers' families live from day-to-day. There is very little chance to put something away for an emergency. If a family missed just one paycheck it may set them back for weeks. In all that time the housewife must manage somehow. The same thing happens when the working man goes out on strike. For weeks and sometimes months she must manage on practically nothing. The miners' wives have a system of storing food and clothes away when their husbands are working steady. In that way, when there is a strike they can live for a while at least on what they have saved up in the way of food and clothes. It takes a lot of experience and training to learn all the tricks and the woman is the only one in a position to learn these "tricks." Corners can be cut in an emergency that you never thought could be cut and you somehow manage.

A woman has to get along on what her husband makes. It doesn't matter how much or how little he brings home. She must decide when to make clothes and when she can afford to buy them. She finds recipes for making economical meals that at the same time look and taste good. The way the family lives, whether there are bill collectors at the door, or food on the table, is dependent on how much money her husband gives her and how she manages it. Although most husbands realize that prices are high, they don't really know how much it takes to keep a family going. It is only the woman who has to live on impossibly little who knows about how to manage finances.

All of this experience prepares a woman to manage when she is on her own. The woman whose husband runs out on her has a pretty rough job on her hands, especially if she has children. If she has relatives who will help her at the beginning then she is considered lucky. But on the whole she has to be both mother and a father to the children. She has no choice about working. She assumes the responsibility of both a man and woman. She supports her family on what she makes, which is usually much less than a man makes. She has less time with her children and sometimes has to be separated from them in order to be able to work. Yet these women manage to bring up their children and start new lives for themselves. They don't sit home and weep. My friend has a neighbor whose husband ran out on her and left her with a child and all the bills. This woman sold all the furniture and with the money took a trip to Puerto Rico to see her mother. It was something to meet her. If she cried, you didn't know about it. She just said that she wasn't going to wait around like a damn fool. She had never done anything like that before but when the time came, she knew just what to do.

They Just Lead Separate Lives

A woman stays at home alone all day. She waits for her husband to come home to tell him of the things that have happened during the day, something that the kids have done or said that shows what wonderful kids they are, or what a hard day she had. She wants to hear what he has gone through and what he thinks about buying this or that for the house. But his life is not in the house. When a man comes home from work, he wants to do nothing. Sometimes he doesn't even want to do any talking. You wait all day for someone to talk to, and then when your husband comes home he picks up the paper and acts as if he doesn't even know you exist. When a woman is home all day, she wants to go out to a show or for a drive on Sunday afternoon. But during the week your husband comes home exhausted and even on weekends he sometimes wants to stay home and relax. He has been away from the house most of his waking hours. Now is his chance to sit around. Women have needs of companionship and understanding that men know nothing about.

If there is not that understanding between men and women about their work and human needs, it is not surprising that many marriages can't make a go of their sex lives, the most delicate phase of their relationship. Their husbands, the people they should be closest to, women are furthest away from. They just lead separate lives.

Women Know Each Other

If women can't turn to their husbands, then they turn to other women. Because of the fact that women lead such similar lives, they know and understand each other. In the neighborhood some women will get very close to others. These women in a court or a street will help each other out if they need help and make the time of day go faster. They talk of things they would not dream of talking to their husbands about, even if their husbands would listen. Who can tell a man how they want to fix up a house or what they want to buy for the children? Things like problems with your husband or financial problems are "common property." The women discuss all the things that affect their lives—whether or not to have children and how many to have, how to save money on clothes, housewares and food, which stores have lower prices, the best method of birth control, sex problems, going to work. In the discussions many things are resolved. Women get new attitudes as a result of hearing other women talk. The women will exclude someone from their group because she is not doing what is expected of her. A mother who neglects her child or does not take care of the house and has no excuse for it will not have the time or confidence of the other women.

Some people call this gossiping but it's much more than that. Women are breaking down the isolation of the home by creating strong ties with other women. It is the only group life a housewife can have and she makes the most of it. The very existence of these ties with other housewives is condemnation of the relations a woman has with her husband, with her work, and with the rest of society. The women come together, talk together, and, in a way, live together. There is no one else they can turn to but themselves. Here is one place where they can decide whom they will be with, where they will be, and what they will do. There is no one who will stand in the way.

The best time of the week in my court is Friday. Everybody cleans house on Friday so they will have less to do on the weekend. After they are finished, in the afternoon, someone will run out for beer and we will sit around and talk and relax and compare notes. The sociability is at its highest and we all feel most relaxed when the work is done. There is a feeling of closeness and kidding around that you can't get anywhere else except with these people that know you and accept you on your own terms.

This is how women are organized. With the experience they have in managing things and with the aid of the other women in their group, they know what to do when they want to take action. The women in a housing project in San Francisco got together to halt the rise in prices. They saw the government wasn't doing anything so they took matters into their own hands. They held meetings and demonstrations and distributed leaflets. No one person organized it. After living with their neighbors in a housing project for so long they knew each other intimately; each other's weaknesses and strengths. The women made price lists up of every store in town and bought at only those stores that had the lowest prices. The whole city knew about "Mama's OPA" and the papers had many articles on it.[1]

---

1 The government department which was supposed to control prices during World War II was the Office of Price Administration—OPA.

There are many times that the housewives take actions that never reach the papers. Women will barricade streets so that their children will have a place to play. The police with tear gas bombs cannot drive them away. Women will pass the word along to other women that on a certain day no woman is to buy meat. They would just walk up to strange women and say, "Don't buy meat on such a day." Women know each other so well that they can talk to a perfect stranger and be sure of being understood. The miners' wives went out on strike to protest the company selling their homes and again to protest the dust in the air of the mining towns. They got the support of their husbands in both cases. Their husbands refused to cross their picket lines.

Women act as a group because they are treated like one. They live the same way on the whole, no matter how different the individual situation may be.

A New Relationship

The most universal organization of women is the action that women take in their own homes. Each woman in her own home is making a revolution. There are some women who don't say much to their husbands or to other women. Yet, when it comes to a showdown, they just go ahead and do what they know is right. Other women argue with their husbands for the things they feel they should have. These arguments mean something to a woman. She is not *just* arguing with her husband. She is showing him and even more important, herself, that she has ideas and desires of her own. Women are constantly telling men however they can that they can't go on in the old way. It is this spirit of independence and self-respect that men admire in women, even when it is directed against themselves. They admire a woman who can stand on her own two feet and doesn't let her husband walk all over her. A woman who doesn't take it from her husband has the respect of other women and she has the respect of her husband as well.

Women are more and more refusing to be just machines for raising children and getting their husbands off to work. They demand more of their husbands in the way of a relationship. If a man cannot change, they will break up the marriage rather than go on living with a stranger. Divorce nowadays is accepted because women have made it acceptable. It is clear that it is not the individual man who is involved. There are too many divorces for that. When a woman gets divorced, although it takes the form of a struggle with an individual man, it is an act opposing the whole way of life men and women must lead in our day.

Women fight the role that men play in the home. This has nothing to do with how much a husband helps his wife or how good he is to the children. No matter how much a husband tries to understand the woman's problems, no matter how well they get along, women fight the way they are forced to live and want to establish a new way of life.

The Working Woman

One of the ways that women show their rejection of their role in society is by going out to work. Many women work today who have never worked before. By going out to work, women have changed their relations with their husbands and children. Along with this, they have given themselves new problems to solve and have found new ways to solve them.

Women have expanded their experiences so that they know what large groups of people are thinking and doing. Fewer and fewer women today are housewives only. Most women at one time or another go to work. Some women go out to work only a few months a year. Some work steady. In any case, they have a picture of the world that they never had before.

Some women that I have worked with say that they work because they can't get along on what their husbands make. This is true especially in the family where the man has no trade and his wages are small. But it is more and more true of everyone. Besides the high cost of living, there is another reason why it is hard to get along on one paycheck today. Women demand much more than they used to. They don't want to go through the awful feeling of being broke that they went through during the depression. They don't want to wash clothes by hand when, with a little extra, they can have the most modern equipment in their homes. Everything now is modern and women want the most modern appliances to work with. About the only thing you can do on one paycheck is exist.

When you are living on a small budget, it is the woman who must bear the brunt of it. She must go long distances to shop. When it becomes necessary to do without, she is usually the first person to forget her own needs.

One of the biggest financial needs that a woman has is some financial independence. They don't want to ask their husbands before they spend any money. They want to have money of their own. To be able to afford new drapes when the old ones are still good but you are tired of looking at them, is a luxury that most women can't afford but all women want. The paycheck that your husband gives you, although you work as hard for it as he does, is never really your own, even though it may be handed to you for the needs of the family. These needs that women have can never be satisfied on the money that the working man alone brings home.

A woman who goes to work in a factory has a feeling of independence not only about the money that is spent, but about the decisions that are made in the house. If you are helping to support the family, you have more right to decide not only what is to be done with the family money, but you now want to have more of a part in other questions that come up in the family which your husband has always decided before. One particular man was so surprised with the rights his wife took since she started to work that he told her to stay home. They got along better that way, he said.

It is not only decisions that a woman feels more independent about. When a woman works she knows that she doesn't have to put up with a lot of things from her husband. If he steps out of line by drinking or going out with other women, then she will up and leave him faster than before. She figures that now, if she has to, she can always support herself.

One of the things that drives women to get jobs is the boredom and loneliness that they would have to live with if they stayed home. Women want to be with other people. As compared to her husband, a woman leads an isolated life in the house by herself. The only company that she has while she is home is the radio and the telephone. In the factory you at least work with other people and get away from the boredom and loneliness that is home life.

The thing that a woman regrets most when she goes out to work is leaving her children. It is true that you want to get away from them for a while, but you don't like to leave them with just anybody. Most of the time you don't know much about how they are being taken care of. If they are older, you don't know who they go around with and what they do with their time. If your child is in a nursery school, you can ask the teacher how the child is doing. Most of the time she will say, "Fine." But that's all. You really don't know how they are being treated or what kind of care they are getting. You always hope the child is doing the right thing but when you work, you are never sure.

There is also the problem of where to leave the child when you work. Many women who are separated from their husbands and have young children, have to board them out. They miss their children who seem to grow up without them. They don't have much say in the way their children are brought up. Other women prefer to depend on neighbors whom they know rather than a nursery school that they know little or nothing about. The reason that a lot of women don't go to work at all is because they have no one reliable to take care of their children.

Wherever She Wants to Be

Women want to be able to decide whether or not to work. If a man tells a woman to work she usually won't. For one thing she feels that if she works when he tells her to then he gets used to it, and sometimes stops working regularly himself. He thinks that she should support him. One woman I know had to stop working because her husband thought that he could go out gambling with the money that she was making. On the other hand, if her husband tells her not to work, that doesn't mean that she will stay home. When a woman goes out to work it is not always with the approval of her husband. Many men resent their wives working. They use as an excuse the fact that the children should stay with their mother. They also say that they are not able to help their wives with the children and with the house and shopping. Others will make it so unbearable by putting the entire burden on their wives that finally the wives will be forced to quit.

Women have to fight those men who believe that a woman's place is in the home, and that is where they should stay. These are the men who don't want their wives to have any independence at all, and who want to be the only ones who bring in a check so they are the only ones with a say in their homes. When a woman goes out to work, they know that she becomes much more of a person in her own right. Women have shown these men that a woman's place is wherever she wants to be.

Those women who want to go on working and whose husbands don't want them to, don't tell their husbands about how hard it is to work. They keep all of that to themselves. One woman on our line at work has to fight to keep working. She has a fourteen-year-old daughter and she says there is nothing to keep her home. Yet her husband, a professional, who makes good money, is constantly asking her to quit. She never shows how tired she is when she gets home and she can't afford to ask him for help or he will make her quit.

There is quite a difference in the feeling toward women working between those women who have to work and those who work because they want to. If a woman works because she wants to, she doesn't have to take as much from the company and she can tell the boss to go to hell with his job, as my neighbor puts it. When she gets tired of working, she knows she can quit, and even if she doesn't quit, the very fact that she can makes her more independent of the company.

Those women who have to work, the single women who are supporting themselves and sometimes their parents, or the divorced women who are supporting their children, must stick to their jobs no matter how they feel or what they feel like doing. When these women get tired of working, they just go right on working. They have no choice. The company usually takes full advantage of this and knows it can depend on these women for Saturday work and overtime. When you are paying ten or fifteen dollars a week for nursery school alone, every penny counts.

Factory work for women is sometimes easy work—that is, it is not hard physically. But, like all factory work, it is dull and monotonous. In certain industries, it is hard physically. You feel in every muscle that you have put in a day's work. The important thing, no matter what kind of work you do, is the people you work with. If the work is easy but dull, then it is the other women who make the day pass at all. If it is hard work, the only thing that keeps you going is the other women who are doing the same thing you are and going through it with you. It is not the work that is so important to you and that makes factory life bearable. It is the people with whom you work that you care about.

There is always something going on at the plant. Either someone is cracking a joke or clowning or you are having a fight with the foreman or lead girl. There is always a discussion going on about something, and everything is talked about. Sex problems or their current affairs, housework and how to manage the children, new dance steps and the latest styles, price control and housing, ways of gaining and losing weight. No matter what you want to talk about, there is someone to talk to. The girls consider each other's feelings and interests.

Unlike the company, the girls care about each other. When one person is out, she is missed and someone usually calls to find out what is the matter. If something is seriously wrong with a particular girl, then her immediate group of friends start a collection to buy her something or to give her money to pay the extra bills. The girls give freely of their time and their money. If a girl is not feeling well a certain day, then the other girls or some special friends will work twice as fast to make up for her work so that she doesn't have to miss time from work. The company never worries about the individual person. They expect, come hell or high water, the same amount of work every day. The girls are the only ones who care about each other and will help you out when you need it.

We—From Now On

When a woman comes home from work at night, there is quite a difference from when a man comes home from work. As soon as she comes home she starts working all over again. A married woman, especially if she has children, can never have the luxury of sitting down and doing nothing. There is dinner to get on the table, the dishes to be washed, the children to be bathed and gotten to bed. She has two jobs. She is a part-time mother and housewife and a full-time wage earner. The weekend which a man takes to relax, for her belongs to the house. And all the things that have been left undone during the week have to be done then.

It's a hard grind, working and having a family. No matter how much your husband helps you or how considerate he is, the main burden of the house is still on the woman's shoulders. Just because a woman goes out to work, it doesn't mean she stops being a housewife.

A woman has a lot more in common with her husband when she works than when she stays home. There is more to talk to him about than there was before. The main barrier is still there, however, and it is still easier to talk to other women than it is to talk to your husband. Yet, things are definitely changed for a couple. For the first time, a woman says, you are not supporting this house. *We are.* And things will have to be *we* from now on.

Union and Company Women

The union and the company try to appear fair by putting up women for supervisory jobs. The shop stewards and the union officials are often women. The lead girls of the company and the foreladies are often taken from the line in plants. But as soon as these girls are taken off the line, they forget the rest of the girls and become agents of the union or the company, very often against the girls. The lead girls usually eat together and go out together and consider themselves better than the rest. They act just like the men supervisors. But they use the fact that they're women to try to win the confidence of the other girls in order to get more production and to keep the girls in line.

One of the lead girls in my plant was asked by the supervisor to get out double production. She said she would never do that to the girls and cried like a baby for days. It never dawned on her that the only way she could get the supervisor to stop pressing her was to get the girls to protest. She handled it herself and in a few days was demanding that the girls produce, using the excuse that she had been pressured into it. Most women feel that when a woman gets to be boss, she is worse than a man. The women who get in as bosses constantly use the fact that they are women to whip the girls into line. The women union officials are the same way.

Men workers talk about how the union is separated from the men. If this is true of the men's unions, it is doubly true of the women's. To many women it seems that the only thing that they do is collect dues and try to keep the girls in line for the company. The initiation fees are way out of proportion to the amounts that the women make and the dues are just as high. In some shops nobody knows who the shop steward is and very few of the girls care. Yet the girls will defend the union if the company attacks it. They know, however, that if anything is to be done, they will have to do it themselves.

Most women look at work as six of one and half a dozen of the other. If it is a choice of staying home in the monotony of the house, then they feel that it is worthwhile working. Some women look forward to the day when they can afford to stay home. When that day comes, they leave the plant only to come right back most of the time. After you have worked out, even for a little while, it is hard to go back into the home. This is what happened to a lot of women during the war, who worked in defense plants. After the war, many were laid off, but some stayed. Those who were laid off and many, many more women who have never worked before are becoming working women. A woman's place is becoming wherever she wants to be.

It is not that women enjoy work. They like the work in neither the home nor the factory. But as compared to being "just a housewife" most women feel that even factory work is preferable. My neighbor went out to work for Christmas money, and because she wanted to get away from the house for a while, but Christmas money was her excuse to her husband. Her three-year-old boy stays with his godparents so her husband has no complaint about her working. Every once in a while, she says she is quitting but she just can't get herself to do it.

Every Woman Knows

More and more today, women are showing by their every action that they can't go on in the old way. They have no confidence any more that what is supposed to work really will, or what is supposed to be their lives, should be. Their husbands, their children, their work, all are in conflict with them. Everything they do, every decision they make, they feel *may* work. Marriage, children, home, none of these things are women sure of any more.

Housewives who have never worked before are waiting until their children are old enough so they can get a job. Women who have always worked are looking forward to the day when they can finally quit. Marriages that have lasted for twenty years are breaking up. Young couples, after six months of marriage decide that they'd better end it now before they have children who will suffer. Young women getting out of high school, instead of running to get married, get a job and an apartment of their own and live independently.

It is not that women don't want to be wives and mothers. They want and need men to share their lives with and every woman wants children. But they feel that if they can't have a human relationship they will have no relationship at all. Women go from being married to being divorced, from being housewives to working out, but nowhere do women see the kind of life that they want for themselves and their families.

Women are finding more and more that there is no way out but a complete change. But one thing is already clear. Things can't go on the way they are. Every woman knows that.

COLUMNS FROM THE NEWSPAPER *CORRESPONDENCE* (1954)

n 1954, I wrote a column, naturally called "A Woman's Place," in every issue of *Correspondence,* the biweekly newspaper that Johnson-Forest was trying to get working-class people to write for. I was a single mother, working in a factory at that time, wiring and soldering radar sets for the military, and coming home in the evening to care for my young son. I had never done journalism before, and I learnt on the job, including reporting how women at the grassroots responded to national and international affairs—if they even knew about them. People were much less aware of "the news" then unless they were directly affected. (I myself never read newspapers until some years later.) I was free to write what I liked, without editorial interference, except for the addition of subtitles. Here are three of these columns.

The first, "Getting Politics Out of the Way," was written in 1954, when the U.S. Supreme Court declared, in the famous case of Brown vs. the Board of Education that "separate but equal"—separate education for Black and white people, which was never equal—was illegal. All kinds of people had to readjust their sights and their behavior and some did it surprisingly quickly.

My neighbor's response all those years ago reported below is a piece of history. It shows not only the turmoil that white people felt, but that within weeks many were able to adjust their behavior from being racist once the government had adjusted *its* behavior from being racist. A great lesson can still be learnt from this.

The second, about the Miss Universe beauty contest, was particularly interesting for me to read almost sixty years later, bearing in mind the women's movement controversy about beauty contests. Clearly I didn't think this was how women should be treated, but I saw some of the reasons women would want to be part of it, and I still do.

I especially remember writing the third, on women's industries. My father was one of those who fought to form a union in Brooklyn, New York, and we were a family deeply committed to the union as our organized power as a working class. But I saw how the union treated us and how much closer the "leadership" was to the management than to us. When I put that down on paper, it was like a revelation to me. Nobody censored me. I was in an organization that really wanted to hear the working-class point of view. Of course I was not the only one who thought that. And by now, it is acknowledged. Almost two decades later I wrote *Women, the Unions, and Work* and *The Perspective of Winning*, which updated and developed these views.

Getting Politics Out of the Way

A lot of parents took their children to school for the first time this September. Like every other September, the yearly ritual is repeated. New pencil boxes and brief cases, kids in the five-and-dime stores buying school supplies, mothers missing their kids (the same mothers who were waiting for school to begin because the kids were getting in everybody's way).

There is the usual shopping for new clothes for the kids to wear on their first day. The girls get new dresses and ribbons in their hair; the boys get new jeans and fresh haircuts. There is the spirit of newness, which are children themselves. The young ones are making their first step out of their mothers' arms and into the world as independent human beings. Even fathers, who act above it all, are hit by the sudden proof that the baby of the family is going into a world only his parents have known up to now.

A Private Affair

I have always thought of kids starting and returning to school, as I am sure a lot of other people have, as a personal matter. That is, it is your child who is affected and your relation with him. No politics, just the yearly shock of growing children. And it would be purely private if politics weren't always entering into people's lives.

This semester, the very simple and private act of taking a child to school is dividing a nation. It is making headlines in the papers. And it is causing no end of discussion among all types of people. The Supreme Court decision outlawing segregation is being tested in the South.

I am sure that other people writing for this paper will have many important things to say about it, as they already have. Except to say that I am very much in favor of the decision, I will leave the discussion to other sections of the paper. I want only to say that the decision made me think again how apparently simple, personal things become increasingly political and social.

Another Political Decision

My neighbors next door are not on the Supreme Court and they certainly are not interested in politics. But they had their own political decision to make on whether education was going to be segregated or not.

Our neighborhood was once all white. Now it is mixed; white, Mexican-American, Negro, and more Negroes are moving in every day. The schools, therefore, where they were once white, are now mixed.

Private School

My next-door neighbors are white. They have a little girl, kindergarten age. About six blocks from our house is a school and my neighbor told me that her daughter wasn't going to that school—orders from her husband. Cathy, if she went, would be "the only white face in the class" and her father just didn't want that to be.

My neighbor inquired about private and religious schools. She found one that would take Cathy—for eight dollars a month. In this school, Cathy would not only not be "the only white face." There would be nothing but "white faces."

A Choice

My neighbor's husband plays golf. It costs him eight dollars a month. He loves golf. He is good at it. They have a little lawn in front of their house, facing my kitchen, and on a Sunday morning, he is out there, golf balls and clubs in hand, practicing. All he would have to do for his daughter to go to private school would be to give up golf, give up that golf money for private school fees. That was quite a decision.

The first morning of school, I stopped in next door. I asked for Cathy. No, Cathy was not home. She was in kindergarten. Which school? Why, the neighborhood school, of course. The one that didn't cost eight dollars. Segregation was important until you got right down to cases.

Through with Politics

My neighbor and I had argued for weeks about discrimination. Now we didn't mention it. The tension was released. We both relaxed. We just sat down and talked about how nervous she was seeing as it was Cathy's first day at school, her first day away from home. After the decision was made, no politics. We went back to normal, two mothers discussing their kids.

I look forward to the day when white and Negro mothers will just be two mothers discussing their kids. But, as with my neighbor, a political decision has to be acted upon and settled before things can be anywhere near normal.

Miss Universe

I watched Miss Universe of 1955 being chosen on television on Friday, July 23. As beauty contests go, this was just another one, except that it was more spectacular and more glamorous. Ordinarily, I wouldn't watch something like that, but as I turned the TV dial, it hit my eye and it was fascinating to see the different types of women and to try to guess whom the judges would pick.

During the week before the finals, TV and movies gave blow-by-blow descriptions of what was happening and just how "lovely" the eighty contestants from all over the world were. As I watched the finals, it struck me that though the women were different types, every one of them looked the same. They all stood the same way, had a similar style walk and had almost the identical smile. To this day, I don't know if it is copying the American style or is just the forced and unnatural international style of all models and beauty contestants.

American Standard

I thought at first they looked so much like Americans because we are too used to seeing people from different countries look different from us. The difference in language doesn't show in a woman's face. But it was clear that for American judges, each country had picked the woman who would be closest to what Americans consider beautiful. As much as Coca-Cola is an international drink, and as much say as America has in the world, so American standards of beauty dominated, at least for the contest.

Of course there was a "type" that was not represented at all. There was not one Negro woman in the beauty contest. This was an American contest in more ways than one.

Not Only Beauty—They Said

The contest was supposed to be not only for beauty, the MC kept saying. It was for poise and stature as well. They even had the women go down the ramp in evening gowns. But the most important outfit was the Catalina swimsuit in exactly the same style for each of the young women.

Besides, I don't see how they could call it anything but a beauty contest. There was no chance to know what the women were like personally. They did no talking, not even hello, so you didn't know what they were thinking or if they even did think.

When Miss United States was finally picked the winner, the judges said that the reason was that the runner-up, Miss Brazil, had two more inches than she should have had around the hips.

Smile for the Camera

They showed one picture where the eighty women were posing together in the sun. Four girls collapsed from the heat and excitement. As they did, there was a slight movement from the other girls, but not much. They still kept that "smile for the camera" look on their faces while the police carried the stricken women away. Being charming, it seems, didn't include forgetting your smile, even when people were collapsing around you. Those who were running the contest probably never thought of postponing the picture taking and giving the girls a break. Business, they say, is business if the business is money or smiles.

The Miss Universe contest was universally American, even to the way Miss Greece was not let into this country until the last minute. To the Immigration Authorities, there was policy to carry out and they carried it out until their boss, Mr. Dulles, OK'd the entry of Miss Greece into this country. Mr. Dulles must have come to the conclusion that a beauty contest is not subversive or Communist.

Everybody Was a Judge

Nobody takes beauty contests very seriously. The day after, everybody I know was having a ball judging who they would have picked. Some thought Miss United States was picked because of politics. Some had their own favorites. It certainly wasn't thought of as any international event, the way it was built up. It was more like picking the winners in a game.

Each time I see one of these contests, they make me a little sick to my stomach that any woman should be judged, not by what she has accomplished or by what she is, but by what she looks like, and that alone. I have often wondered what it would be like in a dressing room with eighty women who are trained to pose, dress their best and worry about their faces and figures more than anything else. To spend your youth that way seems such a waste of time and life. And when I saw them smile continually, not because they felt like it, but because it was part of their job, it made the word smile lose its meaning.

And yet I can understand women doing all this to be different, to get away from just a routine existence, to have a little excitement and to have something they can look back on. And for these reasons, I will bet a lot of women wanted to be in their place.

Women's Industries

Most of the places for women to work in Los Angeles are small TV and radio shops. The work is usually intricate wiring and soldering. Some of it requires a magnifying glass to see what you're working on.

Like any other place in LA, there are people from all over the country, some from Midwestern and southern farms, others from big cities. The women range in age from grandmothers to young girls just out of school on their first jobs. The women run around with their own groups, those who have the same interests, on breaks and at lunch. On the line itself, age, nationality, and background don't matter. When the bell rings, everybody runs for the clock. They walk in. They run out.

No Politics on the Line

Nobody talks politics unless something unusual happens. The daily papers are discussed only when there is a kidnapping or big divorce case or when something like the *I Love Lucy* program is news. They feel that there is nothing they can do about what the politicians are doing, and it just upsets you to think about it. There is a similar attitude to unions.

Lifeless Unions

Most of these radio shops are AF of L.[1] But the only way you know there is a union is by the dues taken out of your check. When you hire in, the personnel man usually has that apologetic tone in his voice when he tells you that you have to join the union in order to get the job. Nobody is that interested in joining.

The union representatives are mostly men, but there are some women representatives. There isn't much difference. Every couple of months, you see them walking through the plant in their Sunday best, enjoying their "tour." Compared with the vitality and energy of the workers in things not connected with work, their "representatives" are like corpses all dressed up.

The Same—But Worse

It's the same all over, but in places like LA, it's worse. The unions were imported here from the east. The women working now didn't help to build them. They got them ready made. And by the time they got them, everything they had stood for once, the unions had lost.

The guys in shipping or in the tool crib remember the unions when they represented something. They have in them the tradition of what the word, union, once

---

1 American Federation of Labor and Congress of Industrial Organizations

meant and how people fought to establish them. They still have hopes it will in some way go back to what it was.

Some say the unions are as they are because there are so many women working and women don't know how to stick together. That is just not true. If women thought that the union could do any good, they would be as active or more active than the men, who aren't very active anyway. The word, union, to the women, is as dirty a word as politics.

Many women are new to plants and plants are new to them. But they are there to stay. They are free of tradition. There is no past, just the present. They judge unions on what they are now. You join like you are hired. Your dues are paid before you get your check. You leave it when you quit or are laid off. It doesn't belong to you. It belongs to the job. All the women see is the difference between what they are supposed to be and what they are.

The company runs the job. They get orders mixed, blueprints jumbled, the wrong wire, cheap solder. That is what creates the strain and makes such physically light work exhausting. There is no way for the women to bring what they know about their work to be a force in the plant and to change the stupid and inhuman way the company runs things.

A Need for Organization

The women want and feel the need for some kind of organization, but they don't look to the unions. If something comes up, they handle it among themselves, at their own tables and in their own groups. Only once do I remember a grievance being taken to the union and then "just to let them know we're still alive." Until they see the possibility of organizing on a plant-wide basis and getting results, they will remain in their own groups, representing themselves as much as possible. They are accomplishing more by taking care of day-to-day problems right on the line than by trying to save a tradition.

AUBREY WILLIAMS AND WILSON HARRIS (1966)

During my almost five years in the West Indies (1958–1962), mainly in Trinidad and Tobago, I worked with CLR James when he edited *The Nation*, biweekly newspaper of the People's National Movement, the political party which led T&T's independence movement. Mainly, I did secretarial work for the editor, was the advertising manager, at times prepared the prime minister's speeches for publication, and edited letters from readers.

These letters were the most testing work and the most rewarding. Often people wrote from country villages I'd never heard of to voice grievances and criticisms. Mostly they were written with pencils that had not been sharp for a while. Their English was also not mine. But the letters were brief, and almost always had something worthwhile to say. It took time and effort to grasp their meaning and then edit so their meaning was clear, while preserving their turn of phrase and style. It was a great training in editing.

I don't have access to these letters or to the (few) articles I wrote then. But some years ago, I read an article on Aubrey Williams, a Guyanese painter, attributed to CLR. In fact I remembered writing it. CLR had done a series of articles on Guyana's 1966 independence celebrations, which we attended. I was impressed with the art show, part of the Caribbean Conference of Writers and Artists celebrating the independence, and when I told CLR, he asked me to report on it and incorporated this into one of his articles.[1]

---

1   *Guyana Dreaming,* excerpt from "An Hour's Harvest of Unique Art," *Guyana Graphic,* June 21, 1966.

It was not unusual in our political network to contribute to each other's work in this way, and this has continued in the Wages for Housework Campaign up to today. Sadly, this piece is all that I have of my scribblings in the Caribbean.

* * *

The walls of the conference room were hung with Guyanese paintings that had been gathered up in about an hour by Donald Locke, himself a painter. He had hung them just before the proceedings were due to begin, using his painter's eye quickly but carefully to gauge the size and center of each panel. Whether or not they were representative of Guyanese paintings was hard to say. But the hour's harvest was distinctly different from anything I had seen in art exhibitions or collections from Trinidad and Jamaica.

The criticism sometimes leveled at West Indian painting, that the colors come straight from the tube, did not apply. Here in Aubrey Williams were the colors of earth and of the beads, feathers and other artifacts of the Amerindians, carefully blended and contrasted. Where in other exhibitions we could pick out the attempt at abstraction, imitating styles and strictures used abroad, these abstracts had roots; and the shapes and forms, we knew, were in the painter's head before he applied the paint. He himself was a product of Guyana with its vast hinterland and a native population.

In the museum the next day the impression was reinforced. Side by side were paintings of Barbados and Guyana, both by Guyanese. The contrast was striking: Barbados with small houses crowded together; Guyana with open savannah and not a house in sight. This reality of Guyanese life, so different from the islands, found expression in more than subject matter. Aubrey Williams and Donald Locke were concerned with the question of space as it confronts the artist: what to do with nothingness; how to lead the eye of the viewer into a vast expanse through the narrow frame of a single painting.

The most individual school of painting to come out of the New World has been Mexican painting. Basing themselves on their native Indian population, their pottery, its color and shape; their dress and their labor, Mexican painters incorporated what they wanted from the Old World and created their own uniqueness: their blues and ochres, their curves and jagged edges, the Mexican silhouette and its movement. It is significant that island painters, seeking to paint the West Indian epic, are sometimes drawn to paint West Indian reality in the plastic language of Mexico. Here were the continental Guyanese discovering their own artistic language springing from their native soil and people.

Once you had seen these pictures, novelist Wilson Harris ceased to be a stranger. He sprang from this "undiscovered" land and the need to shed the routine, the familiar, the safe, with which urbanization cloaked its people. Harris penetrates to the terror of the unknown interior. This is the milieu into which both painter and novelist have plunged in their search for the Guyanese reality.

WOMEN AGAINST THE INDUSTRIAL RELATIONS ACT (1971)[1]

Leaflet of the Notting Hill group, Women's Liberation Workshop. It was reprinted in the issue of Shrew *edited by the Notting Hill group in September of 1971.*

This is an attack on the whole working class, and that includes women. But women in industry have almost no representation on the shop floor. They have always been ignored by men who call themselves militants. Now that we are all attacked these men expect us to join in defense of our class. And we will join. The question is: are they going to join with us? When women are under attack, then the whole working class is under attack. When women are forced to accept low wages, this threatens the higher wages that men have won through struggle.

If the man's pay packet doesn't feed the family, the first to suffer is the woman.

She is the first to go without everything, from food to medical care.

She is the one who has no choice but to work not only at home for no pay but also in factories and offices for low pay.

This Act is the spearhead of an attack upon the working class. Unemployment is next. They have already begun to throw us out of jobs. They tell us women don't "need" to work.

---

1   Introduced by the UK Conservative government, the Industrial Relations Act 1971 attacked waged workers' right to organize and increased the government's emergency powers to deal with strikes considered damaging to the national economy. After much protest, it was repealed by the incoming Labour government in 1974.

<u>First</u>, that is their excuse for offering women only the lowest paid jobs. And because we are discriminated against, we have no choice but to accept.

<u>Second</u>, what they think we "need" is only enough to survive on. Women in the last years have gone out to work for what our rulers call "extras," to bring into our homes a few of the comforts that are THE RIGHT OF EVERYONE. Even so, because of inflation, we have been forced to stay in industry to cover the family's basic survival needs.

<u>Third</u>, millions of women are fed up with the isolation and boredom of their unpaid work at home. We <u>NEED</u> to live a social existence. We <u>NEED</u> to be free of financial dependence on men. But our only escape has been to be exploited worse than men in factories or, harem-like, in typing pools. Black women especially are confined to the lowest paid jobs, and for us nursing is one of the few alternatives to factory work. Once the Immigration Bill becomes law, any struggle we wage will be in spite of the threat of deportation. Whatever work outside the home a woman does, she still has another job waiting for her when she gets home.

We have often had to wage our struggle for equal pay alone. As a result, the government was able to pass an act which gives us equal pay (if it does) only on condition that we are night and day a the disposal of industry. <u>If men had supported us this would never have happened.</u> As it is now, in order to work we have to abandon our children.

We can only defeat the Industrial Relations Act if we are a united force. The only basis for that unity is that the needs of <u>every</u> section of the working class is respected and fought for. The defeats of women have been the defeats of the whole class. THE TIME HAS COME WHEN MEN MUST REALIZE THAT UNLESS THEY SUPPORT US IN OUR STRUGGLE FOR LIBERATION, THEY WILL NEVER BE FREE THEMSELVES.

We want men for the first time to share with us the raising of our children. We therefore demand A SHORTER WORK WEEK FOR ALL. Then <u>nobody</u> has to be sacked.

THE TIME HAS COME WHEN WOMEN MUST NOT WAIT FOR TRADE UNIONS OR ANYBODY ELSE TO WAGE THEIR STRUGGLE. We must organize in the community, in the factory, in the hospital, in the office— wherever we are.

OUR STRUGGLE IS AGAINST THIS ACT AND BEYOND IT, AGAINST THE WHOLE STRUCTURE OF THIS SOCIETY.

THE POWER OF WOMEN AND THE SUBVERSION OF THE COMMUNITY (1972)

I n the summer of 1970, Mariarosa Dalla Costa, whom I had just met, was my house-guest in London, taking a break from lecturing at the University of Padova, Italy. We became good friends. The following summer, I visited her in Padova. She asked about my feminism, knowing that whatever I replied would be informed by the Marxism we shared.

I explained that women's basic weakness was the unwaged housework assigned to us (less mystified then, when fewer women worked outside the home and the house-wife wasn't hidden behind a second job); this work produced capital's entire labor force but was not even considered work. We discussed at length how this ensured women's financial dependence, our poverty, etc.

Two or three days later, I went with her to a meeting she had organized of women from the Left, where she presented a paper she had written almost overnight, inspired by rather than based on our long conversation. I had to wait for a translation to know what it said, learnt "political Italian" in the course of refining the rough translation, and began to reshape it for publication.

A car accident condemned me to three months on crutches, but saved me from having to audio-type (which is how I paid the rent). I had time! Dalla Costa joined me in London and we worked together on the manuscript, beginning in my hospi-tal room, rewriting much of it. Before she left London, I told her to put her name to "Women and the Subversion of the Community"—the piece we had done together—so it would be a weapon against the sexism she suffered.

Having further revised the manuscript, I went back to Italy on crutches, and we finalized the book together. At her suggestion, my 1952 pamphlet *A Woman's Place* was added, and in October 1972 *The Power of Women and the Subversion of the Community* was published by Falling Wall Press in Bristol, England, and at about the same time in Italian by Marsilio Editori, Padova.

While everything in the book leads to wages for housework, it actually comes out against wages for house*wives*. We had both been uncertain about that demand. But when in March 1972, I put forward wages for house*work*, Dalla Costa called from Padova to say how delighted she and the other women were.

In 1974 Dalla Costa wrote in an Italian daily that I was coauthor of *Women and Subversion*, and the 1975 foreword to the 3rd English edition, signed by both our organizations (below), claimed joint authorship.[1]

The book was the launch pad for "the domestic labor debate." Since only Dalla Costa had originally signed the core piece, the book was identified with her, and those in the UK hostile to Wages for Housework used that to deny the connection between my organizing and *Power of Women*, its theoretical basis. At the time this made a lot of work for us.

Dalla Costa and I worked well together across national boundaries until 1977. That year there was a political split (on race) in our international network, and we quietly parted ways.

In preparing to excerpt *Power of Women* for this anthology, I found that the two different orientations between the same covers (which I'd been aware of for some time) were not easy to disentangle. I've excerpted here paragraphs of mine that I consider key, and on which the Wages for Housework Campaign has been built.

* * *

---

1 "Selma James, already a housewife and worker in an electronics factory in the United States in the fifties, is coauthor of that document, not only of 'A Woman's Place,' the section directly signed by her, but also the section entitled 'Women and the Subversion of the Community.' This latter essay is a deepening, enriched by a reading of Marx, of the document that Selma had already written in the fifties making herself 'a vehicle for expressing what women, housewives and factory workers, felt and knew.' And that she herself obviously felt and knew." Mariarosa Dalla Costa, "Non 'cosa scegliere' ma 'come combattere'" (Not what to choose but how to fight), *Il Giorno*, February 5, 1974, 5.

Unfortunately, no Italian edition has reflected this joint authorship. That edition differs from the English in other respects. It's more academic (the title is *Female Power and Social Subversion*), and Dalla Costa's Italian introduction uses some of my introduction to the English edition without attribution. The German translation had the cheek to refer readers to the Italian autonomist Left to better understand our analysis. (In fact it had been directed, at least in part, against their male-dominated politics!) Dalla Costa was not part of that Left when we wrote this book, and I come from a quite different tradition of autonomy that began with the autonomous struggle of Black people and of women in the United States.

Foreword to the 3rd edition, 1975

When this book was first published three years ago, it was already clear that the international movement of women had upset basic assumptions on which this society rested. In confronting what happens in the family and on the street, we have had to confront what happens in the factory, the office, the hospital, the school—in every institution of capitalist society.

This book offered the women's movement a cohesive analysis, drawing on the descriptions by the movement of our diverse grievances. It offered a material foundation for "sisterhood." That material foundation was the social activity, the *work*, which the female personality was shaped to submit to. That work was housework.

In singling out the work of the housewife as that for which women are trained and by which women are defined; in identifying its product as labor power—the working class—this book broke with all those previous analyses of capitalist society which began and ended in the factory, which began and ended with men. Our isolation in the family while doing our work had hidden its social nature. The fact that it brought no wage had hidden that it was work. Serving men and children in wageless isolation had hidden that we were serving capital. Now we know that we are not only indispensable to capitalist production in those countries where we are 45 percent of their waged labor force. We are *always* their indispensable workforce, at home, cleaning, washing and ironing; making, disciplining, and bringing up babies; servicing men physically, sexually, and emotionally.

If our unwaged work is the basis of our powerlessness in relation both to men and to capital, as this book, and our daily experience, confirm, then wages for that work, which alone will make it possible for us to reject that work, must be our lever of power. If our need for a wage and our need to break from our isolation have driven us to a *second* job outside the home, to more work at low pay, then our alternative to isolation and wagelessness must be *a social struggle for the wage*.

This perspective and practice derives directly from the theoretical analysis of this book. But even when the authors understood that Wages for Housework was the perspective, which flowed logically from their analysis, they could not know all its implications. The book has been the starting point not for "a school of thought," but for an international network of organizations, which are campaigning for Wages for Housework.

Some of those who have disagreed with the analysis, and with the perspective of Wages for Housework that flows from it, have said that the perspective may apply to Italy but not to Britain or North America. The fact that an Italian woman, Mariarosa Dalla Costa, signed the main article was proof for them of its geographic limitations. In fact, Dalla Costa and Selma James wrote "Women and the Subversion of the Community" together, as Dalla Costa herself has said publicly many times. The proof of the international implications of the analysis, however, lies not in the national origins of its authors, but in the international campaign for Wages for Housework which has now begun.

Power of Women Collective, Britain

Comitato per il Salario al Lavoro Domestico di Padova
(Padua Wages for Housework Committee)

Introduction

"Women and the Subversion of the Community" is a contribution to *the* question posed by the existence of a growing international movement of women: What is the relation of women to capital and what kind of struggle can we effectively wage to destroy it? We must hastily add that this is not the same as asking: What concessions can we wring from the enemy?—though this is related. To pose the first question is to assume we'll win; to pose the second is to calculate what we can salvage from the wreck of defeat. But in struggling to *win*, plenty can be gained along the way.

Up to now, the women's movement has had to define itself unaided by any serious heritage of Marxist critique of women's relation to the capitalist plan of development and underdevelopment. Quite the opposite. We inherited a distorted and reformist concept of capital itself as a series of *things* which we struggle to plan, control or manage, rather than as a *social relation* which we struggle to destroy.[2] Bypassing that heritage or lack of it, our movement explored the female experience, beginning with what we personally knew it to be. This is how we have been able for the first time on a mass scale to describe with profound insight and cutting precision the degradation of women and the shaping of our personality by forces which intended that we accept this degradation, accept to be quiet and powerless victims. On the basis of these discoveries, two distinct political tendencies have emerged, apparently opposite extremes of the political spectrum within the women's movement.

---

2   "Wakefield discovered that in the Colonies, property in money, means of subsistence, machines and other means of production does not as yet stamp a man as a capitalist if there be wanting the correlative—the wage worker the other man who is compelled to sell himself of his own free will. He discovered that *capital is not a thing but a social relation between persons established by the instrumentality of things*. Mr. Peel, he moans, took with him from England to Swan River, West Australia, means of subsistence and of production to the amount of £50,000. Mr. Peel had the foresight to bring with him, besides, 3,000 persons of the working class, men, women and children. Once arrived at his destination, 'Mr. Peel was left without a servant to make his bed or fetch him water from the river.' Unhappy Mr. Peel who provided for everything except the export of English modes of production to Swan River!" Karl Marx, *Capital*, 1 (Moscow: 1958), 766. (Emphasis ours.)

Among those who have insisted that *caste* and not class was fundamental, some women have asserted that what they call an "economic analysis" could not encompass, nor could a political struggle end, the physical and psychological oppression of women. They reject revolutionary political struggle. Capital is immoral, needs reforms and should be left behind, they say (thereby implying that the reforms are a moral obligation which are themselves a negotiated and above all nonviolent transition to "socialism"), but it is not the only enemy. We must change men and/or ourselves first. So that not only political struggle is rejected; so is liberation for the mass of women who are too busy working and seeing after others to look for a personal solution.

The possible future directions of these politics vary, mainly because this point of view takes a number of forms depending on the stratum of women who hold it. An elite club of this type can remain introverted and isolated—harmless except as it discredits the movement generally. Or it can be a source of those managerial types in every field which the class in charge is looking for to perform for it ruling functions over rebellious women and, god bless equality, over rebellious men too.[3] Integral to this participation in the marginal aspects of ruling, by the way, is an ambition and rivalry up to now primarily identified with men.

But history, past and future, is not simple. We have to note that some of the most incisive discoveries of the movement and in fact its autonomy have come from women who began by basing themselves on a repudiation of class and class struggle. The task of the movement now is to develop a political strategy on the foundations of these discoveries and on the basis of this autonomy.

Most of those who have insisted from the beginning that *class* and not caste was fundamental have been less able to translate our psychological insights into autonomous and revolutionary political action. Beginning with a male definition of class, the liberation of women is reduced to equal pay and a "fairer" and more efficient welfare State.[4] For these women capital is the main enemy but because it is *backward*, not because it *exists*. They don't aim to destroy the capitalist social relation

---

3   The *Financial Times* of March 9, 1971, suggests that many capitalists are missing the opportunity to "use" women in positions of middle management; being "grateful outsiders," women would not only lower the pay structure, "at least in the first instance," but be a "source of renewed energy and vitality" with which to manage the rest of us.

4   If this seems an extreme statement, look at the demands we in England marched for in 1971: equal pay, free twenty-four-hour childcare, equal educational opportunity and free birth control and abortion on demand. Incorporated into a wider struggle, some of these are vital. As they stand, they accept that we not have the children we can't afford; that the State facilities keep the children we can afford for as long as twenty-four hours a day; and that these children have equal chance to be conditioned and trained to sell themselves competitively with each other on the labor market for equal pay. By themselves these are not just co-optable demands. They are capitalist planning. Most of us in the movement never felt these demands expressed where we wanted the movement to go, but in the absence of an independent feminist political framework, we lost by default. The prime architects of these demands were women with a "class analysis."

but only to organize it more rationally. (The extraparliamentary Left in Italy would call this a "socialist" as distinct from a revolutionary position.) What a rationalized capital—equal pay, more and better nurseries, more and better jobs, etc.—can't fix, they call "oppression" which, like Topsy, the orphaned slave child who never knew her parents, "just growed." Oppression disconnected from material relations is a problem of "consciousness"—in this case, psychology masquerading in political jargon. And so the "class analysis" has been used to limit the breadth of the movement's attack and even undermine the movement's autonomy.

The essentially similar liberal nature of these two tendencies, wanting to rationally manage "society" to eliminate "oppression," is not usually apparent until we see the "political" women and these "nonpolitical" women join together on concrete demands or, more often, against revolutionary actions. Most of us in the movement belong to neither of these tendencies and have had a hard time charting a course between them. Both ask us: "Are you a feminist or are you political?"

The "political" women who talk of class are easy to identify. They are the women's liberationists whose first allegiance is not to the women's movement but to organizations of the male-dominated Left. Once strategy and action originate from a source outside of women, women's struggle is measured by how it is presumed to affect men, otherwise known as "the workers," and women's consciousness by whether the forms of struggle they adopt are the forms men have traditionally used.

The "political" women see the rest of us as nonpolitical and this has tended to drive us together in self-protection, obscuring or playing down real political differences among us. These now are beginning to make themselves felt. Groups that call themselves Psychology Groups (I'm not talking here about consciousness raising groups) tend to express the politics of caste most coherently.[5] But whichever quarter they come from, viewing women as a caste and only a caste is a distinct political line, which is increasingly finding political and organizational expression in every

---

5   Psychology itself *by its nature* is a prime weapon of manipulation, i.e., social control, of men, women, and children. It does not acquire another nature when wielded by women in a movement for liberation. Quite the reverse. To the degree that we permit, it manipulates the movement and changes the nature of that to suit its needs. And not only psychology. "Women's liberation needs:

  • to destroy sociology as the ideology of the social services which bases itself on the proposition that this society is "the norm"; if you are a person in rebellion, you are a deviant.

  • to destroy psychology and psychiatry which spend their time convincing us that our "problems" are personal hang-ups and that we must adjust to a lunatic world. These so-called "disciplines" and "sciences" will increasingly incorporate our demands in order more efficiently to redirect our forces into safe channels under their stewardship. Unless we deal with them, they will deal with us.

  • to discredit once and for all social workers, progressive educators, marriage guidance counselors, and the whole army of experts whose function is to keep men, women, and children functioning within the social framework, each by their own special brand of social frontal lobotomy." From "The American Family: Decay and Rebirth," by Selma James, reprinted in *From Feminism to Liberation*, collected by Edith Hoshino Altbach, (Cambridge, MA: Schenkman, 1971), 197–98.

discussion of what to do. In the coming period of intense working-class activity, as we are forced to create our own political framework, casting away secondhand theories of male-dominated socialist movements, the preeminence of caste will be posed as the alternative and will have to be confronted and rejected as well. On this basis alone can the new politics inherent in autonomy find its tongue and its muscle.

This process of development is not unique to the women's movement. The Black movement in the United States (and elsewhere) also began by adopting what appeared to be only a caste position in opposition to the racism of white male-dominated groups. Intellectuals in Harlem and Malcolm X, that great revolutionary, were both nationalists, both appeared to place color above class when the white Left were still chanting variations of "Black and white unite and fight," or "Negroes and Labor must join together." The Black working class was able through this nationalism to *redefine class*: overwhelmingly Black and Labor were synonymous (with no other group was Labor as synonymous—except perhaps with women), the demands of Black people and the forms of struggle created by Black people were the most comprehensive *working-class* demands and the most advanced *working-class* struggle. This struggle was able to attract to itself the best elements among the intellectuals who saw their own persecution as Black people—as a caste—grounded in the exploitation of Black workers. These intellectuals who got caught in the moment of nationalism after the class had moved beyond it saw race in increasingly individual terms and made up that pool from which the State Department could hook the fish of tokenism—appointing a Black as special presidential advisor on slum clearance, for example—and the personnel of a new, more integrated technocracy.

In the same way women for whom caste is the fundamental issue will make the transition to revolutionary feminism based on a redefinition of class or invite integration into the white male power structure.

But "'Marxist' women," as a woman from the movement in New Orleans says, "are just 'Marxist' men in drag." The struggle as they see it is not qualitatively different from the one the organized labor movement *under masculine management* has always commended to women, except that now, appended to the "general struggle," is something called "women's liberation" or "women's struggle" voiced by women themselves.

This "general struggle" I take to mean the class struggle. But there is nothing in capitalism that is not capitalistic, that is, not part of the class struggle. The questions are (a) Are women except when they are waged workers auxiliary to capitalism (as has been assumed) and therefore auxiliary to a more basic, more general struggle against capitalism; and (b) Can anything ever have been "general" which has excluded so many women for so long?

Rejecting on the one hand class subordinated to feminism and on the other feminism subordinated to class, we confronted what (to our shame) has passed for Marxism with the female experience that we have been exploring and struggling to articulate. The result has been a translation of our psychological insights into a critique of the political economy of the exploitation of women, the theoretical basis for a revolutionary and autonomous women's struggle. Based on what we know of *how* we are degraded, we move into the question of *why*, in a depth as far as I know not reached before.

One great achievement of Marx was to show that the specific social relations between people in the production of the necessities of life, relations which spring up without their conscious planning, "behind the backs of *people*" (*Menschen*—previously translated as *men*), distinguish one society from another. That is, in class society, the form of the relation between people through which the ruling class robs the exploited of their labor is unique in each historic epoch, and all other social relations in the society, beginning with the family and including every other institution, reflect that form.

For Marx history was a process of struggle of the exploited, who continually provoke over long periods and in sudden revolutionary leaps changes in the basic social relations of production and in all the institutions which are an expression of these relations. The family, then, was the basic biological unit differing in form from one society to another, directly related to the way people produce. According to him, the family, even before class society, had the subordinated woman as its pivot; class society itself was an extension of the relations between men on the one hand and women and children on the other, an extension, that is, of the man's command over the labor of his woman and his children.

The women's movement has gone into greater detail about the capitalist family. After describing how women are conditioned to be subordinate to men, it has described the family as that institution where the young are repressed from birth to accept the discipline of capitalist relations—which in Marxist terms begins with the discipline of capitalist work. Other women have identified the family as the center of consumption, and yet others have shown that housewives make up a hidden reserve work force: "unemployed" women *work* behind closed doors at home, to be called out when capital needs them elsewhere.

"Women and the Subversion of the Community" affirms all the above, but places them on another basis: the family under capitalism is a center of conditioning, of consumption and of reserve labor, but a center essentially of *social production*. When previously so-called Marxists said that the capitalist family did not produce for capitalism, was not part of social production, it followed that they repudiated women's potential *social power*.[6] Or rather, presuming that women in the home

---

6   Marx himself does not seem to have said anywhere that it was. Why this is so requires more space than is available here and more reading of the man at the expense of his interpreters. Suffice it to say that, first, he is singular in seeing personal consumption as a phase of production: "It is the production and reproduction of that means of production so indispensable to the capitalist: the laborer himself." (*Capital* I: 572.) Second, he alone has given us the tools to make our own analysis. And finally, he never

could not have social power, they could not see that women in the home produced. If your production is vital for capitalism, refusing to produce, refusing to *work*, is a fundamental lever of social power.

Marx's analysis of capitalist production was not a meditation on how the society "ticked." It was a tool to find the way to overthrow it, to find the social forces which, exploited by capital, were subversive to it. Yet it was because he was looking for the forces that would inevitably overthrow capital that he could describe capital's social relations, which are pregnant with working-class subversion. It is because we were looking for *women's* lever of social power among those forces that we were able to uncover that even when women do not work out of their homes, they are vital producers.

The commodity they produce, unlike all other commodities, is unique to capitalism: the living human being—"the laborer himself."

Capital's special way of robbing labor is by paying the worker a wage that is enough to live on (more or less) and to reproduce other workers. But the worker must produce more in the way of commodities than what his wage is worth. The unpaid surplus labor is what the capitalist is in business to accumulate and what gives him increasing power over more and more workers: he pays for some labor to get the rest free so he can command more labor and get even more free, ad infinitum—until we stop him. He buys with wages the right to use the only "thing" the worker has to sell, his or her ability to work. The specific social relation, which is capital, then, is the wage relation. And this wage relation can exist only when the ability to work becomes a saleable commodity. Marx calls this commodity *labor power*.

This is a strange commodity for it is not a thing. The ability to labor resides only in a human being whose life is consumed in the process of producing. First it must be nine months in the womb, must be fed, clothed, and trained; then when it works its bed must be made, its floor swept, its lunchbox prepared, its sexuality not gratified but quietened, its dinner ready when it gets home, even if this is eight in the morning from the night shift. This is how labor power is produced and reproduced when it is daily consumed in the factory or the office. *To describe its basic production and reproduction is to describe women's work.*

The community therefore is not an area of freedom and leisure auxiliary to the factory, where by chance there happen to be women who are degraded as the personal servants of men. The community is the other half of capitalist organization, the other area of hidden capitalist exploitation, *the other, hidden, source of surplus labor.*[7] It

---

was guilty of the nonsense with which Engels, despite his many contributions, has saddled us and which, from the Bolsheviks to Castro, has given a "Marxist" authority to backward and often reactionary policies towards women of revolutionary governments.

7   I said earlier that "Women and the Subversion of the Community" moves into the question of why women are degraded "in a depth as far as I know not reached before." Three previous attempts stand out

becomes increasingly regimented like a factory, what we call a social factory, where the costs and nature of transport, housing, medical care, education, police, are all points of struggle.[8] And this social factory has as its pivot the woman in the home producing labor power as a commodity, *and her struggle not to.*

The demands of the women's movement, then, take on a new and more subversive significance. When we say, for example, that we want control of our own bodies, we are challenging the domination of capital which has transformed our reproductive

---

(and can all be found in *From Feminism to Liberation*.) "The Political Economy of Women's Liberation" by Margaret Benston attempts to answer the same question. It fails, in my view, because it bases itself not on Marx but on Ernest Mandel. Even the few paragraphs of Mandel which Benston quotes are enough to expose the theoretical basis of modern Trotskyist liberalism. We must restrict ourselves here to what he says about women's work in the home, which Benston accepts. "The second group of products in capitalist society which are not commodities but remain simple use-value consists of all things produced in the home. Despite the fact that considerable human labor goes into this type of household production, it still remains a production of use-values and not of commodities. Every time a soup is made or a button sewn on a garment it constitutes production, but it is not production for the market." This is quoted from *An Introduction to Marxist Economic Theory* (Merit, NY: 1967), 10–11. Even the title betrays the falsity of the content: there is no such thing as "Marxist economic theory" or "Marxist political economy" or for that matter "Marxist sociology." Marx negated political economy in theory and the working class negates it in practice. For economics fragments the qualitative relations between people into a compartmentalized and quantified relation between things. When, as under capitalism, our labor power becomes a commodity, we become factors in production, objects, sexual and in every way, which the economists, the sociologists and the rest of the vampires of capitalist science then examine, plan for and try to control).

Juliet Mitchell ("Women—The Longest Revolution") also believes that although women "are fundamental to the human condition, yet in their economic, social and political roles they are marginal" (93). The error of her method, in my view, is that once again an interpreter of Marx, this time Althusser, is her guide. Here separation of economic, social and political roles is conscious policy.

Labor power is a commodity produced by women in the home. It is this commodity that turns *wealth* into *capital.* The buying and selling of this commodity turns the market into a *capitalist* market. Women are not marginal in the home, in the factory, in the hospital, in the office. We are fundamental to the reproduction of capital and fundamental to its destruction.

Peggy Morton of Toronto in a splendid article, "A Woman's Work Is Never Done," points out that the family is the "unit whose function is the *maintenance of and reproduction of labor power* i.e.... the structure of the family is determined by the needs of the economic system, at any given time, for a certain *kind* of labor power" (214). Benston calls, after Engels, for the capitalist industrialization of household jobs as "preconditions" for "true equality in job opportunity and the industrialization of housework is unlikely unless women are leaving the home for jobs" (207). That is, if we get jobs capital will industrialize the areas where, according to her, we only produce use-values and not capital; this wins us the right to be exploited equally with men. With victories like that, we don't need defeats.

On the other hand, Morton is not looking for what concessions we can wring from the enemy but how to destroy him. "All too often we forget why we are organizing women; the purpose of building a mass movement is not to build a mass movement, but to make revolution." Benston, she says, "does not provide any basis on which strategy for a women's movement can be based." The absence of this motive for analysis in the movement generally "encourages a real liberalism among us" (212). Right on.

8   For those who believe the struggle in the social factory is not political, let them note that here, more than in the factory, is the State directly the organizer of the life of the worker, especially if she is a woman, and so here the worker confronts the State more directly, without the intervention of individual capitalists and the mediation of trade unions.

organs as much as our arms and legs into instruments of accumulation of surplus labor; transformed our relations with men, with our children and our very creation of them, into *work productive to this accumulation*.

A Woman's Place, originally published as a pamphlet, was written in 1952 at the height of the Cold War, in Los Angeles, where the immigration of young working men and women had assumed Biblical dimensions.[9] Though it bears my name, I was merely a vehicle for expressing what women, housewives and factory workers, felt and knew as immigrants to the Golden West from the South and East.

It was already clear even then that working outside the home did not make drudgery at home any more appealing, nor liberate us from the responsibility for housework even when it was "shared." It was equally clear that to think of spending our lives packing chocolates, or winding transformers, or wiring televisions was more than we could bear. We rejected both and fought against both. For example, in those days a man's friends would still laugh if they saw him wearing an apron and washing up. We changed that.

There is no doubt that the courage to fight for these changes sprang directly from that paycheck which we so hated to work for. But though we hated the work, for most of us it provided the first opportunity for an independent social experience outside the isolation of the home, and *seemed the only alternative to that isolation*. After the mass entry of women into industry during World War II, and our brutal expulsion between 1945 and 1947, from 1947 when they wanted us again we came back and, with the Korean War (1949), in increasing numbers. For all the reasons outlined in the pamphlet, we wanted money and saw no alternative to demanding jobs.

That we were immigrants from industrial, farming or coal-mining areas made us more dependent on that paycheck, since we had only ourselves to fall back on. But it gave us an advantage too. In the new aircraft and electronics industries of LA, in addition to the standard jobs for women, for example in food and clothing, we—more white women than Black, who were in those days largely denied jobs with higher (subsistence) pay—we managed to achieve new freedom of action. We were unrestrained by fathers and mothers who stayed "back East" or "down South." Trade unions, formed in the East years before by bitter struggle, by the time they were imported West were negotiators for a ten-cents-a-year rise, and were part of the disciplinary apparatus which confronted us on the assembly line and which we paid for in high dues taken out before we ever saw our money. Other traditional forms of "political" organization were either nonexistent or irrelevant and most of us ignored them. In short, we made a clean break with the past.

---

9   Southern California had experienced a huge wave of immigration during the war. Between 1940 and 1946, the population of San Diego (home of shipyards and naval base) had increased by 61 percent, that of LA by 29 percent (*Business Week*, December 20, 1947, 72).

In the women's movement of the late 1960s, the energy of those who refused the old forms of "protection," or who never knew them, finally found massive articulation. Yet twenty years before, in the baldness of our confrontation with capital (directly and via men) we were making our way through what has become increasingly an international experience. This experience taught us: the second job outside of the home is another boss superimposed on the first; a woman's first job is to reproduce other people's labor power, and her second is to reproduce *and sell* her own. So that her struggle in the family and in the factory, the joint organizers of her labor, of her husband's labor and of the future labor of her children, is one whole. The very unity in one person of the two divided aspects of capitalist production presupposes not only a new scope of struggle but an entirely new evaluation of the weight and cruciality of women in that struggle.

These are the themes of "Women and the Subversion of the Community." What was posed by the struggle of so-called "reactionary" or "backward" or at best "nonpolitical" housewives and factory wives in the United States twenty years ago is the starting point for a restatement of Marxist theory and a reorientation of struggle. This theoretical development parallels and expresses and is needed for an entirely new level of struggle which women internationally are in the process of waging.

We've come a long way, baby...

Power to the sisters and therefore to the class.

Padova, July 27, 1972

Women and the Subversion of the Community

We place foremost in these pages the housewife as the central figure... We assume that all women are housewives and even those who work outside the home continue to be housewives. That is, on a world level, it is precisely what is particular to domestic work, not only measured as number of hours and nature of work, but as quality of life and quality of relationships which it generates, that determines a woman's place wherever she is and to whichever class she belongs. We concentrate here on the position of the working-class woman, but this is not to imply that only working-class women are exploited. Rather it is to confirm that the role of the working-class housewife, which we believe has been indispensable to capitalist production, is *the* determinant for the position of all other women. Every analysis of women as a caste, then, must proceed from the analysis of the position of working-class housewives.

...Since Marx, it has been clear that capital rules and develops through the wage, that is, that the foundation of capitalist society was the wage laborer and his or her direct exploitation. What has been neither clear nor assumed by the organizations of the working-class movement is that precisely through the wage has the exploitation of the non-wage laborer been organized. This exploitation has been even more effective because the lack of a wage hid it… *Where women are concerned, their labor appears to be a personal service outside of capital.* The woman seemed only to be suffering from male chauvinism, being pushed around because capitalism meant general "injustice" and "bad and unreasonable behavior"; the few (men) who noticed convinced us that this was "oppression" but not exploitation. But "oppression" hid another and more pervasive aspect of capitalist society. Capital excluded children from the home and sent them to school not only because they are in the way of others' more "productive" labor or only to indoctrinate them. The rule of capital through the wage compels every able-bodied person to function, under the law of division of labor, and to function in ways that are if not immediately, then ultimately profitable to the expansion and extension of the rule of capital. That, fundamentally, is the meaning of school. *Where children are concerned, their labor appears to be learning for their own benefit.*

The Origins of the Capitalist Family

With the advent of capitalism the socialization of production was organized with *the factory* as its center. Those who worked in the new productive center, the factory, received a wage. Those who were excluded did not. Women, children, and the aged lost the relative power that derived from the family's dependence on their labor, *which had been seen to be social and necessary.* Capital, destroying the family and the community and production as one whole, on the one hand has concentrated basic social production in the factory and the office, and on the other has in essence detached the man from the family and turned him into a *wage laborer.* It has put on the man's shoulders the burden of financial responsibility for women, children, the old and the ill, in a word, all those who do not receive wages. From that moment began the expulsion from the home of all those who did not *procreate and service those who worked for wages.* The first to be excluded from the home, after men, were children; they sent children to school. The family ceased to be not only the productive but also the educational center… Capitalism is the first productive system where the children of the exploited are disciplined and educated in institutions organized and controlled by the ruling class.

Confirming the Myth of Female Incapacity

…the isolation from which women have suffered has confirmed to society and to themselves the myth of female incapacity.

It is this myth which has hidden, firstly, that to the degree that the working class has been able to organize mass struggles in the community, rent strikes, struggles against inflation generally, the basis has always been the unceasing informal organization of women there; secondly, that in struggles in the cycle of direct production women's support and organization, formal and informal, has been decisive. At critical moments this unceasing network of women surfaces and develops through the talents, energies and strength of the "incapable female." But the myth does not die. Where women could together with men claim the victory—to survive (during unemployment) or to survive and win (during strikes)—the spoils of the victor belonged to the class "in general." Women rarely if ever got anything specifically for themselves; rarely if ever did the struggle have as an objective in any way altering the power structure of the home and its relation to the factory. Strike or unemployment, a woman's work is never done.

The Homosexuality of the Division of Labor

A power relation precludes any possibility of affection and intimacy. Yet between men and women power as its right *commands* sexual affection and intimacy. In this sense, the gay movement is the most massive attempt to disengage sexuality and power.

But homosexuality generally is at the same time rooted in the framework of capitalist society itself: women at home and men in factories and offices, separated one from the other for the whole day; or a typical factory of a thousand women with ten foremen; or a typing pool (of women, of course) which works for fifty professional men. All these situations are already a homosexual framework of living.

Capital, while it elevates heterosexuality to a religion, at the same time in practice makes it impossible for men and women to be in touch with each other, physically or emotionally—it undermines heterosexuality except as a sexual, economic, and social discipline.

The Refusal of Work

The working-class family is the support of the worker, but as worker, and for that reason the support of capital. On this family depends the support of the class, the survival of the class—but *at the woman's expense against the class itself.* The woman is the slave of a waged slave, and her slavery ensures the slavery of her man. Like the trade union, the family protects the worker, but also ensures that he *and she* will never be anything but workers. And that is why the struggle of the woman of the working class against the family is crucial.

The "Political" Attack against Women

1. Women as consumers

Women do not make the home the center of consumption. The process of consumption is integral to the production of labor power, and if women refused to do the shopping (that is, to spend), this would be strike action. Having said that, however, we must add that those social relationships which women are denied because they are cut off from socially organized labor, they often try to compensate for by buying things. Whether it is adjudged trivial depends on the viewpoint and sex of the judge. Intellectuals buy books, but no one calls this consumption trivial.

We have already said that women buy things for their home because that home is the only proof that they exist. But the idea that frugal consumption is in any way a liberation is as old as capitalism, and comes from the capitalists who always blame the worker's situation on the worker. For years Harlem was told by head-shaking liberals that if Black men would only stop driving Cadillacs (until the finance company took them back), the problem of color would be solved. Until the violence of the struggle—the only fitting reply—provided a measure of social power, that Cadillac was one of the few ways to display the potential for power. This and not "practical economics" caused the liberals pain.

In any case, nothing any of us buys would we need if we were free. Not the food they poison for us, nor the clothes that identify us by class, sex, and generation, nor the houses in which they imprison us.

And that pressure which women place on men is *a defense of the wage, not an attack*. Precisely because women are the slaves of waged slaves, men divide the wage between themselves and the general family expense. If women did not make demands, the general family standard of living could drop to absorb the inflation—the woman of course is the first to do without. Thus unless the woman makes demands, the family is functional to capital in an additional sense to the ones we have listed: it can absorb the fall in the price of labor power. This, therefore, is the most ongoing material way in which women can defend the living standards of the class. And when they go out to political meetings, they will need even more money!

2. Women as rivals

As for women's "rivalry," Frantz Fanon has clarified for the Third World what only racism prevents from being generally applied to the class. The colonized, he says, when they do not organize against their oppressors, attack each other. The woman's pressure for greater consumption may at times express itself in the form of rivalry, but nevertheless as we have said protects the living standards of the class. Which is unlike women's sexual rivalry; that rivalry is rooted in our economic and social dependence on men. To the degree that women live for men, dress for men, work for men, we are manipulated by men through this rivalry.

As for rivalry about our homes, women are trained from birth to be obsessive and possessive about clean and tidy homes. But men cannot have it both ways; they cannot continue to enjoy the privilege of having a private servant and then complain about the effects of privatization. If they continue to complain, we must conclude that their attack on us for rivalry is really an apology for our servitude. If Fanon was not right, that the strife among the colonized is an expression of their low level of organization, then the antagonism is a sign of natural incapacity. When we call a home a ghetto, we could call it a colony governed by indirect rule and be as accurate. The resolution of the antagonism of the colonized to each other lies in autonomous struggle. Women have overcome greater obstacles than rivalry to unite in supporting men in struggles. Where women have been less successful is in transforming and deepening moments of struggle by making of them opportunities to raise our own demands. Autonomous struggle turns the question on its head: not "will women unite to support men," but "will men unite to support women?"

3. Women as divisive

What has prevented previous political intervention by women? Why can we be used in certain circumstances against strikes? Why, in other words, is the class not united? From the beginning of this document we have made central the exclusion of women from socialized production. That is an objective character of capitalist organization: cooperative labor in the factory and office, isolated labor in the home. This is mirrored subjectively by the way workers in industry organize separately from the community. What is the community to do? What are women to do? Support, be appendages to men in the home *and* in the struggle, even form a women's auxiliary to unions. This division and *this kind of division* is the history of the class. At every stage of the struggle the most peripheral to the productive cycle are used against those at the center, so long as the latter ignore the former. This is the history of trade unions, for example, in the United States, when Black workers were used as strikebreakers—never, by the way, as often as white workers were led to believe—Blacks like women are immediately identifiable and reports of strikebreaking reinforce prejudices which arise from objective divisions: the white on the assembly line, the Black sweeping round his feet; or the man on the assembly line, the woman sweeping round his feet when he gets home.

Men when they reject work consider themselves militant, and when we reject our work, these same men consider us nagging wives. When some of us vote Conservative because we have been excluded from political struggle, they think we are backward, while they have voted for parties which didn't even consider that we existed as anything but ballast, and in the process sold them (and us all) down the river.

Women and the Struggle Not to Work

Let us sum up. The role of housewife, behind whose isolation is hidden social labor, must be destroyed. But our alternatives are strictly defined. Up to now, the myth of female incapacity, rooted in this isolated woman dependent on someone else's wage and therefore shaped by someone else's consciousness, has been broken by only one action: the woman getting her own wage, breaking the back of personal economic dependence, making her own independent experience with the world outside the home, performing social labor in a socialized structure, whether the factory or the office, and initiating there her own forms of social rebellion along with the traditional forms of the class. *The advent of the women's movement is a rejection of this alternative.*

Capital itself is seizing upon the same impetus that created a movement—the rejection by millions of women of women's traditional place—to recompose the work force with increasing numbers of women. The movement can only develop in opposition to this. It poses by its very existence and must pose with increasing articulation in action that women refuse the myth of liberation through work.

For we have worked enough. We have chopped billions of tons of cotton, washed billions of dishes, scrubbed billions of floors, typed billions of words, wired billions of radio sets, washed billions of nappies, by hand and in machines. Every time they have "let us in" to some traditionally male enclave, it was to find for us a new level of exploitation. Here again we must make a parallel, different as they are, between underdevelopment in the Third World and underdevelopment in the metropolis—to be more precise, in the kitchens of the metropolis. Capitalist planning proposes to the Third World that it "develop"; that in addition to its present agonies, it too suffer the agony of an industrial counterrevolution. Women in the metropolis have been offered the same "aid." But those of us who have gone out of our homes to work because we had to or for extras or for economic independence have warned the rest: inflation has riveted us to this bloody typing pool or to this assembly line, and in that there is no salvation. We must refuse the development they are offering us. But the struggle of the working woman is not to return to the isolation of the home, appealing as this sometimes may be on Monday morning; any more than the housewife's struggle is to exchange being imprisoned in a house or being clinched to desks or machines, appealing as this sometimes may be compared to the loneliness of the twelfth-story flat.

The challenge to the women's movement is to find modes of struggle which, while they liberate women from the home, at the same time avoid a double slavery and prevent another degree of capitalist control and regimentation. *This ultimately is the dividing line between reformism and revolutionary politics within the women's movement.*

WOMEN, THE UNIONS, AND WORK, OR WHAT IS NOT TO BE DONE (1972)

I wrote *Women, the Unions, and Work* a couple of days before a national conference of the women's liberation movement in Manchester in 1972.

We were about to publish *The Power of Women and the Subversion of the Community* which aimed to identify women's case for an anticapitalist women's movement. While women's groups were springing up everywhere, the Left was urging women to forget all this autonomy, "support the working class" and join the union (or the party) to have our consciousness raised. But some of us *were* working class. I felt strongly that it was time for women to make our own class politics, spelling out why we were organizing independently as women.

Many in the women's liberation movement were there to advance their personal ambition. They were in competition with men and not very interested in fundamental political change. Socialist feminists, on the other hand, although passionately opposed to women's subordination, saw the struggle of women as quite other than the struggle of class—except when women had waged jobs.

A friend sold a number of the hundred duplicated copies of *Women, the Unions, and Work* on the London-to-Manchester coach, so some had read it by the time they arrived.

The paper caused great excitement, even among women who disagreed with it. The demand for wages for housework was one of its six demands and it provoked an explosive workshop discussion. So explosive that it burst its bounds and the whole conference stayed together to discuss wages for housework. Thus began a debate, often bitter, which continues to this day. (This tells us how deep are the issues that divide us.)

After the conference, the Notting Hill (London) Women's Liberation Workshop group, of which I was a member, published *Women, the Unions, and Work* as a pamphlet.

Almost every Left organization or party mobilized against it, and at the next national women's conference in London some months later, there were large banners which said, "A reply to Selma James"—except one which said, "A reply to the reactionary Selma James." Each had a publication with a major article devoted to attacking this terrible thing I had done: I had dared to be critical of the unions and, on top of that, demanded wages for housework which would discourage women from going out to work, so they could have as high a consciousness as men.

Most feminists, whether they identified with the Left or not, were profoundly hostile to women getting a wage for housework from the State because, they said, it would institutionalize women in the home. Many refused to recognize housework as work.

"The Perspective of Winning," written in 1973, sums up months of debate. Through this debate, some of us found out that what had started as a demand was in fact a new political perspective, a class perspective, which began with women. This strengthened the new International Wages for Housework Campaign.

By 1975 the debate was over for us; it was time to put the perspective into practice. The Campaign continued to be treated with contempt and even witch-hunted. This also had its uses. It trained us to keep our focus on grassroots organizing rather than on taking attacks personally and defending ourselves in academic debates. We concentrated instead on building our corner of the movement. It must be noted that with some exceptions feminists in the United States were never as hostile to the Campaign as feminists in the UK.

Reading *Women, the Unions, and Work* now after forty years of campaigning, it's clear that my critique of the unions was too absolute. It takes no account of the possibility of a mass takeover by members, or even of people inside who are fighting to reclaim the unions for their original purpose, as a unifying spearhead of struggle. Such people put facilities and even some funds at the disposal of the union's grassroots as well as the community generally. The problem is that they often exhaust themselves arguing with those at the top and defending themselves against slanders and witch-hunts. We must remind ourselves that a great deal is at stake in unions, both for the working class and for capital, and the pressure on such individuals is great. But if they survive in their rise to the top, keep their principles by keeping in touch with their members and the movement outside—which is very rare—they open the possibility of our reclaiming our own unions.

Even in local government, the media, professional organizations, political parties and both Houses of Parliament, we always find those rare beings who feel their job as insiders is precisely to make the powers of their institutions available to the grassroots who, after all, one way or another pay their wages.

* * *

There are more ways than one in which the women's movement can be co-opted and be cut off from the possibilities of becoming an autonomous and revolutionary political movement. One is that we will assist capitalism to introduce and integrate women into new facets of its exploitative relations. The *Financial Times* of March 9, 1971, has made clear to those backward capitalists who have not realized it yet, how useful we can be:

> The thousands of trained girls who come out of the universities every year are desperately anxious to escape from the triple trap of teaching, nursing, or shorthand-typing... Many of these girls are clearly of high ability, and they constitute a pool from which skilled middle management could be drawn. They would be as hard working and conscientious as only a grateful outsider could be, and it is conceivable that, in spite of the equal pay legislation, they might not cost as much as male equivalents, at least in the first instance. We will use such women, in increasing numbers, when we realize that they exist and feel able to recognize their qualities. Until then, a good deal of talent that is costing a lot of money to train in our universities will continue to be wasted, and British industry will have failed to see a source of renewed energy and vitality that is before its very eyes.

This use of rebellion, for the purpose of developing capital with "renewed energy and vitality," is not new and not confined to women. For capitalism to co-opt every aspect of struggle, to renew itself with our energy and our vitality, and with the active help of a minority of the exploited, is central to its nature. The ex-colonial world whom the British "educated" to self-government, for example, is ruled by "grateful outsiders." We need to examine how we are to be "used" closely and carefully if we are to prevent ourselves from organizing only to assist capitalism to be less backward and in the process further enslaving ourselves, rather than organizing to destroy it which is the only possible process of liberation.

Another connected way of co-option has in some measure already taken place, and its agent has been Left organizations. They have effectively convinced many of us that if we wish to move to working-class women it must be either through them or, more pervasively, through their definitions of the class, their orientations and their kind of actions. It is as though they have stood blocking an open door. They challenge the validity of an autonomous women's movement either directly or—by treating women, an especially exploited section of the class, as marginal—indirectly. For them the "real" working class is white, male and over thirty. Here racism, male supremacy, and age supremacy have a common lineage. They effectively want to make us auxiliary to the "general" struggle—as if *they* represented the generalization of the struggles; as if there could be a generalized struggle without women, without men joining with women for women's demands.

A major issue on which we have swallowed their orientation and been co-opted to defeat our own movement has been on the question of unionizing women.

We are told that we must bring women to what is called a "trade union conscious-ness." This phrase is Lenin's and it comes from a pamphlet called *What Is To Be Done.*[1] In many ways it is a brilliant pamphlet, but it was written in the early days of the Russian movement, in 1902. Lenin learnt from the workers and peasants of Russia in 1905 and 1917 and repudiated a good deal of what he wrote before these two revolu-tions. Left people do not speak of Lenin's later conclusions, and in my view much of what passes for Left theory (and practice) today is stuck in 1902. In 1972 this is a serious charge, and I think it can be proved. They can read Lenin and quote him. But unlike Lenin, they are not able to learn from the actions that workers take.

The most obvious recent action is undoubtedly the miners' strike.[2] I believe many women in the movement have been shaken by this great working-class event. Class action shakes all sections of the population in days or weeks when nothing else has moved them for years. We have all had a leap in consciousness as a result of the *action* of the class. Therefore what we consider possible is expanded. This is the immediate reason for our restlessness. We are not satisfied any more to stand aside and let the world go by. After three years of our movement, Northern Ireland, Zimbabwe, and then this strike, we want to *do* something, but not just anything.[3] We want to build

---

1   But even this, the Left has turned on its head. Lenin's point was that the spontaneous workers' move-ment developed only to the level of "trade union consciousness." The revolutionary party had to bring the workers' movement to revolutionary consciousness. 1) Either the Left assumes that even trade union consciousness must be brought to the working class by intellectuals, or that women are too backward even to arrive spontaneously to where men workers have reached. 2) The conception of bringing revolu-tionary consciousness from outside into the working class was knocked out of Lenin's head first in 1905, then in 1917 and finally in the years that followed when, among other things, he understood the "sponta-neous" fascism which was in the consciousness of petty-bourgeois "socialist" intellectuals. Trotsky under-stood this about Lenin even if his followers do not. See Leon Trotsky, *Stalin* (London: 1947), 57–58.

2   Strike against the National Coal Board, January–February 1972. Since this was written, there was in January–February of 1974 an even more hostile confrontation between the mining community, 260,000 of whom are miners, on the one hand, and the government's policy of freezing pay on the other. In both strikes the mining community was able to use the union and not permit the union to use them. The 1974 strike succeeded in bringing down the (Conservative) government then in power. The year-long strike (1984–1985) by the National Union of Mineworkers led by Arthur Scargill was undermined by most other unions despite great miners' solidarity and public support. The strike was lost and the industry destroyed by the Thatcher government. It opened the way for further defeats of waged workers, including increased unemployment and the weakening of trade unions.

3   Formerly Rhodesia in Southern Africa. I'm referring to actions of the Black population in 1972, which prevented open collaboration between the ruling white minority and the British State. When a British Royal Commission went in January 1972 presumably to hear the voice of the people, they expected to rubber-stamp an agreement between the two governments (aided by Black "leaders" handpicked by white Rhodesia): previously there had been little public sign of Black resistance. But Zimbabweans seized the time and said "no" to the agreement by every means possible. Workers in the mine areas rioted, smiled at TV lenses and shouted, "No!" Black women spoke out at meetings where their white mistresses were present, but where they had the protection of the press cameras of the world. These mistresses were shocked by the lucidity, understanding and boldness of women who, up to that moment, had played ignorant and kept silent. The reaction of the British Establishment was no less surprised. What was at stake for governments was business as usual with the whole of southern Africa. The

a movement, which is at once political and new, one which speaks specifically to the needs of women.

But what has been the basis of this tremendous demonstration of power of the class? After all, this is not the first big strike in the recent period in Britain. The postmen, the dustmen, the electricity workers and many others have demonstrated in action their will to fight. What distinguished the miners is that they didn't depend on their unions but on their own self-organization and methods of struggle. More than once during the strike, the union tried to dictate the terms of struggle. For example, when the union asked workers to man safety crews, or tried to discourage them from violent defense of picket lines, or stood in the way of the women organizing independently. But the mining community went its own *autonomous* way. As a result, it won, among other reasons because in this way it won other workers to its cause.

This is not the first attempt at autonomous class action, but it is the first major success. Almost every recent national strike has been lost or at least drawn because workers allowed or could not prevent their union from "leading" it. Pilkington is the most striking case. And we must remember that 90 percent of all strikes are unofficial, either in spite of or against the unions.

Now at this point, where workers are beginning to wrest from unions control over their own struggle, we are invited to bring women into the unions where they will acquire "trade union consciousness."

What has been the role of trade unions specifically in relation to women?

1. They have helped to maintain unequal rates of pay despite the brave attempts by individual women (and some men) trade unionists to give this issue priority. As a matter of fact, once unions ask for a percentage wage rise, and not *the same rise for all*, they not only confirm inequality of wages but further widen the gap between men and women—and of course between men and men too. Ten percent of £10 = £11. Ten percent of £20 = £22. To them that hath a bit more shall be given a bit more…

They have never organized a struggle for equal pay. In the two great equal pay strikes we know about—and there are plenty we *don't* know about—the women acted independently of the unions. During the Leeds seamstresses' strike the union wrote to the company and told them not to give in to the women.[4] The women had to fight two governors by busting the windows of the union offices.

Black Zimbabwean No was No to apartheid in South Africa as well as Zimbabwe, and No to business as usual.

4   In February of 1970, following the acceptance by the union of a low wage rise discriminating against women, twenty thousand Leeds clothing workers came out on strike. Thousands of women from at least forty-five factories marched from factory to factory calling other workers out, and marched through the streets of Leeds to press their grievance.

At Ford Dagenham (London) in 1967, when the seat cover sewers went out, of course there was no attempt by the union to generalize (that is, bring the men out in support of) a strike which took place because the union had turned their backs on the women. The shop stewards, at the crucial meeting with the Minister of Employment and Productivity, renounced upgrading—which was the demand of the women—and settled for a wage rise which was 8 percent below the average male pay.

2. Grading is the basis for unequal pay where men and women work together. The unions take for granted job categories that have kept women lower paid and will continue to under the equal pay act. Even more, they worry that equal pay for women might "disturb" the wage differentials among different grades of men. The *Guardian* of September 6, 1971, quotes Jack Peel, general secretary of the National Union of Dyers, Bleachers and Textile Workers, talking to an employer, one Eric Booth. Eric says, "If we're not careful this could be very expensive for us." But Jack is more far-seeing. He says, "We could easily upset the men; upset their differentials. The way to avoid this is to go gently along." The question of equal pay is not only about the double exploitation of women and young people. It is about the way capital has carved up the whole class into grades and corresponding wage rates so that groups of workers see their interests as different from other groups—for example, *men in relation to women*.

3. They have not tried very hard to get us into unions. The Night Cleaners were in the degrading position of having to embarrass the Transport and General Workers' Union publicly in order to get "taken in."[5] We're not straightforward like men, you see. We have all these problems of kids and husbands and extreme exploitation. They don't really want us in the unions, although the dues are useful and we don't compete for their union jobs.

Yet note: if there is a rash of strikes or sit-ins for equal pay or for anything else, the unions will be falling over backwards to bring women in. What else does capital have to control workers when they move? How else can they get us to participate in our own exploitation? Who else would we trust but an organization, a movement, formed by us to unite with other workers? And if we are not depending on unions, who else would we depend on but ourselves and other workers? That would be dangerous—for unions and government. It would not be surprising if they were at this moment planning campaigns to recruit women in areas where they have been effectively militant, and planning also to come to our movement for help. Who can do their recruiting among women better than other women!

---

5   Women who clean offices at night could not even get the TGWU officials to meet them because union offices closed at 5 p.m. A night cleaner who was organizing attended a conference on workers' control. Jack Jones, head of the TGWU and then regarded as left-wing, was on the platform and was asked by her from the floor why his union had consistently ignored the Night Cleaners' demand for assistance and membership of the union.

4. But for those of us who are deprived of wages for our work, who are full-time housewives and do not have jobs outside the home, unions don't know we exist. *When capital pays husbands they get two workers, not one.* The unions are organizations which are supposed to protect (some) workers in (some) work institutions. Waged workers have organized unions (not the other way round, by the way—workers organize unions, *not* unions workers) and have organized them to deal with their waged work situation. A housewife's work situation is the home, and every woman who does waged work (except the rich) also does unwaged work, is also a housewife. Yet when husband and father and brother are taking strike decisions, which we have to support, we have no part in deciding the kind of action or the issues on which we fight. We get very little for ourselves—if we win, not even some of the credit. Has anybody pointed out how much *every* strike of men is dependent on the support of women? The unions ensure that the struggle is segregated and women can participate only as auxiliaries. Remember the film, *Salt of the Earth?* In order for the women to be brought actively into the strike and win it, *they had to adjourn the union meeting and have a meeting of the whole community instead. That's where it's at, on a national and international level.*

5. Until recently the capitalist class with the help of unions had convinced men that if they got a rise in pay they got a rise in standard of living. That's not true, and women always knew it. They give men a pay packet on Friday and take it back from us on Saturday at the supermarket. We have to organize the struggle for the other side of wages—against inflation—and that can only be done outside the unions, first because they only deal with the money we get and not with what we have immediately to give back; and second because they limit their fight—such as it is—only to that workplace where you get wages for being there, and not where your work involves giving the money back.

It is not simply that they don't organize the shoppers; it is that the union *prevents* such organization, by following organizationally the way capital is organized: a fragmented class, divided into those who have wages and those who don't. *The unemployed, the old, the ill, children, and housewives are unwaged.* So the unions ignore us and thereby separate us from each other and from the waged. That is, they structurally make a generalized struggle impossible. This is not *because* they are bureaucratized, *this is why:* their functions are to mediate the struggle in industry and keep it separate from struggles elsewhere. Because the most concentrated potential power of the class is at the point of production of commodities, which are things, the unions have convinced the unwaged that only at that point can a struggle be waged at all. This is not so, and the most striking example has been the organization of the Black community. Black people, like women, cannot limit themselves to a struggle in factories.[6]

---

6   All Black people are not men and all women are not white. Yet the movements of Black people and
    women appeared to be struggles of separate sectors of the working class. Knowing more of these

And like women, Black people see the function of the union within the class writ large in its relation to them. For racism and sexism are not aberrations of an otherwise powerful working-class weapon. They are its nature.

You will see by now that I believe in order to have our own politics we must make our own analysis of women *and therefore our own analysis of the whole working-class struggle.* We have been taking so much for granted that happens to be around, and restricting, segregating ourselves to speaking and writing about women, that it looks like we are only supposed to analyze and understand women *after others* (men) have analyzed the class "in general"—excluding us. This is to be male-dominated in the profoundest sense. Because there is no class "in general" which doesn't include *us and all the unwaged.*

I think that some of us who have refused to relate women's struggle to the class struggle have done this in self-defense, in order to get away from the Left analysis of class which left us out completely (and as I have tried to show, was a barrier to men workers carrying out their struggle independent of unions).

In turn some women have been forced to stay in or join Left organizations and suffer continuous humiliation in them in order not to be disconnected from class politics.

Another result of the denial of an autonomous role for the women's movement has been the women who see themselves only as supportive, this time of women and not of men. If we support women's struggles that is a step forward, but if we make no independent contribution, we are either unwilling or unable to use and share what the movement has caused us to learn. Faced with the elitism of the Left, this patronizing has seemed to some women the only alternative.

For all these women a feminist movement based on autonomous class politics is the only viable alternative. Until we create that, we will continue to snipe at each other, and always as a reaction to what men are doing. Now the first thing that will pop into the heads of some of us is the benefit to be derived from unions. There is no doubt that certain slave conditions are done away with when a factory is organized, and usually when workers in factories organize, they organize into unions (or against them). It seems the only alternative to slavery. The whole history of the class is bound up with this institution. But it is the way workers get unions formed, organizing together and almost always going on strike, that abolishes the slave conditions, not the unions. It is their power that brings the union in and it is their power that abolishes slave conditions. The union has become a symbol of this power and has exploited this image and this tradition so as to channel, direct and, where possible, smother the struggle, but the power is the workers'.

---

struggles, we cannot now define these two sectors in this self-contained way. For example, the welfare movement of the 1960s in North America, spearheaded by thousands of Black women demanding wages for housework, was a massive feminist struggle autonomous of the State and of men.

Secondly, if you go into a union or a nonunion factory or office where both men and women are working, you'll almost always see that the men are not as pressed as the women. Their working speed is slower than women's, they take more time in the toilet, to smoke, to breathe. That also has to do, not with unions, but with power: women come into industry less powerful than men, for the obvious reason of their manifold oppression through patriarchy. Their basic wagelessness and resulting dependence on men is the form patriarchy takes under capitalism; and this situation is internalized as the myth of female incapacity, which in turn reinforces the basic situation. But in addition, women have an actual minority status in industry. So they are uncertain not only of their own capacities but of the support they will receive from men and from the unions, which are now identified primarily with men.

The very structure of the unions puts women off. All those rules and regulations and having to talk at meetings and having meetings at night when we are putting our children to bed and washing up, often confirm to us that we are "backward." We know these feelings well. We formed a movement because of them.

Certainly very few women in jobs or out of them feel the union can represent them *as women* who have not an eight-hour but at least a sixteen-hour day.

But if the power of the unions is an expression of the power of the class, and if unions have in essential respects been working against our interests as women and therefore against the working class, then we must organize that power, not those unions. We are in a similar dilemma with the family of the working class…

The struggle of the woman of the working class against the union is so decisive because, like the family, *it protects "the class" at her expense* (and not only hers) and at the expense of offensive action. Like the family, we have nothing to put in its place but the class acting for itself and women as integral, in fact pivotal, to that class.

6. Finally there is the question of women and "unemployment." First of all, we know that only rich women are unemployed—that is, do no work. Whether or not we're in jobs, most of us work like hell. The only thing is that we are unwaged if we don't formally hire ourselves out to a particular capitalist and instead work in our kitchens creating and servicing workers for the capitalist class in general. It is characteristic that the unions and the labor exchanges (i.e. wage slave markets) in Scotland have made a deal not to give jobs to married women. In the explosive situation in Scotland of which the UCS work-in was merely an indication, they—the unions and the government—figure we can be depended upon not to "give trouble."[7] That

---

7   Upper Clyde Shipyards taken over by workers when threatened with closure. They continued to build ships. For more about the tactic of work-ins, see the article about Lip in France in *Falling Wall Book Review* 2, (June–August 1974): "To take over a factory and use it and the congealed labor it contains as a bargaining power, where appropriate, is an excellent and effective tactic. From the Luddites on (and probably before) workers have used the appropriation and destruction of capital which has exploited them as a bargaining lever. In the last years this tactic has been seized on by the Left, parliamentary and antiparliamentary, as

is how we have been used all the time, and we have to prove them wrong or fold up. This damn capitalist class and their damn unions must not be able to count on our quiescence any more over anything. They have made this deal over our heads. They will make or have made others. We are expendable.

And when in Scotland we are kept out of the wage-slave market, it is to keep men from being unemployed just at the moment and in the place where the methods of struggle of Northern Ireland may catch on. This move against women by unions and government is probably as a direct result of the attempt men workers made to take over the employment exchanges at the same time as the UCS work-in was going on. That is, some workers thought that an unwork-in was a better idea than a work-in. No need to say where the unions stand on this when they are desperately trying to shove "We want jobs" placards into workers' hands. You would think it is immoral to be disengaged from exploitation. The only thing "wrong" with unemployment is that you don't get a pay packet.

And this is the heart of the issue. The government, acting in the interests of the capitalist class in general, has created unemployment in the hope that, instead of fighting for *more pay and less work,* we will be glad for the crumbs that the master lets fall from his table. So that the "country" can "progress" over our dead and dying minds and bodies. The unions tell us to worry about productivity and exports while the capitalists are busy exporting their capital all over the world, for example to South Africa (and hope, by the way, to export white unemployed workers behind it). The unions are trying to lead exactly the kind of struggle that would make Ted Heath (except for the mining community, the Northern Irish community and the Zimbabwean community) a happy man: they are demanding jobs.[8] It is the threat of closure of the mines that the government thought would keep the mining community quiet. Instead the people from the mine areas made clear from their strike that they didn't consider spending your life in a mine or scrubbing filthy clothes and nursing people with silicosis was an ideal existence. Their strike meant that they were saying: Take your mines and shove them. They refused to beg for the right to be exploited.

But what about those women who have been deprived of the social experience of socialized work and the relative independence of their own pay packet? It is certainly not as simple in their case.

This "double slavery" of being expected to carry the burden of two jobs, one inside and the other outside the home, is the most dangerous response to our rebellion: capital planned it a long time ago, even before the women's movement surfaced, and

---

their blueprint for the new society. Take over the factory, manage it, and of course work in it. The UCS work-in seemed to breathe life into an ideal. The Lip workers didn't confuse their tactic with their goal. *"Autogestion? Non, autodefense!"* ("Self-management? No, self-defense!") (II). It is probable that that was the standpoint of workers at UCS also, but all the views we heard were those of the leaders.

8   Former Conservative prime minister.

has been organizing it massively. Here is just one example. A confidential report on the employment of women and young persons under eighteen years (revealed in *Socialist Worker*, December 21, 1968) was prepared by the National Joint Advisory Committee, with representatives from the Confederation of British Industries, the nationalized industries, the Ministry of Labour and—guess who?—the TUC.[9] The report stated:

> With the constant introduction of expensive new equipment, shift working will
> no doubt continue to increase so as to maximize the economic return from capital
> investment involved and indeed before committing capital to the purchase of such
> machinery employers want to be assured that shift working will be possible, so as
> to ensure an adequate return.

Can we *now* understand the equal pay act, which gives what they call equal pay on the terms that we work shifts?

The confidential report discussed Section 68 of the Factory Act requiring that all women and young persons in a factory have their breaks at the same time. Section 68, it says, "denies to employers the flexibility in arranging the hours of their women and young persons…so essential in present day conditions." So much for capital's plan-lessness, and our peripheral "use" in industry.

Here is where the movement can be made or broken. We can be the modern suffragettes, only more dangerous to women, since where many of them invited women to vote and be free, we will be inviting them to achieve freedom through work. Or we can break with this reformist aspect of our past and pose a revolutionary alternative.

No doubt there are times when it may seem to women that we have no choice but to demand a second job; or demand that at least we have some choice in the second job we take, especially where we are isolated from women's industries and sweatshops are the only places within miles where a woman can earn enough money to cover the inflation and avoid having to degrade herself by asking her husband for money for tights. But if we limit ourselves to this, if this is our program, our strategy, and we are unable to rise above this level of power, all we are doing is organizing women to be more efficiently and mercilessly exploited.

The question is: what in outline are the alternatives, in organization and in demands?

First, the level of organization of women is low. This is the most obvious reason why women in the movement are tempted to concentrate on bringing women into unions. Here is an institution already functioning and "experienced"—as we are not—which does not have to be built from the ground up. To think in terms of building organizations without traditions (except the traditions of the struggle itself) is to break from other traditions that, among other things, helped prevent a revolutionary

---

9   Trades Union Congress, the central body to which most UK trade unions are affiliated.

women's movement for years. Independent organization—independent of every section of the establishment—is difficult to consider, let alone create, when thousands of women are not in motion.

But the picture is not as gloomy as it appears. There have been dozens if not hundreds of equal pay strikes. The Claimants' Union is gaining in strength and has at its core unsupported mothers. And most recently, the women of the mine areas made the first attempt to organize independently. In addition, if we are not blinded by a "trade union consciousness" ourselves, we can see women even in the worst jobs and most unorganized factories waging their struggle in completely new ways. Here is the *Daily Sketch*, January 18, 1971:

> Thousands of girls quit humdrum factory jobs because they get fed up being treated like "robots."
>
> They complain of monotonous work and impersonal bosses.
>
> The girls become frustrated because the jobs they do make little demand on their abilities and leave no room for personal satisfaction.
>
> These were the main points of a survey by Bradford University into why 65 percent of women quit their jobs in the electronics industry within a few months.

(You see who the universities are working for.)

We are not only victims; we are rebels too. The absenteeism of women is notorious. Instead of workers' control of production, their action is more like workers' control of the struggle, to hell with their production.

So that the first barrier to independent organization, the supposed apathy of women, is not what has been assumed. If we begin to look with women's eyes, respecting what women do and not measuring them as men do, we will see a wealth of rebellion against and refusal of women's work and the relationships and roles they generate.

This is not always organized rebellion and refusal. Well then, let's organize it. The unions don't; they sit on its head.

There appear to be two levels of demands, the issues which arise on a local level, and the general demands which the movement comes to stand for. In reality our movement has suffered from an unnatural separation between the two. The Four Demands we marched for last year [1971] have been on the whole unconnected with individual group activity (in part at least because of the barrenness of those demands).[10]

Our concern must be demands with which the movement articulates in few words the breadth of its rejection of the oppression and exploitation of women. The tension between a local struggle and the stated principles of the movement does not vanish,

---

10 These were: Equal Pay, Equal Educational Opportunity, Twenty-Four-Hour Nurseries, Free Contraception and Abortion on Demand. We commented on these in 1972.

but within each local demand, which mobilizes women wherever they are, the struggle loses its sporadic, provincial, and disconnected character. The demands must raise possibilities of new kinds and areas of action in each local situation from the beginning, and always keep the fundamental issues before our eyes. There is much more to be said about this, but better to move to the proposed demands.

1. WE DEMAND THE RIGHT TO WORK LESS. A shorter workweek for all. Why should anybody work more than twenty hours a week? Housewives are hesitant to ask men after a week of at least forty grinding hours to see after their own children and their own underwear. Yet women do just that, for themselves and for men. When women are threatened with redundancies, the struggle must be for a shorter workweek. (Maybe men will take *our* lead for a change.)

2. WE DEMAND A GUARANTEED INCOME FOR WOMEN AND FOR MEN, WORKING OR NOT WORKING, MARRIED OR NOT. If we raise kids, we have a right to a living wage. The ruling class has glorified motherhood only when there is a pay packet to support it. We work for the capitalist class. Let them pay us, or else we can go to the factories and offices and put our children in their fathers' laps. Let's see if they can make Ford cars and change nappies at the same time. WE DEMAND WAGES FOR HOUSEWORK. All housekeepers are entitled to wages (men too).

3. It is in this context that WE DEMAND CONTROL OF OUR BODIES. If even birth control were free, would that be control? And if we could have free abortions on demand, is that control? What about the children we want and can't afford? We are forced to demand abortion and sterilization as we have been forced to demand jobs. Give us money and give us time, and we'll be in a better position to control our bodies, our minds and our relationships. Free birth control, free abortions for whoever wants them (including our sisters from abroad who are denied even legal abortion—sisterhood is international). WE DEMAND THE RIGHT TO HAVE OR NOT TO HAVE CHILDREN.

But childbearing is not the only function of our bodies that capital controls. At work we make them do what they don't want to do: repeated jerks on an assembly line, constant sitting or standing, breathing fumes and dirt. Work is often painful and dangerous. It is always uncomfortable and tiring. After work your body is too numb for you to feel it as something you can enjoy. For this reason it cannot develop sexually. Our physical feeling is further destroyed by the limited kinds of sexuality and the shallow relationships this society promotes and by the scarcity of times and places where we can make love. Our bodies become a tool for production and reproduction and nothing else.

4. WE DEMAND EQUAL PAY FOR ALL. There is a rate for girls and a rate for boys and a rate for women and a rate for men and a rate for "skilled" and a rate for "unskilled" and a rate in the North and a rate in the South. Whoever works deserves a minimum wage, and that minimum must be the rate of the highest grade.

5. WE DEMAND AN END TO PRICE RISES, including tax, rent, food, and clothing. There is a battle brewing on housing. As usual, with tenants' struggles, women are going to be at the heart: they are the ones who will refuse the rent collector when he knocks at the door during a rent strike. But our intervention can help guarantee that the women will also lead it, instead of being confined to making the tea in the back of the hall while the men make speeches in front.

6. WE DEMAND FREE COMMUNITY CONTROLLED NURSERIES AND CHILDCARE. We are entitled to a social existence without having to take another job out of our homes. Mothers too have a right to work less. Young children as well as women are imprisoned in their homes. But we don't want them to go to a State institution instead. Children, women and men must be able to learn from each other and break the ghetto existence to which they are each confined. We will then begin to destroy the State's authority over our children and our possession of them. In the same way as children are to be wrested from the State, so old people, and the mentally and physically ill must come back to the community's care. We need time and we need money to destroy the prisons in which our children, our grandparents and our sick people are confined.

How do we organize a struggle around these demands? The Claimants' Union has already begun. But the low level of organization of women generally means that there is plenty of hard work to be done.

We begin by uniting what capital has divided. If men have not yet learnt to support the equal pay fight which we have made, it is because their privileges over us—based on the double-edged "privilege" of the wage itself—have blinded them to their class interests. They have always paid dearly for not uniting with us, by being thrown out of jobs to be replaced by "cheaper" female labor. We may still have to confront not only employers, unions and government but men too when we want equal pay. Equal pay for all may win them over to demanding equal pay also among themselves as well as with us. The battle for parity in auto is the class finding its way to just such a struggle.[11]

We can organize with women where they work for wages, where they shop, where they live and work. Women from many industrial estates have shopping areas very

---

11 The battle for parity is the struggle of workers in the car industry throughout Britain to get the same pay. It is an equal pay battle. But the government, the unions and the media guarantee that the phrase "equal pay" be seen as a "woman's issue" rather than the issue of a class of which we happen to be part.

near, where they shop in their dinner hour.[12] They often live close by. We can begin by leafleting in all three places, aiming to organize for their most pressing problems, which are hours of work, wages, inflation, child care, and slavery. Housewives can go to the Social Security [Welfare] offices and demand money, as the women and children from the mine areas did—*we need not wait for the men to strike*, we can ask them to strike to support what *we* are doing.

It is possible that women will feel too weak to act independently of unions (though our job is to emphasize women's potential strength, and there may be pressure on them from many sources—*especially employers*—to go into unions once they take action. At this point it is far from decisive. If we get moving on our demands, even what we can get from the unions will be greater. We all gain confidence and experience. We can have strikes against inflation, rent rises, shift work for women and for men. We can offer to housewives a social existence other than another job—we can offer them the power of the movement and the struggle itself.

Of course this is much easier said than done, though the situation in this country is changing so rapidly that every day more becomes possible. This is meant to begin a discussion of these possibilities, but on our terms.

Nor is this anything like a complete picture of what is taking place in Britain today (or anywhere else), either among workers, or in boardrooms, government offices or TUC headquarters. But it is clear to me and to others too I think that the time has come to make the leap from all that we have learnt in the small group discussions to political activity. We must not allow what we *know* is the female experience to be translated into the secondhand politics of "trade union consciousness," which has been presented to us as the only viable alternative. Goodbye to all that. When 20 percent of the women of a mainly women's factory don't turn up for work on Monday, they are many years beyond the trade union struggle, in fact its mortal enemy. They are struggling not only for better conditions in which to be exploited but against exploitation, against work itself. We in the women's movement should be the last people to believe or act upon the absurd notion that women are incapable of leaping beyond the oppressive institutions that have trapped men. Because we have been ignored and excluded by these institutions it is precisely *we* who are in the position to move beyond them.

One final point. There is a debate that goes on about most of us being "middle-class." Are we? These definitions of class are more sociological than political and must be completely reexamined. In any case, as the Notting Hill *Shrew* put it, to have sisterhood we have to get over the myths that only "working-class" women are oppressed

---

12 Areas completely given over to factories.

and that only "middle-class" women can know they're oppressed.[13] Some women, let's face it, are only in the movement because capitalism is very backward and leaves women out of government and good paying professions. They will eventually have to decide whether or not to fit into the plans that capital and the *Financial Times* have for them. But they must not hold the rest of us back.

A hell of a lot of us are fighting capital not because it is backward but because it exists. We are increasingly aware that the oppression of all women has its roots in the indispensable work, in home, in office, in hospital and in factory, that women perform for capital, sometimes with low wages, most often without wages. We must get over this guilt about having wall-to-wall carpeting and a "good" education—as if they ever taught us anything except to think like them and act for them. Guilt doesn't build a political movement; it inhibits and exhausts it. For guilt becomes sacrifice and sacrifice becomes either martyrdom or bitterness—or both.

The first step in the process of our liberation at this stage is to make our own independent evaluation of the political situation in this country (and later in the world—with the help of women in other countries) on the basis of what our guts and people like those in the mining areas have told us, and then act on it. Then the fact that we are middle-class will not stand in the way of waging the class struggle—but the class struggle as we women define it and as only we can wage it, for the first time in a generalized way. It will take some time, but then Rome wasn't destroyed in a day.

---

13 *Shrew* was the monthly publication of the Women's Liberation Workshop, London. Each member group in turn edited an issue. Reference is to volume 3, issue number 8 (September 1971).

THE PERSPECTIVE OF WINNING (1973)

'Ve been asked to comment on some misunderstandings about the trade unions which have emerged in the explosive discussion following the publication in Britain of *Women, the Unions, and Work* in March 1972. I draw a line immediately between the almost violent opposition of the organizations of the Left and the doubts and disagreements of revolutionary feminists. I deal with the former in passing later on, but they can never be our first concern.

Feminists who are working-class in origin have grown up identifying the defense of their class interests with defense of the unions. Feminists who are not working-class in origin (among whom are those who still consider themselves "middle-class" because their husbands are, though they are full-time unwaged housewives or first generation waged workers—nurses, teachers or other white-collar workers) are nervous that in bypassing or attacking the unions from a feminist perspective they will further separate themselves from the class with which they want to identify, but of which they feel outside.

Both these groups of women assume the unions *are* the working class, as if the working class were identical with and could be subsumed within the unions, of which in any case the majority of the working class internationally—even men—are not members. *But, members or not, the working class is not the unions nor the Labour Party, nor any of the reformist organizations it built by revolutionary struggle.*

* * *

Defense or Attack?

The working class is capital, capital in the form of machines, which are its past labor and in the form of people who are the appendages, directly or indirectly, of those machines. The class is compelled to sell voluntarily its labor power, its capacity for mental and physical activity, its capacity to cooperate socially—its human and animal essence—for wages. It is forced to produce wealth on an ever-expanding scale, and in that way reproduces power against itself, capital, the social relation which is wage slavery. The working class must survive in the agony and humiliation of this relation (which engages every worker, waged and unwaged, white collar or blue, wearing apron or overall). These organizations—unions or parties—are an expression of the attempt of the exploited to defend themselves from the total mastery of capital over them. But this domination, their condition of life, is always driving the working class not merely to survive but to subvert.

The working class is therefore at the same time always anticapital, revolutionary, seeking the power to be autonomous of capital and to destroy itself as a working class. Internationally it confronts itself as capital, it confronts and challenges the social relation which it itself daily reproduces, and attempts to develop its power to break the Gordian Knot of its own slavery. The women's movement is an expression of that search for power. So is the Black movement. So are the movements of school children and students who are resisting their capitalist present and future as workers, as labor power. So are the sabotage, absenteeism, wildcat and official strikes, and slowdowns in the factories. So are the Claimants' and Welfare movements, expressing themselves in nationally known organizations and hundreds of groups (thousands in North America) of unsupported mothers. So is shoplifting and the daily battles of the housewife, "supported" and "unsupported," to do less work and get more money. So is the gay movement as it rejects the sexual division of labor, and lesbian women in particular who undermine the narrow, numbing power relation which passes for sexual expression and which is women's work.

This working-class autonomy always finds expression in the ebb and flow of confrontation. Political parties and trade unions that coalesced at high tide, which froze as they formed, can never keep up with the self-development of the working class, with its insistent pursuit of the power to destroy itself as a working class. The contradiction between the working class as capital, as the reproducer of its own exploitation, and the working class as the gravedigger of this exploitation leaves no room for "moderation." Organizations which no longer express where the working class is going but where it has already been, a level of struggle and goals which it has surpassed, become their opposite, the class enemy. Precisely because they are not grafted onto the class but have come from struggle, it is they who become the most efficient agency to buttress and reinforce the working class as capital, to discipline us to work, and to work us so we will be disciplined. As the working class becomes stronger, so its goals express a more total opposition to capital, a more total expression of its own need; and the more do the agencies of capital reach into the fabric of the working class itself, more difficult to identify, more mystified in their function by their working-class mantle, vocabulary, accent—more dangerous.

The Unions Aren't Joking

The struggle has reached the stage where labor power is massively rejecting work, in the home, in the school, and in the factory—and by factory we mean wherever waged labor is carried on. The unions, the Labour, Socialist, Communist, and most nationalist parties base themselves on the inevitability and necessity and therefore the enforcement of work. They are inseparable from the capitalist organization of work. They are inseparable from the capitalist State and its attempt to plan, control and rationalize every moment of our lives. While they are (at best) mediating or (at worst) openly sabotaging particular struggles, they are closeted with the government (when they are not themselves the government) and the captains of industry (when they are not themselves the captains of industry), planning more efficient ways to exploit and control, devising incentives to get us interested and involved again, even to getting us involved in planning our own exploitation and control. They call it "participation."

The working class is in the position of having to confront, destroy, transcend trade unions and political parties in order to confront, destroy, and transcend itself as capital. When it does not see the possibility of directly and massively confronting, it opts out of work, "politics," "responsibility," and "participation" by turning its back and shutting its ears.

When the women at the Chesebrough Pond's factory in London began to organize themselves, the union man stated his case and ours: "The union only represents people who want to work."

The young woman from Ireland who jabbed the woman next to her in the ribs and said, "He must be joking," had other ideas about why she was spending her precious time away from work going to meetings. *She had another perspective.* That's to say, her only interest in giving up a part of the time when her life did not belong absolutely to capital was to get more time back, was to get her life back, from capital. And when she looked around to find the power to do that, standing opposed to her was the union, ready to defend her, but only if she was ready to continue to accept exploitation as her natural destiny. The unions, unfortunately, are not joking.

In Detroit where I write this it is impossible to dismiss these words on the relation of waged workers to the union as rhetoric. For many years (since the union and its seniority system assisted management in throwing the women out of the big plants) women have been confined to the sweatshops which feed the auto monster of Motown; many of them nonunion, all at low pay and at a speed of work, a level of exploitation, which I remember too well. (*That* is the essence of the "American way of life.") Whether or not there's a union makes a difference. They can't sack you as easily. The pay is union scale—but a woman's rate, because it's probably mainly a woman's factory or you are working in a woman's "classification"—we know the routine, every waged woman does. And there are some insurance benefits for a union member: health care (in a country where you practically have to be a millionaire to afford to get sick) is cheaper. But the speed, if anything, is higher in the union place: they need the health care—work, the speed of the work and the rate of accidents, are killers.

In some cases the company calls in the union to "organize" the workers. In other places the union goes to the company and makes a deal: you let us in, get the dues checked off automatically, and we'll see there are no strikes. In one factory the women rebuffed all organizing drives in the clear consciousness that the union would raise wages and the company would raise production rates with the consent of the union. They chose to work less. Not a big choice, but a choice.

In yet other cases women brave management intimidation to bring in a union themselves, only to complain later about the dues they pay to a union which then helps management to regulate and supervise them. In still others, there is no union, but the workers are dominated and weakened by the knowledge that a union wouldn't help much even if they had one. Whether they pay dues or not, the women and men in the plants here know that as things stand they are trapped for life, and that there is nothing established that they can turn to. They live with mounting frustration, anger, disgust, and self-hatred.

Strikes erupt and so does violence, against foremen, against the machines or against the product in which is buried a piece of your life, against the union, and finally against the State directly when they send in the police to discipline you back to negotiation, back to work, back to slavery.

The United States, you may say, is "different"; it's not like that here. In a limited sense it *is* different in Britain. The incumbent union gangsters don't "bump off" the leader of the opposition, as they did in the coal union in the United States a couple of years back. (And you can imagine what over the years they have done to workers whose only position was their position on the line.) But is it essentially different? Or are we trying to convince ourselves that there is a "British road" to the new society? Is there something less violent and brutal about the masters of capital in Britain (who, incidentally, are the same as the masters of capital in Detroit, Paris, Santiago, Capetown, and Belfast, and the descendants of the masters of the genocidal British Empire)? The trade unions in Britain have not used thugs to beat workers; that is not to *their* credit but to the credit of the working class in Britain, the most experienced in the world.

Feminist Autonomy

Feminist autonomy has appeared to be a separate question from the question of class and this deadlock in the factory, where we are locked between company on one side and union on the other. But our movement by its existence poses autonomy from capital and all its institutions: from the factory, the family, the political parties of Right and Left, the unions of Right and Left—from the State—and, since they act for capital in relation to women, from men. We strive to be autonomous from capital not only because it exploits women more than men but because it exploits. We strive to be autonomous from men to the degree that capital uses men as instruments of that exploitation. Our exploitation has its roots in the home in our unwaged work, producing and reproducing workers. Because of the geographical separation of home and factory, because of the wide disparity in technology between the kitchen sink and the computer or blast furnace, because one job is exclusively for women and the other is identified with men, because one carries a wage and the other does not, there seems no connection between the two.

In reality *the deadlock in the factory is predicated on unwaged exploitation in the home,* on the weakness of the weakest—the unwaged—and on the weakness this separation from the unwaged guarantees in the position of the waged; just as the isolation and wagelessness of housework is predicated on the factory's need for the product of that housework, labor power, without which the factory would cease. It is one circuit of production, organized by capital not only to produce but to appear as two circuits of struggle instead of the one it actually is.

That the woman is unwaged makes her dependent on the wage of a man and reinforces the man's dependence on *his* job. Housewives—within whose isolation is hidden social labor, the labor of producing not objects but human beings, human labor power—enter the factory weak because they are unwaged. And every day that the inflation (which capital has organized but can no longer control) mounts, we are further pushed into that factory or riveted to it if we're already there. *The unions will never get us out unless capital wants us out.* When the factory gates close behind us, or in front of us, the class and its struggle is divided. Either we are trapped at home bearing and rearing children, in wageless isolation, serving men so they can serve capital, our will subordinate to theirs; or we go out of the home for a waged job at low pay, dumping our children at baby-minders or State nurseries and doing a second shift when we get home, our will still subordinate to theirs.

Our feminism grasps finally the totality of exploitation, in the home and out of it, and therefore grasps the totality of working-class struggle, in the home and out of it. *No working-class organization has ever done that before.*

Our struggle against the factory is not only to get out but never to go in. Our struggle against the family is to get out, but not so we are free for the factory.

This is our demand for autonomy, our autonomous class perspective, founded in this total rejection of the capitalist organization of our lives, of our work. Such a rejection is a rejection of defense as a strategy. To keep what we have (which has proved impossible by defense anyway) or inch forward at the speed with which capital can incorporate our demands and raise our productivity at the same time, so we pay back in intensified labor in the home and out of it ("efficiency") more than we have won from them—that is the trade union way: to organize that swindle *is a trade union function.* Our strategy can only be built on taking the offensive *because women will respond to nothing less and because that is the only way to win.* In the most literal sense, women have no time for anything less, and there is no time for anything less. The plans for our complete institutionalization in the factory in addition to the home have long been laid; we are already and increasingly wearing the double chains.

Wages for Housework

The perspective that we counterpose to trade union gradualism is the perspective of wages for housework. It is the demand of women for power, for autonomy against capital. It is the perspective of winning.

To the degree that we organize a struggle for wages for the work we do in the home, we demand that work in the home be considered *as* work which, like all work in capitalist society, is forced work, which we do not for love but because, like every other worker, we and our children would starve if we stopped.

To the degree that we demand a wage and demystify housework, showing it is forced work, we open the possibility of refusing it without guilt. We refuse it with the power to begin to acknowledge and articulate our own needs, and to demand that they be met.

To the degree that we demand wages, we leave the home for a struggle, *not* for another job.

To the degree that we win a wage, we have the power to begin to reject the factory, either by going into it less, by dictating the terms on which we enter, by beginning to come out if we are already institutionalized there. Equal pay begins with having a wage to equalize, a wage *before* we enter the factory, the office, the hospital, the canteen, the bus, or the school.

To the degree that we demand a wage and *demonstrate our power,* we will be able *for the first time massively* to get the support of men for what we demand. This is to reverse a long tradition. Every Left group or party, every trade union told us the best we could do was to unite with the men and support them. And we did—they would have won *nothing* if we hadn't. Now we demand unity on our terms: they must support *us.* But we're neither debating with them nor moralizing at them. We speak to their material class interest. *Men are more disciplined to work for wages because we are their dependents in the home working without wages.*

To the degree that we organize our power, we undermine the power relation that causes and then confirms the chauvinism of men against us. We open the way for their unification with us because we build our confidence, undermine their sense of superiority and *offer them power—but no longer over us.* We break the relation of domination of men workers over women workers in the factory, the hierarchy of labor powers out of the home, which is and must be a reflection of the husband-wife relation in the home—*between all men and all women.*

To the degree that we demand a wage, we demand control of our bodies from capital—whether we are producing children for them, who will become the objects of capitalist machines, or whether our own bodies are the objects of those machines.

To the degree that we demand and win a wage we can refuse to be the army of wageless threatening from outside the factory every struggle of women (and men) inside to work less and get paid more.

To the degree that we win the wage, which will give us financial independence from men, we break the nuclear family founded on the power of the man's wage over women and children. To that degree we have the power to leave intolerable relationships, the power to insist that men share the burdens of the home. But it is also the power to demand of the State the money to reorganize and minimize housework. We make it expensive for them not to pay—our struggle after all is the most expensive item in the capitalist budget.

To the degree that we demand a wage we uncover every moment of our working day and uncover ever-increasing areas which must be waged, and where we can struggle for the wage.

This is our class perspective.

Now let us look at the unions.

To the degree that we organize a struggle against work, women's work of making love for capital or being denied making love by capital; making children for capital or being prevented from making children by capital; making objects for capital and being the objects of capital; the unions will try to take it over and direct it into safe channels under their stewardship—by any means necessary. For the unions are an expression of our function as capital and against our autonomy, the autonomy through which we express that we are anticapital, the gravediggers of capital.

Therefore to the degree that we organize our power, our autonomous power, we will clash with them and with the State power of which they are part. For capital the crisis is never the *thing* that we demand. The crisis for them is our *power* to destroy the social relation and institutions on which *their* power is based. Wages for housework as a perspective is an organizer of power to destroy our dependence, directly or through men, on capital, and on the work this dependence forces us to do. With women there is no separation between living and working; the female experience is twenty-four hours a day of forced labor. That then is the scope of our struggle, the scope of our organization.

The Union of the Left

As we said earlier, the opposition from Left groups to *Women, the Unions, and Work* has centered on the question of the unions. Opposing the pamphlet's position on this, they have of course opposed with equal hostility its alternative perspective, wages for housework. Not one grouping on the Left treated lightly the counterposing of these two political perspectives. It is significant that, though they disagree with each other on many things, they have ignored these disagreements, contradicted each other without comment and organized together in the Women's Liberation Movement to defeat the political tendency whose birth in Britain *Women, the Unions, and Work* signified. They have never concentrated their energies in this way against even avowed anti-Marxist liberals. In this way they have expressed their choice of the "main enemy" in the Women's Liberation Movement; and shown how superficial are the differences among themselves, and between themselves on the one hand and anti-Marxist liberals on the other. They have no fundamental disagreements on women, on the unions, on work and on the State—which is the ultimate and all-pervasive disciplinarian of work which each Left group hopes to become.

That it is through their anti-feminism that such a clarification has surfaced is not accidental. While they are ready to "permit" us to discuss "women's things"—abortion, equal pay (for work of equal value of course), "discrimination" and "equal opportunity"—they find it intolerable that we should counterpose to their Social-Democratic politics (draped in the language of the Bolshevik Party) an analysis *beginning with women* of the entire class struggle. It must have appeared as either empty rhetoric or the height of arrogance that females, and females not within the organizational framework and under the aegis of men, should say, as we did: "The first step in the process of our liberation at this stage is to make our own independent evaluation of the political situation in this country (and later in the world—with the help of women in other countries)." This we have begun to do and find increasingly the Left's analysis of every area of struggle not only inadequate but *against* the working class. Here is a sample of their arguments about the unions during the debate in the last year.

"The unions are reformist but necessary."

Reformist organizations, we must remind these great revolutionaries, are not merely nonrevolutionary. By definition they are *counterrevolutionary*. There are no neutrals in this struggle. Only reformists can defend reformism, or worse, encourage us to extend its power.

"It is not the unions that are reformist but the bureaucracy, the leadership. We must get into the unions and democratize them."

It is not the State but Ted Heath. ("Heath out!" the male Left of both sexes shouted on the Women's Day march of 1973.) It is not the institution of the factory but bad management. ("Workers' Control" they shout, or "Workers' Management," "Democracy on the shop floor!" God forefend we should dream of the abolition of the shop floor, let alone struggle and plan for its abolition.) It is not the family but bad husbands. (Not them, some other man! They are also for democratizing the family. The men, they say, must share the slavery of the home. So they must—until slavery is abolished. They can as little conceive of destroying the institution of the family as they can of the factory. Their plan to abolish the family is to turn it into a factory. That's what it means to call for the State to socialize housework, the State of work discipline in the home and out of it.) It is not "compulsory education," factories for producing disciplined workers, but bad and undemocratic schools. It is not capitalist medicine but bad doctors. It is not the institution of slavery but bad masters. It is not capital but bad capitalists. It is not the capitalist productive process but *what* you produce. (Not they, somebody else, and when they get to power it will be more efficient…) It is not classes but individuals.

What they mean is, it is not a political but a moral struggle, not armed revolution but *moral rearmament,* a better plan for a better, more contented set of slaves.

"But what else is there beside the trade unions?"

Well, there is the class that formed them, "a class always increasing in numbers and disciplined, united, organized by the very mechanism of the process of capitalist production itself."

Transforming the Terms of Struggle

The working class has always created the organizational tools to wage its battles. It is also, particularly in Britain, skilled at knowing when it can use the union, and when it can't but must bypass it. The 1972 strike of the mining community was a classic example of the former; the Leeds clothing workers' strike an attempt at the latter. The media also confuse the unions with the working class, and workers know when the media's attack on the unions is an attack on them. But the heightening of the struggle in Britain has clarified even the heads of the media reporters. *The biggest attack on the unions by the media in recent times is the charge that they cannot discipline their members.*

The organizations which the working class will create—for creativity on a massive international scale can only come from the working class—we cannot predict. But the movement of women is not outside of that class or its creativity. We are part of that revolution—otherwise we are part of the counterrevolution—and we must create the autonomous organizational network with other women, which is an essential ingredient of class power. The autonomous organizational network is based neither on an abstract sisterhood nor on dividing women again by the class of their husbands and fathers, but on the fact that we are all capital's house slaves. Some women will struggle to escape from this individually, by joining with the power of the master. Most of us don't even have any choice but to organize to *destroy* the power of the master. That struggle to destroy the master's power is feminist struggle, the struggle of the unwaged worker against being unwaged and therefore against being a worker.

There may be times when we can use the unions. But that is a *tactic*. Our strategy springs from autonomy so that *we* will not be used as we have been used for so long by a class struggle dominated by men, and managed by the unions that dominate women *and* men.

As we women massively transform the terms of struggle, enlarge the arena of struggle, and increase our power, it becomes increasingly urgent for the feminist movement to decide between women on the one hand and unions and work on the other.

Detroit, May 1973

THE FAMILY ALLOWANCE CAMPAIGN: TACTICS AND STRATEGY (1973)

At the end of 1972, the Tory government issued a paper that aimed to take Family Allowance away from mothers. Since 1948, it had been paid at the post office weekly for each child after the first. The proposal was for it to be paid to the male wage earner rather than the mother, who might never see any of it. The Family Allowance money was to be a part of a tax-credit system for waged workers—those who didn't get wages would not get the tax credit; for example, students or unemployed workers or those on strike.

We organized a campaign within the women's movement to keep the money in women's hands, to increase it, and to pay it for the first child. Even feminists hostile to wages for housework were furious at the government's attack. One well-known feminist journalist interviewed me and said, "I'm against wages for housework, I know Family Allowance is wages for housework, but we can't let them take that money from women." Single mothers on benefits ("Unsupported Mothers") were active in the campaign and demanded family allowance be paid on top of their benefit.

We didn't win this, but we won family allowance staying in women's hands, and the tax-credit system was dropped entirely. Some years later, Family Allowance, now called child benefit, was paid for the first child.

This paper was not a public document. For the sake of unity in the movement, we didn't connect family allowance with women's right to money for the work we do, but for us, Family Allowance was a down payment on what we're owed.

* * *

The Family Allowance campaign was built on the spontaneous response of women in the movement to an escalation of the government's offensive against women (prices, welfare cuts, etc.). It was a response to what the government did, however, and not the result of what we had worked out as a perspective, which we applied to this particular turn of events. This is a statement of fact, not a criticism: strategy can only be worked out on the basis of concrete experience. We now have an excellent opportunity, after eight months of a campaign that has had great success in terms of the response of women and some success in terms of undermining government plans, to begin to draw conclusions from the campaign for strategy generally.

This is not only an opportunity, but an imperative. It is easy to slip from undermining government plans into reshaping them so they operate with fewer snags. To put it bluntly, the campaign can be utilized to make government policy on women more effective; our movement is being linked to the capitalist State by those threads whose fineness hides their strength.

So that the weaknesses and contradictions within the campaign at this stage are far more important than they were at the beginning. These weaknesses must be overcome and the contradictions resolved where possible, first, if we are to prevent being linked in this way, and second, if the work of eight months is not to be a sporadic though massive moment of activity among many other sporadic moments which the movement has known.

1. We dealt with the class issue of tax credits only as it was an attack on women workers who are all full- or part-time unwaged house-workers. Though we stated in our analysis how tax credits were an attack on men, waged and unwaged, no male-dominated "working-class" organization took this up or made any campaign against tax credits as an attack on the male worker.

Along with the Labour Party, of course the TUC supports tax credits. It accepts the taxing of insurance benefits with the proviso: "It would be essential to implement a once-for-all special increase in the rates of NI benefit, to compensate for the effects of such a change." It accepts the end of tax rebates for the sick, unemployed, etc., which this tax credit system wipes out.

If the government decides to withhold tax credits from strikers, however, "(particularly to single-person households)," this "might well lead to outright opposition by the General Council to the whole tax credit scheme." But they're not sure.

The TUC recommends that child credits be paid to the mother. It recognizes that the take-home pay of the father would be reduced by this system. But "the impact on the take-home pay of the father could…be substantially mitigated by a gradual transition to the new situation; thus in the year preceding the introduction of tax credits, child tax allowances could be gradually reduced, and family allowances gradually increased." So that men will gradually get used to a smaller pay packet. (All quotations from TUC Memorandum to the Select Committee, March 14, 1973.)

We are often told in the women's movement to work through or with or for the unions. But those who tell us this have either felt it worthless to try to get the unions active even on behalf of men workers on this issue or, having tried to do so, have largely or absolutely failed. In any case, the campaign has not *and could not be expected* to mobilize men against the tax credit system. Where the attack on tax credits should be coming from all sides, it comes only from one side, the feminist side: the Women's Family Allowance Campaign.

2. We were divided within the campaign on the meaning of taxation as a class issue and on where capitalist wealth comes from. We heard early from the Child Poverty Action Group women who came to our meeting: "Tell me what you want and I'll have it costed" to see if the State could afford it. We had always and repeatedly to make clear that all the capital the State has they have robbed from us, women and men workers. *The question is not whether the State can afford to give it, but whether we can afford to continue to give so much to the State.*

We were therefore divided on whom the State represented. Some women were against that point on the petition, which called for Family Allowance to be made tax-free. They felt that "the rich" would get the Family Allowance and not pay tax on it. Well the rich do not live or die by Family Allowance but by robbing large sums daily from us through our labor in the home and out of it. All workers but the lowest paid and the unwaged are taxed on Family Allowance. Taxation is not a system by which the State distributes income "fairly" but the State's way of robbing the working class after it has finished producing for the week (except women—we never finish).

3. We were divided within the movement on whom the money was for. One women's group in London that held a public meeting on Family Allowance introduced the meeting by saying that Family Allowance was not for the mother but for the children. While we were attempting to make clear that the woman was entitled to the money in her own right, as a human being who is made dependent on men by unwaged work in the home, they were riveting the woman to childcare in order for her to be eligible for Family Allowance. The women we met through the campaign said, "But this is the only money we can call our own." Meanwhile these women from the movement said by implication: This is money for the children that we have no right to spend on ourselves. Thereby they reinforced the guilt housewives suffer: in spending the money their husbands bring home, women are told they are living as parasites off the man since they themselves do not work.

The new proposal, which is attracting liberals from all the political parties is an extension of this money-for-the-child idea. It is called variously Family Responsibility payment and Home Responsibility payment; it aims to keep women at home with under-fives, for example, and by withdrawing payment when children are over five, to force them onto the labor market in order to avoid a substantial drop in living standards and financial independence. See Suzie Fleming, *The Family Allowance Under Attack* (Falling Wall Press & Power of Women Collective, June 1973).

The Red Rag Collective was uncertain about the whole purpose of our campaign and the government's: "Maybe we should press for an increased *children's* allowance, non-means tested, tax free, boosted by return of free school milk, meals, etc." (*Notes Towards a Discussion of the Family Allowance Campaign and Its Implications*, March 1973. They underlined *children's*.)

4. We were late in taking the lead of the Unsupported Mothers whose demand for Family Allowance on top of Social Security payments separated need as we women conceive it from need as the capitalist establishment conceives it. Social Security is calculated on subsistence—as long as we are not starving to death they believe we are not "needy." But money for us is autonomy from men, the right to choose what we eat and when, how much we work and where, where we live, whether or not we have children and under what circumstances and with whom. To demand Family Allowance on top of Social Security is putting our own priorities first, and refusing to be sloughed off with our children by the State because we are refusing both to live in a nuclear family situation with men and also refusing shit jobs at shit wages in addition to housework and childcare.

That the "supported" and "unsupported" mothers began to come together in this campaign, however, on the question of money for women, even in this limited form of Family Allowance, was one of the greatest victories of the campaign and one of the biggest steps forward of the women's movement. For the first time it was practically demonstrable that only a man stands between us.

5. We were never able to clearly and forcibly distinguish ourselves from do-gooders, liberals, and ambitious parliamentarians who were proposing not to eliminate our dependence and poverty, but to regulate wages more efficiently.

Family Allowance was first instituted as a subsidy for low wages on the one hand and as a population control on the other: to control the quantity and quality of future laborers—our children. (See *Social Insurance and Allied Services Report* by Sir William Beveridge, November 1942, known as The Beveridge Report on which the Welfare State was based. See especially pages 153–58.) The State wants to remove Family Allowance because they are now planning to regulate the total wage bill (wages proper, insurance benefits and Social Security) differently and were no longer interested in us as breeders for future factories and kitchens in the same way—they had immigration and bigger machines. The Child Poverty Action Group, for example, like the government, was interested in marshalling people into waged work outside the home to save on Social Security and other benefits. They merely disagree with the government on the most efficacious way to do this. (See again *Family Allowance Under Attack.*) A number of women in the movement were not able to distinguish between the CPAG program to modify the tax credit system, and the determination of the Women's Family Allowance Campaign to have no part of that system, for women or for men.

6. We are allowing the initiative to pass from our hands and the feminist issue to be submerged by State planning, statistical calculations and income tax juggling, which leave the mass of women utterly outside of activity. They won't understand what the "experts" are talking about (that's what expert means), and *to their credit*, they won't care.

Once we are dragged into the intricacies of figures we lose sight of the purpose of the campaign: to mobilize women to get money that they need, not to reform the tax system. At the moment a substantial increase in Family Allowance as a universal right of women is losing ground to the Family Income Supplement, which is a direct wage subsidy to private capital paid by the State to lower paid workers. But the very name makes it appear as a charity from the State, and *the issue of money for women is completely lost in "family income."*

As usual with "benefits" and "allowances" and "supplements," the effect of this is again to hide the source of capitalist wealth. If all the money they have is ours to begin with, then their parliamentary debate on who should get crumbs from the master's table is irrelevant. But they give the impression that there is a budget, which is fixed and unalterable, into which we must fit our wishes, and vie with each other about who will get what they call "a slice of the cake." When one set of workers succeeds in winning something by struggle, they threaten that other workers must take less. But there is no cake, there is no budget, there is only the wealth which we have made and which they have stolen. If they were right, then we would have to say that men's wages are higher because women receive no wage for housework. But this is not so. Men's wages are *lower* than they would be if they had to buy our services.

Men are cheaper workers for capitalists because they don't have to buy the labor we provide in the ninety-nine-hour workweek of the housewife (Chase Manhattan Bank's figure).

Whatever men have been able to win in wages, we *all* fought for. Otherwise wages would be even lower. Whatever we as women win need not be at men's expense unless men are unable to wrest control of their struggle from trade unions, which refuse to fight (or even publicize) the issue of taxes as an additional robbery of working-class labor. Who does not make a fight gets blows. That is the law of the struggle against capitalism.

In order for us now to develop this campaign and not be bogged down in the quicksand of parliamentary politics and (liberal or conservative) economists' figures, we must take our cue from the women whom we have met in the streets. The campaign must state boldly and clearly that we demand Family Allowance:

Because we are entitled to money of our own.

Because we work in the home full-time or part-time without a wage.

Because we get lower wages than men when we work out of the home.

Because unless we have money of our own, marriage is only a polite form of prostitution, and more rape will continue to take place in marriage than in back alleys.

Because we need the power to refuse the job of house servant in "our own" kitchens or somebody else's.

Because we need the power to refuse the worst jobs in industry which we take out of desperation and loneliness.

Because we have demonstrated publicly and consistently that we are ready to begin to overcome that loneliness and isolation by coming to meetings, going petitioning, meeting with other women, in the fight for money of our own.

We must destroy the concept that the State gives the poorest of us—the *unsupported* mother—charity. All mothers, *all housewives*, are unsupported because they do not receive money for their work. We are entitled to a great deal more than the pittance of Family Allowance. We are entitled when we do waged work not to pay *any* taxes. We are entitled to everything.

Family Allowance is not for the family. It is the *woman's* money.

Family Allowance is not an allowance. It is a *right*.

Family Allowance is the woman's right to money.

Women with waged work must receive money for their *entire* workweek, not only the part where the capitalist is breathing down their necks. To posit this perspective is the first strategic step for women to stop him from breathing at all.

July 9, 1973

SEX, RACE, AND CLASS (1974)

R *ace Today*, journal of the Institute of Race Relations (IRR), claimed in its review of *Power of Women* that the women's movement was clearer on race than the Black movement. As a coauthor, I began a letter to dissociate from that view. But the letter kept growing until it was a long article about the relationships between the movements the various sectors had built. This was published as the cover article of the January 1974 issue of the "new" *Race Today* (now independent of the IRR and run by a Black collective), and then as a pamphlet.

* * *

There has been enough confusion generated when sex, race, and class have confronted each other as separate and even conflicting entities. That they are separate entities is self-evident. That they have proven themselves to be not separate, inseparable, is harder to discern. Yet if sex and race are pulled away from class, virtually all that remains is the truncated, provincial, sectarian politics of the white male metropolitan Left. I hope to show in barest outline, first, that the working-class movement is something other than what that Left has ever conceived it to be. Second, locked within the contradiction between the discrete entity of sex or race and the totality of class is the greatest deterrent to working-class power and at the same time the creative energy to achieve that power.

In our book which Avis Brown so generously referred to, we tackled "the relation of women to capital and [the] kind of struggle we [can] effectively wage to destroy it," and draw throughout on the experience of the struggle against capital by Black people.[1] Beginning with the *female* (caste) experience, we redefined class to include women. That redefinition was based on the unwaged labor of the housewife. We put it this way: "Since Marx, it has been clear that capital rules and develops through the wage, that is, that the foundation of capitalist society was the wage laborer and his or her direct exploitation. What has been neither clear nor assumed by the organizations of the working-class movement is that precisely through the wage has the exploitation of the non-wage laborer been organized. This exploitation has been even more effective because the lack of a wage hid it… *Where women are concerned their labor appears to be a personal service outside of capital.*"

But if the relation of caste to class where women are concerned presents itself in a hidden, mystified form, this mystification is not unique to women. Before we confront race, let us take an apparent diversion.

The least powerful in the society are our children, also unwaged in a wage labor society. They were once (and in tribal society for example still are) accepted as an integral part of the productive activity of the community. The work they did was part of the total social labor and was acknowledged as such. Where capital is extending or has extended its rule, children are taken away from others in the community and forced to go to school, against which the number of rebels is growing daily. Is their powerlessness a class question? Is their struggle against school the class struggle? We believe it is. Schools are institutions organized by capital to achieve its purpose through and against the child. "Capital…sent them to school not only because they are in the way of others' more "productive" labor or only to indoctrinate them. The rule of capital through the wage compels every able-bodied person to function, under the law of division of labor, and to function in ways that are if not immediately, then ultimately profitable to the expansion and extension of the rule of capital. That, fundamentally, is the meaning of school. *Where children are concerned, their labor appears to be learning for their own benefit.*"

So here are two sections of the working class whose activities, one in the home, the other in the school, *appear* to be outside of the capitalist wage labor relation because the workers themselves are wageless. *In reality,* their activities are facets of capitalist production and its division of labor.

One, housewives, are involved in the production and (what is the same thing) reproduction of workers, what Marx calls *labor power.* They service those who are daily destroyed by working for wages and who need to be daily renewed; and they care for and discipline those who are being prepared to work when they grow up.

The other, children, are those who from birth are the objects of this care and discipline, who are trained in homes, in schools and in front of the television to be future workers. But this has two aspects.

---

1   "The Colony of the Colonized: Notes on Race, Class and Sex," *Race Today* (June 1973). We later learned that Avis Brown was a pseudonym for A. Sivanandan, who later headed the Institute of Race Relations.

In the first place, for labor power to be reproduced in the form of children, these children must be coerced into accepting discipline and especially the discipline of working, of being exploited in order to be able to eat. In addition, however, they must be disciplined and trained to perform a certain kind of work. The labor that capital wants done is divided and each category parceled out internationally as the life work, the destiny, the identity of specific sets of workers. The phrase often used to describe this is the international division of labor. We will say more of this later, but for now let the West Indian mother of a seven-year-old sum up her son's education with precision: "They're choosing the street sweepers now."

Those of us in the feminist movement who have torn the final veil away from this international capitalist division of labor to expose women's and children's *class* position, which was hidden by the particularity of their *caste* position, learnt a good deal of this from the Black movement. It is not that it is written down anywhere (though we discovered later it was, in what would seem to some a strange place). A mass movement teaches less by what it says than by the power it exercises which, clearing away the debris of appearances, tells it like it is.

Just as the women's movement being "for" women and the rebellion of children being "for" children, appears at first not to be about class:

> The Black movement in the United States (and elsewhere) also began by adopting
> what appeared to be only a caste position in opposition to the racism of white
> male-dominated groups. Intellectuals in Harlem and Malcolm X, that great
> revolutionary, were both nationalists; both appeared to place color above class
> when the white Left were still chanting variations of "Black and white unite
> and fight," or "Negroes and Labor must join together." The Black working class
> were able through this nationalism to *redefine class:* overwhelmingly Black and
> Labor were synonymous (with no other group was Labor as synonymous—except
> perhaps with women), the demands of Blacks and the forms of struggle created by
> Blacks were the most comprehensive *working-class* struggle.

It is not then that the Black movement "wandered off into the class struggle," as Avis says. It *was* the class struggle and this took a while to sink into our consciousness. Why?

One reason is because some of us wore the blinkers of the white male Left, whether we knew it or not. According to them, if the struggle's not in the factory, it's not the *class* struggle. The real bind was that this Left assured us they spoke in the name of Marxism. They threatened that if we broke from them, organizationally or politically, we were breaking with Marx and scientific socialism. What gave us the boldness to break, fearless of the consequences, was the power of the Black movement. We found that redefining class went hand-in-hand with rediscovering a Marx the Left had never understood.

There were deeper reasons too why caste and class seemed contradictory. It appears often that the interests of Blacks are contradicted by the interests of whites, and it is similar with men and women. To grasp the *class* interest when there seems not one but two, three, four, each contradicting the other, seems to be one of the most difficult tasks that confront us in both theory and practice.

Another source of confusion is that not all women, children or Black men are working class. This is only to say that within the movements which these form are layers whose struggle tends to be aimed at moving up in the capitalist hierarchy rather than at destroying it. And so within each movement there is a struggle about which class interest the movement will serve. But this is the history also of white male workers' movements. There is no class "purity," not even in shop floor organizations. The struggle by workers *against* organizations they formed there and in the society generally—trade unions, labor parties, etc.—is the class struggle.

Let's put the relation of caste to class another way. The word "culture" is often used to show that class concepts are narrow, philistine, inhuman. Exactly the opposite is the case. A national culture that has evolved over decades or centuries may appear to deny that society's relation to international capitalism. It is a subject too wide to go into deeply here but one basic point can be quickly clarified.

The life-style unique to themselves that a people develop once they are enmeshed by capitalism, in response to and in rebellion against it, cannot be understood at all except as the totality of their capitalist lives. To delimit culture is to reduce it to a decoration of daily life.[2] Culture is plays and poetry about the exploited; ceasing to wear miniskirts and taking to trousers instead; the clash between the soul of Black Baptism and the guilt and sin of white Protestantism. Culture is also the shrill of the alarm clock that rings at 6 a.m. when a Black woman in London wakes her children to get them ready for the baby-minder. Culture is how cold she feels at the bus stop and then how hot in the crowded bus. Culture is how you feel on Monday morning at eight when you clock in, wishing it was Friday, wishing your life away. Culture is the speed of the line or the weight and smell of dirty hospital sheets, and you meanwhile thinking what to make for tea that night. Culture is making the tea while your man watches the news on the telly.

And culture is an "irrational woman" walking out of the kitchen into the sitting room and without a word turning off the telly "for no reason at all."

From where does this culture spring which is so different from a man's if you are a woman and different too from a white woman's if you are a Black woman? Is it auxiliary to the class struggle (as the white Left has it) or is it more fundamental than the class struggle (as Black nationalists and radical feminists have it) because it

---

2   For the best demystification of culture I know which shows, for example, how West Indian cricket has carried in its heart racial and class conflicts, see CLR James, *Beyond a Boundary* (London: Hutchinson, 1963).

is special to your sex, your race, your age, your nationality, and the moment in time when you are these things?

Our identity, our social roles, the way we are seen, appear to be disconnected from our capitalist functions. To be liberated from them (or through them) appears to be independent of our liberation from capitalist wage slavery. In my view, identity—caste—is the very substance of class.

Here is the "strange place" where we found the key to the relation of class to caste written down most succinctly. Here is where the international division of labor is posed as power relations within the working class. It is Volume 1 of Marx's *Capital*: "Manufacture…develops a hierarchy of labor powers, to which there corresponds a scale of wages. If, on the one hand, the individual laborers are appropriated and annexed for life by a limited function; on the other hand, the various operations of the hierarchy are parceled out among the laborers according to both their natural and their acquired capabilities" (Moscow 1958, 349).

In two sentences is laid out the deep material connection between racism, sexism, national chauvinism and the chauvinism of the generations who are working for wages against children and pensioners who are wageless, who are "dependents."

A hierarchy of labor powers and a scale of wages to correspond. Racism and sexism training us to develop and acquire certain capabilities at the expense of all others. Then these acquired capabilities are taken to be our nature, fixing our functions for life, and fixing also the quality of our mutual relations. So planting cane or tea is not a job for white people and changing nappies is not a job for men and beating children is not violence. Race, sex, age, nation, each an indispensable element of the international division of labor. *Our feminism bases itself on a hitherto invisible stratum of the hierarchy of labor powers—the housewife—to which there corresponds no wage at all.*

To proceed on the basis of a hierarchical structure among waged and unwaged slavery is not, as Avis accuses the working class of doing: "concentrating…exclusively on the economic determinants of the class struggle." The work you do and the wages you receive are not merely "economic" but social determinants, determinants of social power. It is not the working class but organizations which claim to be of and for that class which reduce the continual struggle for social power by that class into "economic determinants"—greater capitalist control for a pittance more a week. Wage rises that unions negotiate often turn out to be wage standstills or even cuts, either through inflation or through more intense exploitation (often in the form of productivity deals) which more than pay the capitalist back for the rise. And so people assume that this was the intention of workers in demanding, for example, more wages, more money, more "universal social power," in the words of Marx.

The power relations of the sexes, races, nations, and generations are precisely, then, particularized forms of class relations. These power relations within the working class weaken us in the power struggle between the classes. They are the particularized forms of indirect rule, one section of the class colonizing another and through this capital imposing its will on us all. One of the reasons why these so-called working-class organizations have been able so to mediate the struggle is that we have, internationally, allowed them to isolate "the working class," which they identify as white, male and over twenty-one, from the rest of us. The unskilled white male worker, an exploited human being who is increasingly disconnected from capital's perspective for him to work, to vote, to participate in its society, he also, racist and sexist though he may be, recognizes himself as the victim of these organizations. But housewives, Black people, young people, workers from the Third World, excluded from the definition of class, have been told that their confrontation with the white male power structure in the metropolis is an "exotic historical accident." Divided by the capitalist organization of society into factory, office, school, plantation, home, and street, we are divided too by the very institutions which claim to represent our struggle collectively as a class.

In the metropolis, the Black movement was the first section of the class massively to take its autonomy from these organizations, and to break out of the containment of the struggle only in the factory. When Black workers burn the center of a city, however, white Left eyes, especially if they are trade union eyes, see race, not class.

The women's movement was the next major movement of the class in the metropolis to find for itself a power base outside the factory as well as in it. Like the Black movement before it, to be organizationally autonomous of capital and its institutions, women and their movement had also to be autonomous of that part of the "hierarchy of labor powers" which capital used specifically against them. For Blacks it was whites. For women it was men. For Black women it is both.

Strange to think that even today, when confronted with the autonomy of the Black movement or the autonomy of the women's movement, there are those who talk about this "dividing the working class." Strange indeed when our experience has told us that in order for the working class to unite in spite of the divisions which are inherent in its very structure—factory versus plantation versus home versus school— those at the lowest levels of the hierarchy must themselves find the key to their weakness, must themselves find the strategy which will attack the point and shatter it, must themselves find their own modes of struggle.

The Black movement has not in our view "integrated into capitalism's plural society" (though many of its "leaders" have); it has not been subsumed to white working-class strategy." (Here I think Avis is confusing white working-class *struggle* with trade union/Labour Party *strategy*. They are mortal enemies, yet they are often taken as identical.) The Black movement has, on the contrary, in the United States challenged and continues to challenge the most powerful capitalist State in the world. The most powerful at home and abroad. When it burnt down the centers of those cities and challenged all constituted authority, it made a way for the rest of the working class everywhere to move in its own specific interests. We women moved. This is neither an accident nor the first time events have happened in this sequence.

It is not an accident because when constituted power was confronted, a new possibility opened for all women. For example, the daughters of men to whom was delegated some of this power saw through the noble mask of education, medicine and the law for which their mothers had sacrificed their lives. Oh yes, marriage to a man with a good salary would be rewarded by a fine house to be imprisoned in, and even a Black servant; they would have privilege for as long as they were attached to that salary which was not their own. But power would remain in the hands of the white male power structure. They had to renounce the privilege even to strike out for power. Many did. On the tide of working-class power, which the Black movement had expressed in the streets, and all women expressed in the day-to-day rebellion in the home, the women's movement came into being.

It is not the first time either that a women's movement received its impetus from the exercise of power by Black people. The Black slave who formed the Abolitionist Movement and organized the Underground Railroad for the escape to the North also gave white women—and again the more privileged of them—a chance, an occasion to transcend the limitations in which the female personality was imprisoned. Women, trained always to do for others, left their homes not to free themselves—that would have been outrageous—but to free "the slave." They were encouraged by Black women, ex-slaves like Sojourner Truth, who suffered as the breeders of labor power on the plantation. But once those white women had taken their first decisive step out of the feminine mould, they confronted more sharply their own situation. They had to defend their right, as women, to speak in public against slavery. They were refused, for example, seating at the Abolitionist conference of 1840 in London because they were women. By 1848 at Seneca Falls, New York, they called their own conference, for women's rights. There was a male speaker. He was a leading Abolitionist. He was Black. He had been a slave. His name was Frederick Douglass.

And when young white women headed South on the Freedom Ride buses in the early 1960s and discovered that their male (white and Black) comrades had a special place for them in the hierarchy of struggle, as capital had in the hierarchy of labor power, history repeated itself—almost. This time it was not for the vote but for a very different goal that they formed a movement. It was a movement for liberation.

The parallels that are drawn between the Black and women's movements can always turn into an 11-plus—a competition over who is more exploited. Our purpose here is not parallels. We are seeking to describe that complex interweaving of forces which is the working class; we are seeking to break down the power relations among us, on which is based the hierarchical rule of international capital. For men cannot represent us as women any more than whites can represent the Black experience. Nor do we seek to convince men of our feminism. Ultimately they will be "convinced" by our power. We offer them what we offer the most privileged women: power over their enemies. The price is an end to their power over us.

The strategy of feminist class struggle is, as we have said, based on the unwaged woman in the home. Whether she also works for wages outside the home, her labor of producing and reproducing the working class weighs her down, weakens her capacity to struggle—she doesn't even have time. Her position in the wage structure is low especially but not only if she is Black. And even if she is relatively well placed in the hierarchy of labor powers (rare enough!), she remains defined as a sexual object of men. Why? Because as long as most women are housewives part of whose function in reproducing labor power is to be the sexual object of men, no woman can escape that identity. We demand wages for the work we do in the home. And that demand for a wage from the State is, first, a demand to be autonomous of men on whom we are now dependent. Secondly, we demand money without working out of the home, and open for the first time the possibility of refusing forced labor both in waged work and in the home itself.

It is here in this strategy that the lines between the revolutionary Black and the revolutionary feminist movements begin to blur. This perspective is founded on the least powerful—the unwaged. Reinforcing capital's international division of labor is a standing army of unemployed who can be shunted from industry to industry, from country to country. The Third World is the most massive repository of this industrial reserve army. (The second most massive is the kitchen in the metropolis.) Port of Spain, Calcutta, Algiers, the Mexican towns south of the U.S. border are the labor power for shit work in Paris, London, Frankfurt, and the farms of California and Florida. What is their role in the revolution? How can the unwaged struggle without the lever of the wage and the factory? We do not pose the answers—we can't. But we pose the questions in a way that assumes that the unemployed have not to go to work in order to subvert capitalist society.

Housewives *working* in the home without a pay packet may also have a job outside of their homes. The subordination to the wage of the man in the home and the subordinating nature of that labor weaken the woman wherever else she is working, and regardless of race. Here is the basis for Black and white women to act together, "supported" or "unsupported," not because the antagonism of race is overcome, but because we both need the autonomy that the wage *and the struggle for the wage* can bring. Black women will know in what organizations (with Black men, with white women, *with both, with neither*) to make that struggle. *No one else can know.*

We don't agree with Avis that "the Black American struggle failed to fulfill its potential as a revolutionary vanguard," if by "vanguard" is meant the basic propellant of class struggle at a particular moment in time. It *has* used the "specificity of its experience—both as a nation and as a class at once—to redefine class and the class struggle itself." Perhaps the theoreticians have not, but then they must never be confused with the movement. Only as a vanguard could that struggle have begun to clarify the central problem of our age: the organizational unity of the working class internationally as we now perceive and define it.

It has been widely presumed that the Vanguard Party on the Leninist model embodies that organizational unity. Since the Leninist model assumes a vanguard expressing the total class interest, it bears no relation to the reality we have been describing, where no one section of the class can express the experience and interest of, and pursue the struggle for, any other section. The formal organizational expression of a general class strategy does not yet anywhere exist.

Let me quote finally from a letter we wrote against one of the organizations of the Italian extraparliamentary Left which, when we had a feminist symposium in Rome last year and excluded men, called us fascists, and attacked us physically:

> The traditional attack on the immigrant worker, especially but not exclusively if he or she is Black (or Southern Italian), is that her presence threatens the gains of the native working class. Exactly the same is said about women in relation to men. The anti-racist (i.e. anti-nationalist and anti-sexist) point of view—the point of view, that is, of struggle—is to discover the organizational weakness which permits the most powerful sections of the class to be divided from the less powerful, thereby allowing capital to play on this division, defeating us. The question is, in fact, one of the basic questions which the class faces today. Where Lenin divided the class between the advanced and the backward, a subjective division, we see the division along the lines of capitalist organization, the more powerful and the less powerful. It is the experience of the less powerful that when workers in a stronger position (that is, men with a wage in relation to women without one, or whites with a higher wage than Blacks) gain a "victory," it may not be a victory for the weaker and may even represent *a defeat for both.* For in the disparity of power within the class is precisely the strength of capital.[3]

How the working class will ultimately unite organizationally, we don't know. We do know that up to now many of us have been told to forget our own needs in some wider interest which was never wide enough to include us. And so we have learnt by bitter experience that *nothing unified and revolutionary will be formed until each section of the exploited will have made its own autonomous power felt.*

Power to the sisters and therefore to the class.

---

3   Signed by Lotta Femminista and the International Feminist Collective, reprinted in *L'Offensiva* (Turin: Musolini, 1972), 18–19.

Postscript

The first paragraph of *Sex, Race, and Class* promises to "show in barest outline [that]… locked within the contradiction between the discrete entity of sex or race and the totality of class is the greatest deterrent to working-class power and at the same time the creative energy to achieve that power." But the pamphlet fails to deliver on this promise to show where the "creative energy to achieve [working-class] power" is to come from. This omission has bothered me for years, so I try to address that here.

We are deprived of enormous energy by the divisions among us. We are so used to the disparities of power and antagonisms among us—sex, race, age, occupation, immigration status, disability, sexual orientation, etc.—that we are not aware of how much our focus and energy go into defending ourselves from being attacked or demeaned through these divisions; and protecting ourselves from being pushed further down the hierarchy by competitors from below or the abuse of power from above. As we overcome, by our struggle, the competition, antagonism, and even violence among us, we liberate energy and focus.

We have already experienced, if only briefly, that when sectors which are ordinarily antagonistic surmount the divisions and act together, we feel elated and many times more powerful, because we are doing less of the soul-destroying and exhausting work of defending ourselves from other sectors. Winning even a temporary taste of unity, makes us more hopeful and confident and powerful.

Thus breaking down the divisions creates an individual and collective force that is no longer inhibited by fear and discouragement, and unlocks our creative capacity to see what is possible, identifying and facing what we need and are deprived of; drawing out the connections with the needs of others; and conceiving of the possibility, even certainty, of winning. That is what a revolution is, which many of us have glimpsed during collective confrontations, but which is rarely mentioned let alone seriously discussed.

Marx described the revolution as the "carnival of the masses"—when those of us whose lives are full of pain on many levels begin to fully enjoy ourselves by individually and collectively taking the enemy on.

If the divisions among us keep capital in power, then overcoming the divisions among us is by definition the destruction of capital, and the transformation of us individually but on a mass scale.

Who do we become when we have by our own effort stopped directing our energy against each other and direct it instead to collectively confronting anything or anyone standing in the way of our freely associating with each other to reshape the world? This is what we thirst to find out.

WAGELESS OF THE WORLD (1975)

T*he Power of Women and the Subversion of the Community* was published in Mexico in 1975 with the following introduction:

> The problem of the revolution is the unity of the working class internationally. The working class is divided by the power of those whose work is waged (men) over those whose work is unwaged (women). But the hierarchy within the working class is by no means confined to the power of men, identified with the wage, over women, identified by wageless and therefore invisible work. There is also the power of the waged worker in the metropolis over the unwaged worker in the Third World. Both are fundamental to the capitalist division of labor nationally and internationally.

In other writing, developing a paragraph of Marx, we approached the hierarchy within the working class this way:

> A hierarchy of labor powers and a scale of wages to correspond. Racism and sexism training us to acquire and develop certain capabilities at the expense of all others. Then these acquired capabilities are taken to be our nature and fix our functions for life, and fix also the quality of our mutual relations. So planting cane or tea is not a job for white people and changing nappies is not a job for men and beating children is not violence. Race, sex, age, nation, each an indispensable element of the international division of labor. *Our feminism bases itself on a hitherto*

invisible stratum of the hierarchy of labor powers—the housewife—to which there corresponds no wage at all.[1]

So that beginning with the wageless work of the housewife, we found ourselves redefining the class struggle in international terms, and most particularly redefining the relation between the working class in the metropolis and the working class in areas of technological underdevelopment. Wageless workers on the land, low-waged workers in the industrial interstices, even lower waged workers in the kitchens of the salaried and the wealthy of the Third World, are divided by power—not by class—from the working class in the metropolis.

Let us demystify not only what divides us as women, but what is the material basis of our unification.

First, where there is a wage the domination of the wage of the man over the woman is international. The reproduction of workers for mines, mills or factories is the product of unwaged female labor everywhere. Each situation of course is unique. In some parts of Africa it is often in the extended tribal family where women perform this unwaged labor for capital. In Zambia, the copper mines are magnanimously and increasingly surrounded by company housing of two- and three-room bungalows. The same in industrial Mexico City: the family is nuclearized and deculturized at one architectural stroke. How efficient to have workers used up daily and reproduced on the spot by other workers (of another sex)! And we are expected to be grateful that government or industry provides us with housing—*our* factories, for which we even pay rent. Again, in Caracas, where the technology to which the oil worker must submit is extremely high, oil production is absolutely dependent on female domestic labor. The following book attempts to show why there is this great discrepancy between the technology of extracting and refining oil and that of extracting and refining oil workers. It shows how the wife of the oil worker is as productive as he is because she daily "directly produces, trains, develops, maintains [and] reproduces labor power itself."[2] These questions, while not the same, are similar to those about the discrepancy between Third World and metropolitan technology in general, and about *who on an international level is productive.*

Second, in most of the world, side by side with women's reproduction of others' labor power when it is daily destroyed *on the land,* is the *use and destruction of women's own labor power on the land.* Often it is not through the wage of the man and the woman's lack of it that her labor is commanded, but *a patriarchal structure that predates capitalist society.* That structure may not yet have undergone *the capitalist reorganization*

---

1 See the previous essay, page 96.
2 "Productive labor would therefore be such labor as produces commodities or directly produces, trains, develops, maintains or reproduces labor power itself." Karl Marx, *Theories of Surplus Value* (London: Lawrence & Wishart, 1969), 172.

of the patriarchy: the patriarchy of the power of the wage. Nevertheless it is *the wage relation internationally* which is commanding the two forms of labor: the reproduction of labor power for the land and the production of the commodities which that land will produce. *In the same way as the proletarian character of the laborer in the home is hidden by the lack of a wage, so the proletarian character of the laborer on the land, "the peasant," land-owning or landless, is hidden by the wagelessness of that labor.*

The majority of Latin American women are either Indian or of Indian extraction, existing on subsistence agriculture and doing a double load of unwaged labor: both as *jornaleras* (day workers), *minifundistas* (smallholders) or *ejiditarias* (collective farm workers), *and* as housewives. The unit of production is the family. Women's work in the home, where they transform primary materials into the few consumer goods of food and clothing, is a fundamental aspect of the production of that family unit.

Even where there is payment in the form of a wage (to *los jornaleros)* or in the form of payment for sale of crops, it is the man who probably receives it. Women and children who work alongside him work for capital through his command. But at least the work of women and children is undisguised; it is recognized as work. Which is more than can be said for the urban housewife who is directly dominated by the wage; her housework, being unwaged, is not considered work at all.

So it is that capital has seized on every mode of production, and on the "train of ancient and venerable prejudices and opinions" which spring from these modes, to exploit all those temporarily trapped in them; and reinforces that exploitation by the prejudices and opinions they generate, from which women suffer most and *in a most specific manner.* To obscure and thus ignore the specific nature of the exploitation of women (and children), and the specific and autonomous nature of the struggles this *must* produce, with the blackmail of universal poverty or universal repression, is to resort to a moralism which in fact is a political attack on the least powerful—and therefore of course on the poorest and most repressed. And when the least powerful are attacked, all the forces of subversion are weakened.

It is impossible to speak of the relation of women to capital *anywhere* without at the same time confronting the question of development versus underdevelopment. It is even more unavoidable when it is women of the Third World of whom we speak, since their situation cannot be wrested from the general context of predominant underdevelopment; rather they are a honed edge with which to approach the Gordian Knot that confronts *all* working-class struggle in the Third World.

Working for Capital

The tendency has been to subsume all those who are not city proletarians under the term "peasant." Once we assume that the basic division within the working class internationally is between the waged and wageless, and that *to be wageless is not necessarily* to *be outside of the capitalist wage relation*, every mode of labor which exists today must be reexamined to determine the social relation which it reproduces: whether there is surplus labor, if that surplus labor is stolen (appropriated by someone other than the laborer), and if so, by whom—in other words, whether and where capital has transformed precapitalist modes of labor into modes of its own self-expansion. Even the subsistence farming family of Mexico, for example, which produces no material surplus may be working usefully for capital; *braceras* and *braceros* provide a cheap and intimidated reserve army of labor, particularly for the farms of California and Texas.[3] Women on that "unproductive" subsistence farm, with our unending work, have produced that army of labor.

Where our product, labor power, is "overpopulating"—that is, where it is rebellious and refusing quietly to starve—the State in the unarmed form of Rockefeller Foundations or the armed form of native or foreign troops and "expeditions" is seeking to "regulate our productivity." Women all over the world are repudiating these controls over our reproductive function, controls which range from mass sterilization to mass genocide of those already born, by planned famines and other more scientific techniques.

Increasingly and in every situation internationally we are demanding the right to have children whose birth is not our agony physically, socially, financially; and the right not to have them if we so desire. Birth control campaigns vulgarly reflect the immediate and long-term brutal interests of the State. In its propaganda, by painting us as victims who don't ourselves know what is good for us, our interests become the excuse to perpetrate its interests against us. The starvation that it organizes or at best allows is blamed on our fertility. We refuse any longer to be reproductive machines to be turned on or off as production plans alter. Having or not having children must be our choice and integral to our individual and social development.

But this is already to demand more than any political parties have ever assumed we in the Third World felt the need to have. We feel many needs because we have learnt many things even when they thought they were teaching us quite different lessons.

In a Mexican village one family may invest in a television. Other families around must pay to see it—must find the money to pay to see it, must find the job or grow the crop *or make the struggle for the wage without the work*, which will yield the money to

---

3   The American State's intimidation of these workers (traditionally with the help of armed vigilantes, official and unofficial) is posed as a protection for native American workers. To its joy, a trade union with membership overwhelmingly of Americans of *bracero* descent has supported the recent clampdown on immigration from Mexico. Which of course only means that the wages of the "illegal" entrant can be even lower. See the *New York Times*, December 2, 1974, "Ruling on Mexican Aliens Stirs Chicanos' Job Fears." Working-class organization, which is confined to national borders and to the trade unionist struggle for jobs always results in our scabbing on each other.

pay to see it. Or reappropriate another just like it or bigger—that is, make a struggle for *the wage without the work* in a way which bypasses the money form.

Once we have seen it, or heard the grating sounds of the inexpensive model of transistor radio in the village or in the field, that person, that family, that community, has stepped beyond any definition of itself as "peasant." When the woman from an area of underdevelopment in the heart of Europe, such as a village in Spain, sees a Hollywood film, the plot is secondary to the technology of the North American kitchen (which, nevertheless, is still the North American *woman's* place). So we are ready to demand in Mexico, Tanzania, India, and Spain all of the wealth that exists but of which we have been deprived. For on the media they tell us about or even show us all the products of technology which Third World peoples are denied. They have sent the media to give one message, but we have absorbed quite another. For we have come to the media with a mind crammed with the refusal of the bitterness of our experience. That media presents a picture, however distorted, of a whole world which peasants of Lenin's day or of Zapata's never knew existed. It pictures a range of goods and therefore a range of possibilities which *nobody* of Lenin's day or of Zapata's knew since they didn't exist *anywhere*. Our experiences as exploited women, urban or rural, Third World or metropolitan, are unique in each case. *Our needs and our desires are increasingly international and universal:* to be free, to be free of the labor that has worn us down over centuries, to be free of domination and dependence on men. We repudiate the assumption that we who are not socialized, collectivized, unionized, are the "backward ones." The backward technology with which they have burdened us is no measure of our own aspirations. And that is our dilemma.

Many well-meaning North Americans who returned from Cuba, having cut their six weeks of cane in the Venceremos brigades, may glorify cane-cutting as once Communist Party visitors to Russia glorified forced collectivization. But who wants to cut cane all their lives? Who wants to do the cooking, washing, child care, when they get home from a day in the fields? Not those who returned after six weeks. What we need instead of the labor is wages, beginning with wages for the work we women have always done without a wage, whether we cook by charcoal or by gas, whether we wash clothes by the river bank, in tubs or in machines. It is our time, our energy, our lives. It is time to put paid to this work.

Refusing Their Development

In the metropolis when we demand a wage from the State, we are told that we can get a wage in the offices or factories, which are waiting to suck up what little of our lives the washing machine has left free. Millions of us are driven there daily by an inflation which is transforming bringing home a wage—and therefore doing a double shift—into another household duty, another chore, another obligation of the wife. In

Mexico, with a 40 percent rate of unemployment or underemployment, to propose that women who want a wage take a second job in factories, offices, etc. (if they don't already have one on the land), is even more laughable. None of us wants that second job, neither those who have it and the pittance of a wage that may go with it, nor those who desperately need a wage despite the sixteen-hour day of the full-time housewife. More work will never sweeten our bitterness. Yet Third World women (in fact *all* women) are told there is no other solution but to accept this "development," to accept, that is, more rationalized exploitation, if they are lucky enough to get it in that sea of wagelessness. There is only one development today in the world, and that is capitalist development, even greater exploitation than we have suffered up to now. That is the price we have traditionally paid for the wage. We will still bear, train and care for the new generation while we are "benefiting" from the assembly line of their development. Also, because so many of us are wageless, they will get the very few they hire cut-rate. Passively to accept that development is to accept a development of slavery, the opposite of its abolition.

For us in the metropolis to demand a wage from the State for the work we are doing in the home is our only real choice, so that we can massively refuse that job and the second, waged, job we do. As capital's crisis deepens it is not clear what place metropolitan women will have in its plans. One thing, however, is already clear. Though we are surrounded by development, they have begun to plead poverty and austerity and are expecting women to be the prime shock absorbers. When we demand Wages for Housework in whatever form—child care which we control, free birth control and abortion which do not sicken, kill, or sterilize us, the socialization of our work on our terms to liberate time for ourselves, and most important, money we can call our own—they now say here what they have always said in the Third World to every demand by women: "The till is empty."

Our great advantage in the metropolis is that the wealth stolen from all of us is where we are, on the spot, to demand back. For those in the Third World, it is infinitely more difficult to demand the return of the wealth that our combined labor has created. For most of us the dilemma is that this wealth is not where we are. This poses enormous problems of organization and mobilization of power. Yet we have no choice. The State of every Third World country that has tried to impose development in the form of "aid" and/or investment has ultimately had to defend that development with arms against the working class. When it is proposed that the road to the new society passes through our increased productivity, the Chilean firing squads are there to block the exits to our own road.[4]

---

4 The Chilean housewife was of course part of the working-class resistance to productivity. Yet that was drowned by the din of a carefully constructed mythology of the Chilean reactionary housewife, which served the Right *and* the Left internationally, not only to obscure the revolutionary struggle of Chilean women but to undercut the struggle of women everywhere. It was in particular the Left's

Since in the past we have lost when we didn't ask enough, we cannot do worse by demanding everything. And though the wealth is not on the spot in the Third World, the agents of its continued expropriation are always close at hand. The State is only partially made up of the government and Rockefeller Foundations; these are the executors outside the factory of the multinational corporations. Together they plan our exploitation, its quality and intensity, as part of an international plan which encompasses every country, females and males, children and adults, the working class employed and unemployed, the waged and unwaged of that class, the urbanized and the ruralized of that class. It is against them, and the (usually U.S.) arms which enforce their plan and their will, that such demands for wages will ultimately have to be made by all of us women. For though the dilemma of the Third World is that the wealth of our combined labor is in the metropolis, the Third World can draw on the wealth of our combined struggle to get it back.

To raise our voices internationally to demand our wage and an end to the work we do, which has brought no wage in the home and very little wage (if any) out of it, to demand that *we* develop and that technology be the servant of *our* development, the opposite of our being at the service of a developing technology the benefits of which we are then denied, is to completely revolutionize the terms of struggle. It is to articulate the internationalization of our struggle and to raise our power at every moment of the international capitalist circuit. The unwaged men must follow our lead; although we will have to fight them for the right to fight capital, that in itself will be a high stage in the revolutionary process.

So, as women in Latin America read of our experience and our analysis, perhaps they will often see themselves; perhaps they will see a future which has been proposed to them finally unromanticized by those who would live it; perhaps they will take confidence from our struggle as we do from theirs, and know how aware we are of our mutual interdependence.

In 1971, we said: "Women of the Third World have not yet spoken of the effects of colonial rule and industrialization on them and on the traditional family. When they do, the horrors we now associate with capitalism and imperialism will gain new dimensions. We need a woman's history of imperialism, and of the division of labor between the industrial and agricultural worlds."[5]

That history has begun to emerge, as a weapon in the developing struggle.

Power to the sisters and therefore to the class internationally.

---

occasion to give vent to their rage at our audacity in organizing without them and against their leadership. [Update 2012: The organizations of relatives, mainly women, of people disappeared or jailed under the military dictatorship in Chile and elsewhere have since obliterated this sexist view. The Mothers of Plaza de Mayo in Argentina, whose courage and determination spearheaded the movement that defeated the dictatorship there, are the most famous, but such women's movements can be found all over the world.]

5   Edith Hoshino Altbach, ed., *From Feminism to Liberation* (Cambridge, MA: Schenkman, 1971), 197.

Note:

The lives of women in Mexico confirms yet again that we understand the wage and all the labor it commands only when we begin with the unique—but by no means exotic—experience of each section of the wageless. "The Marxists" are so mesmerized by the factory that they haven't noticed that Marx (a) states plainly that capital's birth and development began on the backs of the wageless, and (b) that the wage itself is determined at least as much outside of the factory as in it; so that "Taking them as a whole, the general movements of wages are exclusively regulated by the expansion and contraction of the industrial reserve army"—that is, by workers without access to wages.[6] Marx was not a feminist but, unlike "the Marxists," he understood the wage and the lack of it.

---

6 *Capital* 1:637, Moscow, 1958.

HOOKERS IN THE HOUSE OF THE LORD (1983)

This is an account of the 1982 occupation of a London church by sex workers. I was their spokeswoman at the time.

The occupation was a big experience for all who took part. We had to work out every day such practical questions as how to speak the truth but not give the church an excuse to have us tossed out; and how to train individuals who had no previous experience of actions like this so they become part of a collective, effective force. Once learnt, such skills become part of your political equipment, and are universally applicable. I know of no way to learn them except collectively in movement initiatives.

Having to write this article was our chance to spell out for ourselves and others what we did and how we did it. Years later, we heard that a group of sex workers in Canada who were planning to occupy a church had studied the account of our occupation in preparation, and that theirs had been a success.

* * *

On November 17, 1982, the English Collective of Prostitutes (ECP) began an occupation of the Church of the Holy Cross, King's Cross, London, which was to last for twelve days. By our action we were demanding that Local Authorities and society at large stand by prostitutes in their conflict with the police. This is the choice we had been asking feminists to make since we were formed in 1975.

That same year the ECP opened the debate on prostitution within the women's movement with a paper called "For Prostitutes, Against Prostitution." Since then we have taken every opportunity to create a forum for prostitute and nonprostitute women to talk to each other. Women-only ECP public meetings were always packed, always frank and, happily, always more an exchange of experience and feeling than a confrontation of dogmas. The results were rewarding. Our campaign for the rights of prostitute women, with its lobbying and pickets and public meetings and debates, gained increasing interest and support from all kinds of women. Some feminists even came out as prostitutes at conference workshops (though many more still feel it is safer to remain in the closet even in the movement).

In the last couple of years two new factors have made more urgent the choice between prostitutes and police. The urban rebellions, which began in the spring of 1981, attacked racist and brutal policing, making it impossible for anyone in sexual or other politics to remain neutral or silent; neutrality or silence was consent—to racism and to brutality. At the same time, the antipornography tendency as it has grown has lobbied for more State (police) control of explicitly sexual materials, and has often attacked not only the sex industry but those employed by it, treating workers and employers as one entity. No other workers, especially if they're women, are dismissed in this way by the women's movement.

If prostitutes and their work are so unlike other women and their work, then the church Occupation is just an exotic curiosity, not a feminist action whose lessons have general applicability. Let me therefore state the obvious: women who *work* for the sex industry are *workers*. They have those jobs for the same reason that other workers have their jobs: to earn a living.

It is true that sex workers sell a service which we all hope will be connected with intimacy and deep personal feeling. But feminists have been at pains to spell out that sexuality is romanticized to hide how it is sometimes a tragedy or disappointment or danger—or all of these—for women. It is also sometimes a job.

The ECP has argued that there are many more financial considerations in our sexual relations than most of us are prepared to face or at least to articulate to others. This reluctance to admit the connection between sex and money in our own lives can express itself as a prejudice against prostitutes—whose *job* is to connect the two. This prejudice against the women who strip sex of some of its romantic mystique is then reinforced by their illegal status.

The Tradition of Illegal Rebels

Before unions were legal, every trade unionist was illegal, a criminal and probably often a hated or even despised neighbor. Every immigrant who crosses a national boundary for reasons governments don't approve of—to campaign for peace as women have done or to claim a share in accumulated wealth as Third World people have done—is illegal. Being illegal workers, prostitute women are part of this illegal organizing tradition. They get higher wages than women are supposed to have, for work that women are supposed to do for free. Prostitutes are also in a long tradition of resourceful women who have tried to turn sexual exploitation to their own advantage. Women have used their bodies to bargain daughters, sons, husbands, out of concentration camps and border towns; to feed or arm their kin or their movement; and to attain the financial independence necessary to escape from intolerable relationships or situations.

Unless we are aware of what we have in common as women and as workers, we tend to be complicit in the myth that social status equals human value. Our prejudices can reinforce the hierarchy of whose struggle is valid and central and whose is unworthy and marginal: who are "real" women and "real" workers and who are not. On that scale whores are not as important as other more "respectable" workers forming other more acceptable combines—like trade unions. But there is no hierarchy of struggle and nobody's fight is marginal. If you want to change the world, you can start anywhere. And the best place to start is where you are.

By entering Holy Cross, the ECP was breaking ground not only on behalf of all prostitutes but on behalf of those millions of women who are increasingly criminalized by the economic crisis: women who are forced into shoplifting and welfare fraud, women who are having to discover new (sometimes illegal) ways to support themselves, their children, their parents, their movement. (The women who come down from the north of England, where unemployment is even more severe, to work on the streets of King's Cross are called "Thatcher's girls.") In making a case against any woman being criminalized for refusing poverty, and in protecting her rights when she is, the Occupation was a moment of power for all women.

The Occupation embraced more people and wider areas of life than the word "prostitution" usually conveys. But that is because that word is defined not by the women and men whom it condemns but by the prostitution laws and the men and women who make them.

The Laws

The prostitution laws vary from country to country. They are of two basic types: prohibition and legalization. The laws in Britain are prohibition laws: though prostitution is not itself illegal, everything associated with it is.[1]

You can be picked up for soliciting and loitering for the purposes of prostitution if the police say you were seen offering sexual services for a fee. So that for example if a woman in the street asks a man, "Will you sleep with me?" that is perfectly legal. But if he says yes and she tells him that it will cost him £20, that's against the law.

---

1   The prostitution laws have changed since 1983 but not for the better; they are now even more repressive, following the "Swedish model" of State feminism. See http://www.prostitutescollective.net.

If you are cautioned twice by the police, you are labeled a "common prostitute" which sticks with you for life. Once labeled, without a trial, you can then be brought to court and convicted for a prostitution offense on the word of a single officer. As with the "sus"[2] laws, the police need no witness and no complainant. It is their word against that of a "common prostitute."

It is illegal to advertise even discreetly.

Two women working together constitute a brothel.

If a man is financially dependent on you or even (depending on the judge) if you contribute to the upkeep of a home you share with him—whether husband, lover, son, friend—he can be convicted for pimping. (On the other hand, if a husband takes all his wife's earnings to play the horses or to buy books, that's perfectly legal—unless she is a prostitute.) A woman whom you live with who is not a prostitute can be convicted on a separate pimping charge.

In this way the prostitution laws make it virtually impossible for a woman who is a prostitute to live with women or with men without breaking the law.

In some countries the clients are criminalized, and people who are angered that women are sent to prison and their clients go free sometimes feel equality would be achieved if clients too were criminalized. But this is like asking employers to lower men's wages to achieve equal pay: two defeats don't make a victory.

Others who want to see the laws changed sometimes propose legalization, assuming that this is the opposite of criminalization. It is not, and it carries its own dangers. It can be worse than prohibition. Since prostitution is legalized in parts of the United States (Nevada has legalized brothels) and in West Germany (which has legalized red-light areas in every major city), we need not speculate: we can see how it works and what it would mean for us in Britain. In these places, the legalization of prostitution is the legalization of pimping.

In 1981, I visited the Rieperbahn, the famous red-light area of Hamburg, with a prostitute woman. After 6 p.m., women are allowed to work on the street and in clubs and brothels. Called Eros Centers, these brothels are owned by corporations of pimps licensed by the government. Blocks of rooms are then rented to other pimps who then rent individual rooms to prostitute women. The women need their own pimps to protect them from the pimps of other women with whom they are competing for clients to pay, first of all, this enormous overhead of rent. On top of that you pay tax. You also must register with the police as a prostitute, a stigma you can never shake off. It is no wonder then that only 12 percent of the women in West Germany are

---

2   Hated police powers to stop and search on suspicion of criminal intent used mainly against young men of color. When they were finally abolished, they were replaced with similar police powers; these helped provoke widespread multiracial riots in England in August 2011.

legal. Rather than being controlled by landlord, pimp, State doctor (weekly compulsory examinations) and police computer, 88 percent of women prefer to remain illegal.

The brothels in Nevada are more exclusive and isolated. Women are allowed out only after working twenty-one days straight, taking any client day or night as their employers' request. Their children are not with them, and on their ten days off a month, there are restrictions on where in the city they can go. In Nevada, too, most prostitutes remain illegal rather than submit to being imprisoned in these sex factories.

In Britain, when fighting legalization (for example, proposals from Tories on Southampton Council in 1979 to give the pier over to city-run brothels), we have made it clear that prostitute women will not go into brothels run by the State, that is, by the police. One Southampton prostitute told us: "They would have to bring in the army to get us out of our homes into their brothels."

The very existence of these laws, whether legalizing or prohibiting prostitution, determines that women who are not prostitutes will go to great lengths to keep their distance from women who are, and work like hell on their image so as never to be "taken for one." And to the degree that women are divided in this way by the prostitution laws, to that degree prostitutes are vulnerable before these laws. Those who enforce them take advantage of the fact that the prostitute is an outcast among other women first of all. Since if you are a prostitute woman, other women are not particular about what happens to you, *the laws and the people who enforce them are without the restraints of the community's concerns, and they are able to dominate your life.*

Abolition of the Laws

We are campaigning along with prostitutes' organizations in other countries to abolish the prostitution laws. This will not encourage pimping but end it. The isolation the laws impose causes women to be more dependent on men than if we were not divided from each other; this imposed isolation makes it harder for prostitute women to undermine the power of men, even if economic power makes it easier. Once women are not divided by the laws, prostitutes will be in a much more protected position to take the offensive against all kinds of pimping—by landlords, taxi drivers, etc., as well as by individual men.

On the other hand, the laws on pimping have never been effective except as a discipline on prostitutes. Once there are "special" laws, which segregate any group from the rest, equal justice before the law is negated. Ironically, prostitutes and wives are often the least protected. We want all women to be protected by the existing extortion laws, including those two groups now excluded, hookers and wives. And we want all women to be protected from the violence of individual men, in prostitution as well as in marriage. For example, the rape of wives is not illegal *de jure*, and the rape of prostitutes is not illegal *de facto*.[3] The prostitution laws are not about protecting any women but about persecuting and controlling and dividing us. Women have a right to do what we want with our own bodies, and what we as consenting adults do in private is none of the business of governments.

Legal Action by Illegal Women

Having campaigned on this basis since 1975, we published in 1981 an "A-Z for Working Girls," a guide to the laws for prostitutes, their families, friends and supporters, and for women who are considering prostitution to know what they are up against so they can make an informed choice. The following year, in April 1982, we took a giant step. The King's Cross Women's Centre opened its doors to the first women-only legal service in Britain, an ECP initiative.

It soon came to be called Legal Action for Women (LAW). A solicitor or legal worker is available every Thursday evening to any woman wanting legal advice and follow-up representation. It is a unique service where the professional works within the political framework of the campaigning and referral skills of an active women's center. From the beginning all kinds of women came to the center for the service. Local prostitute women immediately used LAW: for custody cases—children taken into care because their mothers were considered unfit; for evictions and other housing matters; and for the wide range of problems they shared with other women who were using the service.

In June, a woman came to plead not guilty. That this was a unique occasion tells you more about the prostitution laws than perhaps anything said so far. Many times women plead guilty when they're not, but this time she was not guilty and said so. Her plea challenged the magistrate to believe a "common prostitute" rather than the police. Such a plea is also a financial gamble: even if you win, the lawyer's fees may cost you more than the fine would have been if you had pleaded guilty. Our lawyer got her legal aid, presented her case as she instructed (another rarity), and she was found not guilty. We informed the local press and let women in our network know.

By September, the already crowded women's center was busy with local prostitute women. There were almost daily meetings to discuss the possibilities of claiming civil rights. Women arrested when shopping or collecting children, or at a bus stop,

---

3   Until 1991, the UK courts considered rape in marriage to be legal; it took 250 years of women's individual and public protest and fifteen years of campaigning by Women Against Rape for it to be acknowledged as a crime. Raping a prostitute was not legal but it was often treated as such by the authorities—"a prostitute can't be raped" and "she is asking for it" were common assumptions. In 1995, two sex workers raped by the same man took a private prosecution after the authorities refused to prosecute. With backing from the English Collective of Prostitutes, Legal Action for Women and Women Against Rape, the women won and the rapist got an eleven-year prison sentence. This case helped to establish that every victim of rape is entitled to the protection of the law, regardless of her occupation or her relationship with her attacker.

wanted to plead not guilty. Even more encouraging, a woman who had a meeting at 3 p.m. might turn up at 2:45 with her support group: the friend who witnessed the illegal arrest and one or two or even three others. All the women would participate in planning the defense and in gauging the attitudes of police and of working women—that is, in evaluating the political climate for their fight. This, remember, was on their working time; it cost them money to meet in this way. All of these women worked independently of pimps.

Aside from legal defense meetings, women came in for a cup of tea or a look at what else the center had on offer (Women Against Rape which meets at our center, seems always to be appealing). Women were anxious to talk about themselves, and long pent-up grievances and indignation against the police came pouring out. "I was drinking a cup of coffee when he arrested me for loitering. You ever heard of picking up punters and drinking coffee at the same time?" Those not used to women organizing might have been surprised at how women who a month before were joking with the police in Argyle Square were now complaining that the police had the audacity to expect that intimacy—now that they had the power to refuse. Encouraged by the center, by LAW and by the one "not guilty" verdict, prostitute women began to construct a minor volcano.

As the excitement mounted, we were able to confront with fairly level heads and even laugh about the special harassment the police had begun to put on women who used the center. Police, in trying to break up the unity which was building, told women the center had police informers, that women were courting trouble by standing up to the police, that they would never get bail if they pleaded not guilty, and that they (the police) and not the center "really understood" prostitutes. Even women filling in the ECP survey on prostitution were threatened. Our academic advisor protested. The police denied it was happening and said it would stop.

Women coped with the threats, and trusted their organization to get them out on bail—arrests were not exactly a new experience. That trust was not misplaced; the ECP was scrupulous and by now experienced with legal defense. Confidence, even in the face of the attacks, continued to grow.

In October another woman's case came to court. Young, Black, with two children, she paid an exorbitant rent in a local hotel. (Quite a few women are in prostitution in order to pay a London rent, especially if they are mothers with young children.)

In court her lawyer asked her how much rent she paid. Eighty-four pounds a week for one room for three of them, she said. The magistrate asked if he'd heard right. "And," she added, "when I don't have to pay that rent, I won't be a prostitute." She was also found not guilty.

The first victory was not a freak. Even if you were a prostitute, if you organized you could win.

The Counterattack

One of the ECP's great strengths is that, despite the laws, its members are not ghettoized. As part of the Wages for Housework Campaign, it is in touch with an international network of both prostitute and nonprostitute women. While the autonomy of prostitute women is protected, we have spent a lot of time drawing the line between separatism of all kinds—building barriers against other women—and autonomy— building networks with other women but keeping tight reins on your own struggle. This hard-won clarity has enabled prostitute women to choose and train nonprostitutes to be the public voice, whenever necessary, of illegals who cannot be public. The women's center also functions by refusing separatism and respecting autonomy. All the groups maintain their independence and still benefit from each other's power and each other's activities. And there are plenty of activities. ECP organizing was by far not the only activity going on at the center during this time. A conference, "Bringing It All Back Home: Black and Immigrant Women Speak Out and Claim Our Rights," was in preparation. All the center groups were helping Housewives in Dialogue, the charity that runs the center, to organize it. It came off on Saturday, November 13.

At that conference about 350 women, mostly immigrant, in the majority Black, heard Nina López of Argentina say:

> You are so vulnerable as an immigrant that you don't want to associate yourself
> with a whole set of people who are also vulnerable… As a member of the English
> Collective of Prostitutes I know very well what it means to be vulnerable and when
> you're a prostitute how you feel about being vulnerable …the kind of treatment
> that Black women get, that's what prostitute women get and even double if you're
> a Black prostitute woman, and this kind of vulnerability, this kind of racism, this
> kind of police assault, police abuse, that you get as a prostitute woman, is just so
> horrendous that a lot of immigrants don't want to associate with prostitutes. They
> think, well, if that's the treatment they get, I've got enough with my own treatment
> without associating with this other set of people and making it worse.

The point was taken by women who hadn't come expecting to hear, and certainly not to empathize with, a speaker from a prostitutes' group. For the first time the case for Black and immigrant prostitute women was put to the women's movement. This was the fruit of the organizing at the center. About half the women working on the game in King's Cross were Black, and that fact was exactly reflected in those who came in to organize. The fact that the center houses Black Women for Wages for Housework helped both Black and white women to make it their base, and ensured that the racism Black prostitutes faced would not remain invisible.[4]

---

4   Now renamed Women of Color in the Global Women's Strike.

After the conference we were hoping for a bit of rest. A number of cases were pending and we were still short of the kind of devoted lawyers we needed, lawyers for whom getting justice for clients and not their own careers was the first consideration. We had written to all the lawyers we heard might be sympathetic, and slowly we were getting responses.

Sunday, the day after the conference, women were at the center preparing the WAR survey on women's safety for the computer. A woman who had been raped was brought in by a local resident and WAR took her to the police. She was white, her boyfriend was Black. The police kept her for hours, said she was a prostitute (and therefore she wasn't raped) and that her boyfriend was a pimp. She had no convictions for prostitution nor was there any other evidence to indicate that she was. It was a complete invention. The police also refused to go to the scene of the crime even though she told them of evidence there which could identify the rapist. It seemed clear that the police might not be sorry to have a rapist loose in the vicinity of our center. We got her out of the hands of the police but not before she had been intimidated into signing a paper saying there had not been a rape. The following day her boyfriend was picked up for pimping (later he was found not guilty).

Monday morning, I was to go to court with a woman pleading not guilty. A single mother with a disabled child, she had dropped into the center on her way home and our logbook, which records every visitor, said so. As she left the center she was arrested. At the court, I found she was in a panic because the witness who had seen the arrest was herself appearing on a trumped-up probation charge in a court at the other end of London. Her closest friend, a woman from the north of England, was in court with her: she had just heard that her mother with whom her six-year-old son lived had been visited first by the police and told that her daughter was a prostitute (which freaked the old woman out completely). Then the Social Services came to say, in front of her grandson, that she was too old to be taking care of him, and that he would be taken from her and put into care. The boy begged his granny not to let them take him away. He had an attack of asthma and had to be taken into hospital.

The defendant herself had her hands full. The police were watching her house to get her boyfriend, who lived with her, for pimping, and they eventually did get him.

We had always tried to develop friends in high places; if you're illegal you are particularly dependent on those with some power who can intervene for you, questioning the gross discrimination you are likely to suffer at the hands of the powers that be. We needed them now.

The case was postponed and we all went back to the center, to call a lawyer, a Member of Parliament and others who might help. But we were very worried women.

All of us had been able to cope when women who were organizing were arrested on any pretext—even women sitting in the park would get nicked for loitering—or refused bail for pleading not guilty. Splitting up families, terrorizing children, arresting boyfriends who were not pimps and could be jailed for years, was a different story altogether. The police were obviously now intending to concentrate their considerable forces and connections on breaking "the girls' union," as the ECP came to be called. In my experience, having to respond to many more attacks than you have forces for is a formula for disaster. You get tired and then you get demoralized and then you begin to quarrel among yourselves and then you make bad decisions, based on a sense of weakness and failure. If we didn't do something quickly, tired as we already were, we might win individual battles but we'd lose the war. We were racking our brains for a precedent—what had other women (or men) done in similar circumstances? The occupation of the churches in France in 1975, which was led by the French Collective of Prostitutes (which is where we got our name from and the inspiration to form), came to mind. Sitting in the center wondering what to do next, someone whispered to the woman next to her, "Maybe we should occupy a church."

There was enthusiasm in the whispered reply. We agreed to think about it.

On Tuesday all day we quietly polled people whom we trusted to be discreet. The response was positive. Spending twenty-hour hours in a church we would enter for sanctuary would call attention to what was going on and would hopefully restrain the hand of the police by the light that would be shone on them. Then we could continue with our legal defenses and our organizing.

On Wednesday afternoon, we called a meeting at the center and asked people to bring their sleeping bags and their children. The very close network of the ECP was there and three infants, including my granddaughter. We put it to the meeting that we had decided to occupy a church, without mentioning which one. Most women were enthusiastic: "Finally, some action." We asked anyone who was not ready to enter the church to leave then. One of the women, saying she had to pick up her children, left and never came back. But she could not have told the police the name of the church we intended entering because she didn't know. If our plan got out before we were inside, we could have been occupying cells instead of pews.

Going to Church

We prepared for our entry. We made a banner big enough to be strung from one spire to another across the roof of the church, saying "Mothers Need Money. End Police Illegality and Racism in King's Cross. English Collective of Prostitutes." We'd bought fifty black masks; in that way prostitute and nonprostitute women would not be distinguishable from each other, and press photos of either would not be dangerous. We wrote a statement explaining why we were entering the church and listing our demands:

1. An end to illegal arrests of prostitutes
2. An end to police threats, blackmail, harassment, and racism
3. Hands off our children—we don't want our kids in care
4. An end to arrests of boyfriends, husbands, sons
5. Arrest rapists and pimps instead
6. Immediate protection, welfare, housing for women who want to get off the game

We ended the statement with an appeal for MPs and local councilors to come and hear our case, and a special call for all women to come to speak with us. We set up a support unit at the center whose first task was to call the press and whose second was to inform our network in England and in other countries of what we were doing.

A number of people who had been involved in the conference joined the support unit. One who worked particularly hard was Andaiye, in England from Guyana to set up an international tribunal to investigate the government's assassination of Dr. Walter Rodney, leader of her organization, the Working People's Alliance. She postponed all she was doing and worked for the Occupation until it was on its feet. (Walter had been a friend of mine; that rebel would have loved it.)

The English Collective of Prostitutes was accompanied into the church by Women Against Rape and Black Women for Wages for Housework—both organizations share the center with us—since we were driven to seek sanctuary by a combination of issues: rape, racism, and the prostitution laws. We were uncertain of our safety and were glad to have two "respectable" women's groups with us.

We entered in twos and threes towards the end of the church service, when we knew the doors would be open. By the time the service was over there were about fifteen of us with sleeping bags and blankets sitting at the back. The priest came over to ask if something was wrong, and we told him we were staying overnight and why.

We locked the doors of the church that night. The next morning we were up at 7 a.m. Nappies were changed and tea made. We put the church in perfect order, stowing the bedclothes neatly and discreetly in the back corner, opened the door for the 8 o'clock service and sat silently in the back pews.

When the service was over, we locked the door in the usual way, looked at each other and immediately and unanimously decided that we weren't leaving. The Occupation of the church had well and truly begun.

By about 7 a.m. that morning the press had begun to arrive. We sent them away till after the church service was over. They came back about 9 a.m. and we carried out our plan: the two women at the door (invariably smokers since smoking was allowed only in that little vestibule) instructed pressmen to show their credentials at the center; when a woman from the support unit returned with them, we opened the church door. Eventually the press of the world turned up, and we held press conferences every day. At one of these early press conferences the vicar was delighted to be included, and he spoke in support of us. Since he was supportive, the media were relatively fair. His support didn't last, however, and most of Fleet Street were delighted in a couple of days to get back to denigrating "vice girls" and trivializing our action.[5]

Despite this, the press let people know it was happening, and they could make their own judgment. Once people knew, especially through television news, the visitors began to arrive.

Local residents dropped in, or stayed after service to talk to us. Some brought flowers, or tea, or toilet paper, and many put a donation in our collection box, which stood at the back with a display of our literature and a guest book.

There was a steady stream of individuals, mainly women, some students, some friends like Jackie Forster of Sappho, one of the oldest lesbian organizations in Britain, who came to help. (The ECP goes back a long way with Jackie and Sappho's Tuesday evenings. Each time Jackie invited us to speak there, there were always one or two lesbian women who gave us a special welcome, making it clear they worked as prostitutes.)

People came out of a healthy curiosity (what *is* a church occupation?), to express support and to find out what they could do to help. Gay male friends later ran a crèche for us, and they and others cooked hot dinners. (Kentucky Fried as a steady diet is abrasive to the budget—we were not earning—as well as to the lining of the gut.) We were regularly brought two large pots, one for meat eaters, one for vegetarians, which would be collected, with the cost, when empty, since our entire water supply came from a tiny wash basin in the loo.[6]

Quite a few Black women came. One Black woman, in her request to Paul Boateng, chairman of the Greater London Council Police Committee,[7] to meet our demands, spelled out that the prostitution laws are to young Black women what the "sus" laws are to young Black men. This was a real breakthrough for us. After years of work, we could begin to see the illegality and racism of the police against hookers being lifted out of the exotic, even the erotic, where it could be dismissed and ridiculed; and onto the deadly serious terrain we share with others who are up against the law.

The first Saturday, exactly a week after the conference, and three days into the Occupation, there was a meeting of Black women in the church—which was large enough to accommodate twenty or thirty people meeting in one corner while the rest carried on speaking to the press, discussing with visitors, walking crying babies,

---

5   For decades, most UK newspapers were based in London's Fleet Street. This is no longer the case.
6   Toilet.
7   At the time this was the elected authority responsible for the police.

sweeping the floor, writing press releases, making tea or coffee, and coming and going to shops, launderettes, and speaking engagements.

The Collective Process

Our most important activity was the morning strategy meeting. Sometimes we had another meeting in the evening. Any woman in the church who was not press was invited to participate. These meetings had to accomplish a number of tasks:

- *They assessed our power:* was the vicar about to call the police or would the publicity we had generated stay his hand? (We never argued with the armchair generals who when they visited chastened us for using the establishment media. If you are organizing anything, the media are almost always indispensable because they, not we, have the power of the word. Despite half-truths, lies, and trivializations, media attention was our greatest protection.)
- *They decided our next moves:* what to do, when, how and who to do it?
- *They got us all on the same wavelength:* so each of us was able to function autonomously and responsibly for the rest of the day, when we were lobbying or speaking publicly or giving interviews, often on our own. This was no time to be either lacking in confidence or doing your own thing; a mistake might invite the police to do theirs.

These meetings, which were a collective unraveling of events, to figure out what was really going on, and the translation of overall strategy into immediate tactics, were daily culminations of the great learning experience we were creating. I'm tempted to say that no one ever learnt so much in a church until I remember that the church is traditionally the place women have been permitted, even encouraged, to visit; there they may have found the privacy denied them at home where they were always on call; there they could sort out their most intimate thoughts and problems, and could bring their search for an understanding of themselves and their world. We built on that tradition and transformed it by our collective contemplation.

Visitors, especially elected officials, also got a church education.

They heard first-hand how the police were protecting pimps. When threatened with having their kneecaps broken if they didn't hand over their money regularly, women would go to the police, describe the man, the car, and the license plate, and the police would tell them: "Come back when your kneecaps are broken." For a couple of days there was always a pimp in a doorway from which he could see both the center door and the church door, watching all who came and went from both. The police could not have missed seeing these pimps since they were also watching the center and the church. (We were reminded that the French women were thrown out of their churches in 1975 when police and pimps came in together to get them out.) No woman was allowed to leave the church alone, and we kept track of them when they left. Those inside who were prostitutes were used to being in danger without being able to call on the police for help. The rest of us continued to learn.

One of the visitors was Juliet from Molesworth Peace Camp, who stayed for a couple of hours, quietly absorbing the scene. Next afternoon she returned with her bedroll to spend some days.

Other peace campaigners were to join us. One woman was on her way to Greenham Common Women's Peace Camp and we sent a message to say that we wanted the military budget to come to women so that no woman need ever be a prostitute; therefore campaigning hookers were also part of the peace movement.[8] Not long after, three women from Greenham came with their bedrolls.

There was for us a deep affirmation of our own action in their warm and unassuming support. They believed in putting their politics into practice; and they are convinced that there isn't anything more worthwhile than doing that. They are not passing through the peace movement as a step to one's real life work, as some women have passed through women's groups on their way to careers and personal power. They're in it till we win because this is the most worthwhile and personally rewarding way to spend your life. They felt a responsibility to others who were also openly challenging the State's right to power. We felt in the most profound sense that we were not alone. This has sustained us through many dark days since.

We later learnt from Juliet that she had originally visited us because she had got a message from a Greenham friend to the effect that "Whores and lesbians have taken over a church. Things are really moving!" As always with people who are themselves organizing, they grasped the significance of others' actions. They focused on the outcasts among us; that these were organizing, and together, was clearly exciting and inspiring to them.

In a few days prostitute women from other red-light areas began to drop in, to see who we were (as opposed to who the media said we were) and what was happening. We soon issued Occupation bulletins, which we distributed in other neighborhoods, and by mail. In this way, the word was spread and the establishment version of events counteracted. We later heard that prostitutes all over Britain knew how to read the media. Typical was: "No social workers would be sleeping on the floor of a cold church for me. I knew it was the real thing!" To express solidarity, women still working on the street in King's Cross wore ECP badges. One night, all the women in Argyle Square wore masks. The next day there were some great tales of women defiantly arrested with masks on.

---

8   See *Marx and Feminism*, note 30 (page 159 in this volume).

Demanding a Monitor

On the whole, however, with the glare of publicity, arrests had dramatically dropped. Police illegality and racism fare better in the shadows. But we knew that when we no longer had the church as a power base and the media had moved on, there would be retaliatory arrests. Early in the Occupation, when Valerie Wise and Paul Boateng, chairs of the Greater London Council Women's and Police Committees, came to the Occupation, the possibility of retaliation was already in our minds. Since the police in London are in the hands of the Home Office, not (as elsewhere in Britain) supposedly answerable to local government, they told us they could do no more than publicly support us. Our response was: then give us a monitor. This became our central demand.

Now a lot of people have been monitoring the police since the 1981 urban rebellions, but these monitor after the event. For example, if you are beaten in custody, you report that to a monitoring unit—which may not get you justice immediately but is useful in documenting that your experience is neither unique, nor the charge of an eccentric or a troublemaker.

Our idea was different. We wanted a monitor to watch the police in order to prevent the illegal arrests and victimization, to try to make sure they didn't happen in the first place. We were confident that if the police were monitored in this way, the number of arrests would fall dramatically. Then a comparison of arrest figures with and without a monitor would help to substantiate our claim of illegality.

We were of course rebuked for adding to our demands. We wondered at people who were surprised, even alarmed, that women with an occupation felt more powerful and were more demanding than women without one.

We had I suppose put ourselves on display, and laid ourselves open to anyone's judgment. We were not unaware of that. But we were also in a unique position to do some observing ourselves. Necessarily rapid judgments became strikingly accurate. The only visitor to get a round of applause from this critical audience was Tony Benn.

Late on Saturday night Tony, leader of the left wing of the Labour Party, and Caroline Benn, his wife and political partner, came to the church at the request of our Bristol ECP branch. Caroline sat with us; Tony faced us and asked what was going on and what we wanted him to do. We got no grilling, no condescension, no nervousness that we would take them to unorthodox and therefore unsavory places. He listened to our story and immediately made the parallel with a factory sit-in. *He was the only visitor to compare us with other working-class people.* When he had grasped our views and demands, he took out his pocket tape machine and dictated letters to the MPs for Camden and to the Home Secretary who is responsible for the Metropolitan Police. We corrected them; he rolled the tape back and redictated the corrected passages. That's when he got the applause.

A couple of weeks later we got the copies with a note reporting to us what had been the responses—virtually nothing. When we thanked him months later, he wrote back, "I was *proud* to help."

As well as a monitor, we wanted meetings with the police and with Members of Parliament; and finally, with someone in the Housing and Social Services Departments of Camden Council to whom we could refer for help any woman who wanted to leave prostitution. It was about time that those who professed to be against prostitution put their money, their social services and their housing, where their mouth was.

These demands we negotiated through Kate Allen, chair of the Camden Women's Committee, who had been supportive from the beginning. She had worked to convey our demands to others, and to help us to win support. By Monday, November 29, we had interviewed the woman who we were told would monitor the police in Argyle Square for one month, her wage to be paid by Camden Council. It was agreed that she would report any illegal arrests she witnessed during that time, along with the comparative figures for arrests before, during and after the Occupation. We had got firm promises that all our other demands would also be met.

Winning

We had won. Helen Buckingham, who has been the only prostitute woman in Britain who has come out in order to campaign, and who with her infant son had spent at least eight hours in the church every day, had bought scented furniture wax as we neared victory. By the time we left for our press conference that Monday evening, she had polished every pew, and others had swept and put the church back into the order in which we had found it. It was cleaner and shinier than when we had entered and it smelled like lilacs.

We were very sorry to leave. Many more people use our cramped women's center than use that spacious church, and we had put it to such good use. We look at "our church" longingly each time we pass her.

Our lives had literally stopped for twelve days: the milkman had not been paid, the post not collected and money not earned. We were physically exhausted and we craved a bath and a bed. Yet we were loath to reenter the flat atmosphere of daily life. We dreaded slipping away from the authentic and collective life inside the church, back into the harness and blinkers of daily routine. In masks we had glimpsed what could happen: we created change. Taking off the masks, our collective power was as hidden as the reality to which it had penetrated. Going back to work—housework, whoring, office work, school work—is never a victory. It was hard to remember we had won.

Many people helped us to win, first of all of course those who came to the church to express support. We shall not forget Father Wheatley, former vicar of Holy Cross and our dear friend, who was our first visitor.[9] He came as soon as he got our message. Nor will we forget he was chased out, told in front of us to "Get out! Get out!" by the present vicar, Father Trevor Richardson, who felt so threatened by goodness.

We had hot meals and other help from Payday Men's Network. They're part of an international network of men who support the Wages for Housework Campaign and who are against all unpaid work.

There was a support picket of prostitutes in Venice, Italy, along with Payday there. There were protests in a number of U.S. cities by the Wages for Housework Campaign: in Boston to the British Consul, in Philadelphia in front of British Airways. There was a picket in San Francisco by the U.S. PROStitutes Collective. We got a joint cable from the Green Party, the Arc (a refuge for prostitutes) and the Wages for Housework Campaign in Hamburg; and a cable from the Alliance for the Safety of Prostitutes (ASP) in Vancouver, Canada. We got telegrams and letters from within the UK. All of these were terribly important. They gave us confidence and courage, and discouraged those tempted to call the police against us or in any case ditch us so we could more easily be levered out: we were protected by this evidence that people everywhere were interested in our fate.

The Monitor's Report—a Careerist's Charter

Towards the end of the Occupation, it was clear that Kate Allen was under great pressure from other politicians to get us out, and that she was weakening fast in her support for us. Just before Christmas, barely a month after we came out of the church, she, as chair of Camden Council's Women's Committee, called a meeting of local social services and feminist groups to discuss setting up legal services for prostitutes without any reference to the one we had built and had stood up to the police to preserve. This was a shock, but even then we didn't expect the political brutality, which was to come.

The monitor's Report was released on January 20, 1983. It did not mention the Occupation, and anyone reading it now would never suspect that her job was the product of our struggle. Making us invisible was not an oversight. It was an invitation

---

9   Father Wheatley, now the Right Reverend Bishop of Edmonton, was the vicar of Holy Cross Church
     until earlier 1982. For him everyone was worthy of compassion and help. He invited the ECP to meet-
     ings with local residents and businesses to bring the community together. He once famously wrote
     that he considered himself a member of the ECP. We saw him a year later when he chaired my Marx
     and Feminism lecture in another church, and in 2010, when he accepted our invitation to visit the new
     women's center building.

to careerists to professionalize and depoliticize the legal and other services prostitute women had created as campaigning tools. In this way, our own tools would be refashioned into weapons against us.

The monitor's Report had no comparative figures for police arrests; that is, no numbers of arrests when the police were monitored and when they were not. After all that had happened, evidence for—or against—our claims of victimization had been sidestepped. We demanded to know why these figures were not in the Report, and were told privately that the police had refused to release them—a crucial fact, damning of the police, which was omitted from the Report and never mentioned anywhere in public.

Elsewhere we are analyzing this Report, including the useful information it contained. What is important here is that because the prostitutes are not acknowledged as having made it happen, the Report is a careerist's charter: others need not refer proposals about prostitutes and prostitution to prostitutes.

Prostitution has always been a political football, and prostitutes, like other minorities, have often been made the scapegoats for injustices and deprivations governments impose or at least refuse to relieve us of. This is the history of King's Cross, a red-light area since the nineteenth century. Understanding this, we had always made the case for all residents to have more resources: more nursery places, more parks and more police protection for all women against violence. This we believed was the only honest response to genuine grievances, the only reasonable basis for prostitute and nonprostitute residents not to be at each other's throats in this working-class, inner-city area.

But this made local councilors and the local MP even more anxious to split us from other residents and to ensure that others in King's Cross did not take direct action as we had done. The best way for politicians to defeat prostitutes and deflect the pressure of nonprostitute local people was to encourage residents to attack us and get the police to do the rest. Considering that the area has a National Front history, and that we had over the years resisted some residents' calls for saturation policing, it was not an impossible or even a difficult task. The local MP, Frank Dobson, took the tenants' leaders to meet with Sir Kenneth Newman, Chief Constable of the Metropolitan Police, late of the Royal Ulster Constabulary of Northern Ireland. The cooperation that followed between some tenants and police resulted in a thousand arrests of prostitute women between January and March, and fines for each conviction of up to £150, with seven days to pay.

By February, the head of the Women's Committee support unit, with the backing of feminist lawyers and women from the antiporn lobby, told us to give up our legal service. They were ready, they said, to get money from Camden and the GLC to create another one instead. The pretext was that nonprostitute residents would not use Legal Action for Women because prostitutes used it. The new service, which would create new highly paid jobs, and which they demanded we put all our expertise into creating, would be "confidential"—which turned out to mean that "no one would know" if prostitutes used it too. We now face an unholy alliance between unscrupulous politicians (male and female), police, right-wing local residents and careerists who identify as feminists. *What we are witnessing before our very eyes is the process whereby women's struggle is hidden from history and transformed into an industry, jobs for the girls.* "Feminists" making a career off prostitution has become a new branch of the sex industry and is as much pimping off women as men have ever done.

In the course of defending ourselves from this concerted and growing attack on LAW and on our center, we have discovered that the phenomenon of careerism in the movement is not so new, not so rare, and very well known and understood by a lot of people. They have also seen women juggling for position and power at other women's expense; working to turn the new Women's Committees in London's local government, with the help of ambitious or weak or simply unprincipled politicians, into career opportunity centers—all in the name of feminism. Many more women than we expected—local residents, feminists, legal workers, immigrants, Black women—have had to confront the same experience in the course of their own ongoing efforts. They have understood what we are facing and have made their support for us public. We may be under attack, but we are not isolated.

One of our jobs now is to chronicle the process whereby "feminists" in the State arrange what Virginia Woolf in *Three Guineas* called "brain prostitution"—women who sell ideas and other intellectual services, in this case to defeat women up against police illegality and racism. Such a chronicle will be useful for the women's movement and its allies in every other movement for social change, each of which, if it is seriously seeking change, finds itself up against the same State and the same ambitious types. With this history in our hands, we can ask the Women's Liberation Movement again, this time with the confidence and wisdom born of the Occupation: choose between prostitutes and police, between "bad" women and bad laws, between whores and careerists, between the State and the women confronting it for justice.

August 1st, 1983, 150th Anniversary of the abolition of slavery in the British colonies.

First published in *Feminist Action* 1, ed. Joy Holland, (London: Battle Axe Books, 1984). This was written in consultation with the ECP, but I take responsibility for deficiencies. We tried to steer clear of heavy academic references, but every quotation and statement of fact is verifiable in the files of the women's center. LAW, the legal service for all women, continues. For those who want to know more about the laws, prostitute women and the struggle between the two, contact the ECP.

JEAN RHYS
(1983)

T his is an excerpt from *The Ladies and the Mammies—Jane Austen and Jean Rhys*,[1] based on a speech at the Cheltenham Literary Festival (November 4, 1979) entitled "Ms. Jane Austen." My theme was the women of the Great House in both Austen's novels and in *Wide Sargasso Sea*, Rhys's novel written a century and a half later. Rhys, a light-skinned Caribbean woman (with, she says, a "colored" grandmother), writes the story of Charlotte Brontë's mad woman in the attic (*Jane Eyre*), explaining how she got there and what drove her mad. For the first time the white West Indian woman in the attic wrests the account of her life back from the racist Charlotte and speaks for herself. The historic antagonisms of sex, race, and class, hidden in Brontë's account, are not only revealed but dissected.

* * *

A woman began to write in Europe, a white woman from the West Indian island of Dominica. She was discovered by Ford Madox Ford, an American novelist also living in Europe. We have to remember that until recently New World writers and artists came to Europe, especially to Paris, to be part of the artists' community there. A white West Indian would be just one more "foreigner" who had come to the artistic mecca.

Ford was enthusiastic about Jean Rhys's "singular instinct for form" which was "possessed by singularly few writers of English and by almost no English women

---

1 Bristol: Falling Wall Press, 1983.

writers." By that he meant that she could write as few men could. In fact she wrote as no men could. He was also excited that "coming from the Antilles [she had] a terrifying insight and a terrific—an almost lurid!—passion for stating the case of the underdog."[2] More than he knew, she was herself an underdog, which might explain her insight and her passion.

In the dozen or so years from the late 1920s to World War II, Jean Rhys published a book of short stories and four novels. While some of the stories are set in the West Indies, all four novels take place in Europe. With the exception of *Voyage in the Dark* (1934), the women are European and there is no hint that the writer is not European too.

But there is one thing foreign about all four of the novels. Jean Rhys's central character—whether English or Continental, and in the case of *Voyage in the Dark*, West Indian—is not a native of the country she is living in. The crisis of being an immigrant, an alien, is not the major theme, however.

These novels are about how women are aliens and how, because the cards are stacked against us, we don't stand a chance. The novels have in common the isolation, defeat, and hopelessness of the heroine. Each personifies the female condition; and each is the perfect victim, unable or unwilling to defend herself. Unable because, being foreign, she is outside the terms of reference of the dominant culture and does not know how. Unwilling because she will not fight for *things* that are withheld, nor tailor her case according to what her opponent will understand and respect, but which is not the truth, nor be brutally honest for the sole purpose of self-defense. Her sense of proportion is out of kilter; she operates under a completely impractical set of priorities. These—alien set of standards, terms of reference, sense of proportion—leave the heroine defenseless against domination by men and exploitation by anyone.

Her problem is most certainly not her consciousness. Nothing—neither nuance nor substantive act of social domination by men—escapes articulation. But she does not fight back. Knowing deeply what is happening and having neither defense nor allies is a formula for suicide. Jean Rhys's heroines are not physically protective of themselves either.

Voyage in the Dark, the third novel, tells us that its heroine, though taken for European because she is white, is in fact a young West Indian in England. Ms. Rhys opens the book with a description of how it feels to this young chorus girl (a job Jean Rhys did too) to be in Europe, which reads like a poetic preview of all the interviews

---

2 Ford Madox Ford in "Preface to a Selection of Stories" from *The Left Bank* (London: Jonathan Cape, 1972), reprinted in *Tigers Are Better-Looking* (London: Penguin Books, 1972), 138. Here is the rest of the sentence: "she has let her pen loose on the Left Banks of the Old World—on its [jails], its studios, its salons, its cafes, its criminals, its *midinettes*—with a bias of admiration for its *midinettes* and of sympathy for its lawbreakers."

with West Indians who came later to Britain in the 1940s and '50s. Anna Morgan, the heroine, is speaking in the first person. These are the book's first lines:

> It was as if a curtain had fallen, hiding everything I had ever known. It was almost like being born again. The colors were different, the smells different, the feeling things gave you right down inside yourself was different. Not just the difference between heat, cold; light, darkness; purple, grey. But a difference in the way I was frightened and the way I was happy.[3]

Anna's age makes her more defenseless than the others, but she has always been vulnerable, since she was a child, a white child in a Black country, torn between identifying with the Black people, especially the Black women who cared for her and who sustained her, and with the white society that she inherits through her family and her race. Once she is in Europe she is cut off from Francine, the servant at home, the woman who tells her what she needs to know when her menstrual cycle begins, who nurses her when she has a fever, whom she loves more than anyone; who mothered her, but as a job. Thus her great love for Francine can only be expressed obliquely:

"The thing about Francine was that when I was with her I was happy."[4]

Anna is torn between defending her Creole mother from the charge that she was "colored" and desperately wishing to end her own ambiguity: she has "always wanted to be Black." "Being Black is warm and gay, being white is cold and sad."[5]

But no one knows these things about Anna, and the people around her wouldn't understand if she told them. They are English, they have many crises—mainly about money—but they seem to know who they are and who they are not. One character tells her regularly how much she hates "dirty foreigners."

Anna is kept by a wealthy man with whom she falls in love—despite warnings from other women who also live by being kept by men; and when he tires of her, she is devastated. Her first response is not to leave her room or eat or even change her clothes. Unable/unwilling to apply to the man for the money he has offered, she drifts into more overt forms of prostitution. This way of supporting herself is neither more brutal nor more venal than the other relationships she witnesses or herself experiences.

Anna's father is dead and Hester, her English stepmother, makes clear that Anna's association with men excludes her from Hester's acceptance and from her acceptance by English Society. Hester traces this immorality to Anna's affinity with Black people. "I always did my best for you and I never got any thanks for it. I tried to teach you to talk like a lady and behave like a lady and not like a nigger and of course I couldn't do it."[6]

---

3 Jean Rhys, *Voyage in the Dark* (Harmondsworth: Penguin Books, 1969), 7.
4 Ibid., 58.
5 Ibid., 27.
6 Ibid., 56.

Jean Rhys disappeared from view for some years. Francis Wyndham tells us: "The few people who remembered their admiration for these books, and those even fewer who (like myself) were introduced to them later and with great difficulty managed to obtain second-hand copies, for a while formed a small but passionate band. But nobody could find her; and nobody would reprint the novels."[7] As a result of a radio dramatization of one of them in the late 1950s, she was traced to Devon in the west of England. She was at work on a new novel. It seems that "For many years [she was] haunted by the figure of the first Mrs. Rochester—the mad wife in *Jane Eyre*," the character whom we know only from Mr. Rochester's biased and racist descriptions.[8][9]

The first Mrs. Rochester had many attractions for Ms. Rhys from Roseau, Dominica. She too is a white West Indian who has ended up in Europe. She is not only a "foreigner," but the victim, the underdog personified; entirely defined by and in the power of a man, her white English husband Rochester. Charlotte Brontë's Mrs. Rochester is the epitome of all Jean Rhys's heroines, but seen from the point of view of their tormentors. In her West Indian novel, Ms. Rhys sets out to tell the other side of the story, to make Mrs. Rochester's case, to refute English literature's distorted account. In the process, Rochester's character gains new depth and evokes in us a deeper compassion.

To accomplish this, Jean Rhys left the Europe of Parisian cafes and London bedsits. The West Indies is no longer a flashback or an idealization, the internal point of reference in her private voyage in the dark. In *Wide Sargasso Sea,* Jean Rhys went home.

Antoinette is born an outcast. A white child from a Great House in a predominantly Black society, and thus cut off from the great majority of the population except

7 Jean Rhys, *Wide Sargasso Sea* (London: Andre Deutsch, 1966), 11.

8 Mr. Rochester, in explaining to Jane Eyre why he married Bertha Antoinette (which Ms. Rhys has transformed into Antoinette Bertha, putting her Creole name first), says to her: "Her family wished to secure me because I was of a good race." (Charlotte Brontë, *Jane Eyre* [London: Penguin, 1966], 332.) If there is any doubt about whether this is also his view of race, a few pages later, speaking of his life since his wife's madness, he spelled it out: "Hiring a mistress is the next worse thing to buying a slave: both are often by nature, and always by position, inferior." Charlotte Brontë has Jane say: "I felt the truth of these words." (339).

9 It is worth recording how Jean Rhys felt about her rediscovery. When in 1966 she got the W.H. Smith Award for *Wide Sargasso Sea,* she commented, "It has come too late." If she had been recognized earlier, she might have made another life for herself. A. Alvarez in the *Observer* (May 20, 1979) said Ms. Rhys is "one of the finest British writers of this century" and in reviewing *Wide Sargasso Sea* originally in the *New York Times Book Review* (quoted in the *New York Times,* May 17, 1979, by Herbert Mitgang), he said that she was "quite simply, the best living English novelist." Ms. Rhys was a West Indian. That is what she is fighting to establish in *Wide Sargasso Sea.* To deny her that is to call her Bertha when her name is Antoinette. Mr. Alvarez then went on to say that "although her range is narrow, there is no one else writing who combines such emotional penetration and formal artistry or approaches her unemphatic, unblinking truthfulness." My case is made: women are always said to provide a narrow range; as I wrote in another context, men's "wider" range is "never wide enough to include us." Ms. Rhys's attempt to penetrate the most crucial divisions of our time, those of sex, race, and class, is entirely overlooked. It is enough to break a writer's heart and to inspire a movement among the readers.

through the mistress-servant relationship, later she becomes a West Indian woman in Europe. To describe her as a white West Indian is also to say that the framework of her personality, her thinking, her attitudes, are shaped by Black people, especially by those Black girls she played with as a child, and by those Black women who raised her, nursing her in sickness and in health. In the United States this Black woman, from the time of slavery, has traditionally been called "mammy." Audiences internationally will know that historical figure from the absurd but celebrated movie *Gone with the Wind*. One of the reasons that film had picket lines in front of movie theatres when it was first shown in 1939 in the United States was precisely because of its racist glorification of the mammy figure.

The title of the novel, *Wide Sargasso Sea*, is painfully appropriate. The Sargasso Sea is in the North Atlantic and, according to the *Encyclopedia Britannica* (1960), "was first reported by Columbus, who crossed it on his initial 'West Indies' voyage." It also tells us that "the widely credited story of ships becoming helplessly embedded in the floating seaweed which fill it are disproved"; but it remains a perfect image for the tangled weed and murky depths traversed in the social voyage between the West Indies and Europe.

The Sargasso Sea was launched on its modern history with the first thrust of imperial conquest and the Middle Passage, the traffic in slaves. But it was party to a whole new history with what George Lamming has called "Columbus in reverse," the migration of thousands of West Indians to England, in a voyage of another kind of discovery. Mrs. Rochester had come much earlier.[10]

Her name is Antoinette Bertha Cosway and she is born a daughter of the slave owning class. She grows up just after the abolition of slavery, her home a white island in a furious and rebellious Black sea. She witnesses the burning down of Coulibri, her home, by liberated Black people who are no longer disciplined by the lash.

All that is familiar entirely destroyed; all the beauty which hid the brutality burnt away. One last hope appears: her Black friend, daughter of a friend of her mother's servant:

> Then, not so far off, I saw Tia and her mother and I ran to her, for she was all that was left of my life as it had been. We had eaten the same food, slept side by side, bathed in the same river. As I ran, I thought, I will live with Tia and I will be like her. Not to leave Coulibri. Not to go. Not. When I was close I saw the jagged stone in her hand but I did not see her throw it. I did not feel it either, only something wet, running down my face. I looked at her and I saw her face crumple up as she began to cry. We stared at each other, blood on my face, tears on hers. It was as if I saw myself. Like in a looking glass.[11]

---

10 G. Lamming, *The Pleasures of Exile* (London: Michael Joseph, 1960).
11 *Wide Sargasso Sea*, 45.

Divided from Tia, she is divided from herself. At this moment of powerlessness, she sees reflected in Tia both sides of her dilemma, clearly and simultaneously: in Tia's tear-stained face and in the stone she has thrown; in Tia's attachment to her and rejection of her; all this has been revealed by the act of burning down the Great House.

Here I believe is the source of the peculiar vulnerability of Jean Rhys's heroines in previous novels. The woman, the foreigner, the alien, always the same person, is taken by European readers to be European, prefiguring later novels and plays by Existentialists of the isolated and the rootless.

But Jean Rhys's heroine is not European. She is West Indian. And though she is white, she is less the descendant of Hester, her English stepmother, than of Francine, her West Indian mammy. Tia is her sister under the skin. Divided from Tia by the history of slavery and the racial chasm, this woman begins life divided from herself. In the novels she wanders through Europe, first as a young, then as a mature, and finally as an ageing woman, but never able to mobilize herself to fight back. It is because she is divided at the root of her being that she lacks the strength, the sustenance, the positive confirmation of her right to be autonomous, to survive, to flourish. As a woman she is particularly under attack; as a woman she has no wife or girlfriend to mitigate her loss and to confirm her life right.

Her dilemma as a woman is one with her dilemma as a white West Indian. The separation of race and sex as political categories has limited use when they are aspects of one personality, in fiction and in life. These two aspects of herself shed light on each other and emphasize the grossly uneven balance of power the heroine is always up against.

Jean Rhys is a West Indian woman writer, in perception, in preoccupation and in prose. While these two strands were divided in earlier work, in *Wide Sargasso Sea* Ms. Rhys is able to put them together for the first time. They reinforce each other. Neither is a metaphor or symbol for the other; both demand joint resolution.

Antoinette is raised in convents and learns to live with her tragedy. She grows into a beautiful woman and inherits a fortune from her English stepfather when he dies. Rochester, the second son of an English Great House, has no money of his own; he therefore must find money to marry where he can. His father sends him to the West Indies to find a Creole heiress, as was not uncommon in the nineteenth century, and he finds Antoinette.

He does not love Antoinette Bertha Cosway. He has married for money, not love. But unlike the *woman* who marries for money, the money he marries becomes his. Once he has it, he sets out to destroy his wife.

He resents her local associations, her only independent source of power. He feels hostility from this strange place of which his wife is a part. The people are still shaped by wild tropical beauty; still aware of more than the rational, still in contact with creative impulses not mediated by money. And so is she. These embarrass him, make *him* the stranger, and challenge him as a man and as a European. Ms. Rhys has him speak for himself: "everything around me was hostile… The trees were threatening and the shadows of the trees moving slowly over the floor menaced me. That green menace. I had felt it ever since I saw this place. There was nothing I knew, nothing to comfort me."[12] He feels these people have some secret he cannot know, which his wife shares with the servants; she is like them, part of them, not his. "The feeling of something unknown and hostile was very strong. 'I feel very much a stranger here,' I said. 'I feel that this place is my enemy and on your side.'"[13]

The Sargasso Sea has sharpened but not invented the division between them. Men are often threatened by the independent power base of the women they marry. Rochester defends himself by evoking the social power he has as a man and as a European to vent his hostility on Antoinette. He renames her. He refuses to call her Antoinette and instead calls her Bertha. Here is the European identifying the Third World woman; here is the man defining his wife. He succeeds in his campaign of attack; she is entirely defeated and he calls her defeat madness. The effort exhausts him, and only then does he tell us how he, the European upper class man, defines sanity: "All the mad conflicting emotions had gone and left me wearied and empty. Sane."[14]

Earlier, he has described his childhood: "How old was I when I learned to hide what I felt? A very small boy. Six, five, even earlier. It was necessary, I was told, and that view I have always accepted."[15]

It is his acceptance of repression, his "sanity," that has defeated Antoinette. He takes her to England where he is entirely in charge, thanks to her money, and then he locks her away; she is driven to madness by that.

Over the years, Antoinette has a recurring dream. The first time she has it she is still in the West Indies, and on each of the other two occasions, more of the story is revealed. She is always trying to find out what she is supposed to do, and she is always going somewhere with a stranger. The first time: "Someone who hated me was with me."[16]

The second time, she is "following the man who is with me…I follow him, sick with fear but I make no effort to save myself."[17]

She sees a flight of steps, the top of which is her destination. She has the dream again after years of being imprisoned in the attic: "That was the third time I had my

---

12 Ibid., 149.
13 Ibid., 129.
14 Ibid., 172.
15 Ibid., 103.
16 Ibid., 26.
17 Ibid., 59.

dream, and it ended. I know now that the flight of steps leads to this room where I lie watching the woman asleep with her head on her arms."[18]

Sometimes when Grace Poole falls asleep or drinks herself to sleep while on duty (because it's a lonely job ensuring other people's loneliness), Antoinette, this insane Mrs. Rochester, escapes:

> In my dream I waited till she began to snore, then I got up, took the keys and let myself out with a candle in my hand. It was easier this time than ever before and I walked as though I were flying. All the people who had been staying in the house had gone, for the bedroom doors were shut, but it seemed to me that someone was following me, someone was chasing me, laughing. Sometimes I looked to the right or to the left but I never looked behind me for I did not want to see that ghost of a woman whom they say haunts this place.[19]

The "ghost" is herself; she has heard them talk about her without knowing it was she they were talking about. But it is also the person she has been—a ghost—being discussed by the person she is becoming. She is no longer the passive victim. She acts. She is not "sane" like Rochester; she does not accept repression. She fights against it. The protagonist has exorcised the ghost of the victim. Finally. But she has not left the past behind; instead she will remember what this victim found out in her captivity: "At last I was in the hall where a lamp was burning. I remember that when I came. A lamp and the dark staircase and the veil over my face. They think I don't remember but I do."[20]

Even those whose history has never been chronicled have a long memory:

> There was a door to the right, I opened it and went in. It was a large room with a red carpet and red curtains. Everything else was white. I sat down on a couch to look at it and it seemed sad and cold and empty to me, like a church without an altar. I wished to see it clearly so I lit all the candles, and there were many. I lit them carefully from the one I was carrying but I couldn't reach up to the chandelier. Then I looked round for the altar for with so many candles and so much red, the room reminded me of a church. Then I heard a clock ticking and it was made of gold. Gold is the idol they worship.[21]

She is beginning to understand now what motivates the strange people whose voices have come from the other side of the attic door over the years, and who have imprisoned her. They are motivated by money. Antoinette is afraid of being discovered. (All of this, you remember, is her dream.) But she is not discovered, and she sinks

---

18 Ibid., 187.
19 Ibid.
20 Ibid., 187–88.
21 Ibid., 188.

back on to a couch. Then in her mind's eye she is transported back home: "Suddenly I was in Aunt Cora's room. I saw the sunlight coming through the window, the tree outside and the shadows of the leaves on the floor, but I saw the wax candles too and I hated them."[22]

It is tragic for her to have this manufactured substitute for the natural sunlight from which she has been taken. She hates England, she hates the cold and the damp, she hates the household in which she has been imprisoned, and she hates the personification of all this, her husband Rochester. All of her anger now is focused on the artificial light of the candles:

> So I knocked them all down. I laughed when I saw the lovely color spreading so fast, but I did not stay to watch it. I went into the hall again with the tall candle in my hand. It was then that I saw her—the ghost. The woman with streaming hair. She was surrounded by a gilt frame but I knew her. I dropped the candle I was carrying and it caught the end of a table-cloth and I saw flames shoot up. As I ran or perhaps floated or flew I called help me Christophine help me and looking behind me I saw that I had been helped.[23]

Christophine was her Black mammy in the West Indies who tried to help Antoinette but whose mystic powers were not enough to save her from Rochester because she was too white. It is to Christophine that she has always gone for help. She receives her help again, and goes on:

> There were more candles on a table and I took one of them and ran up the first flight of stairs and the second. On the second floor I threw away the candle. But I did not stay to watch. I ran up the last flight of stairs and along the passage. I passed the room where they brought me yesterday or the day before yesterday, I don't remember. Perhaps it was quite long ago for I seemed to know the house quite well.[24]

We have known the Great House for a long time, those of us in England, in the United States, in the West Indies. "I knew how to get away from the heat and the shouting, for there was shouting now."[25] Now, we remember the scene when her own Coulibri was burnt down. Then she had said: "…they roared as we came out, then there was another roar behind us."[26]

This time she hears the shouting, not in terror, but in tranquility, the first she has known: "When I was out on the battlements it was cool and I could hardly hear

22 Ibid.
23 Ibid., 188–99.
24 Ibid., 189.
25 Ibid.
26 Ibid., 41.

them. I sat there quietly. I don't know how long I sat. Then I turned round and saw the sky. It was red and all my life was in it."[27]

She has been burning this house down in her dream and by that act her whole life is coming to her, coming together, finally. Not only that room, but everything that she has lived through, as a woman, as a white West Indian, as an immigrant to Britain. Now she begins to face her past, the past of the descendant of the slave owner, the daughter of one Great House and the wife of another. "I saw the grandfather clock and Aunt Cora's patchwork, all colors, I saw the orchids and the stephanotis and the jasmine and the tree of life in flames."[28]

The Caribbean is fire itself in these images—confirming and encouraging her in what she is doing in this England place:

> I saw the chandelier and the red carpet downstairs and the bamboos and the tree ferns, the gold ferns and the silver, and the soft green velvet of the moss on the garden wall. I saw my doll's house and the books and the picture of the Miller's Daughter. I heard the parrot call as he did when he saw a stranger, *Qui est là? Qui est là?* [in her native Patois, derived from the French] and the man who hated me [Rochester] was calling too, Bertha! Bertha![29]

To the last he would identify her, but she has already moved beyond his reach. Only his voice is left as a presence. She is now *identifying herself.* From being the object of Rochester's power, Antoinette is transforming herself into the subject, by grasping the power to determine her own actions and her own fate. "The wind caught my hair and it streamed out like wings. It might bear me up, I thought, if I jumped to those hard stones. But when I looked over the edge I saw the pool at Coulibri. Tia was there."[30]

In her dream she is home again, on the plantation that had burnt down around her, not the one she is burning down around herself. And Tia, the Black child who was her friend, and from whom she was divided; Tia, who rejected her to go for her own power, is there with her.

"She beckoned to me and when I hesitated, she laughed. I heard her say, 'You frightened?' And I heard the man's voice, 'Bertha! Bertha!'"[31]

Here are her two choices. On the one hand Rochester, who has driven her sanity from her, dragged her from her home and imprisoned her in a shrine to gold; Rochester is calling Bertha back to his control. And on the other hand Tia, the Black girl, her people, her childhood friend who embodies her personal history

27 Ibid., 189.
28 Ibid.
29 Ibid.
30 Ibid.
31 Ibid., 190.

and her social history as a West Indian; Tia beckons and invites Antoinette to join her and be free of this man. The truth is often hidden for centuries and then bursts upon us in an intense moment. "All this I saw and heard in a fraction of a second. And the sky so red. Someone screamed and I thought, *Why did I scream?* I called 'Tia!' and jumped and woke."[32] She wakes now that she has decided between them.[33]

---

32 Ibid.

33 Edward Kamau Brathwaite, the very distinguished poet from Barbados, has commented in *Contradictory Omens* (Savacou Working Paper Reprint 1, Mona, Jamaica, 1982, 36) on this crucial passage: "'The jump' here is a jump to death; so that Antoinette wakes to death, not to life; for life would have meant dreaming in the reality of madness in a cold castle in England. But death was also her allegiance to the carefully detailed exotic fantasy of the West Indies. In fact, neither world is 'real.' They exist inside the head. Tia was not and never could have been her friend. No matter what Jean Rhys might have made Antoinette think, Tia was historically separated from her by this kind of paralogue." And he quotes a passage that makes abundantly clear the racism of the white West Indian. Wally Look Lai of Trinidad in "The Road to Thornfield Hall" (*New Beacon Reviews*, Collection One, edited by John La Rose [London: 1968]) responded differently: "Antoinette's act of burning Thornfield Hall down, and her leap from the battlements, far from being acts of self-destruction, were attempts to do the very opposite: to save herself from an existence which had become a form of death, and to restore to her life the only possibility which she had come finally to see as capable of leading to fulfillment... Antoinette's leap was her first attempt to take command of, and redirect, the forces which had hitherto dictated the direction of her life." I quote so extensively because the question is vital: can Black and white women join together, or is the Sargasso Sea which divides us so impenetrable that Ms. Rhys's representation of the joining must remain only fiction? If cultural differences are what divide us, then women would never be with men, so different are the "personal and group attitudes, behavior and perception" (Brathwaite, 48) of the sexes, women's culture from men's. This is why Antoinette had to get away from Rochester. I don't believe that "Tia was not and never could have been [Antoinette's] friend." The hatred that is produced by the divisions of sex, race, class, age, nation, etc., has never been able to stamp out communication, even love, between us, and never will. What is decisive is that Jean Rhys *did not have Tia jump to Antoinette, but Antoinette to Tia.* As women have waited for men, so Black women have waited for white women—and for everyone. George Lamming concludes *Natives of My Person* with the wives who are waiting for their men (whom they do not know are dead), discussing why they wait. One woman explains: "We are a future they must learn." Women do wait for men to learn—but we do not passively wait; we act against them and speed up the education process! I do not believe that any of us waits for those who have oppressed us, quietly hoping for them to change. We act and force them to change.

Tia's people, Black people, burnt Antoinette's Great House to the ground. That was the beginning of the education. I believe that is "real." Rochester's cruelty is also "real." Antoinette acts and burns down Rochester's mansion. That is why Tia, who has always been waiting, finally welcomes Antoinette; for Antoinette has met her conditions: her first leap is to burn down Thornfield Hall. Jumping to Tia is the logical second leap. Mr. Look Lai implies that in the context of what was possible for Antoinette, jumping to her death was a victory. I agree. George Lamming in *Of Age and Innocence*, where the West Indian myth of the Tribe Boys, and their massive jump into the sea when they could not defeat the slave masters any other way, is recorded as the triumph it was. Suicide, in literature and life, can also be an act of defiance. *Wide Sargasso Sea* is a novel, a creation, a work of fiction. Its relevance to life is demonstrated by the heat generated in this debate about "jumping to Tia." In the final analysis, whatever Jean Rhys meant or did not mean, whatever Antoinette or Tia did or did not do, we cannot allow, on pain of mass destruction, that the Sargasso or any other sea should keep us apart. Jean Rhys's vision must be of the future reality.

Now something happened between Jean Rhys's writing of novels in the 1920s and '30s and her writing of this novel in the '50s (published in 1966). What happened was, first, a massive movement for Third World independence and, secondly, a massive West Indian immigration into Britain. Her people had come—the Tias and the Francines and the Christophines—and they were stronger than they had been when she left them in the West Indies in the early part of this century. She would have heard English racism against them—she was rediscovered by Francis Wyndham in 1958, the year of the Nottingham and Notting Hill riots against Black people; and she would have felt that she herself was under attack. But she would not have felt alone. This was a new source of power finally to confront all the misery and isolation and loneliness that she had worked to record and articulate in her earlier novels. She had been an outcast as a woman, as a West Indian in Europe, as a white West Indian. She had ended her novels in defeat because she herself was born in defeat.

Now another power enters her writing arm. Her heroine is no longer the passive victim that history has tried to make her. Now Antoinette is able to move against the arrogant, racist, and brutal metropolis and against the arrogant, racist, and brutal man who personifies it—Mr. Rochester. Many years before, she had said, "I will live with Tia and I will be like her." But first she had to let Tia know the terms on which she planned for them to be together. All she had offered Tia before was the domination of her white skin. But as Antoinette burns down the Great House which imprisons her—as Tia had burnt down the Great House which was the center of her exploitation—Tia welcomes her home.

A Last Note

In the course of writing this book, I appreciated Jean Rhys in a new way. *Wide Sargasso Sea* has 190 pages of words, and each one was weighed and considered in relation to every other in a way that I have never seen except in a poem. It *is* a poem, and, to paraphrase its author, all her life was in it.

How much this is literally true can be seen from her unfinished autobiography, *Smile Please* (1979). From the portrait of her mother and their antagonistic relationship, to her descriptions of Black people, and her own feelings of being an outcast among white and Black, even to the vegetation, the parrot, the patchwork quilt—the West Indian terrain of *Wide Sargasso Sea* is shown to be drawn from her own life there. Ms. Rhys, from childhood in the West Indies and adulthood in Europe, had many scores to settle and her creation of Antoinette was for the purpose of settling them. She wanted to burn down all that Rochester symbolized on her own behalf as a West Indian woman, and she wanted us to know.

In the original Brontë story of Jane Eyre, the first Mrs. Rochester's maiden name was Mason. Ms. Rhys gives Antoinette another name so that both her mother and father are Creole and the European Mason is the stepfather. The name she gives her is Cosway—or causeway, the bridge between the Third World and Europe, between one race and another, a causeway from defeat to victory. I believe it is a triumph for us as women, for all of us as citizens of the world.

MARX AND FEMINISM (1983)

I was invited in 1983 by Rev Kenneth Leech of the Jubilee Group, Church of England, to participate in their annual series of Lent lectures. That year they were marking the centenary of the death of Karl Marx.

I aimed to be accurate about Marx's analysis of exploitation in a way that was accessible to a willing reader. When feminism asserted that "the personal is political" it usually conveyed that women's personal grievances were also political. I wanted to use this occasion to show that the reverse was also true; that the political was profoundly personal, shaping our lives, and that applying Marx's analysis of capitalism to the relations between women and men illuminates them.

* * *

First about the title. I asked that this talk be called "Marx and Feminism" rather than "Marxism and Feminism" because Marxism is disputed territory. Just what it means, and whom it means, vary greatly from one political circle to another. But we can go to Marx and find out some of what he said. Then we can test his specific relevance to women, and to organizing within the women's movement. That is what I plan to do, bearing in mind that Marx's analysis of capitalist production was not a meditation on how the society "ticked." It was a tool to find the way to overthrow it.[1]

---

1   Introduction to *Power of Women*, 10.

Since Marx concentrated on dissecting capitalism in order to fashion an organizing tool, it follows that he makes the most sense in the context of organizing, where his ideas can be tested and—if they are to remain viable—developed.

I must declare an interest early. His analysis has been indispensable to my organizing. He penetrates capitalist reality, including in my own life and, from what I can see, in other people's, as no one else does, and helps keep me focused on that reality by warding off invasions of the enemy's logic, excuses, and invitations to egomania.[2] I am profoundly grateful for that help.

Which leads to my second point by way of introduction. While this year is the hundredth anniversary of the death of Marx, which I am honored to be called on to celebrate with you in this way, it happens to be another anniversary. Today is ten years to the day since I was arrested in a sit-in of women and children at the main London post office in Trafalgar Square, when the Wages for Housework Campaign took its first public actions: protesting the government's attempts to take Family Allowance away from women and put it into men's hands.[3] It seems entirely appropriate for me to celebrate that occasion—one is not arrested every day (at least not yet, though there are signs in this country that it may soon come to that)—to celebrate that occasion, together with the Marx centenary, here in this church.

And that leads to my third and final introductory point. You may know that some of us have got unusually intimate with churches in the last few months. I was fortunate enough to spend twelve days in November 1982 in the Church of the Holy Cross, King's Cross, with about fifteen or twenty other women.[4] And we liked it there. As a matter of fact, we liked it so much that the vicar (who was not exactly friendly) had a lot of trouble getting us out.

Thus before we plunge into the substance of the topic, you know something of the terrain from which the ideas spring that you are about to consider.

The women's movement began in the late 1960s and early '70s—that is, this new women's movement. There is always a women's movement; women are always privately saying "No," and from time to time organizing publicly to say "No." But the vocal and visible massive movement that we know today began then, in a number of countries almost at once. There are some things that it made clear right away: that we were subject to domestic slavery; that we were often financially dependent on men; that we didn't have equal pay; that we didn't control the reproductive processes which went

---

2   Such reliance on others is a tradition in some societies. The Indian philosopher Patanjali, for example, talks about the need for ongoing "reliable testimony" in order to make valid judgments. Marx, I think, gives us "reliable testimony."

3   We won and mothers kept the money. For the history of the campaign that won Family Allowance in the UK, see the introductory essay by S. Fleming in *The Disinherited Family* by Eleanor Rathbone (Bristol: Falling Wall Press, 1986).

4   See *Hookers in the House of the Lord*, page 110 in this volume.

on in our own bodies; that we were the victims of sexual exploitation of many kinds; and that we were much more likely to be passive and much less likely to be effective compared to men—in a word, that we had colonized lives and personalities. And the question was not long after posed: what relationship does all this bear to class and class struggle as it had been traditionally defined and passed on to us by the Left?

On the one hand: how much are men to blame? Are they the sole beneficiaries of our exploitation? Are they the enemy, men one class and women another?[5] On the other hand: what is the relationship of our demands as women to class? Equal pay may be about workers, but is abortion, sterilization, housework, rape, divorce, child custody and care, lesbianism, dress, personality, orgasms?[6] The question ultimately came down to: who is "the working class" and what income level, work, political issues, demands, and actions distinguish it? The question could not have been more basic and more obvious, but it was almost never clearly articulated, because even posing it then challenged everybody: not only the State, but the Left establishment, even the Left *alternative* establishment.[7] And because they were challenged, they worked overtime to dismiss, with the charge of ignorance or even betrayal, any of us who dared to ask. Marx, they said, had answered a hundred years before; surely that was enough! Under such pressure, clarity—even putting questions to yourself clearly—is hard won.

Now many things were happening at the same time as the women's movement was forming itself. Other movements were also flexing their muscles and by their existence posing the same question for their sector, which made the business of defining the working class even more urgent and generally important. Others, even men if they were not in factories, were also told they were not working-class. And even some "workers" could be dismissed as "marginal," "peripheral," i.e., not central, insignificant, unable to influence the course of history or to have more than a minimal effect even in the struggle for their own liberation. Liberation was dependent on a separate, other, unrelated force: "the real working class."

---

5   This is a view popular with separatists: that is, feminists who believe that men—and sometimes women who are with men, including with male children—are the enemy. What follows from separatism is often an attack on all men in theory, and in practice—because they have the least perks and power to bestow—on Black, Third World, and working-class men.

6   I have not mentioned welfare in this catalogue because in the United States the massive women's movement, led by Black single mothers for wages for housework in the form of welfare, was virtually ignored by the new Women's Liberation Movement, in the same way as its proabortion wing at first ignored the fight against forced sterilization. (Much the same was true in Britain, although here women in the Claimants' Unions pressed their case in Women's Liberation, with some success.)

7   Capital and its State have their own reasons for promoting the Left definition of the "working class." To them, "Small [less numerous and therefore less powerful] is beautiful" is an extremely convenient view of the working class. Thus they try to convince almost everyone that s/he is "middle-class." But why do we believe it? Since (thanks to the Left) "working class" implies downtrodden, futureless, backward victims, and few of us wants to see ourselves in that defeated way, we often find the middle-class label necessary to self-respect.

This was the time of urban rebellions, in the United States in particular, where millions of people challenged the American State, the most powerful and oppressive in the world. (Mind you, it has competition, but it wins.) The people who challenged that State's power in the streets of its own major cities as well as in Third World countries like Vietnam (Vietnam was the most spectacular, but it was happening in many places) were also not traditionally considered to be part of "the working class."

Sections of the Left tried to minimize the importance and the effect of these struggles, in order to protect "their" working class (which it seems, had a closed shop on effectiveness) and prevent it, apparently, from being upstaged. Others, mainly academics, even some who called themselves Marxists, seized this opportunity to say that Marx may have been right once but he was now passé. The working class are not the "gravediggers of capitalism," as he had said; they were never going to do anything; they had all sold out—they had refrigerators.

We can laugh at that now, but they did literally say that, especially about the working class in the United States. These others, Black people (presumably the ones without fridges), students, "peasants," they were the ones with the consciousness and the will to take on the job of overthrowing capitalism, to the exclusion of, even in spite of, "the working class." Marxists and anti-Marxists alike asked us to choose between "the workers" and "the others."

In the midst of this confusion, some of us were clever enough to look for ourselves at what Marx had to say. We were not satisfied with analyses in jargon of what he "really meant"; or assertions by learned academics that the young Marx—German poet and philosopher—was superior to the mature Marx—German immigrant to England, organizer, and theoretician. It did not pass our notice that it was academics who carried the greatest weight in defining what Marxism was to be. From universities they head organizations of the Left and write the books that the Left studies, discusses, and commends to us.

We refused also to be satisfied with what Marxist governments, which rule at least half the world's population,[8] said Marx was about. The emphasis and interpretations of governments are shaped by their need to retain power. Thus Third World governments may need to defend the Russian or the Chinese brand of brutality on which they depend for defense and aid, even if they would prefer not to. "Put not your trust in princes" applies even to Marxist princes.

Those of us who read Marx found out a number of things. It is not possible to go into all of them here, but some basics should be generally known, and since Marx is not hard to understand (and is a brilliant and exciting exponent of his views), it is not difficult or painful to know them. I will summarize very briefly some things that I believe are fundamental, and then relate them to the women's movement as we know

---

8   The Eastern European regimes were still in power in 1983.

it, and to other sectors of society which are also visibly organizing and also defined out of the working class. To define, or rather redefine, who are the working class is an ambitious goal. Luckily, the truth can usually be expressed simply.

Marx said that what distinguishes one society from another is the way in which human beings relate to each other in the course of working to reproduce ourselves: to survive and to develop as human beings. What distinguishes the social relations in which we reproduce ourselves in capitalist society is the wage relation: work previously done for a feudal lord or a slave master takes the form of waged work for an employer. But, he said, it is not our work that we sell for wages. It is our ability to work that the employer buys. Marx calls this ability to work *labor power*. By buying the use of our labor power, the employer buys the right to tell us what to do for a fixed time, for the forty or fifty hours a week that it belongs to him, and to own all of what we produce in that time. He gets as much as possible out of us during that agreed time.

In part of that time, let's say two, three, or four hours a day, we are able to produce the equivalent of the wages he pays us: we receive what we produce in that time in the form of wages. Thus that time is paid time, that work is paid work.

For the rest of the day, what we produce is kept by the employer. Thus for the rest of the working day we work for free.

I'll repeat that, since this is the nub of Marx's work (which, by the way, he fully understood quite late in his productive life). In part of our working day, we produce enough for the employer to cover our wages, his cost for hiring our labor power. The product of that part of the day is paid to us; thus in that part of the day, we do paid work. We continue to produce for the rest of the day, but the employer keeps that. So for that part of the day we are not paid: for that part of the day we do unpaid work. Marx called that *exploitation*.

That is the heart of all that Marx said. When he had grasped this, it focused all he had said before. The social relation which is capital is, according to him, that capital owns and does what it likes with our labor time and its product.

The ratio of unpaid work time to paid work time he called the *rate of exploitation*. So that if in four hours of an eight-hour day, you produce enough to pay your wages, and in the other four hours you work for free, the rate of exploitation is 100 percent: you do twice as much as you get paid for doing. You produce 100 percent more than you get paid for.[9]

---

9 Readers should know that I am using my own language except where I say otherwise in order for the analysis to be accessible and quickly graspable. While my exposition of Marx's theory of value is not inaccurate, it is of course incomplete: my aim is merely to make the basic connection between unwaged "women's work" and the waged working day. The reader who goes to chapters 4–9 of *Capital*, 1, will be richly rewarded. Marx himself connects the reproduction of labor power directly with the reproduction of capital in chapter 23. "By converting part of his capital into labor-power, the capitalist… kills two birds with one stone. He profits not only by what he receives from the worker, but also by what he gives him. The capital given in return for labor-power is converted into means of subsistence

But capitalist appearances are deceptive. The wage you get looks like payment for the whole day. The wage, which keeps you alive and able to continue to work, hides the unpaid part of your working day, hides that there is an unpaid part. You feel ripped off, but it's hard to put your finger on what appears to be a fair exchange. This "fair exchange"—of labor power (which works a whole day) for wages (which pays for only part of the day)—hides robbery.

Now, ever since society was divided into classes (and it wasn't always), the working day had a paid portion and an unpaid portion. Those of us who were serfs worked for ourselves only after we had finished working on the land and the crops of the feudal master. When we worked on the land assigned to us we were paid—with what we had ourselves produced, which kept us alive and able to continue to work. When we worked for the feudal lord on his land, we worked for free—for the right to keep what we grew on our own patch.

Those of us who were slaves did paid work too: the master had to give us food and clothing and shelter, not much but some, to keep us alive and working, and what we produced in one part of our working day paid for this. But the rest of the time during which we expended our labor power was unpaid time: its product was kept by the master; no part of it came back to us in any form.

Thus the capitalist way, paying us wages for the daily or weekly or monthly sale of our labor power to keep us alive and working, is merely the latest form of dividing the working day between paid and unpaid labor so the ruling class can appropriate, can steal, our labor time. But it has wide implications.

There is a book on rape by a feminist called *Against Our Will*.[10] It is, among other deficiencies, a very racist book. Yet the title sums up precisely what Marx had to say about waged work in capitalist society. It is against our will. He's very witty and very precise: we are "compelled to sell [our labor power] voluntarily."[11] We are forced to

---

which have to be consumed to reproduce the muscles, nerves, bones and brains of existing workers, and to bring new workers into existence. Within the limits of what is absolutely necessary, therefore, the individual consumption of the working class is the reconversion of the means of subsistence given by capital in return for labor-power into fresh labor-power which capital is then again able to exploit. It is the production and reproduction of the capitalist's most indispensable means of production: the worker" (572). Readers should also be aware that the rate of exploitation of 100 percent is a nineteenth-century anachronism. Computer technology makes it possible for wages to be produced in minutes; many of us work for free most of the day. Thus the rate of exploitation today runs in the thousands of percents. This is not merely a point of information (and aggravation). Marx's theory of communism as "the end of labor" was premised on the inevitable development of such a technology. Here is yet another area of Marx's work which has been largely ignored. The Left on the whole prefers to campaign for the right to work rather than for the right not to work. All references to vol. 1 of *Capital* are to the 1958 Moscow edition.

10 Susan Brownmiller (Harmondsworth: Penguin Books, 1986).

11 "It is not enough that the conditions of labor are concentrated in a mass, in the shape of capital, at the one pole of society, while at the other are grouped masses of men, who have nothing to sell but their labor power. *Neither is it enough that they are compelled to sell it voluntarily.* The advance of capitalist

do it, and we do it freely. Only by doing this work to acquire a wage do we have the right, the social power—the money—to eat. Free choice under capitalism is the right to choose between forced labor and destitution.

Marx goes further. Doing forced labor is the condition of our survival at the cost of our development. When capital buys the use of our labor power, it is in charge of our working, of our activity for most of our waking hours. It is not only what we produce which capital takes, from which we are "alienated." It takes our possibilities. We are alienated from our own capacities, our ability to be creative, our ability to shape and reshape ourselves. Capital takes who we could be and limits us to who we are. *It takes our time, which happens to be our life.* It takes us. We belong to it—not so different from the serf or the slave.

Virtually all other activities are a preparation for work or a recuperation from it.[12] That, Marx says, is the wage relation, labor power sold as a commodity in exchange for a wage. That is the terrain on which are shaped our personalities and all our relationships, private and public, personal and political, for the entire twenty-four hours of the day.

As the wage relation becomes the dominant form of stealing unpaid labor, the wage begins to dominate all relationships. For Marx, *capital is a social relation not only between classes but between all individuals.* All the relationships in society are transformed on the basis of this capitalist way in which human beings are exploited in the course of working to survive and develop. The most obvious, pervasive, and fundamental change is that we relate to each other through things. Exchangeable with everything, money connects human beings. *The Communist Manifesto* had put it this way: "The bourgeoisie…has left remaining no other nexus between man and man than naked self-interest, than callous 'cash payment'… It has resolved personal worth into exchange value."[13]

---

production develops a working class, which by education, tradition, habit, looks upon the conditions of that mode of production as self-evident laws of nature" (our emphasis). "Bloody Legislation Against the Expropriated, from the End of the Fifteenth Century. Forcing Down of Wages by Acts of Parliament" (*Capital* I: 737).

12 "Employed or not, we spend twenty-four hours a day working for capital in the social factory. Waged laborers spend their remaining hours 'after work' reproducing themselves to return to work. Eating, sleeping, drinking, movies, screwing are all essential work, which we do in order to be prepared for the next day's labor. These same functions are perhaps even more essential for the 'unemployed' so they will not turn their violence against capital" (Beth Ingber, Sidney Ross, Sam Weinstein, et al., "The Social Factory," in *Falling Wall Review* 5, ed. Jeremy Mulford [Bristol: Falling Wall Press, 1976], 3. "The wages for housework perspective…has allowed us to understand the 24-hour working day of the international working class and the need to struggle on that level. This is the debt that the whole movement owes to revolutionary feminism" (1–2).

13 "The bourgeoisie where it has got the upper hand…has left remaining no other nexus between man and man than naked self-interest, than callous 'cash payment.' It has drowned the most heavenly ecstasies of religious fervor, of chivalrous enthusiasms, of philistine sentimentalism, in the icy waters of egotistical calculation. It has resolved personal worth into exchange value, and in place of the numberless

The mature Marx was more precise. Our relationships are objectified, embodied in objects. The commodities we produce are "fetishized," that is, these things, in relating to each other through exchange, express our connection to each other no matter how far apart we are, and mediate between us no matter how near we are:

> Since the producers do not come into social contact with each other until they exchange their products, the specific social character of each producer's labor does not show itself except in the act of exchange. In other words, the labor of the individual asserts itself as a part of the labor of society, only by means of the relations which the act of exchange establishes directly between the products, and indirectly, through them, between the producers. To the latter, therefore, the relations connecting the labor of one individual with that of the rest appear, not as direct social relations between individuals at work, but as what they really are, material relations between persons and social relations between things.[14]

We are now so used to relating in this way that we take it for granted. But to allow the last three hundred years of our history under capitalism and the personalities we have developed because we were born and raised to live with and through the "cash nexus," to be considered "natural" to us is clearly absurd. Yet it is the object of most sociology, psychology, journalism, writing of history, even of conventional medical and dietary dogma, to establish and confirm that who we are at this moment in time is all we can be; that our capitalist selves are "human nature" and our capitalist lives the inevitable product of that nature.

Marx's accomplishments were considerable. He described the quality of the social relationship between labor power and capital, and then measured just how ripped off we are by it. How ripped off we are in things is a measure of how ripped off we are as individual human beings and as a society. Marx explained what exploitation was—how it alienated us from our abilities and possibilities and from the product of our labor, how it came to take place, what were its implications—*and then he quantified it.* The class struggle is in essence to end exploitation and to transform the quality of our lives: we don't wish to spend any of our precious time submitting to an alien—an alienating—will. But the form the class struggle takes is the daily war over the quantity of our lives which we are forced to give or can resist giving: how much exploitation we can organize to refuse, how much of our labor time will be paid and how much unpaid, how much or how little we will produce in how much time.

---

indefeasible chartered freedoms, has set up that single, unconscionable freedom—free trade. In one word, for exploitation, veiled by religious and political illusions, it has substituted naked, shameless, direct, brutal exploitation." Karl Marx and Frederick Engels, "Manifesto of the Communist Party" in *The Revolution of 1848: Marx's Political Writings*, vol. 1 (Penguin: 1973), 70.

14 *Capital* 1: 72–73.

In 1969 and 1970, reading in Volume 1 of *Capital* all about this uniquely capitalist commodity labor power, I realized that this was the special commodity which housework produced. Being ignorant, I thought everybody knew and I was angry that they had neglected to tell us. It was a surprise to find that the obvious view—that women were the producers of everyone's labor power, everyone's ability to work and to be exploited—was new. In the course of spelling out the implications of this (and in the process shocking some well-meaning left-wing people out of their political minds), I tried to describe the work that produced and reproduced labor power, the general sale of which defines a society as capitalist:

> This is a strange commodity for it is not a thing. The ability to labor resides only
> in a human being whose life is consumed in the process of producing. First it
> must be nine months in the womb, must be fed, clothed, trained. Then when it
> works, its bed must be made, its floors swept, its lunchbox prepared, its sexuality
> not gratified but quietened, its dinner ready when it gets home even if this is eight
> in the morning from the night shift. This is how labor power is produced and
> reproduced when it is daily consumed in the factory or the office. To describe its
> basic production and reproduction is to describe women's work.[15]

I invented the word "unwaged" to describe this "women's work," this housework.[16] Although we got no wage for doing it, it wasn't entirely unpaid—remember? For some we are paid in the form of food, clothing and shelter. But we get no money in our own right for expending our labor power in producing other people's labor power. We are deprived of money of our own, wages which are ours by right, acknowledgement of and reward for a contribution to social labor. Without recognition of what we contribute, we lack the socially accepted justification to claim autonomy as individuals. Without money of our own, we lack the power to take that autonomy.

But though it brings no wage, this work is not outside the wage relation. We are neither serfs nor slaves. The wage and the wage relation, often in the form of a man's wage, commands the work we do; the wage and the wage relation dominates the society we do this work for, and thus most directly dominates us.

The wage relation is not only a power relation between waged worker and employer but between those workers who do and those workers who do not have wages. This is the material basis of the social antagonism between the sexes. Whether or not we are in a relationship with men, let alone a dependent relationship, women's dependence in the society generally sets the terms of the relationship between all men and all women. Whether or not money passes hands between any particular individuals, the "cash nexus" binds the sexes to each other and into society. Women, the

---

15 Introduction to *Power of Women*, included in this volume.
16 The words "unwaged" and "wageless" were first used in *Sex, Race, and Class*, included in this volume.

poorer sex, are the socially weaker sex; men, more powerful financially, can exercise social power against us in every area of life.

Since when housework is unwaged no money passes hands as it does between employer and waged worker, it appears to be a strictly private matter, on the woman's part a labor of love, in keeping with the compliant and generous female nature. Thus the capitalist theory of "human nature" glorifies and praises women's poverty and hides our unwaged slavery. Hidden with it is the fact that we work for the employing class, which uses our product as an inexhaustible source of unpaid—and unwaged— labor. But in the same way that the work of those who are waged is forced labor; in the same way that they have little opportunity because of this labor to learn, to invent, to create and to develop and exercise talents; in that same way the producers of labor power without a wage are also doing forced labor, are also deprived of their time and their possibilities.

The work we do, housework, is also against our will; we too are compelled by economic necessity to sell our labor power voluntarily. And though we sell it to the same employer, it is usually through another employee, attaching ourselves to a man's wage, and becoming his dependent. In reproducing him and the children who will one day replace him—and us—we are protecting and enhancing capital's investment in him and in ourselves.

There are many things I like about Marx. One of them is that he is so confident of our case, and he has grounded it so well, that he did not hesitate to spell out our weaknesses. He was not worried about being critical of workers. He speaks at one point of how, in addition to the man selling his own labor power for a wage, when his wife and children are also introduced into the factory he sells them as well. The man, he says, becomes a slave dealer.[17] For Marx, our case does not rest on working-class moral superiority, or on anyone's moral virtues or lack of them, but on the justice of our case against exploitation, and on how, despite weaknesses, ignorance, superstitions, and prejudices, our collective struggle enables each of us to lift ourselves out of what capital has done to us.

There is therefore no need to glorify "the worker" as a heroic and blameless victim; no need to hide or excuse the violence that is the framework of working-class

---

17 "Previously, the workman sold his own labour-power, which he disposed of nominally as a free agent. Now he sells wife and child. He has become a slave-dealer. The demand for children's labour often resembles in form the inquiries for Negro slaves, such as were formerly to be read among the advertisements in American journals." (*Capital* 1: 396) Marx adds this important footnote: "In striking contrast with the great fact, that the shortening of the hours of labour of women and children in English factories was exacted from capital by the male operatives, we find in the latest reports of the Children's Employment Commission traits of the operative parents in relation to the traffic in children, that are truly revolting and thoroughly like slave-dealing. But the Pharisee of a capitalist, as may be seen from the same reports, denounces this brutality which he himself creates, perpetuates, and exploits, and which he moreover baptizes 'freedom of labor.'"

life; no need to mythologize the working class as the fount of humanism. Marx wasn't worried that the revolution would fail because workers—in this case husbands and fathers—were guilty of brutality against other workers—in this case wives and children. We are brutal to each other all the time. We are compelled to sell ourselves—what we are and what we can be—voluntarily, compelled to spend our waking lives in activities which we have not chosen or designed, an alien will imposed on us, directly and through others, from birth. This is the violence that we are forced to endure.

We absorb violence from those above and then often let it out on those less powerful than we are. If the man is waged and the person he lives with is dependent, even in part, on his wage, and in exchange has as her life's work to serve him so that he is fit to do the work he does against his will, then wife-beating is not a mystery. In that hostile environment where within this power relation each is trying to survive and to cut down on the amount of work that they are compelled to do against their will, what's astonishing is that men and women even talk to each other, let alone live together and even love each other.

It is also important to see that once men are identified as those who have the wage (or should have if they don't), and women as those who don't have a wage (and don't need to even if they do), almost any man can get women to reproduce him, to cook his eggs, make his bed, comfort him, and sleep with him. In very crucial respects, women are part of the male wage.[18] We come with the male pay packet because we traditionally lack our own.

Being part of another worker's wage is the fate not only of women in relation to men. Some years ago I compared the wage rates of skilled white workers in Johannesburg with skilled workers (largely white but some Black, and all men) in Detroit working for the same employers: Chrysler. White workers in *apartheid* South Africa were getting a great deal less than their counterparts in Detroit. Yet their

---

18 That women's unwaged work will make up for both men's low wages and the lowering, through cuts in social services, of the "social wage," has long been central to the Wages for Housework Campaign. In 1976 we wrote: "Working class resistance to work, waged and unwaged, has thrown profits into crisis on a world level. In response, trade unions and governments have together constructed an attack to which women are central. Prices are raised, real wages are cut, and social services are run down or abolished... Between the Labour Party and the unions, women face the most concerted attack since the Second World War. We are being sent back home without a wage to work twice as hard as before. Our 'flexible' working day at home is stretched to breaking point, cushioning the impact of the State's attack on others. The State calculates that our unwaged housework will bridge every gap in wages and social services. Every plan they make is premised on our work" (Introduction by the London Wages for Housework Committee to *Women, the Unions, and Work*). This view is by now more generally accepted. It is now clear that Margaret Thatcher's "community care" and David Cameron's "big society" result either in more unwaged work for women, or in women being condemned for those in need of care bearing the brunt of women's refusal of the extra work. This is the dilemma that women as carers have always faced. See "The Home in the Hospital" in *All Work and No Pay*, eds. W. Edmund and S. Fleming (Bristol: Falling Wall Press, 1975).

standard of living was in many respects higher. Black South Africans are part of their wage. Capital can pay whites less because a whole set of goods and services—a whole set of Black labor—is commanded by the white wage. Many of us in the world who are from sectors which tend to be unwaged, and are therefore low-waged, are part of someone else's wage.[19]

In fact, if we give it a moment's thought, we will realize that on a world level the number of people who get any wages at all is tiny. Most of us are unwaged, and many of us because of this must work under the command of other workers who stand as foremen—even sometimes employers—in relation to us.[20] Thus though the few (the "have-littles") have the wage and the many (the "have-nots") do not, all of us are dominated by it and by the struggle to survive through it.

This conflict on an international level between the waged minority and the unwaged majority has appeared as a conflict between different classes, rather than between different sectors within the same class. The implication is that the conflict between us is irreconcilable. I want to cite two quotations from Marx, the first on how these divisions within the working class, these power relations, were built into the process of production in the first place, and the second on how he saw the development of these divisions.

Marx was first of all describing "manufacture," an early stage of capitalism (manu = hand), later superseded by the "machinofacture" of large-scale industry. Manufacture, he says: "develops a hierarchy of labor powers, to which there corresponds a scale of wages. The individual workers are appropriated and annexed for life by a limited function; while the various operations of the hierarchy of labor powers are parcelled out among the workers according to both their natural and their acquired capacities."[21]

So here was capital organizing production politically; organizing for one worker to be above, and therefore against, another; creating a hierarchy of skills, money and social power. (Marx had already said that an "individual carries his social power… in his pocket.")[22]

---

19 And this is not an accidental offshoot of differentials. The struggle over the depression of one sector's wages is *always* the struggle over other sectors' wages. Thus low—unequal—pay for women is what keeps men's wages down.

20 For example, in many Third World countries, nurses, teachers, and other waged workers may well be able to afford servants. Because of horrendous rates of unemployment (30, 40, even 50 percent), domestic workers' wages are notoriously starvation wages. Marx made clear that "Taking them as a whole, the general movements of wages are exclusively regulated by the expansion and contraction of the industrial reserve army…" *Capital* 1: 637.

21 *Capital* 1: 349.

22 "The power, which each individual exercises over the activity of others or over social wealth exists in him as the owner of exchange values, of money. The individual carries his social power, as well as his bond with society, in his pocket…" Karl Marx, *Grundrisse: Foundations of the Critique of Political Economy* (Harmondsworth: Penguin, 1973), 157.

He then shows how the hierarchy was reorganized when machines replaced hand production:

> Along with the tool, the skill of the worker in handling it passes over to the machine. [Your skill is now objectified—embodied in an object—thus lowering your value to capital. On the other hand, this is also potentially useful:] The capabilities of the tool are emancipated from the restraints inseparable from human labor power. This destroys the technical foundation on which the division of labor in manufacture was based [the hierarchy of labor powers we described above]. Hence, in the place of the hierarchy of specialized workers that characterizes manufacture, there appears, in the automatic factory, a tendency to equalize and reduce to an identical level every kind of work that has to be done by the minders of the machine.[23]

Now, he didn't use the word "automatic" as we use it today. He meant that with steam power, you didn't turn the machine by hand; the steam turned it automatically; and the power for each machine derived from a central source independent of the individual machine operator. No longer was an operation dependent on the size or strength or even the skill of the operator. The machine now equalized us. Does that mean the end of the hierarchy? Quite the contrary. He continues: "in place of the artificially produced distinctions between the specialized workers, it is natural differences of age and sex that predominate."[24]

So that the hierarchical wedge, first inserted between men and men, dividing them from each other on the basis of skill, is at a later stage inserted between men and women and children. Biological differences become social divisions. Capital was able to divide the single workplace, and then whole branches of industry, and eventually the whole world in similar ways. In capital's hands, *the division of labor is first and foremost the division of laborers, on an international scale.*

In 1973, we drew the conclusion for the extension of that division of laborers from the waged workplace to the society generally:

> A hierarchy of labor powers and a scale of wages to correspond. Racism and sexism training us to acquire and develop certain capabilities at the expense of others. [You learn to pull a lever but that's all you learn. You do not learn a million other things because your time and your energy are consumed and your will is sapped by your enforced submission to pulling that lever. Or changing that nappy.] Then these acquired capabilities are taken to be our nature and fix our functions for life, and fix also the quality of our mutual relations. [They think we are made for this work. Worse: some part of us thinks so too.] So planting cane

---

23 *Capital* I: 420.
24 *Sex, Race, and Class* above.

or tea is not a job for white people, and changing nappies is not a job for men, and beating children is not violence. Race, sex, age, nation, each an indispensable element of the international division of labor. *Our feminism bases itself on a hitherto invisible stratum of the hierarchy of labor powers—the housewife—to which there corresponds no wage at all.*[25]

You can see how useful Marx has been to the Wages for Housework Campaign. There are feminists who take pleasure in denigrating and dismissing him. The excuse they sometimes give is that he was a man, or that he was a male chauvinistic pig. He can be defended from this charge, but what if it were true? Surely it is worth hearing what men think is wrong with the world (especially men dedicated to the destruction of capital!), even if they are sexist, since we can't win without them. And if you exclude the sexists and the racists and the ageists, etc., who is left? Which of us is "pure"? In any case, I don't think the elevation of women is dependent on the denigration of men. It is at best self-indulgent to reduce Marx in this way. Frankly, I am suspicious.

We are all aware of how much hostility there is to Marx by those who rule us precisely because he is such a power for us against them that a century after his death he continues to make them nervous. Thus it is extremely saleable to be anti-Marx. You can make a career that way. You can get a job, or a research grant, or invitations to important conferences, important dinners—at the very least, important wine and cheese parties. I don't say that's the only motivation of those who dismiss Marx, but it is no discouragement.

I cannot show that the hierarchy of labor powers was a focus of Marx's. I found these two quotations; I was feeling my way to such a view when I came upon them. It was because Marx was scrupulous about putting down all he saw the mode of production to be that he described the hierarchy as integral to it. But he draws no organizational conclusion from it. He concentrated on the condition general to all of us: what we shared rather than what divided us was what we needed most to address. A certain kind of political organization flows from that. He formed the First International. He fought for "workers of all countries [to] unite" in an organization together. Considering how divided we were, based on the division of labor and on other historical and geographical divisions, it was new and revolutionary to establish our commonality. He did that work.

In the hundred years since his death, it is perfectly clear that, while unity is as central today, that unity will be built only in the process of attacking and destroying

25 One great change since Marx is the role that immigration has played and is playing in the unification of the working class on an international level. "One thing we [immigrants] offer is that we transport struggles from one part of the world to another… Immigration is the network along which the international travels." Margaret Prescod, addressing the conference "Bringing It All Back Home: Black and Immigrant Women Speak Out and Claim Our Rights," November 13, 1982, in *Strangers & Sisters: Women, Race and Immigration*, ed. Selma James (Bristol: Falling Wall Press, 1986), 85.

the hierarchy. Our struggles have often suffered when we united in organizations dominated by more powerful sectors of the working class. Thus increasingly we have organized ourselves very specifically against the hierarchy: the Black movement, the women's movement, the movements of Third World peoples and specifically of Third World women, the movements of women and men with disabilities, the movements of lesbian women and gay men, the movement of ex-mental patients, prisoners, ex-prisoners, parents of children with cancer, prostitute women, transvestites, welfare recipients, students, farmers, "farmers' wives"…the list is endless and continues to grow: all kinds of movements which presume that each sector has a specific attack to make on capitalist society that only it can make in organizations that only it can form and within which only it can sort out and even fight out who and what are its friends, enemies, needs, strategy, tactics.

The existence of these movements confirms that the hierarchy does not cease at the factory gates. Born in the need to subordinate the will of the working class to the will of capital, the hierarchy extends up to stratify managements and bureaucracies and down to stratify factories and farms and families. The whole society is involved in the division of labor and in the hierarchy, the division of the laborers. Wherever we are, our moves are adapted—or subversive—to the specific levels of the hierarchy in which we are enmeshed, the niche our sector is squeezed into, even on a street, even in a tenants' association, even in King's Cross between those of us who are prostitutes, those of us who are clients, and those of us who are neither: a red-light area is one of the many points of conflict between various sectors of the working class, which we as a working class are confronting in the only way we can, by each sector making its own direct and specific attack on capital and its State.

Once we do that, however, we come into immediate conflict with those sectors of the working class which stand above us and for capital in relation to us.[26] Yes, we do. There is no question that if we are Black we find ourselves confronting white people. If we are women we find ourselves against men. And if we are Black women we find ourselves against Black men and white men and white women. If we are children we find ourselves against our exploited mothers who stand against our exploited fathers who stand against employers and other more powerful women and men. That is the fabric of the world in which we live. That is the structure of exploitation, of the working class and of the social relation, which is capital. It is a very complicated hierarchy and demands a very complicated network of organizations to destroy it, *which millions of us have been forming.*

That is the vital point. Not merely do we face an enormous and complicated task, but also we have tackled it. *That is why we now know so much about the hierarchy.* We did

---

26 And with those in our own sector who are bought off or at least are for sale. Careerism in the women's movement is the greatest threat to it, and in fact draws the class line within it.

not invent these divisions (though we were accused of splitting the working class when we formed autonomous organizations to deal with them). They were invented, and continue to be reinvented, along with the rest of the mode of production, by capital. But now that we massively confront these divisions in an increasingly organized way, the hierarchy can no longer be denied—a giant step in the process of its destruction.

Now I want to draw two conclusions.

First, everything that I have been saying assumes that the wage (what capital pays us) is the crucial point of conflict between us and capital. They want the money; so do we. They want the money because they want to force us to work. We want the money because we don't want to be forced to work. We understand each other perfectly; we just disagree. When the Wages for Housework Campaign began in 1972 it was precisely to make visible and to advance the struggle for wages by those of us who are unwaged. Other unwaged sectors besides women have also articulated their wage demands. When Black people in the United States said they wanted reparations for slavery, it was back pay. And they said so.[27] Everywhere in all kinds of ways the unwaged are quantifying our exploitation.

But the wage is not only money. It comes also in the form of goods and services. The Tories are robbing us of a National Health Service; that's our wage. We take a wage cut every time they cut any social service. That's our social wage, what we get in the form of services, which we try not to pay again for, either in time or money.

And the wage is what we refuse to give in time. Winning half an hour, fifteen minutes, sometimes even five minutes, in the waged workplace—those of you who know factories will know that five minutes can be a lot of your time to reclaim— you get a wage rise of five minutes: you take five minutes of your life back from the vultures. The Wages for Housework Campaign has articulated that struggle over the wage on the part of the unwaged worker, beginning with women, a struggle which, because the protagonist does unwaged work, has been invisible or at any rate not the "real" class struggle.[28]

Second, the autonomous organizations which we have created have shown, as I say, that without this autonomy all the former Internationals, even Marx's First International, could not express the needs of all of us but instead reflected the hierarchy within the working class, confirming it; expressed the needs of the most powerful sectors (of course only partially) often at the expense of the weaker. I was reading a manuscript recently about meetings in Germany in the 1920s where Rosa Luxembourg,

---

27 The most eminent early advocate of back pay for the Black community in the United States was Martin Luther King Jr.: "No amount of gold could provide an adequate compensation for the exploitation and humiliation of the Negro in America down through the centuries. Not all the wealth of this affluent society could meet the bill. Yet a price can be placed on unpaid wages," *Why We Can't Wait* (New York: Mentor Books, 1964), 137.

28 Fleming, *Disinherited Family.*

a great woman, a great revolutionary, was trying to convince women against their will to have more babies so that the working class could be more numerous and thus stronger. Shocking! That is where the Party, the organization which purported to represent every sector but never did and never could, led even her.

The independent organizations and movements we have founded put forward our own demands and discipline and educate more powerful sectors of the working class *to see their interest in uniting with us*. Because—and Marx was, of course, absolutely right about this, as about most things—the point of organizing is to unite. The question is: who unites with whom? Do we unite with the men or do they unite with us? Do "Black and white unite and fight," that is, Black people unite with white people, as the old Left used to have it, or white with Black as the Black movement insists?

Those with more power must unite with those of us with less because we know better what their interests are than they know themselves. Oh yes, we certainly do. Women know, for example, which of men's "victories" are victories for us, and which are defeats for us and therefore ultimately for them. We also know how much we have contributed to all victories, and how much men owe us for that.

In 1973 we said: "How the working class will ultimately unite organizationally we don't know."[29] This was a useful political statement. It didn't presume to have all the answers, and said so, aware that nothing depended on any of us having the answers. But it needs a little updating. One thing that has happened in the past two or three years which is most encouraging is some indication of how these movements can ultimately come together, or at least how they are beginning to come together. I think they are coming together in the peace movement, especially because of the action of the women of Greenham and what they have spawned in all of us.[30] Woman-led, the best of it Third World oriented, Peace and Money—though this latter is only just

---

29 *Sex, Race, and Class* above.
30 Greenham Common Women's Peace Camp was set up in 1981 outside a U.S. military base in Berkshire, England, to protest against the siting of cruise nuclear missiles there. The base had a number of entrances, or gates, and women camped outside each gate, which they named with a color. The Communist Party wanted Greenham to be aligned with the East; which would have suited the United States too, since such alignment would have compromised Greenham's opposition to the West's missiles. And neither superpower was happy with an antiwar women's space whose work was "the monthly stopping of the cruise convoys, the daily evictions, the arrests, the court appearances, the imprisonments, and their involvement with the support groups." (See Margaretta D'Arcy's "Power to the Sisters!" in *Awkward Corners*, eds. M. D'Arcy and John Arden, [London: Methuen, 1988], 231). Worse: thousands responded when they called periodically for women to come to Greenham. We worked with Yellow Gate, supporting their fight to keep Greenham nonaligned, and to make it antiracist. Racism became an issue when women of color joined the support—would they be welcomed and protected from police racism by the white majority? Were peace and antiracism bound together or not? When Margaretta, veteran of the Irish nationalist Armagh and H-Block campaign, actress and playwright, who lived for weeks at a time at Yellow Gate, wrote the account of the battle for nonalignment and antiracism quoted above, the pro-Soviet women tried to stop its publication. The

beginning to be spelled out. Not only must they not make bombs, but the money they have been using on arms must go to the poorest of both the Third World and the metropolis: to women and children, to those with disabilities, to the elderly…to the unwaged. We all want that, and we all know we need that, and we are all increasingly ready to accept the leadership of women on that. That is a giant step forward, which gives me a lot of courage and reaffirms my confidence—with Marx—that working-class power is inevitable.

Camp closed in 2000—it had succeeded in getting the base shut down and the cruise missiles flown back to the United States. The common was returned to the public.

Passport photo with son Sam,
before leaving for the UK, 1954.
Photo copyright Selma James

Selma and CLR
James, Guyana,
1958.
Photo copyright
Selma James

English Collective of Prostitutes church Occupation, London, 1982. Caroline Benn (front row second from left) and Tony Benn, Member of Parliament, visited Saturday night.
Photo Crossroads AV Collective

Clotil Walcott, National Union of Domestic Employees and Wages for Housework Campaign, Trinidad & Tobago, 1925-2007.
Photo Crossroads AV Collective

With Egyptian feminist
writer Nawal El Saadawi,
UN World Conference on
Women, Nairobi, Kenya,
1985.
Photo Crossroads AV
Collective

GWS mothers' march, London, March 2011.
Photo Peter Marshall

With Phoebe Jones (GWS Philadelphia) and Lt. Ehren Watada, the first U.S. army officer who refused to go to Iraq, Olympia, Washington, October 2006. Photo Crossroads AV Collective (U.S.)

GWS International Gathering, London, February 2009. People came from Bolivia, China, France, Guyana, India, Ireland, Italy, Peru, Tanzania, Turkey, UK, and U.S.
Photo Crossroads AV Collective

Actor-activist Danny Glover at a Global Women's Strike press conference on Haiti and Venezuela, London, 2004. From left: Margaret Prescod (Los Angeles), James and Nina López (London), and Andaiye (Guyana).
Photo Crossroads AV Collective

With Niki Adams and Lord Ramsbotham, former HM Chief Inspector of Prisons at the House of Lords launch of Mumia Abu-Jamal's *Jailhouse Lawyers*, London, June 2011. Photo Crossroads AV Collective

Speaking at Occupy London Stock Exchange (OLSX), October 2011.
Photo Crossroads AV Collective

GWS mothers' march, Red Thread, Mahdia, Guyana, 2010.
African and Indian women from the coast join with Indigenous
women in the Interior.
Photo Red Thread

At the Aristide Foundation for Democracy, Haiti, March 2011.
Photo Aristide Foundation for Democracy

Speaking at "Why Anti-Capitalism?" workshop, Tent City University, OLSX,
November 2011. The other speaker is trade unionist Sam Weinstein.
Photo Crossroads AV Collective

The Strike has been organizing with parents, mainly mothers, whose children have been taken into care because of poverty, racism, imprisonment, homelessness, and domestic violence—in Philadelphia and in Los Angeles (above, 2011).
Photo Crossroads AV Collective LA

Leddy Mozombite Linares (domestic workers union SINTTRAHOL, Peru) and Manju Gardia (Nawa Chhattisgarh Mahila Samiti, India), both part of the GWS network, London, 2009.
Photo Crossroads AV Collective

THE GLOBAL KITCHEN (1985)

I n 1985, women from a number of countries in our international network attended the Final Conference of the UN Decade for Women in Nairobi, Kenya. *The Global Kitchen* was written, literally, on the eve of our departure. It made the case for women's unwaged work globally to be counted in national statistics. We took it to the UN conference to get governments there to agree, and with hard work, we succeeded. (See *The UN Decade for Women: An Offer We Couldn't Refuse* below.) This is an excerpt. The title was taken from an article by Clotil Walcott.[1]

* * *

"What Have You Been Doing All Day?"

Women do two-thirds of the world's work, receive 5 percent of world income, and own less than 1 percent of world assets.

The above figures, computed by the International Labour Office in 1980 and often cited by the United Nations, tell us a great deal, and not only about women. That

---

1 Mother, factory worker, founder of the National Union of Domestic Employees (NUDE), and point of reference for the Wages for Housework Campaign in Trinidad and Tobago. After meeting the Campaign at an international conference, she immediately drew out the connection between the uncounted work of unwaged housewives and the low pay and gross exploitation of the millions of domestic workers working long hours in other people's kitchens. The Strike has organized with domestic workers in a number of countries ever since. Clotil Walcott died in 2007 in her eighties, and is sorely missed. NUDE continues as a trade union of domestic and other low-waged workers.

women do twice the work of men is basic information about both sexes, as children and as adults. What follows aims to begin uncovering the implications of this information for the global facts of all our lives.

Incredibly, few official figures indicate women do anywhere near that amount of work. Most statistics claim the opposite, that women on the whole work much less than men, and that many if not most women "don't work" at all. In the United States in 1979, only 51 percent of adult women were "in the labor force," 48 percent in China and France; in Latin America only 14 percent of the total female population was counted as workers in 1975. In Britain 40 percent of women are in the paid labor force now. In some parts of the world, women's participation in the "labor force" is actually dropping. In Peru it fell from 28 percent in 1950 to 12 percent in 1970. In Africa, 32 percent of women were considered to be in the labor force in 1950; only 24 percent in 1980; yet 60–80 percent of the agricultural work is done by women, work which produces, among other things, up to 90 percent of all the food.[2]

Most of the two-thirds, then, refers to work that is not ordinarily counted as work by governments that compute how much a country produces. The basic government statistic is the Gross National Product or GNP. Most of women's work is left out.

What does this work consist of? Some of it is the housework metropolitan women do "privately"—that is, enclosed within the family. Views about the nature, quantity and value of this work vary widely and almost always spark fierce controversy. For example, some feminists believe that childcare is not "housework," or that work for a "fit but demanding husband…is both unnecessary and demeaning," while "looking after a baby or an invalid" is not.[3] This asserts a widely held view that, while children may be entitled to the care women bestow, most men and other women are capable of caring for themselves and it is habit, culture or just backwardness which keeps women enslaved by this work. Not surprising then that the Advisory Council on the Status of Women in Canada reported they get "many telephone calls from housewives who feel the women's movement is putting them down."

Most women know that a basic element of housework is managing the tensions of and servicing in every other way those—women and men—who do waged work, school work, housework, and those distraught by unemployment; they know that work in the home is precisely to ensure that work outside and life generally goes on uninterrupted:

> throughout the world, in both developed and developing countries, women are the
> mainstay of the hidden support economy which allows the rest of the economy to
> function and which is not mentioned in national accounts, which does not appear

---

2   *New Internationalist*, August 1980, 10; G.N. Lamming, *Women in Agricultural Co-operatives: Constraints and Limitation to Full Participation* (Rome: FAO, 1983), 6; Ibid.

3   *Spare Rib*, March 1981, 25.

in census reports and which is not clearly reflected in the social and economic indicators.[4]

The family functions as a soak pit to absorb expressions of anger that are not allowed elsewhere.[5]

How to draw the line between housework and childcare? Is feeding children, laundering their clothes, cleaning their rooms, changing their beds, buying their clothes housework or childcare? In Britain the estimated fifty hours a week "basic childcare" includes only some of these physical tasks and specifically excludes explaining and listening, trips to the park, etc.[6] In order fully to describe work we are still in the process of discovering and finding words for, definitions of housework must be seen to supplement rather than negate each other.

We know what a woman does all day most fully when, perhaps through illness, she is not on duty: even the most insensitive among us sees what she usually does when she is no longer doing it and we have to find others to do it, try to live without it, buy replacement services, or do it ourselves. One estimate puts these services at "3,000–4,000 unsalaried hours a year" or sixty to eighty hours a week for "the average Western housewife."

While metropolitan feminists may differ in definitions of housework or, more to the point, in views about its economic and social importance to society and the State, as well as to individual men, they share with other women a universal and deep hostility to the identity imposed on women by this unwaged "women's work." Solutions vary. The women's movement has expressed increasing determination to do much less of it, and some to make the State pay women so we will have the economic power to refuse it.

Women in Third World countries are almost never referred to as "housewives" but as "peasants" or "farmers." Yet the major part of unseen and uncounted housework is done in the nonindustrial world. In the discussion in North America and Britain which began in 1972 in response to the claim that housework is "productive," the woman in the nonmetropolitan world has been almost entirely invisible. This intense self-absorption is tragically common and allows some metropolitan feminists to ignore all who seem irrelevant to their own future. Even development workers tend to avoid focusing on Third World housework or considering that Third World women are housewives too.

Yet since housework is dismissed as so trivial and mindless, so marginal and unnecessary, and the people who do it are so often identified with their work, that

---

4   "The Invisible Woman," *The UNESCO Courier*, July 1980.

5   *Southern Africa Research Service* (Johannesburg) 27 (June 1983): 41, quoted in *For Their Triumphs and Their Tears*, by H. Bernstein (1985), 45.

6   David Piachaud, *Round About Fifty Hours a Week: The Time Costs of Children* (Child Poverty Action Group, 1984), 19.

it may be out of respect, even charity, that Third World women escape this demeaning identity. On the other hand, some women consider being a housewife a privilege which Third World women are denied.

But who do they think does housework in the Third World?

A rural woman from Tanzania:

> I am 39 years old, which is quite old for our people. I think of my own life as having been long and strenuous. Thirteen births have more or less worn me out. Some of the children died as infants, while seven are still alive. It is the same in most of the families around here: about half of the children never grow up... Most of my mature life I have had to care for a baby in addition to all other work in the house and in the field.[7]

Headed "A Hundred Hour Week in Latin America," the ILO's *Women at Work* reports the huge burden in the cities:

> A recent survey organized by the ILO Regional Office for Latin America and the Caribbean on unremunerated domestic work in eight countries has revealed surprising results that merit reflection on the condition of women in society... In the overwhelming majority of cases, the hours of work at home far exceed those of women who work outside the home, according to the surveys and other studies which support this evidence. Some examples are striking. In Argentina the homeworker works on average 68.9 hours a week, that is almost ten hours a day. In low-income families in Bolivia domestic work involves a total of 15.5 hours daily on average, including Sundays and holidays. In the case of Chile, whilst economically active women devote what is already the considerable time of 57 hours 19 minutes on average to work outside the home, homemakers spend the amazing amount of about 99 hours each week on domestic tasks.[8]

In La Paz, Bolivia, women queue for up to twenty-four hours to have bottles of gas for cooking filled. In Guyana "the food line...is the longest line you can find anywhere ...A man here, a man there, sometimes some children, but women from back to front...we have to go and line up from three to four o'clock in the morning to attempt to get food."[9]

The technology of the average European working-class kitchen is obviously far behind the technology of industry and war. Where those employed will be paid according to the expenditure of their time, technology must free employers of labor costs, and is capital intensive. But the labor intensity of housewives' work is of no interest to those who do not pay for any of it.

---

7   "My Husband, My Master," *New Internationalist* 25 (March 1975): 6–7.

8   Krishna Ahooja-Patel, ed. *1/85* (Geneva: Office for Women Workers' Questions, ILO), 10–11.

9   *Strangers & Sisters: Women, Race and Immigration* (Bristol: Falling Wall Press, 1985), 168.

What can we say then of how the time of the Third World woman is valued? The rural woman especially may be cooking on a wood or charcoal fire for which she must gather the fuel, must wash her clothes by the side of the river—if she is lucky enough to live within walking distance of a river—and in any case spend up to four hours a day collecting water. If metropolitan women wasting time is not a major economic concern, what can be said about how the time of the Third World woman—which happens to be her life, which she can never reappropriate—is dissipated, wasted, squandered, in the absence of the most rudimentary technology, beginning with water pipes?

Gathering water and fuel for the fire is identified as women's responsibility as much as the cooking to be done on it. And so is much of the planting, tending, and harvesting of the food she will cook. Most of this work, carried on by most of the three-quarters of the world's women who live in the Third World has no official recognition. Children, when they are old enough, especially if they are girls, help their mother. "A girl is only a few years old when she is sent for the first time with a bucket or pot to collect water."[10] And because they help the invisible worker, their work also vanishes.

Elsewhere we have spelled out how the entire Tanzanian economy, and many Third World economies, is carried on the backs of rural women.[11] What is unique about Tanzania is that its basic independence document, the *Arusha Declaration*, pushes forward some basic truths about this work. Such a level of truth is at least somewhat effective. Tanzanian women who do waged work get 79 percent of men's wages, a higher proportion than in any other Third World country, and much higher than in the United States (66 percent in 1980).

It is not only in the Third World that women do unwaged agricultural work. According to the Council of Europe, 90 percent of those regularly employed in agriculture are "family workers," the majority of whom are "farmers' wives."[12] It has been traditional in North America and elsewhere for "the farmer's wife" to manage the poultry (the "egg money" may be the only family earnings the woman gets into her own hand) and the kitchen garden, preserving what she grows against the hard times of winter, and to be unpaid farm laborer when needed.

Women's unwaged work is more pervasive and varied than any one person or study has ever calculated or computed. In the last years its extent and importance have begun to be publicly acknowledged. The following is from a long piece cataloguing the work observed among women friends in a couple of weeks by a major columnist in England:

> A son had to be taken to hospital and once there sat with for four hours so that he
> would feel easy in uneasy circumstances... A daughter needed a birthday party to

---

10   "My Husband, My Master."
11   President Julius Nyerere, *The Arusha Declaration*, Tanzania 1967.
12   *Women at Work*, 10.

mark a coming-of-age. A mother-in-law had to be written to with news of family doings and inquiries as to aching feet and general well-being... A child's school had to be visited for talks with teachers... A sister had to be given hours of time to support her through impending divorce, a brother had to be listened to through the woes of impending redundancy. A neighbor eased her loneliness with a chat about greenfly on the roses. A housebound relative had ill-fitting shoes returned to a shop. A friend's child had to be babysat while the mother took herself to the doctor. Another friend wanted comfort about an erring child... [W]e appear to be blind to that network which is just below the surface of every hostile activity; so essential to human happiness and even to human existence that it is counted as a reflex happening, like breathing. And yet that whole network is most carefully and lovingly woven, erected, repaired, serviced and staffed by the unpaid women at home. If it were not for them (and women who have paid jobs and still service the net because they are women) I verily believe that civilized life as we know it would simply collapse.[13]

Voluntary organizations from church societies to library support groups, from food co-ops to disaster appeals, from tenants associations to groups for improved, supplementary and antiracist education for children, are often the inventions and initiatives of women and always depend on woman power for their day-to-day functioning, perseverance and continuance.

On some of this voluntary work depends the survival of individuals and whole communities. But history rarely records such historical achievements. For example, in Britain in 1939 the Women's Voluntary Service was responsible for the evacuation of one and a half million people in a single day.[14] Women alive to tell the tale will explain that meals on wheels and other social services to neighbors during the Great Depression were the invention, organization, and unpaid voluntary work of women. The Welfare State was a victory because it acknowledged that work, paid for it and accepted the responsibility for its continuance.

Monetarism in Britain, which aims at cutting State expenditure, is returning to the law of survival of the richest, and putting that work back on to women. The government of Margaret Thatcher calls it "community care" and "Victorian values," which not only hides that it is work but makes it women's moral obligation. When women's work is not counted—not even mentioned—it is still counted on. By 1976, in England the direction was clear:

We are being sent back home without a wage to work twice as hard as before. Our "flexible" working day at home is stretching to breaking point... The State calculates

---

13 Jill Tweedie, "The Unacknowledged Network That Makes the World Go Round," *Guardian*, June 15, 1978.
14 R. Broad and S. Fleming, ed., *Nella Last's War* (Bristol: Failing Wall Press, 1981), 9.

that our unwaged housework will bridge every gap in wages and social services. Every plan they make is premised on our work. They have tried to use women to subsidize men's wages, to make up in extra work at home for the drop in money coming in.[15]

Caring for others is accomplished by a dazzling array of skills in an endless variety of circumstances. As well as cooking, shopping, cleaning and laundering, planting, tending and harvesting for others, women comfort and guide, nurse and teach, arrange and advise, discipline and encourage, fight for and pacify. This skilled work, which requires judgment and above all self-discipline and selflessness, is most often performed within the family. Taxing and exhausting under any circumstances, this service work, this emotional housework, has an additional emotional cost when it is done for and on behalf of those whom the woman is emotionally involved with. But all this is expected of women by everyone: friends and neighbors, workmates, employers (why else is the secretary called the "office wife"?), as well as family; this emotional work is done both outside and inside the home. For example, unknown men have been confident enough to ask a woman in a public place for a smile to cheer them on their way.

There are more references to this work, its extent and its cost to women, in fiction than in economic textbooks. One of the most extraordinary is Virginia Woolf's description in *To the Lighthouse* of Mrs. Ramsay's academic husband "demanding sympathy" and Mrs. Ramsay working to reassure his ego. The metaphor of metal raping flesh is used to describe his insistent need and her work satisfying it: "into this delicious fecundity, this fountain and spray of life, the fatal sterility of the male plunged itself, like a beak of brass, barren and bare."[16]

To ensure that the intention is not passed over or misunderstood, the same metaphor with slight variations is repeated. And when Mr. Ramsay was "Filled with her words," he was "like a child who drops off satisfied"—here the metaphor is of a nursing infant; while Mrs. Ramsay has worked until "the whole fabric [of her being] fell in exhaustion upon itself..."

The literary rape to describe the demand for emotional work approaches the more literal but just as common rape in marriage. The New York Prostitutes' Collective:

> Women in our industry have been told we encourage rape. To single out porn or prostitution as the cause of rape and sexual violence is a veiled attack on those of us who, as part of the movement for women's financial independence, are getting paid for what all women are expected to provide for free. Taking care of men's sexual and emotional needs, often at the expense of our own, is work... Rape begins at home where too many women and children can't say "no" to the rapist who pays the rent.[17]

---

15 See *Women, the Unions, and Work.*

16 Virginia Woolf, *To the Lighthouse* (New York: Penguin), 38–40.

17 *Village Voice,* January 1981, 7–13.

At what age are women first saddled with this work? In Third World countries in particular, the work of children, and most especially girl children, is a vital part of the family's subsistence calculation, both in rural village and urban slum:

> Survival…often depends on having children to bring in extra food or money for the family… [D]emographers have calculated that a rural child at the age of 10 or even 8 can bring a net food or income benefit to the family. Children, for example, herd animals, fetch water, firewood and dung, transplant rice, glean fields, and cut stubble… For each such family, the number of children determines the number of workers it can field to support itself. If the family has little or no land, its income might depend on the number of children that can be hired out as laborers in the fields of others.[18]

A survey in rural Zambia and Zimbabwe found children aged seven to fifteen working in farming for about quarter of the time worked by women. The surveys generally don't differentiate between boys and girls.

But whatever work boys do on the land, and this varies from country to country, it is a fairly universal truth that, while their brothers are at liberty, girls are expected to do housework. According to the Food and Agriculture Organization, girls in Zaire aged between ten and fourteen do 55 percent as much work as adult women.[19]

In rural Bangladesh children under ten years old do up to three and a half hours housework a day, girls aged thirteen to fifteen years old, seven hours a day. In Chile, children aged seven to ten years old act as heads of household—taking responsibility for housework and looking after younger children.

These statistics do not specify which sex carries the burden of housework. It would be astonishing if it were equally shared, flying in the face of everything else we know and have seen or heard in life, books, films, photographs, and personal accounts. A Tanzanian mother reports that "boys have no obligations in the home. They just run around and play while the girls work just as hard as their parents."

It is no wonder that a rural schoolboy in the French Congo was told by a European economist, "If your sister goes to school, you won't have anything to eat but your fountain pen." Working-class resistance to compulsory education in Britain (and perhaps in the world) was based on a similar dependence on child labor.

This vital work done by Third World children, together with the expectation that those who survive childhood—and because of poverty many will not—will "provide minimal old age security for the parents," making it a matter of economic and physical

---

18　Frances Moore Lappé, Joseph Collins, and Cary Fowler, *Food First: Beyond the Myth of Scarcity* (London: Sphere Books, 1982), 33.

19　*Women in Agriculture*, FAO Fact Sheet, May 1983.

survival that women bear many children. We stress that Third World women's bearing and raising these children is part of the work women do to ensure the survival of everyone. Yet "for many mothers, so often undernourished, the burden of yet another pregnancy and child outweighs any prospective gain from an additional laborer in the family."[20]

On the one hand, the husband demanding that she make babies, and on the other plans to sterilize her.[21] The State and the husband controlling women—an international power relation. Yet we are sometimes told that if women get a wage for housework, men and the State might be able to use it to control us.

Interviewing rural women in Tunisia, the Sudan, Kenya, Sri Lanka, Mexico, and Egypt, a UN social worker "found that it is not women who need to be convinced to have fewer children. In each of the six very different cultures she repeatedly heard variations of 'I'm tired. Look at me. I am nothing but a beast working in the fields and bearing all the children. I don't want any more but my husband says I must have as many as come.'"[22]

The sexual division of labor and the international power relations between the sexes are inseparable from housework—I would say based on it. As we have seen, women and girls everywhere are expected to do a mountain of work on which the survival of the human race and of all our possibilities are founded. When we consider the repression that continuous open-ended service to others requires, we realize it must begin early to begin at all. The housework that girls do not only contributes when they do it. It is a training for a life of servitude, a question of the very nature and differentiation of the personalities of the sexes. Women are not born housewives, but can only become housewives because we are trained to it almost from birth. We then see that "Our childhood is a preparation for martyrdom."[23] Men are not born housewives either; they are not only not trained to do this work but trained to expect it from females of almost every age.

Since those who work under our command have less power than we do—or they wouldn't work under our command—they always enjoy our contempt in some measure. Women do at least twice the work of men, which both gives rise to and perfectly mirrors the power relations between the sexes.

The movement of women internationally has put the description, counting and evaluation of women's work on the economic and political agendas of the world.

---

20 Lappé et al., *Food First*.
21 London *Evening Standard*, May 11, 1977, 15. "Population control is needed to maintain the normal operation of U.S. commercial interests around the world." Dr. R.T. Ravenholt, director of U.S. Office of Population of the State Dept. Management Program at Washington University, St. Louis, to sterilize 100 million Third World women.
22 Lappé et al., *Food First*.
23 *The Power of Women and the Subversion of the Community*

Below are some of the unofficial estimates which are beginning to proliferate on the work women are forced to do against our will, on pain of violence, destitution, disgrace, and starvation.

It may be useful to note that for all this information to have been gathered and to be made increasingly available, is a major victory. It is important that we take this information in and resist being overwhelmed by women's legacy of overwork, poverty, and every other variety of violence and injustice; so overwhelmed that we don't see women's struggle against these burdens and how we can build on it.

Your Money or Your Life

Now when I hear, or read in the press, about a big burglary or the theft of thousands of rands by Blacks, young or old, men or women, I often express the desire that they will not be caught. I suspect that I am not the only one to find myself changing in this way. It is a change forced on me, certainly not chosen, and it is one I bitterly resent. In the South African situation, I have often had cause to halt and reflect: Who is robbing whom in this country?

Take a mother in domestic service from 6 a.m. to 6 p.m. or even later earning barely R80 a month. Is not this a case of exploitation? Would it be surprising if such a mother, with full family responsibilities and the best intentions in the world, should be tempted to make good her needs by stealing from the employer?

Who in this case is the first to display tendencies of theft? Is it employer or employee?[24]

In all these estimates of the value of women's work—and there are many more compiled from Scandinavia to China—one omission is glaring: the value of women's agricultural work. Yet in many countries women's (and children's) subsistence food production is the mainstay of whole communities. In fact, it is increasingly accepted that the famine in Ethiopia and the Sudan, in which thirty million people's lives are threatened, five times the number of Jewish people who died at the hand of European racists, is directly attributable to the land being taken out of the hands of women, out of the hands of those who were guaranteed to make it productive to the survival of the community.

The apparent cause of the omission of the value of women's work on the land seems to be the pervasive provincialism of metropolitan people generally and the narrow specialization which is the habit (passing as the rigors) of most academic work. Academia, the "leaders" in thought, usually trail behind history, collecting facts and footnotes only when a field of human endeavor or concern has been made an acceptable arena for study by the efforts of others.

---

24 Ellen Kuzwayo, *Call Me Woman* (Women's Press, 1985).

Every time one employer succeeds in raising the productivity of "his" workers, that becomes the standard that other employers must try to make "their" workers meet, and even overtake. Either that or they go to the wall in the competition on the world market. The latest, highest productivity is the labor time, which becomes the standard all employers must make "their" workers meet, the necessary production time, the "socially necessary labor time." Because of competition between employers on the one hand, and between workers and employers on the other, the amount is always going down: as soon as we win a rise in pay or a lowering of the workweek, the employer tries to make it back by increasing our workload or the intensity of our work to drive the standard—the cost to himself—further down, and production—the cost to "his" workers—further up.

Where employers are concerned, there is no urgency to cut down on the time spent in unwaged work—after all, they don't pay for it: "If you are not paid by the hour…nobody cares how long it takes you to do your work."[25] That is why the technology even of the metropolitan home is so far behind that of industry and war.

It is the ultimate mystification of our work to reduce it to the goods and services that undoubtedly housework does churn out. But the aim of these goods and these services is the production of people. Our work is the production of the human race and that means overwhelmingly the human workforce, the basic ingredient of all industry, all agriculture, all services, all profit, and all war; as well as of all the movements for social justice, social change, and peace. We produce the commodity that is sold for wages, labor power, not merely biologically but physically, socially, and emotionally. What is the value of that?

The estimates of the value of our work which are beginning to appear reflect in general not only the replacement value of the woman who does an enormous variety of jobs, but a woman who cannot be replaced. Can we live without the emotional work in particular which saves us from suicide or at least minor acts of self-destruction every day on the one hand; and which builds movements on the other?

But estimates of Third World women's work are in inverse proportion to the amount of work they do. If and when women's unwaged work is counted in the gross national product of any country, by whatever method of calculation, even if it reflects the value of our work to others, it cannot reflect either the value of our time to ourselves or indeed the value of our product to anyone.

How can there be any measure of the alienation of time, in the age of star wars and moon walks, represented by the dusty walk in hot sun to fetch water in a calabash or a clay pot or a tin pail with a child on your back? How to quantify the cost of birthing ten children when three of them may not survive due to the virulence of the

---

25 *Power of Women*, 35.

measles virus where regular meals are a luxury? Whatever is the value of this work in economic terms to those who have not even been obliged to notice it was happening, the lives of humans are valuable to themselves and this ultimately is the lever to organize on a global level against any kitchen which imposes any slavery.

The Cost to Women

The first consequence of women's work being "nonmarket" and "nonmonetarized" that is to say, uncounted, unrecognized and unwaged, is that women must do it with virtually no technical help. This means such a quantity of time in order to eke out survival, such a number of childbirths, and such utter fatigue, that women's lives are literally consumed in the process of performing this "nonwork" through which whole areas of the world hang on to survival.

While this is much more literally true of the non-Western world, the South, it is truer of the North than Northern governments admit. As unemployment in Europe grows, the poverty of women (and children) is the first sign of the deterioration of working-class standards of living.

While this is increasingly the concern of feminists, who now speak of the "feminization of poverty" (but to be fair, poverty has always been a women's issue), it is usually duly added to the growing list of injustices which woman's flesh is heir to, and which the women's movement is devoted to cataloguing and removing.

Confronted injustice by injustice, however, in single-issue lobbies and campaigns, it is possible to believe that there is something inherently wrong with women and our consciousness or with men and their consciousness or with both.

The sexual division of labor and the contempt for women which it fosters, like charity, begins at home, then pervades the society and is reflected in everything from wage rates to literacy rates.

It is important for us to be clear that this is deeply connected with the great wage differentials and the hidden work at home, and it is easy to see it. It is common knowledge that the jobs women do outside the home tend to be extensions of work in the home, beginning with domestic work in someone else's kitchen, and caring for someone else's children.

It is just as important that we reject the view of ourselves, which our poverty and lack of social power impose on us. The habit of blaming women for what we are forced to endure is a common one. The usual way it is done among women who may consider themselves feminists is to complain that women have a low level of consciousness. We are proposing to start at the other end: we have problems with workload and bank accounts and land ownership and child custody. Let us deal with spelling out the need for visibility of these, and then we will see where our heads have reached.

The standard of living of North and South vary widely. What does not vary is that whatever the standard, women are the poorer and the socially weaker sex. Once we know that this weakness is the product of how much we are forced to do and how little we are forced to accept for it, we cease to believe that our lack of power is either inherent or cultural. It is important for us always to bear in mind, despite pressure to the contrary among those who want to keep women divided, that whatever injustices to women or to anyone else that traditional societies were guilty of, the imperial powers have used that and encouraged that and codified that and even insisted on that. "I firmly believe that the reasons for the lower status of women in [Arab] societies, and the lack of opportunities for progress afforded to them, are not due to Islam, but rather to certain economic and political forces, namely those of foreign imperialism operating mainly from outside, and of the reactionary classes operating from inside."[26]

But for those who insist on attributing the particularity of women's situation to culture, it might be useful to consider—again—a novel, but this time by a man.

One product of the independence movements in the former colonies has been remarkable fiction writing. African literature is more accessible than some because it is often in English. Novel after novel seeks to work out the relationship between traditional society and women's position within it on the one hand, and imperial conquest and then postindependence on the other. The implication of some books seems to be that the traditional division between the sexes, and women's subordination to men, were what allowed such rapid imperial conquest. (That is, it was all women's fault.) One novelist in particular concerns himself with the fate of women. One of his heroines wishes to bridge the gap between what Western society has to offer and the tribal life she also loves. Another is a single mother exploited in every way by the new independent regime. He is not tentative in describing that exploitation. Here is a description of a woman searching everywhere for a job in an office. She is telling the story about herself in the third person:

> She enters another office. She finds there another Mr. Boss. The smiles are the same, the questions are the same, the rendezvous is the same—and the target is still Kareendi's thighs. The Modern Love Bar and Lodging has become the main employment bureau for girls, and women's thighs are the tables on which contracts are signed... Modern problems are resolved with the aid of thighs.[27]

Escaping from Mr. Boss or, if we must, submitting, are both work that we want the world to know we are fighting to refuse. Recording both what we endure and how we oppose it makes our case for all our entitlements.

---

26 Nawal El Saadawi, *The Hidden Face of Eve* (London: Zed Books, 1980).

27 Ngugi Wa Thiong'o, *Devil on the Cross* (London: Heinemanm, 1982).

STRANGERS AND SISTERS: WOMEN, RACE, AND IMMIGRATION (1985)

I n 1984, a one-day women's conference was organized from our center on race and immigration. Immigrant women, rather than the voluntary sector (better known now as NGOs) and social workers, were the panelists. It was the first time that immigrant women from a number of countries had spoken publicly not only about fighting to stay, but about what it meant to leave home for Britain. It was inspired by *Black Women: Bringing It All Back Home,* which was the first time some issues had been raised: "the uprooting of everything you've ever known, to go someplace else, not really knowing what's ahead of you."[1] At the end the audience of three hundred was so moved by the truth of personal (but also political) experiences that had been spoken that for some minutes it did not disperse. It was as though a community had coalesced in that long day and people were loath to dissolve it by leaving the hall.

I edited the book of conference panels and discussion. This is an excerpt from the introduction, followed by "Evaluation: Making Trouble, Making History," about what we can achieve by critiquing our own events.

* * *

---

1   Margaret Prescod, *Black Women: Bringing It All Back Home* (Bristol: Falling Wall Press, 1986). From Barbados to Brooklyn, from Jamaica to England, two accounts of girlhood in the Caribbean, the upheaval of leaving and the conflicts of being an immigrant.

The Wages for Housework Campaign has always spelled out the connection between the unwaged and invisible work of women, and the work, waged and unwaged, of immigrants, women, and men.

We also insisted that those of us who are immigrants, wherever we come from and wherever we go, are attacking the racism and provincialism carefully nurtured among every working class, by bringing another world—usually the Third World—with us into metropolitan centers. One side of immigration, we said, is that it is an element of State planning—using immigrants to undercut the wages, working conditions and living standards which have been won by the native working class, and to disorganize resistance. The other side is how immigrants—as much those from Malaga in southern Spain as those from Port of Spain in Trinidad—use immigration as a method of reappropriating their own wealth, stolen from them at home and accumulated in the industrial metropolis. Immigrants are in Britain, we knew, not for the weather but for the wealth. Because much of it has been produced by their own and their ancestors' labor, that wealth is as much theirs by right as those whose history of exploitation has never left Britain.

The work of women is basic, first, to organizing for themselves and others to become immigrants, and then to transforming their communities from victims of the State plan into a network of reappropriators. That work is hidden, as most of women's unwaged work always, everywhere, is hidden.

The First Quantification of Women's Work

The great debate which has raged in the women's movement about why we are (or could be) together as women despite a thousand divisions, is (or at least can be) ended by the UN figures that women do two-thirds of the world's work, get 5 percent of the income and own 1 percent of the assets.[2] This is basic information, the raw material from which is constructed the social weakness of women. It is the first quantification of sexism, a tangible measure of just how ripped off women are internationally.[3] The work and the poverty of women and our struggle against both constitute the material basis of the women's movement, what we had always claimed is the basis of women's relation to capital: women's exploitation.

---

2 *Women at Work,* International Labor Office Newsbulletin Geneva, no. 1 (1980): v. The two-thirds figure originated in this journal.

3 Capitalist society turns everything, including human skills and abilities, into commodities whose value *is quantified* on the price tag or in the wage packet. The amount we are to be exploited is meticulously planned for and constantly *measured* and evaluated in stock exchanges, banks, boardrooms, cabinet meetings, at foxhunts, and over dinner. Even, for all we know, in bed. In general, men do not work as hard as women; the differences in amount of work and income and in degree of exploitation are *quantifiable.* To the degree that we quantify our exploitation, to that degree we can measure not only how much we lose but what we win, and frame our demands accordingly. As a strategy, quantification began with Marx, whose early work was a description of the effects of exploitation and whose later work quantified this exploitation, showing how it resulted in the alienation he had previously named and described.

Such a quantification is a weapon against the work. One way to refuse it is to refuse to let it go on unnoticed. We began to publicize the UN figures.

From the perspective of women's work, all issues are transformed. Take for example immigration.

How much work do women do to make immigration possible, to make possible the rebuilding of the community in a new town, city, country; among other races; speaking other languages; with different food, dress, customs, education, religions, hierarchies? What is the hidden cost—hidden because women pay it and are not paid for doing it—when the family and community have to confront and survive the economic and social consequences of racism, while the woman on whom such survival depends may be under attack as a woman even from within her own community?

Such questions begin to drag out of the shadows the mountain of work, which has defined women's condition, as well as the mountain of work which is assigned to immigrants, particularly if we are Black, always if we are women.

For though as women we share overwork and poverty, yet race, immigration and other divides determine what kind of work we do, how much we do, under what circumstances and for what returns. While the UN figures quantify the sexual division of labor, there is also a racial division of labor, an immigrant/native division of labor, and so on, which have rarely been quantified.

In fact, every division among us expresses the division of labor: the quantity of work and the wages or lack of wages mapped out for each particular sector. Depending on who we are—what combination of sex, race, age, nation, physical dis/ability, and so on—we are pushed into one or other of these niches which seems our natural destiny rather than our job. To allow even one of these aspects of our identity to be denied by anyone is to allow them to falsify or at least obscure our social position and our workload, which they do most often to falsify and hide the power relations between us and them.

Work—Not Just Another Issue

Generally in the self-proclaimed women's movement, our waged work is only one of many unconnected issues. Our unwaged work on the land and in the kitchen is hardly a concern at all of many feminists. The same is true of most political men of every hue and complexion. For neither of these, is this tortuous two-thirds of the world's work ever included in definitions of either sexual or racial violence, though it is both. Work is not just another issue, one of many ingredients of "oppression," one item on a list of grievances which add up to women's inferior position. Work is not one branch of a blighted tree, each branch having equal claim to treatment in the cause of women's—or anyone else's—liberation. Work—the activity women and men are forced to perform to survive—is the essence of capitalism, which must be destroyed root and branch. This work is what saps our time and our energy, which happen to be our life. Work confines us, defines us and shapes our relationships. For women, to the degree that the work we do is to care for, nurture, train, and nourish others, physically and socially, work is also our relationships. Because work is how we spend our lives and how we relate, work shapes our consciousness of ourselves and of each other. Women are seen as naturally low-waged or unwaged servants, by men, and by the entire society, starting with our own children. In fact and in consciousness, the work we do, women and men, is the essence of our slavery.

Neglecting women's work has wide implications for every aspect of struggle. For example, without a quantification of women's work, the case against imperialism, the multinationals, the military-industrial complex, has a basic weakness, a tragic flaw. Why they conquer, what they steal, and how much they are exploiting whom, in factory, farm, and family, are calculated on an incomplete reckoning at best. At worst, such a false reckoning conceals the most bitter truths about one of the two sexes, about the relations between men and women, and about every aspect of politics and economics.

The neglect of immigrants' work, but immigrant women's work in particular, is a basic weakness of every antideportation campaign. The movement has often made the case that because most immigrants are of "working age," those of us who are immigrants contribute more to the economy per capita than natives, who tend to be older; and that in any case we are doing jobs the natives have refused to do. This is true but it postdates our contribution.

In 1978 three immigrant women's organizations together led a campaign to try to prevent the loss of child benefit to immigrant parents whose children were not in Britain. This £70m a year was to be denied to parents who had already been denied their children by immigration procedures and rules, and racism. The basic premise of the Child Benefit For All Campaign was that immigrants have always been working for Britain, first in the colonies and ex-colonies, and then in Britain itself. This work roots the claim for the right to stay and for rights to the Welfare State not in abstract justice only but in very concrete debts outstanding. "Once this work and pain are highlighted, we also see that we are owed far more than we owe."[4]

Women's unwaged work all over the world has produced this army of immigrants, women, and men. While housework everywhere is consuming and endless, in the Third World it is generally accomplished without running water at home or at all, without State health care, education, welfare. Immigrant women came to metropolitan countries precisely to refuse this housework.

---

4 Solveig Francis, "Until women have spoken…" Introduction to *Black Women: Bringing It All Back Home* cited above.

Many generations of Third World women have paid heavily so that Britain and other metropolitan countries could have a reserve labor force ready and waiting in the wings, so to speak, for when it was needed. That poorer nations subsidize richer ones by exporting immigrant labor power has been noted before. That it is women's unwaged work in Third World conditions of economic and technological poverty that has produced this labor power, and that this is a subsidy extracted specifically from women by international capital, is rarely if ever noted. The State never mentions the work on which it has been so dependent. And neither, in general, does the movement.

That women should be seen as appendages of men in immigration legislation and be threatened with deportation if they lose that connection, is directly attributable to the invisibility of their work.

It is vital for us as women that the economic and social foundations laid by our unwaged housework, fieldwork, community work, office work, and much more, in every society, finally be acknowledged.

Women's unwaged work appears nowhere in any country's gross national product (now referred to as the gross domestic product), which is supposed to quantify the total amount of a country's goods and services. Those who claim to lead us in the struggle against exploitation, including of course trade unions, seem just as reticent to mention the two-thirds we do, the 5 percent we are given for it, and the mere 1 percent of assets we own. Women's unwaged work? Hard. Maybe even tragic. But marginal. Unproductive. They should get a job.

And so, women (and children) who bear the burden of this work and poverty are omitted from every consideration of entitlement. Dismissed as much by militant antisexists as by militant anticapitalists and antiracists, and even by those who pride themselves that they are all three.

In dismissing or ignoring the UN figures, two-thirds of the case against capitalism, racism, imperialism and sexism—against the racist, imperialist patriarchy—and two-thirds of the proof that there is a material basis for sisterhood, that we have a basis for common struggle as women and as workers internationally, is also dismissed.

In particular, the struggle of Black women day to day, to cut down on this work, and where it is unavoidable to get it done and still survive, remains largely invisible and unrecognized.

Women's Justice Work

While it is public knowledge that Black people, and particularly young Black men, are regularly harassed, falsely arrested, and beaten by the police, there is rarely a mention of the women—mothers and sisters, wives and lovers—who go back and forth to courts and prisons, who organize defense committees and attend their meetings sometimes on winter nights after long days cleaning hospitals; or who deliver to prison cells, along with home cooking and cigarettes (and at times unwelcome words of advice), the laundered shirts, so that the accused—son, brother, husband, or lover—can appear before his persecutors dressed in the community's care and support.[5]

It was such women who picketed the Old Bailey, London's Central Criminal Court, a few years ago during the trial of the Islington 18, Black youths unjustly accused of a variety of petty crimes. Families, mainly mothers and sisters, of these youths, organized a Defense Committee and did everything humanly possibly to force the defense lawyers to take instructions, to do what the defendants wanted and needed done. In order to call public attention to the laziness and arrogance of the lawyers towards their clients, and to their cowardice in standing up to the court on their clients' behalf, the mothers' placards demanded that the legal fees that lawyers were collecting for their sloth be paid instead to those who had done most of the defending—the families. It is rare for the work of Black women to surface in this way.

Neither feminist separatism nor nationalism, by country or by race, has noticed the women who have provided the backbone of every struggle. Thus sustained, Asian communities, women and men, have defended themselves from attack not only on the streets but in the waged workplace, beginning as far back as 1965 with the Courtaulds' strike in Preston, Lancashire, against two men having to tend three machines instead of one each, thus resisting Courtaulds' new plan for all its factories which it was trying on with immigrants.

Women's cooking, caring, supporting—their organization—made it possible for the women and the men at Imperial Typewriters in Leicester to take on the National Front physically and drive them away; and for Jayaben Desai and the sisters and brothers she led at Grunwick to wage their more famous but no more dramatic struggle.[6]

Such caring and supporting behind the scenes, since it is just women doing just physical and emotional housework, remains largely uncounted, unhonored and unsung by every movement. Suffering such invisibility, especially if you lack the language, you are assumed to be passive, helpless, unaware, and incapable, the stereotypic victim, rather than the survivor and protagonist, an identity that your actions and accomplishments could earn you if you were white and a man.

---

5 Even the police admit this. In the report of the Policy Studies Institute, *Police and People in London*, published in four volumes in 1984, the Metropolitan Police are accused of racism, sexism, framing suspects, drunkenness, etc. Since the study was commissioned and paid for by the Met, they did not deny its findings. After the first headlines, the media dropped the subject and never returned to it.

6 Grunwick Photo Processing Plant in London, UK, was a small firm employing mainly Asian women. In 1976 Jayaben Desai and others walked out in protest against poor pay and working conditions and forced overtime, and demanded union recognition. The strike lasted nearly two years and attracted massive support—eight thousand people picketed at one point—and police violence. It lost, but established that Asian women were fighters like the rest.

Few among us appreciate how weak we—any of us—would be without this work and how much it protects us from. In passing laws and inventing rules and procedures aimed at keeping families divided, the British State is showing more recognition for the work of women than many of those on our side. They who preach the holiness of the family know exactly when it is in their interests to split it up. They are well aware that the presence and support of the kinship network, which women's work builds, nourishes, and sustains, greatly strengthens any struggle against them.[7]

Elsewhere we have spelled out how the survival of the family is dependent on the woman's slavery. On the other hand, women know very well when the family is our protection, when the breakup of the family by the State is an attack on us. It is therefore *always* in our interest to have in our power the decision to protect or to destroy the family, which, after all, rests on our labor.

Separatism—A Strategy for Defeat

Excluding or treating as marginal the mountain of work, the two-thirds, serves to reinforce the racism of white "feminist" politics and the sexism of male politics. When the workload we as women share is invisible, it is not hard to believe what all kinds of people impress on us in all kinds of ways, that Black and white women have "different" problems and therefore want different things. It is not a long racist jump from there to the claim that, while Black women want money, white women want "higher things"; or that while Black women want to be housewives whom some feminists despise, white women want jobs outside the home, a more respected ambition in their hierarchy of desires.

The truth of course is that Black and white women both want choices, to be able to have, given their particular circumstances, whatever will mean less work and more money, less than two-thirds, more than 5 percent; and that every woman is in the best—the only—position to evaluate just what her own needs and circumstances are.[8]

On the whole, working-class women, whatever their race, tend to make similar choices; and so do the minority of women of whatever race with just a bit more power, who often demand in the name of all women what they want for themselves.

---

7   The laws which prevent women from bringing husbands and intended husbands into Britain are not more sexist, not more of an attack on women than the procedures which keep wives and children in Pakistan or Bangladesh waiting for years, or forever, when they do not pass the British Consul's trial-by-fire interviews. Both are aimed at preventing a unified family.

8   The entire debate in the women's movement about wages for housework is centered here. Feminists who oppose it almost always detach work from class and economics when it is unwaged and when it is done by women. We are told that a wage would not free us but would institutionalize us in the home doing this trivial, uneconomic, unsocial, unproductive nonactivity. Rather, they say, housewives should get a job. An extremely impractical suggestion in a period of high unemployment, and a very metropolitan one: what would they tell Tanzanian women?

When they demand equality in our name they may end up with careers. For the rest of us, "equality" may mean—and has often meant—just another lousy job on top of the housework. A bit more power makes some people think they are more than a bit more "advanced." If poorer women don't want what this "advanced" minority demand, then this minority—which has the power to define us—claims we have a low consciousness.

Feminism without the work we have in common on the one hand and the different workloads that divide us on the other; without the poverty we share on the one hand and the hierarchy of wages on the other; such a feminism tends to be so vacant and so narrow that race and immigration are treated as complications which get in the way of "the struggle against the patriarchy"—which is how much of feminism is defined.

Defining the enemy as patriarchy—the power relation between men and women—while ignoring the multitude of other power relations—such as those based on class, race, and nationality—impels many feminists into narrow, unfeeling, and racist corners. It is an arrogant and one-dimensional view of humanity and of the crisis of survival we share.

The theory of the patriarchy, in targeting men as the enemy without attacking work or profit-making, leaves the military-industrial complex, which thrives on everyone's work, all three-thirds, free to do as it likes with all of us. Such kindness to the powers that be is worth money. There are careers, grants, invitations to international conferences and access to the best academic circles to be found in such selective separatism. The theory of the patriarchy cut off from and prioritized over class, race, etc., is a scabs' charter.

It is also a formula for defeat. The idea that, by cutting ourselves off from those men who share one or another aspect of our exploitation, our struggle against that exploitation will be strengthened, is as absurd as it sounds. It is also dangerous. We need the support and protection of other sectors. Whoever suggests that we reject the support of others, women or men, for whatever excuse, intends us to be the isolated victims of divide and rule again, this time in the name of the purity of our own movements.

Based as it is on the inevitability of divisions, separatism is a self-fulfilling prophesy: it pits individuals and groups against each other and then complains that they cannot unite.

No one should have to qualify as a "real" feminist by how she dresses, who she sleeps with, who and what she loves and hates; or as "real" Black people, "real" workers, "real" lesbians… There is no competition for reality. We are all real—real women with real tragedies, which we are confronting the best we know how with real struggle.

Immigration: The Network Along Which the International Travels

Immigrants—women or men—are seen as strangers. In Europe, so are Black people, immigrant or not. Yet race and immigration have been major issues in the making of British capital at home and abroad, as well as the making of the working class at home and abroad. That is to say, while race and racism had always been a vital component of British imperial rule abroad, we are led to believe that Black people, and the racial clash within Britain, are both new arrivals.

In the same way, while we know that deportation from one colony of the Empire to another was commonplace—for example, West Indian "outside agitators" deported from one island back to the island where they were born—it is generally assumed that deportation as a basic and widespread tool of State discipline within Britain is as recent as the 1962 Immigration Act and the increasingly repressive Acts which followed; that deportation is basically about race.

It is beginning to be known that one of the by-products of the British trade in slaves and of slavery itself was a Black population in Britain beginning as far back as the 1570s. By 1772, it was estimated that of a population of nine million in England and Wales, about fourteen to fifteen thousand were Black.[9] Few of those people ever left these shores and so, aside from old Black communities in places like Liverpool and Cardiff, those thousands must have become the ancestors of many British people today, some of whom, because they have white skins seem not to be aware of (or at least don't acknowledge) their African roots. (Some would have Asian roots, the descendants of later arrivals.) Hints of this ancestry can appear anywhere, and I will not forget being taken aback by a white face of obvious African derivation on the television spewing out racism in a plummy accent on behalf of the Monday Club, the extreme right of the Conservative Party. Upper class hooligans may also have Black roots.

Deportation or threats of it also have a long history in Britain. Queen Elizabeth I deported Black subjects on the pretext that they were taking food from white ones. Two centuries later, the word "transportation" was a euphemism for the deportation to the colonies of working-class troublemakers, most of them convicted of crimes of poverty. In the process, the racial balance in the colonies of Virginia, Australia, etc., was changed, which the colonizers considered an additional bonus.

"Transportation" was also the method of punishing more organized and subversive forms of working-class resistance. The Tolpuddle Martyrs—farm laborers, to this day Britain's wretched of the earth—were convicted of swearing an oath not to scab on each other, and to constitute themselves as a trade union. For this they were "transported" to Australia; 1984 was the 150th anniversary of their historic deportation. It

---

9   Peter Fryer, *Staying Power* (London: Pluto, 1984), 68. Other estimates went as low as ten thousand and as high as twenty thousand in London alone.

is not irrelevant to us today that they were allowed to return after two years of their seven-year sentence, so strong was the antideportation campaign waged on their behalf in England, and the men's own organizing which began almost immediately after they arrived in Australia.

Immigrants today facing deportation or the threat of it, which turns any claim for common rights into an act of bravery, have never been seen as the political descendants of those earlier working-class heroes.

There are examples in our own time also. Organizing sanctuary for immigrants and refugees within the United States for people from Central America is helping to build a network of support against U.S. intervention and destabilization.

Confronting Power Relations

The Wages for Housework Campaign has spent a lot of time confronting the power relations among ourselves and with others as they surface in the course of our campaigning, spelling out the varied, pernicious, and subtle forms they take; and working out ways to organize against them.

This process is never completed, of course; the way any of us relates to anyone else is hardly a question of intention only but of the very structure of society, the very structure of our lives which are founded on the divisions of work and wealth among us, pitting us against each other to compete for basic needs.

Given this pervasive competition, attacking and demeaning or at best ignoring the needs and claims and pain and struggle of others—beginning with children— appears to all of us, again and again, as a necessity for our survival.

We will not end racism—which assumes that any other human being, on whatever pretext, wants less, needs less, or deserves less than we do—until the society based on competition of needs is completely transformed. Nevertheless, we *can* work together against this competition in a productive and satisfying way. But it is *work*. It is *hard* work. Which, if we are serious about uniting, we have to be prepared to do.

This work is not separate or apart from organizing but central to it. Only in this way can we confront our own and each other's racism as a crucial part of our struggle. This helps ensure that our demands speak to the needs of other sectors, and that our anger is directed against the State which divides us, rather than against each other. We in the Wages for Housework Campaign consider ourselves experts at this way of organizing.

Power to the sisters and therefore to the class.

Evaluation: Making Trouble, Making History

As the work of the conference began long before the actual event, so the work did not end when the conference was over. The concluding stage was our customary evaluation meeting. Recording the aims and purposes of this evaluation process here will help explain the methods as well as the purpose of our organizing, and will complete the conference picture.

Evaluation is not less necessary if an event is successful. Our evaluation meeting always seeks to integrate the big moments with the ongoing day-to-day work of the Women's Centre. It is a thorough postmortem, an organizing tool we've used since the Wages for Housework Campaign first had public events in the mid-1970s. A public event is a test of your analysis, your tactics and strategy, and the quality—the abilities, skills, clarity, and focus—of your people. Success or failure, meeting or demonstration, organized by us or jointly with others, after the rush is over we sit down among ourselves and with other interested participants and break it down. Being women, who are doing two-thirds of the world's work and who have fewer resources than men with which to organize, we must get as much as possible out of every investment of our most scarce and precious commodity, our labor time. Something as major as a conference must be scraped clean of its meanings and uses, like a bowl of food when you're broke.

The evaluation meetings seek again and again to answer the same questions, and to do this, they have the same simple format: report and discussions. The questions aim to uncover the basic facts of political life around us and among us, to pool information and to reach conclusions about the terrain of our struggle, conclusions which we try to make as precise and practical as possible.

The raw material for the picture we build up is basically what each of us has observed and lived through. Because you're usually working during your own event, it is only later, by exchanging experiences, impressions, and anecdotes with others, that you get to hear about what you missed, and only then can you arrive at an overall view. The discussions branch out to any concerns and information which any woman can show to be remotely connected: there are an infinite number of bits and pieces which make up the answers we are putting together collectively and in each individual mind. Since we don't presume ever to have all the answers, and for the purposes of evaluation presume to have even fewer, every evaluation meeting begins with the great expectation that we will be at least a little wiser at the end. If we are evaluating a success, it begins also with great excitement.

The meeting looks first of all to register our victories: how much we achieved of what we set out to do; what we learnt preparing it and throughout; what talents were revealed among us and in others; how much different sectors of women (and occasionally men) learnt from each other, saw common interests, and worked together, who ordinarily would not have; how, and how much we weakened the case of those who wield power against us; what long-term effects we can expect or should keep our eyes open for.

Spelling out what a political occasion has won is part of our survival strategy:[10] for a group whose existence is always under attack because it stands out against the Establishment, working out methods to maintain yourself is decisive. The methods you choose also reflect what your organization stands for.

For example, many pressure groups which claim to be anti-Establishment hold out the promise of money and power as prizes for the most ambitious and cleverest members. That has become their reason for existence, shaping their policies and their practices: they are cautious with their members' future. Such pressure groups are a traditional step in the career ladder of British society: people who aspire to be MPs, for example, make their name by rising to the top in organizations which fight for the needy, with caution, good manners, and moderation.

On the other hand, almost every shade of the Left promises its members State power as the ultimate reward when "the workers" realize whom they must follow.

The race relations industry and the newer but no less deadly gender relations industry are not essentially different from these two sectors of the ambitious.

The evaluation meeting where we first of all count our victories is vital to maintaining us as who we are: campaigners who reject this careerism, measuring our success by the effectiveness of what we do, rather than by whether personal bank accounts grow—a dominating motive, ironically, among many feminists who deny that money is important!

The Wages for Housework Campaign is extremely interested in money, but knowing it is social power, we also know that when only a few get it at the expense of the rest of us, we are further divided.

Counting our victories, we make our work count and we quantify its effectiveness. As with women's more private—but no less political—housework, most of our organizing work is invisible. Along with acknowledged politics, such as writing leaflets or setting up meetings, is the political housework of drawing people out, discovering and encouraging their skills and talents, breaking down barriers to people identifying with each other and finding a basis on which to propose they move together—all of which require time and concentration, energy and skill—and above all compassion. Women do this work especially well, not because it is natural to us but because we are trained within the family almost from birth to do it. Yet this political housework, the cement of any movement (and there is never enough of it), is rarely seen

---

10 There are of course other parts of our survival strategy. The Campaign's international network has always been decisive in warding off provincialism, nationalism, and racism. It has also given us access to many more victories and thus more power than if we accepted the boundaries that governments set. Goodwill and even good works are not enough to build and maintain such an international network. It requires constant hard work and attention to all the pitfalls of grassroots organizing beyond national ghettoes. But that is another, and even longer, story.

and even more rarely considered work. The evaluation process lifts this work from obscurity, appreciating its productivity, quantifying its results.

Counting our victories we appropriate our own history.

With the growth of women's power, the history of all kinds of contributions by women, as individuals and as a sex—in literature, language, art, music, politics, religion, agriculture, science, etc.—has at last begun to surface. For the record, women are not the only sufferers at the hands of historians. The Great Man theory of history hides not only Great Women but defines almost everyone out of greatness.

Specifically, the invisibility of women's work as organizers—which includes every woman rather than just "Great Women" (writers, scientists, painters, and so on)— itself reflects a class bias, a career bias, in the women's movement, itself perpetuates a historical censorship in another form.

The evaluation process is part of righting the historical wrong which condemns most of us, women and men, to an unimaginative and unproductive past and, by implication, to a destiny of more of the same, *by preventing the same thing from happening to the history we are making now, at this very moment.*

We are in a stronger position to do that at present than ever before. Among other things, we know (or should know) more about *how* our history is swallowed up by others with more power: how politicians live off "their" reforms which we lobbied, cajoled and pressured them into; how the media lies, distorts, trivializes, and hides altogether; how the same view out of the mouth of a white/man carries more weight than out of the mouth of the Black/woman who first worked it out. In metropolitan countries we often have literacy and weapons of our own based on that literacy which record our ideas, our struggle, our successes: leaflets, newsletters, and—much more rarely—even books.

But grassroots women (and men) don't know ourselves the history we are making, and this is the greatest deterrent to our recording it. Such lack of self-consciousness is one of the most debilitating effects of the power of education and the media against us. We must regretfully add that the Left on the whole reinforces it. Having had it drummed into us from birth that we can't influence events and must submit to authority, and having almost always been forced to submit, we are trained not to appreciate our own effect or the effect of other people like ourselves. When we do succeed in breaking out, appreciating our experiences, articulating our thoughts, we can rarely get them into recognized and widespread channels; and even then, they are almost unrecognizable: hacked to pieces, stripped of essentials, and dismissed with a sophisticated phrase implying that they are irrational ravings. Later we see them regurgitated from the mouths of journalists or others on the make as if fresh from their minds; and we sit quietly grieving, tragically defeated: the product of our struggle, our gut and our mind, robbed from us and spouted against us by those who had scoffed and jeered, to confirm our incapacity and backwardness.

This is a common experience. It is a matter of life and death for any working-class organization but especially a women's organization not to allow itself to be subverted by such intellectual imperialism and plunder.

Our actions are under similar attack. What we do, we are told, has no impact since we are just a few, or a few dozen, or a few hundred, or even—as with recent peace demonstrations—just a few hundred thousand. There are, we are told, always more on the other side, and sensible, straight, white, respectable, police-loving, work-loving people they are—*real* housewives and mothers worthy of the name, local residents, not "outside agitators" (which we are everywhere!) like us. And yet governments adjust their arguments because of these "few," but in such a way as to conceal our impact, to keep us from knowing our own power: how we made them shift, how the majority are *moved* by us, are *like* us, *are* us; how in some measure we are changing the balance of power, changing the world; how in making trouble we are making history.[11]

Our evaluation meetings aim precisely to record how much history we have made, how much power we have wielded and how much potential power we might have as a result of what we and others have done.

We and others. For in developing the habit of awareness of your own historical acquisitions and potential, you learn also to respect and understand other women's and men's struggles. You become aware, through conscious appreciation of your own experience, of the problems they had to overcome and what, despite these problems, their efforts have won, for themselves and also for you. In this way, you prevent yourself from being used to cover up others' contributions to the history of the movement—the women's movement, the immigrants' movement, the gay movement, the labor movement, etc.—the working-class movement. We have, after all, one history that we are reappropriating, protecting, recording; one tradition of struggle that we are advancing; from which common pool each of us draws our power and to which we all contribute.

But we can only protect the achievements of every sector of the movement by evaluating and quantifying from the bottom up. Although we are one, we are also many, which is less than one, less than unified. We can never afford to lose sight of the power divisions among us.

To give an example from our current experience, we are raising money for the mining communities during their present strike because we know that if they lose,

---

11 Perhaps the most convincing proof of how effective the peace movement and other movements have been is the degree of illegality the government is prepared to engage in, in order to spy on us, infiltrate, hack our phones, and who knows what else.

we all lose, and if they win, we win with them. But all the money we raise goes to the women, who then have the bargaining power of the purse strings. Miners are confronting government and police for all of us, but that does not mean that we can afford to forget the power men wield over and against women. The strike does not absolve them of wife-beating, queer-bashing, racism, etc. We insist that they acknowledge how dependent they are, and have always been, on the women of the mining communities.

Since the miners are asking for—and getting—our support for their struggle now, we will be in a better position in future to demand *their* support, but only if we establish with them now that it is on the basis of our autonomy that we support their strike. Such an *exchange of power*, where we are strengthened by what others do on their own behalf, is always taking place among sectors of the movement confronting the powers that be. What ensures that there is an exchange of power *both ways*, between the more vulnerable and those who are socially more powerful, is the autonomous organization of the less powerful. The women in the mining communities are deriving great strength from autonomous organizations of women such as ours (and say so publicly), to build their own autonomy from men and from the union: for the men as strikers on the one hand, and against the men as wife-beaters—as scabs on women—on the other. Our autonomous organizations are always involved in threading their way through this contradiction, between the slavery we share with the more powerful and their managerial relationship to us. *The work of balancing these opposites is the price of winning.*

So that the habit of identifying our own victories and claiming them, and identifying and acknowledging other people's victories, are what the evaluation meetings should achieve; a way of laying the basis for working together with others whose level of power is different from our own but whom we need in order to win. Which was the purpose of the conference in the first place: discovering common ground not between women and men, but among women, Black and white, immigrants and natives. The sectors may change. The process and the goal are always the same.

Last but by no means least, our evaluation meetings invite anyone attending to complain about and criticize any part of what anyone did, didn't do or left half done for the event. In this way, one woman can be critical of another in a direct and positive framework, which prevents necessarily negative comment from festering internally into personal resentments and rivalry. (For the record, there were a number of criticisms of colleagues' work at the conference, ranging from how the books were displayed to what time people turned up in the morning and whether they carried out jobs they had volunteered for carefully, well and promptly.)

Taking what each of us does seriously enough to spend our precious time constructively criticizing it, is another expression of our respect for each other's time and work, of our self-respect as women, and of our collectivity. In the process we set the terms of relationships among us, adjust our tactics and reexamine our division of labor. Each individual trains her judgment and becomes more autonomous, more conscious of herself as protagonist with skills and capacities—more able to stand up for herself anywhere. If political life is not also personally rewarding in this way, is not individually educative, exciting, power- and confidence-building, it is just another piece of alienating work, just another capitalist tragedy, which can lead to burnout, dropout or an excuse for careerism. So far the Wages for Housework Campaign has suffered very little from these.

THE UN DECADE FOR WOMEN: AN OFFER WE COULDN'T REFUSE (1986)

I was asked by Kofi Hadjor, founder and editor of *Third World Book Review* (London), to help with the education of his core of young African women. Young people were turning away from political involvement as the movement of the 1960s receded under Thatcher and Reagan. He decided that I should write a review of the UN Decade for Women, which the young women had dismissed as unworthy of their attention. Many European feminists had also dismissed it. But most grassroots women in the Third World would not turn down the offer of a global forum where they could meet each other, try to make their case to governments and maybe even to the media. We see over and over how those of us with the least power seize any occasion that might lift us out of economic and social desperation. The UN provided unique opportunities of that kind, especially while the Group of 77—the bloc of governments of the South—was a strong caucus within it.

Kofi thought his colleagues would not consider what a Western woman had to say, so I used the name Fahnbulleh to disguise my non-African origins, borrowed from a Liberian colleague. I never found out the impact this review had on them but having another look at that decade from the bottom up was a learning experience for me (and I hope for others).

The article first appeared in *Third World Women's News* 1 (1986).

* * *

The UN Decade for Women is over. Its last and highest drama was played out in July of 1985 when more than fifteen thousand women—some say twenty thousand— crowded onto the campus of the University of Nairobi, intent on being part of its history.

In Britain, the close of the Decade was hardly reported. A women's newspaper was dismissive, headlining with: "NAIROBI—you didn't go? me neither!" implying that lack of interest was a mark of radical feminist chic.[1]

In 1975, International Women's Year, it was widely assumed that the movement couldn't use such State initiatives without "selling out." In 1974, just a year before, a conference on population, with the prominent input of the Rockefeller family, had planned how many children women's bodies would be allowed or coerced into produc- ing according to their color, country and class. Was the Decade to provide window- dressing for such plans? Or, worse, was it an exercise to get us to work even harder? We knew the Decade for Women was a result of the rise of the women's movement, but it was organized by governments, not the movement. Could we use it? Could we even prevent it from using us?

The Decade's themes—"Equality, Development, Peace"—reflected the usual UN *ménage à trois.* "Equality" reflected the U.S. self-image as the land of equal opportu- nity. It also verbalized the aspirations of its powerful career feminist lobby (which had won a female vice-presidential candidate in 1984 and which, as we shall see, includes the president's daughter). "Peace" was shorthand for the image the Soviets promote, according to which women have no problems internal to that society, only those imposed by external enemies. (The Soviet government had the audacity to claim this throughout the Decade even as Soviet women were describing how they "suffer from equality.")[2] Symbolically sandwiched between these two was "Development," which summed up the aspirations of Third World governments.

This consensus on themes for the Decade, like much else in power politics, could only be achieved by imprecision. For example, to whom are the poorest of the Third World's women to be equal? Third World men?

Mexico 1975

This obvious and crucial question was raised obliquely at the first UN World Conference of Women, held in International Women's Year (Mexico City, June 19– July 2, 1975), when the Decade was formally agreed. (It began officially on January 1, 1976.) Mexican President Echeverria at the opening session asked, what good was it "to recognize solemnly that all women have an equal right to education and

---

1   *Outwrite Women's Newspaper,* July–August 1985. The British government seemed to work overtime for women in Britain not to know about the Decade. Four of the six UK delegates to Nairobi were members of the House of Lords, which has to be a government statement of contempt for us lesser mortals.

2   Carola Hansson and Karin Liden, *Moscow Women: Thirteen Interviews* (London: Allison & Busby, 1985), 24.

employment if these requirements cannot be satisfied in most parts of the world?" He pointed for answers to the New International Economic Order which the Group of 77—the Third World bloc at the UN—had passed in 1974, a program for economic independence from imperialism as Third World governments define it. This document was to be referred to many times in the Women's Decade as embodying the economic changes that we would want to see. Not insignificantly, it doesn't mention women.

The Mexico conference, chaired by a man, agreed a World Plan of Action drafted in a committee chaired by a woman. But the woman was Princess Ashraf Pahlavi of Iran, sister of the Shah. Nevertheless, concerns of grassroots women traditionally ignored by governments found their way into the World Plan. Paragraph 46, for example, which listed what the World Plan aimed to achieve in the Decade, included *Recognition of the economic value of women's work in the home, in domestic food production and marketing, and in voluntary activities not traditionally remunerated.*

Much of the World Plan spoke to those concerned primarily with changing "social attitudes" rather than the economic order. But recognizing "the economic value of women's work" spoke also to women who might deny they were feminists and to a women's movement which doesn't call itself that—in other words, to most of the world's women whose first concern is how hard they work, and how this invisible work keeps them poor. Over and over, the Decade confirmed that this overwork and poverty were the major issues for women worldwide.

How did such a paragraph, representing as it did the concerns of the disenfranchised majority of women, manage to get past the Princess and others like her? The answer to that question holds the key to how women made use of the Decade. But that the paragraph did get past her establishes first of all that women did make use of it.

The Tribune Was the Movement Talking to the Movement

There was other evidence too that the women of the world were entering "their" Decade. The UN's Economic and Social Council confers "consultative status" on nongovernmental organizations (NGOs), which can show that they represent significant interest groups in the international community, and that their aims enhance those of the UN. (The YWCA, for example, has consultative status.) A committee of such women's NGOs organized the Tribune, an alternative meeting to run parallel with the official conference in Mexico City. Over six thousand women from all over the world beamed in on this Tribune, turning it into the largest meeting ever held by and about women. While Saudi Arabia's misogynist views ("Women have more equality than men...") were tolerated at the official conference, the Tribune was the movement talking to the movement.

Or at least some strata of the movement. After all, who could afford to go? Many had of course come from the United States, the host country's imperial neighbor north of the border. Others came from further afield. The backbone, however, were Mexican women and other Latinas, some of them grassroots women whose fares had been paid by grant aid. Sensing the unique power of their numbers, the Tribune participants demanded that the official conference be accountable to them, and publicized their conviction that women's issues are inseparable from economic and political reality (which the U.S. government in particular spent the Decade denying).

This the first international women's meeting also confronted a basic conflict within the organized women's movement everywhere, between women faced with dire poverty and overwork, and women who have a secure economic base. The more powerful (who in Mexico City were by no means exclusively metropolitan women) inevitably raise issues which, when not connected or proportioned to others' poverty, may seem a luxury. If you are on the poverty line, you defend yourself from such issues, not because you are not interested in (for example) sexual choices, but because these concerns feel like—and often are—an attack on your priorities, pushing your survival down, even off, the agenda. On the other hand, defending your survival priorities may take the form of an attack on sexual choices, or higher education, or divorce rights— none of which you have the economic power even to contemplate. In Mexico City, there was a bitter clash of priorities, which, though muted in the rest of the Decade, was never stilled.

Women Facing Dire Poverty Clashed with Women Who Had a Secure Economic Base

In fact this open clash was unique: the grassroots woman has had little chance to confront the more privileged woman with her own global perspective, and this clash won something. By the 1980 Mid-Decade Conference, women like Domitila Barrios de Chúngara, an organizer of the Housewives Committee among Bolivian miners' wives, who first caught public attention in Mexico, had become an international point of reference.[3]

The Mid-Decade event was originally to be in Iran. (How much did Princess Ashraf's high placed lobbying have to do with that?) A revolution intervened.

---

3   Having heard her speak in Mexico, Moema Viezzer helped Domitila (as she is known) to write an account of her life and a statement of her views. This has been translated into many languages (published in English as *Let me Speak!* [London: Stage 1, 1978]). It was in fact Domitila who led the attack at Mexico City against the women who prioritized lesbianism ("Those weren't my interests"); who considered men the enemy; and "who defend prostitution, birth control, and all those things, [who] wanted to impose their ideas as basic problems to be discussed in the Tribunal. For us they were real problems, but not the main ones. For example, when they spoke of birth control, they said that we shouldn't have so many children living in such poverty, because we didn't even have enough to feed them. And they wanted to see birth control as something which would solve all the problems of humanity and malnutrition…our government prefers to see things their way, to justify the low level of life of the Bolivian people and the very low wages it pays the workers. And so they resort to indiscriminate birth control." (*Let Me Speak!*, 198)

Times had changed in other ways. The news was out that the Decade conferences were ideal for picking up information and for "networking." Exactly what that meant to different sectors of women varied greatly, as we hope to make clear.

Copenhagen 1980

For all kinds of reasons, Copenhagen, the city chosen, attracted over eight thousand women to the NGO event, now named the Forum. Among these were European grassroots organizers who had scraped the fare together (the price of an air ticket to Mexico had ruled it out of bounds to most Europeans, but Copenhagen was accessible to the mainland by car and ferry), as well as representatives of women's organizations and government-sponsored academics and politicians from many Third World countries.

The sharpest and most pervasive clash at the NGO Forum was between Third World and metropolitan women. Fiercest on the question of Zionism, it emerged on many other issues.

Female circumcision for example. Some metropolitan feminists proposed a campaign against it with little or no reference to the women most affected. No doubt this arrogance was encouraged by the knowledge that such imperialism-cum-charity can easily get Establishment approval and therefore funding.[4] But with the power of an international arena, African and Arab women kept the leadership of their own struggle. Circumcision as a Western feminist money spinner and power trip was, at least temporarily, held at bay.

Unlike both sex tourism and "female sexual slavery." "Concerned sisters" are still working hand in glove with Interpol and every other repressive and reactionary force, to prevent mainly South Asian women from crossing national boundaries to work as prostitutes, or to prevent men crossing, bringing money to be their clients. These feminists devote themselves to raising the morals—and removing the financial choices—of the poorest. They rarely if ever attack either the economic circumstances which make prostitution an attractive or even the only choice, or the institutionalized pimping and persecution of prostitutes by the police and other powerful forces.

Feminist academics and moralists were supported by the substantial contingent of Japanese women—who, though excited to escape traditional submission, seemed determined to preserve a traditional power: keeping husbands and incomes at home. They had big workshops against prostitution tourism from Japan to Thailand or Korea,

---

4   *Newsweek*, in their issue of July 22, 1985, during the Nairobi conference, showed how useful such issues are to imperial capitalism: "longstanding cultural traditions—dowry systems, female infanticide and religious prohibitions against family planning—have kept women in developing nations centuries behind their counterparts in the developed world." The exploitation of women is not perpetrated by multinationals but "cultural traditions"! What *Newsweek* doesn't say is that these traditions are a form of political repression of women which imperialism has promoted and strengthened to ensure its own domination of both women and men.

where the women are poorer and less powerful than themselves. Travel on behalf of another Japanese tradition—imperialism in Asia, which had helped impoverish these women—had no critics.

Whatever the motive, and many contradictory ones were comfortable in tandem, the zealous activity to "protect" Third World women from tapping metropolitan men's money had to be seen to be believed. The workshops of the International Prostitutes Collective, which pulled together the strong presence of prostitute women, from Brazil to West Germany, attracted the largest crowds but couldn't defeat the anti–sex tourism/propolice lobby. There is too much ambiguity in the Third World itself about women, moralism and money.[5]

African and Arab Women Kept the Leadership of Their Own Struggle

The confrontation over Zionism pervaded both the Forum and the official government conference. At the Forum, arrogant Israeli women, some occasionally accompanied by men they obviously aimed to please, clashed with Arab women in all kinds of workshops and events. Third World/left-wing women supported Palestine. Middle-class Jewish-American women, taken aback by the universal hostility of the Third World presence to their support for the Israeli State, had to be regularly reassured at State Department briefings, whose line was: let's discuss women, not politics—in other words, not Zionism.[6]

Anti-Zionism could have been even more effective. At a UN conference on women, the Palestinian and other liberation struggles were on the whole still not presented from the point of view of women, even when presented by women. It is self-defeating in any context for a liberation movement not to spell out the crushing weight of work, poverty and subservience to which planned underdevelopment and

---

5   That is to say, those who defend the violence and immorality of poverty do so by steering clear of the issue and instead attack as immoral the ways the impoverished find to survive. However, there is a growing body of literature which takes a more realistic point of view. See for example Khin Thitsa, *Providence and Prostitution: Image and Reality for Women in Buddhist Thailand* (London: Change, 1982) and Janet M. Bujra, "Production, Property, Prostitution: Sexual Politics in Yumbe [Kenya], in *Third World Lives of Struggle,* ed. H. Johnson and H. Bernstein (London: Heinemann/Open University, 1982). See also documents of the English Collective of Prostitutes, particularly about Copenhagen. See also petition circulated in Nairobi calling for the release of imprisoned street workers in Kenya. "The prostitutes of Kenya's 'Sunshine City' have not been asked to send any delegates to neither the Non-Governmental Nairobi Forum nor the official UN Conference. Instead they have for the last two weeks been systematically chased by Kenya police and put behind bars." The women who organized the petition were nameless, but the International Prostitutes Collective circulated it and five hundred non-Kenya and a few brave Kenya sisters put their names to it. It was passed anonymously to Margaret Kenyatta, chair of the official conference, via the press.

6   The Heritage Foundation, a CIA think tank, published a document, "A U.S. Policy for the U.N. Conference on Women," photocopies of which were fairly widely circulated before Nairobi. Keep politics out of women's affairs, it said.

imperial conquest and occupation have reduced women in particular. Keeping women's specific interests invisible inhibits the specific attack on imperialism which only Third World women can make, and only Third World women can rally other women to join.

Despite this weakness in the Third World camp, to which we will return, the visibility of Third World women's concerns was increasing.

Women Do Two-Thirds of the World's Work

Factual papers and surveys—only eighteen in Mexico—proliferated in Copenhagen, many describing rural women's condition: the hours spent daily fetching fuel and water, the absence of women's health care and of help with seed, advice, technology... The UN figure, that women do two-thirds of the world's work for 10 percent of the income and 1 percent of the assets appeared for the first time. It had come from the International Labour Office (ILO), a UN associate organization based in Geneva, in particular from its Office of Women Workers' Questions. The editorial of the first issue of its *Newsbulletin*, prepared for Copenhagen, and edited by Krishna Ahooja-Patel from India, had this to say:

> Most women are permanently working, but not permanently employed in the workforce. It is this difference between work and employment which is a major issue today. That they constitute half of the population is a demographic fact. That they perform one-third of the total work hours in the market is also making an entry into official statistics. More recent calculations based on ILO and UN data show that women receive about 5 percent of the world's income; and that their income is so low that most women have no margin for saving and hence for any assets. Therefore, they have no independent control of directing income-generating activity. If quantified, it would not be surprising that they own perhaps not even 1 percent of reproducible world assets.

Beyond the market, inequalities get even sharper when the nonmarket activity of women is brought into the picture. There, their input of labor amounts to twice as many work hours as in the market. It is this large chunk of unpaid labor that the market has not measured nor has society recognized. What is the size of the problem? What is the nature of women's work? To what extent and degree do they participate in the economy? In what manner are they economically rewarded and what are the tasks they perform in society as "free services"?[7]

The reader will notice that the ILO figures were somewhat modified by the UN: the 5 percent of income raised to 10 percent for no visible reason. Even so, they remain a brief but uniquely relevant description of the basics of life for women. Some women took it upon themselves to single out these figures from among dozens of others, and publicize them, first at the Forum and then everywhere.

---

7   *Women at Work*, ILO Newsbulletin 1 (1980): v.

Daily Meetings of Hundreds

The Forum, peppered with political activists who had digested the experience of Mexico in the following five years of the growth of the women's movement, offered a more organized challenge to the government conference than the 1975 Tribune had done. Within a few days, there were daily meetings of hundreds to work out how to directly influence the official meeting. Out of these meetings came the Issues Committee, which compiled any and all demands Forum women wished the assembled governments to consider. Lucille Mair, Jamaican spokeswoman for the Group of 77 in Mexico, and now chair of the government conference in Copenhagen, welcomed a meeting with the Issues Committee, accepting and acknowledging their comprehensive list of concerns. This committee, coordinated by Wilmette Brown, an Afro-American, had both a Jewish woman and an Arab woman who worked well together—though they would not be photographed next to each other. There is much to be learnt from this vignette of one sober and successful little committee.

The Program of Action, basic document of the official government conference, carried forward the demand raised in Mexico on recognition of the unremunerated work women do, with two important changes. First, it aimed to count in the gross national product women's work "in the home, on the farm and in other fields," which was invisible—without remuneration or quantification. Second, the term "worker" was to be redefined to include women who do this invisible work. Adding agricultural work and targeting the GNP transformed the relevance of the 1975 proposal.

It was not passed, but it had a unifying impact among many diverse groups at the Forum. And it was not forgotten.

A lot of cash and prestige accrue to a country that is chosen as the site for a major international event. Kenya won the tender for the final Decade conference. It had advantages for governments of both East and West even over the Shah's Iran: not only a repressive regime with Third World credentials but also, as the center for the UN in Africa, a bureaucratic infrastructure—photocopying and other rudimentary information technology plus appropriate creature comforts such as restaurants with international cuisine. On the pretext that Kenya lacked adequate accommodation for thousands of women, and probably in response to how near the 1980 NGO Forum got to influencing the official government conference, there was an attempt to dispense with the NGO event in 1985. But it was soon clear that at least ten thousand women had registered to invade Nairobi if they had to bring tents, many of them Americans of African descent who were delighted to combine a trip "back to Africa" with a chance to make common cause with other Third World sisters. The British and other governments which had worked hard to exclude the women of the world from their own decade conference, retreated.

Nairobi 1985

In the event, the Forum attendance was between fifteen and twenty thousand, of which Kenya women were about four thousand strong: the determination of local Kenya women to use this world gathering of women on their doorstep was born of a desperation far greater than that of local Danish women at Copenhagen. Cleaners and caterers at the University of Nairobi, where the Forum was held, as well as participants from the countryside, went out of their way to make contact, to register their presence, even to thank us for coming. Kenya women were "slaves," they said; they work so hard and the men have so much power over them, which the government upholds. The presence of thousands of women, they said, would leave them stronger. A surprising number of Nairobi women had read the novels in Gikuyu of the banned Kenya writer, Ngugi wa Thiong'o, which describe the sexual and other exploitation of women in Kenya by the new ruling class and by men in general. These women engaged immediately with all the issues usually considered "Western": from wages for housework to peace to sexual choices. For example, the lesbian workshops, which the Kenya government tried to ban,[8] were packed with African women asking the most explicit questions. Here as everywhere, Third World women showed their determination to know all that the world had to offer, every choice, every possibility. The Dutch women led in the presentation of lesbian issues. But whereas in Holland you can still get away with lesbian separatism, no one at the Forum suggested that lesbianism was a strategy for liberation. Not in Nairobi. In Nairobi, only the wealthy and those they have corrupted would dare ignore women's poverty and overwork as the central issue.

The Campus Swarmed with Armed Police

African women were ready for everything. The problem was that Kenya women in particular were gagged. It is illegal in Kenya to criticize the government. To minimize the impact of thousands of women from all over the world on the police State of Kenya, the campus swarmed with police armed not only with hand weapons but machine guns. Even workshops were not out of bounds to armed men. Report after report of Nairobi, verbal and written, has omitted this. In Nairobi, women from the Women's International Democratic Federation even expressed gratitude for the Kenya government's "protection." Demonstrations against the Marcos dictatorship in the Philippines which was still in power, or against the Contras in Nicaragua—even against *apartheid*—none was permitted to flow off the campus and into the streets, into the consciousness of the media, of the official conference, of the people of Kenya.

The wide participation of academia seemed to be another part of the strategy to keep the Forum contained and its impact smothered: local women did not have the

---

8   But which Dame Nita Barrow, convener of the Forum, did not allow the authorities to do. In fact Dame Nita kept remarkable order with a relatively light touch.

power to challenge the government, and academics were not about to. Workshops abounded on development, research, etc., where those who had studied, were studying, or for the right fee would be glad to study anybody anywhere, could compare references and enhance job prospects. There was also a wide presence of the social planning and welfare industries, such as migrant and refugee services, planned parenthood, adult education. Workshops now were multicultural: academics were far more integrated across national and racial boundaries than at Copenhagen. But though the Decade had made it impossible for metropolitan professional women to exclude Third World women from academic and service industries, little else had changed: the view from the bottom—whether Third World or metropolitan—was still hard to find. When found, it was dynamite.

Introducing a workshop on "Linking Research and Training with Activist Groups: Who Sets the Agenda?" the chair said that academics needed activist links to do research on rural women properly. But there was a speaker whose starting point was not what academics needed. Ela Bhatt, founder of the Self Employed Women's Association (SEWA) of India, with about forty thousand members—home-based pieceworkers and street-based vendors, hawkers, laborers, etc.—described how SEWA had made academia useful to those whom it makes a living by observing and analyzing. "Experts call them 'unorganized sectors,'" said Ms. Bhatt, "but I wouldn't."

Most Research Doesn't Aim to Forge Weapons for Women's Struggle

Here are some notes on her stunning ten-minute presentation:

> We started surveys and questionnaires for ourselves to know more about the women. In this way, we gathered data about their living conditions and gave it to the press. It was the first time public attention was drawn to these women, which helped make us visible. Since the investigators were from the same community, the same women who were being questioned, that gave us more credibility and also helped us when we called meetings, because everyone had been visited in their own home by an investigator. It was a two-way process. As we did the survey, they got to know us and then could see that the women who did the survey are now coming back to do something about it. It wasn't "research." When we saw the survey results, we needed university help. For example, amongst the hand-cart pullers, we found several cases of miscarriage and then we approached the Health Institute to redesign hand-carts. The academics took ages but they did it… Another example. The police stopped a woman with an overloaded cart and broke her knees with the impact. For the first time a woman went to court for compensation. A test case. The court was favorable but wanted a basis for calculating compensation. So we went to the university for a study of a fair wage

for cart pullers, and they gave us 25 rupees which we couldn't win. We told them
to bring down their valuation to 15 rupees, and we won that.

Most research did not aim, as SEWA's did, to forge weapons for working-class women's struggle. Nevertheless, by the end of a decade which had been a bonanza for academics, there had been gathered—and we could appropriate—the most massive and irrefutable statistical evidence about women ever assembled. On almost any conceivable scale of measurement, we had the proof that women contributed far more to society than men and got less back.

The Facts of Life for the World's Women Poured Out

From lasting childbirth debilities to lack of contraception (50 million abortions a year), from twice the work to more malnourishment and higher death rates of infant girls, from lower rates of schooling to higher rates of illiteracy, from lack of land rights to lack of inheritance rights, from most of the unwaged work to the lowest-waged work, no area of private or public life in any country treats a woman with the respect, rights or social esteem of her father, husband, brother, son—no matter how little these receive, she receives less. The UN statistic from Copenhagen was the starting point of many papers, including the official UN document, *The State of the World's Women 1985*.

For the first time in history [in International Women's Year, 1975] the eyes of the world were focused on that half of its population who, by virtue of an accident of birth, perform two-thirds of the world's work, receive one tenth of its income and own less than one hundredth of its property... Over the last year the United Nations has been compiling the results of a questionnaire completed by 121 governments reviewing and appraising the position of women in their countries. At the same time United Nations' agencies have themselves been amassing a fund of independent research from all over the world to complete the picture. The results of these two parallel investigations are summarized in this Report on *The State of the World's Women 1985*.

The findings reveal: that women do almost all the world's domestic work which, together with their additional work outside the home, means most women work a double day; that women grow around half of the world's food, but own hardly any land, find it difficult to get loans and are overlooked by agricultural advisors and projects; that women are one third of the world's official labor force, but are concentrated in the lowest-paid occupations and are more vulnerable to unemployment than men; that, although there are some signs that the wage gap is closing slightly, women still earn less than three quarters of the wage of men doing similar work; that women provide more health care than all the health services put together...

The results point, again and again, to the major underlying cause of women's inequality. A woman's domestic role as a wife and mother—which is vital to the well-being of the whole of society, which consumes around half of her time and her energy—is unpaid and undervalued.

The Famine Stretched to Within Fifty Miles of Nairobi

Women's groups, churches, think tanks, and universities also poured out the facts of women's lives, in documents, booklets, charts, and posters, illustrating the outrageous, even killing, length of their working day and other key statistics.[9]

This mass of data began finally to overflow into the age-old information vacuum, making it impossible any longer to deny women's relation to "political issues": how over and over women's suffering proves to be the key to children's and men's suffering, and how tackling women's disadvantage proves to be the key to Third World survival. Take the famine: "It is now becoming clear that a factor contributing to Africa's acute food shortage is the way women have been systematically excluded from access to land and from control of modern agriculture."[10]

Patches of that famine stretched down to within fifty miles of the government conference in Nairobi, but it was not debated at that conference. Why not? Could one reason have been that a major cause of the famine—the gross disadvantage of women farmers, not least in Kenya—made spelling out the "female connection" too explosive? Whatever the reason, the African Establishment, rooted in part in men's power over land ownership and use, got off easy. So did the multinationals, which thrive on this power relation between African women and men. And so did the governments of the North, which didn't have to put their hands in their pockets.

South African Women's Autonomy Will Transform Every Women's Movement Worldwide

The chador on the face of history also concealed women's contribution to the struggle. Oliver Tambo, speaking for the African National Congress in Nairobi, pledged to destroy *apartheid* "so that South African women can join their sisters in the long march to Equality, Development and Peace." Many of us know that the *apartheid* State requires that an African woman's passbook is signed by husband or son, giving African men a secondary but significant share in its power over her movements. We have noted the silence of liberation movements on all such issues where men allow their power over women to be used by the imperial State to divide and rule them both; and are quite aware of one of its consequences: that South African women, for example, must invest much energy into defending themselves against African men on the *apartheid* chain of command. Once our anti-imperialist politics begin with women, we can see how, in the painful years before the 1985 explosion, it was women from Crossroads and other squatter towns who kept the fire of revolt public and

---

9 Of course there were also the glossy self-congratulatory brochures produced by governments on how well "their" women had done and how much credit they could take for it. But these have not lasted. On the other hand, Decade documents such as *The State of the World's Women 1985* have become reference works.

10 *The State of the World's Women*, 6.

massified. Are these heroines really still to "join their sisters" or have their struggles been providing leadership to their sisters as well as—pardon me—their brothers? Is anyone ready to welcome—and defend—the tidal wave of South African women's autonomy, which is so obviously on the way, and which will help transform every women's movement worldwide?

The state of emergency in South Africa was declared just before the Nairobi conference. The United States knew it could not avoid a direct attack on apartheid in *Forward Looking Strategies for the Advancement of Women to the Year 2000,* the final Decade document which was debated by the government conference. But the question of Zionism was still negotiable.

Anti-Zionism in the Peace Tent

Zionism had been an explosive issue in Forum workshops. It even exploded in the Peace Tent, which called itself "the International Feminist Alternative to Men's Conflict and War."When Fawzia Hassouna, a Palestinian activist, invited three Jewish women to join her on a panel of four, and one of them, Selma James, called Zionism "the theory and practice of imperialism and racism," pro-Zionist women dropped their pursuit of peace. That Israel was trading in arms with both El Salvador and South Africa had even its supporters embarrassed.

At the government conference, Nawal El Saadawi led a walkout of Arab women when Israel rose to speak at the plenary session. It was clear that the final vote on *Forward Looking Strategies* would be a cliffhanger. The impasse was the usual: Maureen Reagan, appointed by her father to head the U.S. delegation, made clear that the paragraph equating Zionism with racism was not acceptable. The chair, Margaret Kenyatta, another daughter of a famous father and his spitting image, during a recess asked the Soviet Union and the Group of 77 if they would drop the word Zionism for the sake of consensus to get *Forward Looking Strategies* agreed.[11] How many promises and threats bought that consensus we cannot know. We do know that the Soviet Union politely deferred to Kenya, its Third World host; and once it had, the Group of 77 acquiesced.

It must be noted that at an international conference on women which was split on the question of Zionism, the specific situation of Palestinian—or indeed Israeli—women as women hardly arose. In addition, while there were women in the PLO delegation (which had observer status at the government conference), in the final confrontation that last night, the caucus was male and aged over fifty. Patriarchs.

Counting Women's Unremunerated Work

Still, the passage of *Forward Looking Strategies* at 5 a.m., Saturday, July 27, was a victory. It contains 372 paragraphs, many of which women will be working to implement in

---

11 Jomo Kenyatta, the first prime minister of independent Kenya.

the coming years. Paragraph 120 in particular, calling for official measurement of women's staggering load of work, and therefore recognition of this enormous but invisible economic and social contribution, has already been singled out.

Nairobi was the last chance to commit governments internationally to counting women's work. The Wages for Housework Campaign had been working on this since before Mexico: it was they who had lifted the two-thirds figure from one of a number of statistics in Copenhagen, to international prominence. In Nairobi, while WFH was spreading the word at the Forum ("Women Count—Count Women's Work"), Housewives in Dialogue (HinD), an NGO which had just got consultative status, was at the government conference tackling (amongst others) Paragraph 120. After infighting in pre-Nairobi preparatory committees, the issue of quantifying women's work had emerged vaguer and weaker than in Mexico and Copenhagen. But despite having been warned that Paragraph 120 would never be passed if the GNP was put back into it, HinD women presented to almost all of the over 150 government delegations an amended Paragraph 120 which now read:

> The remunerated and, in particular, the unremunerated contributions of women
> to all aspects and sectors of development should be recognized, and appropriate
> efforts should be made to measure and reflect these contributions in national
> accounts and economic statistics and in the gross national product. Concrete
> steps should be taken to quantify the unremunerated contribution of women to
> agriculture, food production, reproduction and household activities.

The delegates, now mainly women (they were mostly men in Mexico), had little trouble grasping the usefulness and urgency of acknowledging, by measuring, women's contribution to each national economy. But the Soviet Union seemed to be militantly hostile to any mention of the workload of the liberated socialist woman. And the United States was just as hostile to quantifying the workload of the liberated American woman—and also determined not to give Third World women any quantification of *their* exploitation, which could inspire claims against imperialist wealth. No country dependent on either power wanted to be seen championing the amendment. At the last moment, Rosalind Forde, delegate from Sierra Leone, with great tact, put it forward. And once it was put on the table, no one wanted to be seen opposing. Seconded by women delegates from Jordan and Uganda, it was agreed.

Many rejoiced, and even Betty Friedan, who rarely praises what she hasn't proposed, admitted this was the central victory of Nairobi.

Forward Looking Strategies was ratified by the General Assembly of the UN in New York on November 19, 1985. Because of its importance to Third World women in particular, some governments and NGOs want Paragraph 120 singled out for implementation. Because of its popularity, Maureen Reagan is on the one hand publicly claiming it as her own (despite informal U.S. opposition in Nairobi) and on the other privately trying to delay implementation.[12] *A luta continua.*

Was the Decade worthwhile? It was, to those who have least and who dare not bypass any chance to register their claims; to those who participated in the Decade in order to build an international movement; and to those who were rewarded with the visible growth, at every Decade event, national and international, of networks among the grassroots. The Decade made us an offer which gave us a chance. Most of us can't afford to refuse a chance—we have too few—even when it comes booby-trapped in invitations from governments.

A Growing Women's Movement in Cities, Towns, and Villages

The UN is not a government but a coalition of governments where many forces meet in its committees and its corridors to bargain their agendas. A few women—some, nameless international civil servants; others, famous individuals or representing prestigious organizations, even governments—saw the Decade as their chance to slip some home truths into the official records, to champion the cause of working-class women, grassroots women, rural women—whose voices never echo in the corridors of power.

The Decade also inspired some grassroots women themselves, inexperienced in the use of official statements, documents and statistics, to learn the skills of influencing those who walk those corridors, from verbal confrontation to written statement, to the most delicate lobbying, as appropriate. After a decade of practice, some now could gracefully—and effectively—tiptoe through the minefield of international power blocs without losing either their heads or their grassroots purpose. These women derived their strength from the thousands who flocked to meet each other at three international gatherings and numerous national and local events all over the world, and from a growing women's movement in cities, towns and villages everywhere. The UN organized the Decade for governments but, despite what cynics say, the women of the world also used it for themselves.

---

12 It was opposed by Allen Keyes, Maureen Reagan's second in command in the U.S. delegation. An Afro-American, it was rumored that shortly after the conference he took a job helping South Africa with its public image.

THE CHALLENGE OF DIVERSITY: REFLECTIONS ON A CONFERENCE (1990)

As part of a North American tour in the spring of 1990, I was asked to sum up a conference of the Women's Studies departments of the Claremont Colleges, at Scripps College in Los Angeles (The Challenge of Diversity—Race, Ethnicity, Class, and Gender in Higher Education, March 24, 1990). About three hundred people attended. My summation provoked some very plain speaking from the audience. It also inspired the formation of an organizing group to deal with some troubling and unresolved racist incidents in employment, in the recent past.

* * *

It's hard to know precisely how to be useful, but while commenting and perhaps being critical, I wanted to say from the start that though guilt is often a component of discussion on racism or sexism, my aim is not to guilt-trip anybody. I don't think guilt is constructive.

I think what I was trying to find out as I sat listening hard is what you were trying to do here these two days: what you thought of the establishments you work in as teachers or as students, and what if anything you were trying to make happen in them. But I had to consider the context of the conference.

You are living and working in the greatest imperial power the world has ever known. There has been little or no recognition at this conference that this is the United States, which is now coming together with the USSR (and maybe others) to form the *United State*, which will dominate the entire world, manipulate the mind to manipulate the wealth of the entire world. And if your work as teacher, as learner, as explorer, as observer, as protestor, as initiator—as changer of yourself and others— is being done in the *United State*, then you have some serious problems because on the whole that State will try to fund only what helps it or at least doesn't challenge it. (More of this later.) And so the other consideration that I felt was missing in the discussion yesterday, at least in the plenary sessions, was money. It's not a dirty word, especially for those of us who don't have much. [Laughter and applause]

There is often the view in academia that once you mention money, you're no longer discussing the higher things of life. But a lot of us have no choice because since we haven't got enough money, the higher things may be withheld from us. You were discussing power yesterday without discussing money. It's impossible to discuss power seriously without discussing money, since money is, according to Marx, the "universal equivalent," the embodiment of social power. You may think that it shouldn't be, but it is. These seem to me to be important elements of the context within which to evaluate our deliberations.

Another element is the lies which surround us everywhere. Now I am of this soil, but as the sister has said, I've lived away since 1955, in Britain and for five years in the West Indies. And from outside, the United States looks very different from how it looks inside. (I see the sister from Cuba shaking her head in agreement.) It looks very different. And when we walked here for the first time, Margaret Prescod and I, we admired the beautiful shrubbery on campus—there's an assumption that the ivory tower of academia is surrounded by beauty and tranquility so you can think.[1] In fact it's so you won't think! [Laughter] It can divide you from the world; it can ghettoize you.

And there was not enough awareness, I think, during the conference of what you are being deprived of if you in academia are cut off from those of us who are outside, from the whole world outside. There is a causal relationship between our being and our consciousness: the world we experience *in general* tends to shape what we think and think about, especially if we do not consciously act to mitigate the power of that tendency. Academia seems to imply, if it doesn't state baldly, that you are uniquely capable of rising above your being, above your actual circumstances. During the conference I didn't hear a great deal about people's actual experiences, which does tend to imply that you considered they were not material to what we were discussing. I'm going to mention a few issues that must be basic to your circumstances.

No small matter: what are you funded to do? Are you doing it? Do you want to do it? If you don't, can you avoid doing it? That, it seems to me, has to be asked.[2] I

---

1 Margaret Prescod of Women of Color in the Global Women's Strike, Los Angeles, who had arranged for me to sum up the conference.

2 "Scientists, in exchange for funding, agree to be on call. Given this arrangement it's no wonder that the Government promulgates the image of scientists as objective and detached; this only enhances the

realize that asking those questions in this way I am no longer talking to everybody. That was the problem I had this morning trying to get this summary together: how can I talk to everybody? In fact I can't. I'm talking to those people who want to tackle these serious questions. That's how it is. And to give you some idea of the unreal image of the world which is presented to us in the media and everywhere around us, which discourages any serious probing (it's really getting to me, I haven't been back in the United States since 1987; I thought it was bad then), I see my Black granddaughter learning race relations from the *Bill Cosby Show*. This is deeply upsetting. [Laughter] This Care Bears reading of life in these United States creates enormous difficulty if you're trying to explore even the most obvious areas of your own reality.

For example, this conference was called The Challenge of Diversity. But we've been discussing *divisions*, not diversity. And when divisions are called "diversity," the problems become cultural and no one need address how and why we are divided, because we are not divided; we are "diverse": we differ merely in cultural premises or practices. But some of these "cultural" premises and practices are racist. And some are sexist. And they often undermine people at the university, let alone people outside. So how can you avoid naming the divisions among us as part of addressing what to do about them?

I had some difficulty in a workshop yesterday because I got the impression that although people saw that sexism and racism were connected, the way they saw the connection gave no overall picture of the society. This frustrates people who want more than descriptions, who want change. I'll try to explain what I mean.

What we've been trying to do in the International Wages for Housework Campaign is to develop a unified view of the world, that is, a holistic view of all the divisions among us and how they connect, in order to build the movement to undermine these divisions. That's different from assuming that there is one track for race, and a parallel track for gender and a parallel track for sexual preference, and one for disability. And one track for those of us who are white-haired and therefore can't think anymore. And one for those of us who are very young and therefore haven't thought yet. And one track for those of us who are teachers. And one for those of us who are students. And yet another for lesbian students, and who are single mothers, and who have just got off welfare or are going to get on it as soon as we finish our course.

---

values of science as a source of legitimacy for public policies. In fact, though, research priorities, laboratory practices and scientific hierarchies are all shaped by scientists' endless quest for research funds and, ultimately, by what the Government is willing to pay for... Co-opted by the state, scientists are little inclined to question research priorities and their relevance to social needs. Highly vulnerable, they are unlikely to use their power to challenge the state's controversial policies." Dorothy Nelkin, "Scientists in a Golden Cage," *The New York Times Book Review*, April 8, 1990 (review of *A Fragile Power: Scientists and the State*, by Chandra Mukerji [Princeton University Press]).

We are divided in many, many ways. Economic divisions must result in diversity of habit and practice, what we eat, how we dress, etc. Naming and examining those divisions, we can come to a unified conception of the real relations among us, both subtle and stark.

There was the view expressed here (and it is widely held everywhere) that those who work at a university as students or teachers are not workers. I wonder why you think that. Do you not work? Some of the work you do is for wages, some work is unwaged, but either way it's work you do.[3]

Basic to exploring divisions is finding your relationship to other people who work. The hierarchy of race is pervasive, and some of us know a lot about it; it can provide a handle into how the hierarchy of a divided society operates in relation to everyone. We're talking about divisions of sex, race, class, etc., which comprise a hierarchy of work and wealth. The more wealth you have, the less work you must do. We know that. And the people at the bottom have least and must do most, and they're women and children of color. The place to start to undermine and attack the hierarchy is where you are, but with awareness of and in synch with how it is being attacked and undermined, from the bottom up—because liberation doesn't come from the top down.

For example, the reason that there are Women's Studies and Black Studies and Latino Studies in universities is that starting in the 1960s and '70s people outside began to demand that the mess of racism and then sexism practiced and taught here be cleaned up. And we can be eternally grateful to those movements and always be accountable to them for what we do here. The people inside did plenty, but the initiative and the power of negation of the old and repressive poured in from outside, most especially from the movements of people of color. Some of those "outsiders" were then let in (often to cool them out, but that's another story). This history seems temporarily to have sunk without trace, but it will surface again.

The women's movement has resulted in some women getting careers in colleges, in the media, and in organizations which claim to monitor and lobby on behalf of justice. Through plans like this, "women's wages"—sexism—are structured into and enforced by the institutions of the Establishment, including those which now have women highly placed within them, even heading them. We have heard nothing from any of these women, feminists or not, in protest against this con or others like it. Rather than refusing the Establishment plan based on sexism (or racism or...), women have often lent it credibility by their silent presence. Their acquiescent presence is part of their job.

---

3   "In the City University [of New York] something called the Seek Program was established...largely for poor students and minorities. The vast majority of them were women, including women on welfare... Beginning in 1966, every few weeks these students would receive some wages, a stipend...for going to school. 'Just for going to school.' But that's another full-time job." Prescod, *Black Women*, 31.

So what we have to consider very carefully is the answer to the question: what are we doing here? Are we rubber-stamping here? Are we becoming, while professing to principle, even radicalism, a kind of camouflage for what may be going on here? Or are we accountable to the movement, which put us here, using the standards of that movement as the mirror and the measure for what we choose to do and what we refuse to hide behind our skirts?

Somebody asked in discussion yesterday: who decides what feminism is? Well, feminists do. But there are a lot of women who don't consider themselves feminists for whom feminism has come to stand for the double day. It has come to stand for liberation through work. Liberation through work? The right to work? For women? That is the only right women have ever been guaranteed. [Laughter]

How can we liberate ourselves by more work? In the United States, Black women, Latina Women, Asian women and many white working-class women have always worked outside the home, in factories and in fields. They have never been able to sit down in their own kitchen for fifteen minutes together—you cannot seriously suggest to those women that they will be liberated by a job. You can't. But that may be what the Establishment needs you to do right now. And your job for the movement is to find out how not to do that in a way that is relevant to all kinds of women so that they will protect you; because as soon as you try to undercut that plan, someone will try to undercut your funding. And then you will need community people to come in to help you to keep your funding so you can continue to help us. That is one small example of how to overcome the divisions.

Now I'm going to comment about a few specific things I heard or saw.

There was a reference to Virginia Woolf yesterday, which I was not comfortable with. As far as I know, the antiracism of Virginia Woolf has never been explored. There is no time to do that today, but I must at least register that on race, as on so much else, Virginia was not a typical white European feminist, but stood against much of what that sector of women has come to stand for. Virginia Woolf wanted the military budget for women.

She made the case for middle-class women. She said it should come to women as wages for the housework we did; that that was a better way to spend the money. I can't see an argument against it. In *Three Guineas*, the only extensive nonfiction book she ever wrote, she made this central. But the case she makes for wages for housework, spelled out most brilliantly in this extraordinary book, seems not to interest—may even be censored out by—her admirers.[4]

---

4 Virginia Woolf made it clear that her demand was for wages for housework to be paid to the mothers, wives, and daughters "of educated men." She was convinced that as a middle-class woman she didn't have the right to make demands on behalf of working-class women. It must also be noted that she wrote *Three Guineas* while a campaign led by Eleanor Rathbone for wages for housework for working-class women was raging in Britain. This campaign resulted in the winning of the Family Allowance

When the great economist of capitalism John Maynard Keynes read *Three Guineas*, the case for money going to fight the war to be paid to women instead, according to a recent biography he was "dismissive."[5] But one of the many connected arguments of Virginia's case was that it would save us from what joining the learned professions would do to us. It would, she said, enable us to avoid "the poison tree of intellectual harlotry."[6]

When women entered the professions, they were involved in "brain prostitution"; you had, for example, "to write at the command of another person what you do not want to write for the sake of money. But to sell a brain is worse than to sell a body for when the body seller has sold her momentary pleasure she takes good care that the matter shall end there. But when a brain seller has sold her brain, its anemic, vicious and diseased progeny are let loose upon the world to infect and corrupt and sow the seeds of disease in others."[7]

She said that. That's not what Virginia Woolf is known for, but that's what she said after living fifty-five years in the world. Unfortunately, when women die they're not able to say to those who write about them: "Just read the whole thing." [Laughter] If we had money of our own before entering the professions, she said, then we could refuse the prostitution that professional men have been forced into in order to support their families, and at the same time we could more easily refuse the wars we had supported men in waging.

I think Virginia can be tremendously useful to us, to all of us, women of color, Third World women, white women, and men on our side, because she gives us the strength to demand more of what we're entitled to. And the strength also to refuse to replicate or allow other women to replicate what we have been attacking men for doing and being.

---

from 1946, money paid weekly to all mothers in the UK for each child as a statutory right. (See "The Family Allowance Campaign: Tactics and Strategy" above.) Virginia Woolf and Eleanor Rathbone are two components of the history of the wages for housework movement in Britain which our Campaign has put together with the 1960s welfare rights movement in the United States and elsewhere. The whole, at least theoretically, is greater than the sum of its parts.

5   Lyndall Gordon, *Virginia Woolf: A Writer's Life* (New York/London: Norton: 1985), 258.

6   Virginia Woolf, *Three Guineas* (New York: Penguin 1982), 114.

7   Her point was not that we should not enter the professions but that, with financial independence we could dictate the terms of our work in these professions. In fact, we would be in a better position in any job we took, waged or unwaged. Secondly, women generally would have far more power to publicize and impose their collective will on the employers of career women and on the career women themselves. As it is, women who rise in the economic and social hierarchy exercise their new power as they choose, often without reference to the needs of other women or of any grassroots people. They are not accountable, and they are not asked to be. Other women are expected to rejoice when they rise to new heights without making any commitment to how they will exercise power. When Prime Minister Major chose no women for his cabinet there was a storm from Tory lady Members of Parliament, and even Labour women parliamentarians complained. There was not a mention of what a Tory woman in the cabinet would stand for.

I'll give one more example of what is happening today between feminists in the professions and nonfeminists outside of the professions, and then perhaps we could just go on to speak about what we can do in a more concrete way.

As my very generous chair has said, the Wages for Housework Campaign has been trying to get governments to count women's unwaged work in the gross national product. And in 1985 at the World Conference of the UN Decade for Women in Nairobi, we got the UN to agree to count it; all the governments agreed in principle to Paragraph 120 of *Forward Looking Strategies for the Advancement of Women*, the UN document which summed up the UN Decade for Women. Of course a chasm exists between commitment in principle and implementation in practice, and most governments have done very little. So we have been lobbying, etc., and in fact some women present today have taken Time Off with us on or around October 24, our annual international mobilization to press governments everywhere to implement Paragraph 120.

And just as I was coming to the States at the end of February, some women from the Campaign in Trinidad and Tobago and in England attended a special session of the UN Commission on the Status of Women in Vienna. The Commission discussed what to prioritize of the 1985 UN decisions. It seemed to our deputation that some key countries on the Commission didn't want Paragraph 120, counting women's unwaged work, to be prioritized. At the Nairobi conference, Alan Keyes, U.S. representative to the UN (a Black man who shortly after took a job as lobbyist for the South African government), had told Margaret Prescod that the United States was against Paragraph 120 because as soon as women, especially from the Third World, find out how much their unwaged work is worth, they would come to the United States demanding the money. Which no doubt they will. They should. [Laughter] Because the question of course is not how much the Third World owes the banks but how much the banks owe the Third World, beginning with women.[8]

Anyway, in Vienna it was clear that Western governments didn't want to count women's unwaged work in the GNP. Not only Third World women but their own harem, so to speak, were going to demand the money they were owed as soon as they

---

8 "The Third World is estimated to have sent some $43 billion back to its developed country creditors this year, the fifth successive year in which net financial flows have been from poor countries to rich, the World Bank's annual 'Debt Tables' show today...the heavily indebted countries are still suffering declining output and living standards as a result of their debt burdens... The existence of substantial net flows of resources to the rich countries is a major factor depressing the growth of the Third World. The debtors can only generate dollars for debt service by running enormous surpluses of exports over imports, which in turn means sharply curtailing domestic spending and growth." ("Third World Pays $43 billion Back to Its Rich Creditors," *Guardian*, December 19, 1988). "The pace at which developing countries have been transferring money back to the richer nations accelerated dramatically last year, hitting a record total of $50.1 billion, up almost $12 billion from 1987, the World Bank reveals in its annual report to be released on Monday... The outflow of $50.1 billion from all developing countries in 1988 represented the difference between new lending of $92.3 billion and repayments of principal and interest of $142.4 billion." (Poor "Pay" $50 Billion to Rich," *International Herald Tribune*, September 18, 1989, 17).

had the ocular proof of the value of their unwaged work. So governments—in the age of feminism represented in Vienna predominantly by women—spoke little and vaguely about counting women's work and much and clearly about getting women out to work, and about more employment opportunities and career promotion for women at the UN. You know what that means? That means a trade-off: soft-pedaling counting all women's unwaged work in exchange for a few jobs for women in the UN. That trade-off is acceptable to many ambitious women calling themselves feminists.

And this is the hook on which people have been hanging in every movement. Every time we build a movement a few people get jobs, and those who get the jobs claim that this was the objective of the movement, this was the change. And indeed, when we look closer, we see that this was *one* of the aims: to get people into positions of power in order to carry out the changes we want. But those who get the jobs, in order to move still higher in the pay and power scale, or even just to keep the jobs, transmute the aims and needs of the whole movement into the aim and needs of the sisterhood of brain prostitutes. Movements permit this because they have not resolved which end of the class hierarchy they will serve, the top or the bottom end. But we are moved to prevent it—first of all, like Virginia, by calling it, by making clear what is happening with as much precision as we can manage. Precision in exploring the obstacles to women's liberation is hardly encompassed by replacing "sex" with "gender." It may be useful in itself, but it can give the impression that we're getting down to brass tacks even as we sidestep anything sharp and pointed.

There's a lot of imprecision. And I found one reason for it yesterday in a workshop. I'm not an academic, and I didn't go to university. Anyway, in this very academic workshop something was raised which people agreed with, and then someone else said the exact opposite and people agreed with that also, and then they concluded: both are true! [Laughter] You can't have both. You can't have both an attack on racism and a discussion about whether racism even exists. One negates, discredits, the other. You have to decide. There are many times when you connect opposites, but that depends on what you're talking about: racism and antiracism are not compatible opposites. That is to disconnect ideas and language from the life-and-death struggle which they exist to explain and articulate. No, that way you can deceive yourself that you are thinking but in fact you're "Double-Think"-ing. We must be scrupulous: it is past Orwell's *1984*, and Big Sister has joined Big Brother in the hierarchy. There was a lot of such abstraction on race in the workshop yesterday. And there were some who knew very well what was going on; you have to stand your ground against it; you can't let it pass without dissent. You can't allow blatant racism to pass as reasonable academic speculation.

That's another important consideration: if you have a position, you have to stand your ground. You don't have to be rude, but it may help to be angry—in a controlled way, of course. [Laughter] These are not *only* abstractions; either they describe our reality or they mystify it, repressing opposition. Either way, they have an impact on our lives, which makes me take them personally. But not so that I lose the ability to choose my response, and not in order to justify self-indulgence, where my response becomes central, and the issue—"the thing itself"—is lost as the focus for response.[9]

And one criticism of the speech the night before last, which was grappling with the question of race. The speaker referred to white people as "my people." They can't be. They can't be. [General laughter] I don't know how to even begin to explain. There are times when "my people" is acceptable, but if you say white people are "my people" you are saying other people, people of color, are not "my people." That describes your choice, not what a racist society has foisted upon you. You must stop it. And you must stop it here, not only because you're going to be invaded from outside just now—there's a new movement coming up which will not tolerate that—but because such a position can drive you crazy: you may wind up in a schizophrenic state where you will be unable to go on with your lives and you will wind up just counting your paycheck. [Laughter]

We want to hold together but not at the expense of hiding the real divisions among us. Only with such clarity can we actually come together as we are not together now.

A number of very fine things were said yesterday—I'm not mentioning too many of those. I'm trying to put forward a point of view which aims to provide a context for what was said about your specific situations which I cannot know.

Someone said that white people say Black people are "them," but they never say that they are referring to Black people. (Was that person responding to "my people"?) Startling and profound. Now that is exactly the starting point of work I'm doing on the Brontës, and of my case against what has become feminism. Perhaps I can illustrate through the Brontë work that this political framework doesn't narrow you; it can widen you. Nor does it force you into political activity in the usual sense, but it does help you to deal with the political relationships we are involved in all the time—I mean, dealing with the divisions among us; that's tough and steady political activity demanded by just about anything you're doing. And it can help you to think clearly about anything. The Brontës are my jogging for thinking.

Feminists are in love with Charlotte Brontë. Yet the great summation of the travails of Charlotte's Jane Eyre was: "Reader, I married him." Reader, I married the boss. No, listen, that's just not good enough! [Laughter] Charlotte Brontë was a

---

9   "One has only to skim those old forgotten novels and listen to the tone of voice in which they are written to divine that the writer was meeting criticism… She met that criticism as her temperament dictated, with docility and diffidence, or with anger and emphasis. It does not matter which it was; she was thinking of something other than the thing itself," Virginia Woolf, *A Room of One's Own* (London: Granada, 1983), 71.

flaming racist. If you want to know where she stands, compare her with her sister, the antiracist Emily Brontë, who said, "I *am* Heathcliff": I am that man of color, who had been a street urchin. And that's just the beginning of what I think we have to do, not only if we are white, but whoever we are. We have to identify entirely with those with less power than ourselves: not only are we "with them"; we *are* "them." That way lies power for all of us, the end of the divisions, the end of the hierarchy and the flowering of real diversity and individuality.

There was discussion yesterday of the role of white men in maintaining sexism and racism. In 1977, in Trafalgar Square in London, Women Against Rape, which the Campaign helped launch, put government and industry on trial for rape and conspiracy to rape—first of all by spending our money for the defense budget so we were too poor to defend ourselves against, among other things, being dragged into war. And our case against these defendants was: you uphold men's power over women in order to uphold your power over everyone. Dig. That doesn't let men off the hook, but it's not labeling men as the enemy either. Treating white men as the enemy doesn't undermine the hierarchy. It just makes room for some women to move up a few rungs. The "economic and political institutions which govern us," into which is structured and which enforce sexism and racism, can incorporate token women and token Black people and Hispanics and Native Americans, and Asians, and all this without fundamentally altering either structure or purpose.

One other thing about men. For a number of years now I've been a point of reference for Payday, an international network of men against all unwaged work who are working with and in support of our Campaign. And I've found that in many ways they're exactly like women—except in relation to women. [Laughter] They're as worried as we are, as insecure as we are, as indecisive as we are, they're almost as enslaved as we are—but not in relation to us. I raise this to illustrate that there is less diversity among us than the divisions lead us to expect; the divisions hide our commonality.

Now what follows from all this? The precision which I think we should work to achieve, and the clarity it affords, comes from making connections with the rest of the world, not from the academic ivory tower. You have a base here and of course you must keep it. But you must share it; together with the community you can work out the terms and defend them. It is everyone's right to have information and exchange ideas. Open admissions was a breakthrough struggle of the 1960s from which came Black Studies and then Women's Studies, etc. In any case, to embrace the world is not a sacrifice. We have a basis to be together as women: acknowledging the invisible work you share with other women which as professionals you are invited to deny but which, being women, you yourselves are (sometimes invisibly) coerced to do.

The UN has said we women do two-thirds of the world's work for 10 percent—the ILO says five percent—of the income. That means that we women do an enormous amount of work—twice as much as men. Ah, but different sectors of women do different quantities of work in exchange for different incomes. So on the one hand we can see that whether we're washing clothes by the side of the river, or in a washing machine, it's the women who are doing the laundry, and this is what we have in common; on the other hand, there's a big divide between those of us using a washing machine and those of us using stones by the river side. That's the duality within which we're always working; without acknowledging this, we cannot proceed, except upwardly alone and against other women, other people of color, other sexual preferences, other workers.

And exploring the double day for other women, which contributes so much to that two-thirds figure in North America, has to begin with exploring the double day for women here. It seems to me you should find out how much work women on campus are doing, students and lecturers and typists and cleaners, etc. And how much work men are doing; they should be encouraged to spell out what that work is—after they have listened to the work that we do.

So when we are dealing with divisions, we're dealing with power relations based on who has the money and who is doing the work. And it is impossible to look these power relations in the eye without asking: what work am I doing? That's a terribly important question. From that you can begin to connect yourself with others in the world who are also doing this work. You have perhaps been told that as a woman in academia, you are irretrievably cut off from other women. But in fact every night you go home to a kitchen, I'm sure you do. Or else some other woman goes to work in your kitchen, and you have to deal with the fact that your study of women is made possible by her work in your kitchen. That's an irony surfacing in Britain: feminists hostile to wages for housework pay another woman wages to do their housework. But if this woman had wages for her own housework, she wouldn't do anybody else's. And sometimes I think some people oppose wages for housework because it would raise the price of servants. [Laughter]

So you begin with who you are and that opens the way to connect with who everybody else is and where the movement is and how to be an outpost of it, and how to try not to be an outpost of those who fund you for alien and unhelpful purposes. Which is usually the military-industrial complex, internationally, West and East together.

(By the way, in one discussion someone said that people outside academia don't think theoretically. I'm not even sure that it's useful to think theoretically as that's ordinarily defined and practiced. But we can be sure that thinking work is going on outside: generalizing and comparing and contrasting and drawing out connections.

Many realities are far more obvious outside than within the halls of ivy. Although there is not time to prove it here, I'm convinced that the most profound thought and the clearest articulation of reality spring from collective, social action by people whose eye contact with reality is not on the whole mediated by learned tomes. When new ideas and directions first take shape as integral parts of movements, it's the rare academic writing them up who references where they come from.)

The movement in Eastern Europe has a lot to teach us. And I'll end with that. The women in Eastern Europe were told (as we are) that liberation was found in a job outside the home. They're exhausted. Three of us from the Wages for Housework Campaign went to a women's peace conference in Moscow in 1987, and the Soviet women talked about how desperate they are. That's the first thing we have to learn from them. We could have learnt it from women in any Third World country or even Third World area of this metropolitan country—there's a lot of Third World in the United States. (And by the way, your attitude to the Third World begins with your attitude to the Third World in the metropolis. If, for example, you're not dealing with immigration, please don't tell us how sorry you feel about the children in Africa.) [Applause]

The other lesson to come from Eastern Europe recently, which is a source of great hope, is that nowadays things can change quickly. Now I'm wary of calling myself a "Marxist," because I don't trust what that is, after a hundred years of disinformation and "interpretation" and Stalinism; but Marx himself is—literally—my main man. And one of his very clever observations was: revolution comes like a thief in the night. That is, rapidly, unexpectedly, when you're not looking. He said that over a century ago. But events in Eastern Europe seem to have stolen upon us almost literally overnight. Our problem is getting our minds to keep up with such a rapidly and massively changing reality. Despite distance and division, we *are* them, and their actions are transforming *our* personalities and *our* relationships, and our consciousness of what is possible for *us*. There are still those who say: "Well, there's no help and it's not going to come for years and there's eight years of Reagan and now four years of Bush and who knows who's going to get elected next time, and it's going to go on and on and on like this." That disaster view is also a lazy, comforting view: it gives permission to do nothing.

I believe Marx worked on two time scales: one that it's going to happen tomorrow and one that it's not. [Laughter] Yes. Wise, I think. One that it's going happen tomorrow and therefore we have to be hopeful; and one that it's not going to happen tomorrow so we have to dig in for the long haul. But you can't do one or the other; you must do both.

Because *something* is going to happen tomorrow, you see. The only thing we don't know is what. And now we know that within hours you can have thousands of people in the street and the police may not fire on them because they are too many. This is the world in which we live, where thousands of people, and in fact millions, people you had thought didn't "think theoretically" or at all, and unlike the professors haven't worked it out and so they can't know where they're at, and they're apathetic, and backward, and their consciousness is low, and they all come out on the streets and say "no," and nobody can take yes for an answer, because they have said "no" in such massive numbers that the world does change one little bit and the professors run for a grant to analyze what they couldn't foresee, let alone create.

And if that is the context of all our lives, then what we have to worry about is what *we* are doing, whether *we* are making the connections, whether *we* are apathetic and—yes—backward, and how much faster we have to run to keep up with a moving reality we, along with millions everywhere, are determined to transform, shaking the base of the hierarchy and letting it all hang out.

Thank you.

WOMEN'S UNWAGED WORK: THE HEART OF THE INFORMAL SECTOR (1991)

S olveig Francis and I represented the movement to get unwaged work counted at INSTRAW's Consultative Meeting of Experts on Macro-Economic Policy Analysis for Women's Participation in the Informal Sector, Rome March 19, 1991.[1]

* * *

At the 1985 World Conference of the UN Decade for Women in Nairobi, Housewives in Dialogue presented evidence, which helped government delegates to agree to the amended Paragraph 120 of Forward-Looking Strategies. Paragraph 120 commits governments to counting in the GNP women's "unremunerated"—unpaid or unwaged—work in "agriculture, food production, reproduction, and household activities." The International Wages for Housework Campaign pioneered for almost two decades of grassroots campaigning and determined lobbying, the elaboration of the implications of unwaged work which, though uncounted, is counted on by every individual and institution. There are signs that we are moving slowly but surely towards implementation: pilot projects, such as that on Measuring Unpaid Household Work in Australia; a national policy in Trinidad and Tobago; a Bill in the British Parliament; a resolution in the European Parliament; and Recommendation V by the 1990 UN Commission on the Status of Women that counting women's unwaged work be

---

1   INSTRAW: United Nations International Research and Training Institute for the Advancement of Women.

prioritized in national policies by 1995, and that methods of counting be developed by the UN.

The Present

Despite this progress towards acknowledging unwaged work, which is estimated to produce as much as 50 percent of GNP, Third World women are urged to "get into the development process," and metropolitan women are urged to get "out to work."[2] In fact, with the economic crisis which for women never seems to cease, fewer and fewer women anywhere can afford to refuse to work at least two jobs. The so-called "double day" is an international phenomenon that ironically goes hand in hand with the "feminization of poverty": a rise in workload, a fall in living standards. But while women in metropolitan countries who do two jobs—housework and work outside the home—get one wage, women in Third World countries, even with two jobs—housework and, for example, subsistence farming—can still be without wages and even perhaps without food. To add insult to injury, the woman anywhere who doesn't secure a wage may enter statistics as "economically inactive."

In 1982, the ILO, "for purposes of international comparisons, [classified] all members of the armed forces…as employed." On the other hand, they introduced "a separate category…to account for persons not economically active but contributing to output and welfare. This category includes homemakers, community and volunteer workers and persons engaged in certain subsistence activities…"[3] The person whose business is death is named a worker, but the person whose business is life is not.

This definition of work and productiveness says much about the priorities which have resulted in, or at least permitted, the increase of world poverty in the 1980s and the death, injury, or dislocation of 80 million people in 105 wars from 1945 up to but not including the Gulf War.[4]

Despite such "disregard" and "discounting," every sector of every economy is dependent on women's unwaged housework for its basic ingredient: its workforce.[5] Unwaged housework is the heart of every economic sector, formal, informal, waged or unwaged, not merely presenting commerce and industry with a new generation of workers, but each day reproducing the human mind and muscle which have been exhausted and consumed by the day's work. Overwhelmingly, the burden of this reproductive work has been carried by the female half of humanity, consuming our

2   Valuing Domestic Activities, Second ECE/INSTRAW Joint Meeting on Statistics of Women, UN, Economic Commission for Europe, Geneva, November 1989, 2.

3   Labour Force, Employment, Unemployment and Underemployment, Report II ICLS/13/11 Thirteenth International Conference of Labour Statisticians, ILO 1982, 42.

4   World Bank 1990 World Development Report, cited in the *Independent* (UK), July 19, 1990, 21. "Five million civilians have died in recent conflicts," *Guardian*, January 29, 1991, 9.

5   "We have been oppressed a great deal, we have been exploited a great deal, we have been disregarded a great deal." From *The Arusha Declaration*, Tanzania, February 5, 1967.

time—which happens to be our life. And yet this work is hidden from history, politics, and economic statistics.

In order to meet reproductive obligations to family and community, women daily face a mass of unavoidable immediate tasks. The woman who has to cook the food may have to grow it first. In this situation, agricultural work is indistinguishable from reproductive work. Some metropolitan definitions of housework are too narrow to encompass this reality. Definitions rarely include time squandered in waiting rooms and standing on queues that bleed not only hours but months and years from the life of women; in some areas of the world, older women, whose time has less exchange value, are condemned to do this vital but tedious work. All of it must be counted.

The line between the unwaged sector and the informal sector is often blurred and sometimes cannot be traced at all. If a rural woman's subsistence crop is good, she may sell the surplus. She may do two or three hours of laundry or other domestic work for those better off, fitting this around her own housework. When it is suggested that some of this work be counted, women ask: why not all? Each division of her labor rests on the others; each segment of the day, and of the year, is integral to her survival and to the survival of those dependent on her work. To single out any part as worthier than any other is to misinterpret and misrepresent the living reality that statistics should aim to profile.

Women would welcome help with any of it and deserve help with all of it. But in order to command help, and shift the prevailing standards by which women's lives and work are valued—or more often undervalued, even unvalued—all of it must be recognized. It is impossible to achieve the objectives of this consultative meeting, namely to identify and analyze the patterns, problems, and constraints of women's work in the informal sector, and prepare guidelines for policy measures, without quantifying the cost to the woman—in time and energy—of her entire working day.

The Past

It may be useful to recall that the informal sector and even the question of development, as international questions, arose in the second half of the twentieth century. In 1947, India, the jewel in the British Crown, became independent. A decade later, the Gold Coast became Ghana, the first Black African country to break from colonial rule. It was at first assumed that once political independence had been achieved, the aspirations of the population had been met. But then what was called "the revolution in rising expectations" made clear that political independence aimed at more than a flag, a national anthem, and local personnel inheriting positions of power and prestige vacated by the imperialists. The formerly colonized people wanted to enter what appeared to be a wonderland of consumer goods, which the transistor radio—not dependent on electrification, and therefore able to leap wide expanses at a single bound—was anxious to advertise to them. The pressure from this explosion of hopes was used to propel the economies of newly independent countries further into the money economy. When exchange value became the measure of wealth, power moved from the farmer in the countryside—often a woman—to the city, and women found themselves deprived of their economic power base. There is evidence that women fought such diminution of power with all their might. Esther Boserup's pioneering work already indicated in the 1960s how women defended themselves against the erosion of their traditional power. African women, market traders for centuries, demanded money.

There are many reports from Africa about husbands whose wives refuse to help them in the production of cash crops, or to perform household chores, unless they are paid for their work.

Boserup also indicates women's resistance to the formal sector, which trades cash crops for food, putting money (at least for a while) in men's hands but not necessarily food in the family's mouths.

Other reports concern women who refuse to help their husbands in the cultivation of cash crops because they want to grow only their own food crops. This is considered an obstacle to the progress from subsistence agriculture to commercial production for the market. In the Bwamba region of Uganda, for instance, women's preference for growing subsistence crops is held to be an important factor restraining the cultivation of cash crops.[6]

The statistics that exclude the unwaged woman as a worker reflect the dominant market view that the work she does, on which her social power and her very survival depend, is standing in the way of "progress." "Progress" has won, among other consequences, depriving many rural women of a living from the land (but not freeing such women from agricultural work). Women have therefore tried in every possible way to enter the waged sector. In Third World and metropolitan world, this thirst by women for the economic and social independence of waged work has been misread, as if it were the work, rather than the independence, which was the goal. Women may be delighted to gain waged employment, especially on payday, but they're less thrilled on Monday morning after a weekend of housework. Despite great efforts to get to the work in order to get to the wages, including by becoming "economic refugees"—immigrants—hundreds or even thousands of miles from home, for millions of women (and men), the informal sector is as far up as they go, even in metropolitan countries. One occupation that many must turn to yet again is housework.

Clotil Walcott of the National Union of Domestic Employees (NUDE) of Trinidad and Tobago reports that because women's housework and childcare are not counted as work, paid domestic workers are not considered to be workers. The results

---

6   Esther Boserup, *Woman's Role in Economic Development* (London: Earthscan Publications, 1970), 64.

are catastrophic: protective labor legislation excludes them; recognition as a trade union and bargaining rights are denied; women are at the mercy of employers; wages are kept low; state pensions and benefits don't exist or are minimized; the Convention on the Elimination of All Forms of Discrimination Against Women is violated.

This devaluation of domestic workers is replicated internationally. As a consequence, women must take on additional informal work, such as prostitution, with its burden of criminalization, that is, further devaluation. In 1987 the ILO decided not to list prostitution as a job in the International Standard of Classification of Occupations. Yet this (primarily) "women's work" keeps many families alive, and in some Asian economies is a high earner of foreign currency, in Thailand the largest single foreign currency earner.[7]

NUDE in Trinidad brings together waged with unwaged house workers and both with unrepresented fast food workers, making the connections that strengthen each while retaining the uniqueness of each. Similarly, the Self Employed Women's Association (SEWA) in India has been enormously effective in wielding the collective bargaining power of forty thousand self-employed women in the informal sector—street traders, porters. Ela Bhatt, its founder, described this sector in Nairobi in 1985 to an audience of academics: "Experts call them 'unorganized sectors,' but I wouldn't."

While women crawl their way up into the informal sector, capital-intensive enterprises develop by moving down to rest on it. The industrial miracle of Japan,[8] the economy most famous for developing in the twentieth century, is a classic example. Subcontractors employ casual labor, mainly women, whose low wages and poor working conditions are a subsidy to the industrial giants for which they make components. Thus unseen women in precarious employment are the miracle workers who bestow permanent employment on men. This "dual industrial structure," the formal resting directly on the informal, is spreading with Japanese investment, carrying this aspect of planned underdevelopment to metropolitan countries.[9]

And how to distinguish work in the informal sector from the work of women employed by multinationals operating in Free Trade Zones? Women, often treated

---

7 Thanh-Dam Thong, *Sex, Money and Morality: Prostitution and Tourism in South East Asia* (London: Zed Books, 1990), 163.

8 Japan is considered a miracle because the level of capital investment and of a habitually disciplined workforce required for a technologically advanced economy (as opposed to one or two advanced industries) is so tremendous. In present circumstances, most Third World countries haven't a hope of "catching up with the West," to use Stalin's formulation of his development goal, in pursuit of which it is estimated that he killed between 20 and 40 million people.

9 Mary Saso, *Women in the Japanese Workplace* (London: Hilary Shipman, 1990), 81. See also *The Independent*, March 11, 1991, "Japan is the world's richest poor country... Because of the country's bias towards production instead of consumption, some of the benefits that consumers take for granted in other developing countries are just missing here. Only 42 percent of households in Japan were connected to the sewers. And 13 percent of households have no bath."

as casual workers and working without labor protection codes, form up to 95 percent of this work force.[10]

The Future

To sum up. The housewife producing the labor force is considered marginal. The informal sector is considered marginal. Subsistence farming is considered marginal. We now know that this work is not marginal to the economy. But the people who do it have less social power to insist that their needs be met and are therefore called "marginal." What can statistics do to help?

Statistics shape and reflect a hierarchy of social values by the categories into which people, their activities and their products are placed, and by what is being measured— and not measured. Statistics on women can only reflect their needs by counting their entire working day and what they gain from it.

When we say that women's unwaged work should be counted, we mean that the actual number of hours women work should be quantified, and that the output of this work should be valued and included in the GNP. And since a woman's working day is often, especially in Third World countries, supplemented by children's work, this work too must be quantified and valued. The gulf widens between expenditure of time and energy on the one hand, and output and return on the other, the further we get from metropolitan centers, but is always wider for women than for men within the same social sector or class.

This dual counting would allow a redefinition of the term "worker" to include and name those who do the most work, and it would prioritize confronting the disparities between effort and output or return (where these are different) on the other. These disparities make women and children the poorest everywhere.

The level of Northern military technology is dazzling; yet in the South there are scant resources for piped water, solar cookers and nonpolluting technology which would both relieve the burden of labor and protect the environment. Counting women's unwaged work would value a woman's time by valuing the cost to her in hours of her life that she spends in trying to ensure everyone's survival. This cost is borne by women not only where starvation is imminent but where life is less threatened but still a grim struggle. This encompasses most of the world's population, Third World and metropolitan, including Third World in the metropolis and metropolis in the Third World.

Such a cost accounting would make clear that communities need not justify their claim to survival by proving their productiveness. The disparity between labor and productivity reflects not on them but on social and economic priorities that counting and renaming women's work would help transform.

---

10 "Women Working Worldwide, the International Division of Labour in the Electronics, Clothing and Textile Industry," War on Want (UK), 1988.

THE MILK OF
HUMAN KINDNESS
(2002)

We had urged for some years the recognition of women's vital work of breastfeeding and babies' right to this vital first food, rather than beginning life with formula, the first junk food. On this basis we were invited to an international breastfeeding conference in Arusha, Tanzania. This occasion became a deadline to publish *The Milk of Human Kindness*.[1] (When you are an organizer, you need such deadlines; daily pressures ensure that you never find time for the long-term writing and publishing work.)

To dismiss caring work, which is overwhelmingly the work of women, is to dismiss the reproduction of human beings. Nowhere is this more obvious than when mothers breastfeed the newborn. There have been famous international campaigns against the murderous formula companies (though there are none prominent as we write, and UK Prime Minister Tony Blair invited Nestlé—the worst offender—to advertise at New Labour's annual party conferences). Less well known are the constant struggles, for example of African village women resisting pressure from governments fronting for manufacturers, to retain the right to feed the young in the traditional (and free) way and to keep them alive. The conference was an eye-opener, enabling us to glimpse the way NGOs build empires; and the way African women must struggle against them.

* * *

---

1 Solveig Francis, Selma James, Phoebe Jones Schellenberg, and Nina López, *The Milk of Human Kindness: Defending Breastfeeding from the Global Market and the AIDS Industry* (London: Crossroads Books, 2002).

A Society of Carers—Preface to the First Edition
With Phoebe Jones Schellenberg

This book is right on time. In heralding the invaluable contribution women who breastfeed make to society and to the economy, it speaks to this moment in the new millennium when all the social and economic priorities we have inherited are being questioned by all kinds of people around the world.

This accounts for the new awareness of the life-and-death struggle with the baby milk formula industry, to try to prevent the deaths of at least four thousand babies every day because they were not breastfed.

The contest has not been of equal forces.

On one side is the global market, which lacks neither resources nor influence. In the market's powerful judgment, what does not pass through its exchange to leave behind some profit is not work and cannot have a high social priority.

On the other side are women worldwide, most of whom don't even have a small wage most of the time. We have repeatedly had to insist that the production of life and the caring for it, work we do outside the market, has economic as well as social value.

Mothers feeding infants, in fact all caring work outside any money exchange, is basic to human survival—not exactly a marginal achievement. What, we must ask in our own defense and in society's, is more important than this? Yet as more and more women have gone out to waged work in both industrial and nonindustrial countries, the unwaged work mothers and other women continue—or try to continue—to do has been downgraded as a social priority. The market has set the terms for how caring is evaluated and has dismissed the claims of unwaged carers, and first of all mothers.

Since the market refuses to come to the mother—to value her contribution, meet her needs and help her to meet the needs of the new generation (or at least not sabotage her efforts!)—the book takes the mother to the market, not to "get a job" but to demonstrate that she already has one and to prove even to the market that it is a productive one. If serving the needs of the individual from birth (and in fact from conception) is to be dismissed as an optional extra, we can counter this by a balance sheet of caring, demonstrating that even by the standards of costs, risks, investments, savings, product promotion, and competition, breastfeeding makes a massive economic contribution.

This book, then, sets out to quantify and to value economically as well as socially the caring work of breastfeeding: how much time it takes and how much this time and effort are worth—in every sense. It brings together a dazzling range of measurements: what society gains from breastfeeding, in the saving of life, health, well-being, and relationships; and what it loses when we lose the natural resource of breastfeeding—from the waste of our time to the destruction of our environment. Once all the monetary measurements and estimates that can be found are brought together, we glimpse the truly immense value of what has been devalued, and the loss we have all suffered with the catastrophic decline in breastfeeding, where only one in three babies around the globe is fully breastfed.

It cannot go unremarked that since the work of caring (outside the market, and increasingly within it) is identified with women—who do so much of it—every word, action or policy which demeans this work, also demeans women, our time and our priorities. It makes invisible women's efforts to protect those we have expended time and energy bringing into life and/or caring for, while we struggle to gain independent lives for ourselves, during an era of unprecedented destruction and devastation. Thus a balance sheet on support for versus sabotage of this caring work is also a balance sheet on women and on the society generally.

We also confront the question of women's "biological nature." Women are often identified with the work we do, work which most of the time has not one thing to do with our biology—there is nothing unique to women's bodies that makes us cleaners! And when as with breastfeeding the work is biological as well as social, since breastfeeding is a relationship as well as a physical process, we have reason to fear its promotion: is this yet another trap to reduce us to our physical function so we can be institutionalized, confirmed, in unwaged work and in a lower social status? Are we again to be the giving sex, from whom can be demanded an endless outpouring of the milk of human kindness by various takers? At this moment of global reevaluation, we must again consider what is biological as opposed to what is social (to the degree that we can know this), how we want to deal with both, and how we want society to deal with us.

Up to now, our biological contribution has been a liability. We were the "natural" sex and, unlike men, were assumed to be governed by our hormones—to the detriment of our status. Men could think; women could bear children; nobody could be expected to do both! This identification of men as rational versus women as emotional beings, was used to justify every sexist discrimination, from unequal pay to the claim that we invite rape even as we shout "No!"

Some have been nervous even to mention our needs when men did not share them, since this could weaken our chances, especially on the job market. The Nordic governments at the International Labour Office, justifying the employers' attack on paid breastfeeding breaks, claimed that such breaks were unfair to men, and would undermine women's chances of job security, advancement, etc. For them, women employees had no rights as mothers. For them, if women wanted equity, we had to disregard or suppress our biological nature, or hide the work it imposes.

Women have had to make clear that demanding childcare has nothing to do with biology, but with society's responsibilities to carers and to children. By the degraded standards that prevail, we have a chance of winning childcare only when it frees us for "real" work, never when we need it to have time and energy for ourselves.

In self-defense, many of us, when we saw no other way to refuse the use of our biology to attack our possibilities and limit our destiny, insisted that we were "equal to men." But men had fewer (if any) caring responsibilities, did not get pregnant or breastfeed—had few (if any) biological or social barriers to full and constant participation in what the market says is the real business of life: working in it and for it. We were encouraged to believe our biological contribution was an affliction, and to blame our bodies rather than a sexist society for the discrimination we suffered.[2] So much are our natural powers to be suppressed that in the following pages we discover, among other amazing information, that industry is working on genetically modifying cows to produce a substitute milk nearer breast milk than formula. What's wrong with ours—except that we don't have to buy it?

Even having children has been under threat. The fertility rate in industrial countries has fallen from 2.8 children per woman in 1960 to 1.58 in 1997, not only because we were trying to shed the enormous burden of parenting work—overwhelmingly it is mothers who do parenting.[3] It was also because having economic independence from men almost always required that we go out to work. Every child made it more expensive and more exhausting to do that.

When the women's movement began in the 1960s, childcare at public events became a commonplace for the first time. We could be more socially, politically, artistically active even when we had children. Breastfeeding, natural childbirth, and other awareness of our bodies' functions and possibilities were again on the agenda—along with thinking and protesting!

Yet as the years passed, we were repeatedly told that the road to liberation, especially in industrial countries, had to pass through paid work outside the home. (Many of us had been there for years.) One manifestation of the dominance of that perspective was the enormous feminist resources and energy that went into the proabortion movement. Most of us agree that the right to refuse a pregnancy is vital, but choice does not end there. The right to have children and to have economic and other support to enable this, was rarely a feminist demand. It was at times problematic to get active support for the struggle by Third World women, and in the United States by women of color and the poorest of white women, against forced sterilization.

Not only sexism but racism played a part in discrediting breastfeeding. Women in Third World countries often have no access to clean water for formula. Thus for their babies formula feeding may be a death warrant. Yet if women are considered physical as opposed to thinking beings, then women of color in nonindustrial countries are even more likely to be demeaned by doing biological work. Further proof

---

2   "One reason why some mothers dislike breastfeeding is that they feel that breastfeeding—and childbirth too—is something 'primitive', too elemental an experience for a civilized woman to enjoy." S. Kitzinger, *The Experience of Childbirth*, 4th ed. (London: Penguin, 1978), 271.

3   UNICEF, *State of the World's Children*, OUP (1994), 8. *New York Times*, May 4, 2000, A8.

of this "backwardness" may be how long many babies are breastfed, how much time they spend next to their mothers' bodies, and no doubt how happy they are with this arrangement.

Such sexist and racist stereotypes are based on trusting "scientific experts" over "backward" women who believe "old wives' tales"; what is manufactured, labeled, and advertised versus what a woman's body produces. It is an indication of how, and how much, what passes for science is prioritized; we are encouraged to distrust what generations of experience have taught us nature can do, and which the most disinterested science confirms.

The book demonstrates that, ironically, breast milk has the lowest economic value where it has the highest social and life-supporting value, in the Third World. This grotesque disparity parallels the 1995 study on the economic costs of global warming, which calculated that one life in industrial countries was worth fifteen lives in Third World countries.[4] One commentator said: "*By placing such a low value on the lives of most of the world's people, they seem to endorse the economics of genocide.*"[5] Doesn't the same apply to the devaluing and undervaluing of breastfeeding described here?

Why do women who contribute by producing the whole workforce have to plead for maternity leave that would allow them to recuperate from childbirth, get to know their children and their children to know them, and feed babies the best possible food? Why are such basic and humane demands so controversial? What qualifies those who favor formula to deny the overwhelming evidence and individual personal experience that favor breast milk?

The wealth of information assembled here also strengthens the case for acknowledging women as perhaps the greatest producers of food. The individual production and one-to-one delivery of breast milk often goes hand in hand with subsistence farming on small plots of land "too small to count," perhaps with a few chickens, a goat or cow, and individuals' endeavors day in day out which benefit mainly those with little political clout or social status. Entire communities are surviving on that work—up to 80 percent of the food consumed in Africa is grown by women almost all outside the market. Are those of us who spend long hours of every day in this work also "too small to count"?

Not long ago we wrote:

A rural woman in Africa may have a toddler on her back as she sows, hoes, harvests, grinds, prepares, cooks and cleans up, on top of spending up to five hours a day collecting the water and fuel for cooking (and then is somehow supposed to find the time for a little small enterprise). A rural woman in the U.S. may be out in the fields or in the garden, making sure the children and the pets are safely

---

4   By the Intergovernmental Panel on Climate Change, Geneva.
5   *Independent on Sunday,* July 23, 1995, 2.

away from the machinery, keeping track of the load in the laundry and the pie in the oven while considering how the new calf is doing, or even how to keep the farm in the family's hands as her neighbors are losing theirs—and figuring out how to possibly console them for their loss. Meanwhile, statistically speaking, these two women in Africa and the U.S. are considered "economically inactive."[6]

Between breastfeeding and agricultural work, women are feeding the world!

In making this new and powerful case for acknowledgement of and support for breastfeeding, the case is also made for support for all mothers. This must include women who are combining waged work and breastfeeding. But while the status of mothers is central to the status of all women and girls, almost all women of every age are doing unwaged caring work, and all this work must be recognized.

Counting, valuing, acknowledging, and supporting (including with wages and pensions) unwaged and low-waged care giving—beginning with breastfeeding— opens the way for more choices for women, and fewer penalties for the biological burdens which fall to us.

The book mentions the hormones which flow in mother and child during breast- feeding, among other things encouraging the mother to enjoy her child and helping both of them to digest their food (no real surprise that these go together). There are two possible approaches to this biological process. Either nothing must be allowed to interfere with this life-enhancing process; or it must be pushed aside to make way for "more important things." The formula companies would replace this process with the product they wish to sell us. Global marketeers would halt it in favor of work they want us to do for them.

Breastfeeding is between mother and child. But it need not exclude men from being involved in care. In the raging global debate on priorities, the work identified as men's is also passing through an "agonizing reappraisal." What does it do to them? to the environment? to the possibility of a caring relationship with their partners? with their children? to their sharing of work in the home and in the community with women who have not only borne the bulk of this burden, but have been expected also to be at men's disposal so men could be at the disposal of their employers?

The movement for the right to breastfeed, which this book is fortifying with global information, is not only a rejection of the imposition of formula feeding; it urges society to prioritize the caring for infants and for mothers, and by implication caring also for each other: women and children and men, of any age and in any place. The name for this is relationships. What if that became the social priority which mate- rial production would serve?

---

6   Phoebe Jones Schellenberg, Valuing Rural Women's Work, Second International Conference on Women in Agriculture, Washington, DC, June 1998.

VENEZUELA (2004–2005)

We have been working with grassroots people in Venezuela since July 2002 when the National Women's Institute (INAMUJER) invited the Global Women's Strike to attend their *encuentro*. They were the first to appeal for international solidarity after defeating the U.S.-backed coup against the government of President Hugo Chávez in April of that year.

In August 2004, the Strike was asked to send international observers for a referendum to confirm President Chávez in power (he won with a landslide). Five of us went, from England, Guyana, Peru, and the United States. While there, friends took us to see the work of grassroots groups, mostly run by women. They told us over and over how professionals were undermining their movement.

In Venezuela the revolution's success and its security in the face of possible U.S. military intervention were dependent on the grassroots mobilization growing rather than being discouraged.

On our return home we were determined to make known and get support for the mobilizing we had seen. The result was the *Guardian* article of August 13, and later a film, *Talking of Power*, the third the Strike had made about the revolution. (The other two were *Venezuela: a Twenty-First Century Revolution*, and *Enter the Oil Workers*.)

In the second article, Nina López and I spelled out how dependent the revolution is on resisting the managerial class, which was trying to exhaust and demoralize the grassroots into submission.

An Antidote for Apathy

(*Guardian*, August 13, 2004)

Venezuela's president has achieved a level of grassroots participation our politicians can only dream of.

Increasing numbers of people, especially the young, seem disconnected from an electoral process that they feel, does not represent them. This is part of a general cynicism about every aspect of public life.

Venezuela has many problems, but this is not one of them. Its big trouble—but also its great possibility—is that it has oil; it is the fifth largest exporter. The United States depends on it and thus wants control over it. But the Venezuelan government needs the oil revenue, which U.S. multinationals (among others) siphoned off for decades, for its efforts to abolish poverty. Hugo Chávez was elected to do just that in 1998, despite almost all of the media campaigning against him.

Participation in politics especially at the grassroots has skyrocketed. A new constitution was passed with more than 70 percent of the vote, and there have been several elections to ratify various aspects of the government's program. Even government opponents who had organized a coup in 2002 (it failed) have now resorted to the ballot, collecting 2.4 million signatures—many of them suspect—to trigger a referendum against President Chávez, which will be held on Sunday.

For Venezuela's participatory democracy, which works from the bottom up, the ballot is only a first step. People represent themselves rather than wait to be represented by others, traditionally of a higher class and lighter skin. Working-class sectors, usually the least active, are now centrally involved.

Chávez has based himself on this *pueblo protagónico*—the grassroots as protagonists. He knows that the changes he was elected to make can only be achieved with, and protected by, popular participation.

Chávez has understood the potential power of women as primary carers. Four months of continuous lobbying got women the constitution they wanted. Among its antisexist, antiracist provisions, it recognizes women's unwaged caring work as economically productive, entitling housewives to social security. No surprise then that in 2002 women of African and Indigenous descent led the millions who descended from the hills to reverse the coup (by a mainly white élite and the CIA), thereby saving their constitution, their president, their democracy, their revolution.

In a country where 65 percent of households are headed by women, it is they who are the majority in government education and health campaigns: who are users as well as those who nurse, train and educate. Again, women are the majority in the land, water and health committees which sort out how the millions of people who built homes on squatted land can be given ownership, how water supplies are to be improved, and what health care is needed.

Despite oil, 80 percent of Venezuelan people are poor, and the Women's Development Bank (Banmujer) is needed to move the bottom up. Unlike other microcredit banks, such as the Grameen in Bangladesh, its interest rates are government-subsidized. Banmujer, "the different bank," is based on developing cooperation among women. Credits can only be obtained if women get together to work out a project which is both viable and what the local community wants and needs.

As Banmujer president Nora Castañeda explains: "We are building an economy at the service of human beings, not human beings at the service of the economy. And since 70 percent of the world's poor are women, women must be central to economic change to eliminate poverty."

In this oil-producing country 65 percent of basic food is imported. President Chávez has placed much emphasis on regenerating agriculture and repopulating the countryside, so that Venezuelans can feed themselves and are no longer dependent on imports or vulnerable to blockades which could starve them out. After all, you can't drink oil.

Most importantly, the oil revenue is increasingly used for social programs as well as agriculture: to enable change in the lives of the most who have least. People feel that the oil industry, nationalized decades ago, is finally theirs. The oil workers have created committees to work out how the industry is to be run and for whose benefit, even what to do about the pollution their product causes.

The government has turned the referendum, regarded by Venezuelans as an imperialist attempt to oust Chávez, into an even wider expression of the popular will. The small electoral squads, again mainly women who know the community and whom the community knows, are checking identity cards to weed out the names of those who have died or are under age, and register all who are entitled to vote, so that this time there will be little opportunity for electoral fraud. The turnout is expected to be 85 percent.

Some, especially the well-off, see the political engagement of the whole population as a threat to the status quo. Exactly. But since, increasingly, people find representative government doesn't represent them, it may be the wave of the present.

The Grassroots Revolution and the Managerial Class

with Nina López

Many of us in Britain feel that whether or not we vote, we are unlikely to unseat this widely hated warmongering prime minister [Tony Blair]. Others of us look to other countries where people have been able to resist the U.S. onslaught on which the British government models its own actions.

In Venezuela democracy has taken on a new meaning as people expect to act on their own collective behalf. In 1998 they elected Hugo Chávez as president despite a hostile campaigning media. Faithful to his constitutional mandate, Chávez has refused to privatize and hand over to U.S. multinationals the vast oil and water reserves that belong to the population. Instead he wants to "eliminate poverty by giving power to the poor"—the great majority. He faces U.S.-backed coups and assassination attempts. But his popularity is greater than ever. The constitution uniquely gives the electorate the power to recall any official halfway through their term of office. In August 2004 Venezuelans used it to ratify Chávez as president with a 59 percent to 41 percent landslide.

But what about the 41 percent who voted against him?

This would of course include the relatively small élite, which was until Chávez in charge of Venezuela's considerable oil revenue. They refused to accept the referendum results, despite President Carter, the Organization of American States and over one hundred independent international observers, all verifying the transparency and validity of the results. The former rulers were further defeated in the October regional elections which won the Chavistas twenty out of twenty-two state governments.

But the élite have friends abroad among the political and financial power fraternity, especially in the United States where Condoleezza Rice has again threatened Chávez, accusing him of "destabilizing the region." The Venezuelan élite will be encouraged to continue to object to the redistribution of wealth which challenges the structure of economic power—untold wealth at one pole and a majority in shantytowns at the other.

Venezuela's middle classes too have usually opposed Chávez's antipoverty programs. They complain that it is "dictatorial" for Chávez to have bypassed State institutions, replacing them with structures based on the direct participation of the most excluded sectors.

Dr. Thaïs Ojeda, who is a member of *Clase Media en Positivo* (Middle Class Positive), which sees itself as part of *el proceso* (the process of change), claims it is the institutions that have blocked the reforms. She is deeply critical of her peers:

> For the two years after Chávez was first elected, the government worked through
> the institutions. Chávez thought that doctors and educators, whom you expect
> to be most socially aware, would support changes that were for the good of the
> majority. But they didn't. Only 2 percent of doctors support *el proceso*, and obstacles
> were put in the way of ideas, orders, directives that came from the Minister
> of Health or of Education so they never got implemented, never reached the
> grassroots. In response, the government set up a parallel system of neighborhood
> health clinics and education campaigns.

Known as the missions, these are implemented by the users, and first of all by women who as society's main carers are most engaged with health and well-being in the community. The government has also relied on over fourteen thousand Cuban doctors to serve in the shantytowns. They live in people's homes and work with Venezuelan nurses as part of each neighborhood's Health Committee.

Ojeda's own political training has a source deep in modern Venezuelan history. Her father Fabricio headed the Democratic Front that defeated the 1950s dictatorship. Two years later he resigned from parliament in protest at the corruption of the elected parties. He was imprisoned and then assassinated in 1966, when his daughter was a child.

Most professionals have so far refused to bow to the will of the majority who, like Chávez, are the color of their servants—the majority they have despised enough to ignore all their lives. Caring professionals never assumed they were to care for those who could not pay.

Ojeda: "I come from State hospitals, I know. Doctors are paid for six or eight hours' work but the pay is low so they work two or three hours and spend the rest in private hospitals for higher pay. Previously the State didn't care if you provided good healthcare."

Now it does, and a new crop of doctors is being trained in Cuba to minister to all Venezuelans.

We were astonished that not long after the vote, Chávez made a direct appeal to the 41 percent who voted against him, truly unique for a head of state with such a huge majority. He told the mayors and governors who won the October elections with him not to sit on their laurels:

> The people, some of the people, have elected us, but we have not won. I'll say we
> have won when this revolution succeeds…We look at the regional elections and
> at the referendum, we see that many people voted for the opposition… In some

states we only won by a few thousand votes. Yet in those states, as everywhere in the country, the majority of the population are poor or lower middle class. We must consider this carefully... Instead of condemning and witch-hunting, we must talk and convince them... These results force us to look again at the work of the parties, the leaders, the militants, the government officials...We cannot afford the luxury of allowing the oligarchy to keep 40 percent of the population captive.

Many of those who voted against Chávez are professionals and small business people. In a society where the hierarchy is shifting daily, their monopoly on skills is not guaranteed. Ojeda believes that "As grassroots people get the skills that education provides they will begin to replace those professionals who never did anything for them, and many professionals will leave the country."

Some may well decide to take the plane to Miami. But some are likely to be drawn by the promise, the energy and above all the excitement of this massive movement. And even those who are not may be educated by their own revolutionary children: another generation comfortable with, even excited by, a gradual but accumulating seismic shift in power.

SIXTH GLOBAL WOMEN'S STRIKE CALL (2005)

E very year since 1999, the Global Women's Strike has sent out a call to action for March 8, International Women's Day. We invite women and women's organizations, and men, to take action to strengthen what they are working for, and in support of the Strike's demands. These demands were agreed over months of open meetings of women and of men. The central demand is *payment for all caring work*. In the first IWD in the new millennium, women in over sixty countries took part. This is the 2005 call.

End Poverty and War—Invest in Caring Not Killing! A Living Wage for All Our Work and Pay Equity in the Global Market

Dear sisters and brothers,

Every International Women's Day since 2000, women in over sixty countries have taken all kinds of grassroots actions to demand together that society Invest in Caring Not Killing, and that the money squandered on war is spent instead on what our communities need. The Strike has grown stronger in these five years, especially in countries of the global South, and women, and increasingly men, now take action throughout the year. We have seen how working across national boundaries with others in struggles for justice empowers us all.

Opposing war and ending poverty are inseparable. The recent horrendous tsunami killed almost three hundred thousand people, but every day many thousands die from starvation, disease, global warming, and war—all man-made disasters caused by the rule of money and the market. Governments and their beloved multinationals talk a lot of hot air about ending poverty but they never even mention giving us the money we need. The twin terrors of poverty and war are profitable, so it's against their interest to end either. Only we ourselves, beginning with women the carers who struggle every day to sustain life, working the hardest for least, can make this life-saving change. The Strike is our way of mobilizing for this.

We are not asking for charity but demanding what we have earned: *A Living Wage for All our Work*. And waged workers are entitled to the same pay, women and men, in whatever country: *Pay Equity in the Global Market*. This is the Strike's program to end poverty as well as sexism and racism.

The Strike always aims to bring women (and men) together across many divisions. It begins with those of us who are invisible as workers: mothers and other caregivers, grassroots activists; subsistence, migrant, and family farmers; those struggling on disability benefits, welfare, social security; child laborers; immigrants with or without papers; bonded laborers; domestic and homecare workers; sex workers; prisoners and ex-prisoners; *refuseniks*; students; rape survivors and others working for justice; community volunteers and more; whatever our sex, race, nationality, religion, age, sexual choice… Demanding global pay equity and wages for all the work we do, strengthens all workers, waged and unwaged, by making visible our contribution and our power to unite.

Men's support and participation internationally is coordinated by Payday, a multiracial network of men. They have not only supported women's Strike actions, but have also organized with women and men refusing the military and its lethal and repressive work, from the United States and the UK to Israel and Eritrea. The "poverty draft"—those driven to join the army by economic necessity, mainly people of color and immigrants—enables the United States to make "endless war." Thus those refusing the military are a vital part of the movement to end not only war but poverty. Payday will be launching its film *Refusing to Kill* about women and men refusing to be torturers, rapists, and murderers for the military.

The Bolivarian Revolution of Venezuela and the resistance to the U.S.-French coup in Haiti are important points of reference for the Strike. Both are largely woman-led, though that is not often admitted. The Strike will be launching its third film on Venezuela—the extraordinary experience they are making shows that what the grassroots wants and is demanding everywhere is achievable.

Many of us are shocked that Bush and his genocidal henchmen are in charge of the largest military machine in the world for four more years. But as Joe Hill, a great working-class fighter, said when he was framed for murder by the U.S. police and got the death sentence, "Don't mourn. Organize!"

Power to the sisters and brothers to stop the world and change it!

Global Women's Strike International Demands:

Payment for all caring work - in wages, pensions, land & other resources. What is more valuable than raising children & caring for others? Invest in life & welfare, not military budgets & prisons.

Pay equity for all, women & men, in the global market.

Food security for all, starting with breastfeeding mothers, paid maternity leave and maternity breaks. Stop penalizing us for being women.

Cancel "Third World" debt. The South owes nothing, it is owed.

Accessible clean water, healthcare, housing, transport, literacy.

Nonpolluting energy & technology which shorten the hours we must work. We all need cookers, fridges, washing machines, computers, & time off!

Protection & asylum from all violence & persecution, including by family members & those in positions of authority.

Freedom of movement. Capital travels freely, why not people?

REDISCOVERING NYERERE'S TANZANIA (2007–2009)

Julius Nyerere, leader of Tanzania's independence struggle and then its first president, was the only head of state to offer his country an economic and political program for development that was anticapitalist, nonaligned, and based on grassroots self-activity. He had spelled this program out in the *Arusha Declaration* in 1967. Central to it was *ujamaa*, a form of traditional African communalism, variously translated as "familyhood" or "African socialism," updated and developed to meet the needs of the new Tanzania. He had been explaining the importance of *ujamaa* to Tanzanians since before independence.

Anti-imperialists everywhere recognized the *Declaration* as a document relevant not only to Tanzania but to all newly independent African countries and some thought more generally: it was proposing development that avoided reenslavement via the capitalist market.

It must be noted that not even the most astute and dedicated supporters of Nyerere's *Declaration* had as far as I know ever even mentioned what it says about Tanzanian women working much harder than men—and the profound implications of this for development.

As the movement that had won independence lost momentum, in fact was being defeated, the *Declaration* was neglected and almost forgotten. Younger Tanzanians were unfamiliar with this great leadership from their past.

We had for years wanted to make the *Arusha Declaration* available again, and in 2007, on its fortieth anniversary, we republished it. We invited Madaraka Nyerere, the president's youngest son, to come to London for its republication. (The copies he took home were the first time many Tanzanians had ever set eyes on the *Declaration*.)

In the course of advertising this historic event, we got to know Noreen and Ralph Ibbott who told us about the extraordinary Ruvuma Development Association (RDA) and its seventeen villages. In response to Nyerere's call for *ujamaa*, in 1961 a group of rural people had begun to create an *ujamaa* society that, like the *Declaration*, had also been forgotten. The Ibbotts with their four young children (the youngest was born there) had lived and worked with great dedication in RDA's lead village—making their skills and knowledge freely accessible to the villagers and scrupulously taking leadership from them.

We had never heard of the RDA. We soon learnt how much not only the *Declaration*, but "Socialism and Rural Development" and other key Nyerere writings had been shaped by what the grassroots was actually achieving with the RDA, and what they were teaching Nyerere. Since we only learnt about the RDA after the 2007 republication of the *Declaration*, it is barely mentioned in this introduction to it.

The 1970 manuscript by Ralph Ibbott about how the RDA was built, and then in 1969 destroyed by Nyerere's party against his will, had lain in his drawer for forty years. We are preparing it for publication for the first time. The people of Tanzania—women, children, and men—will then finally get the credit they deserve for the leadership they gave President Nyerere, which he in turn was wise enough to appreciate. Nyerere drew out the principles that were hammered out collectively by the grassroots in the course of creating the RDA, and offered them to the world, first of all in the *Arusha Declaration*. What Nyerere didn't do was credit the grassroots source of his *Declaration*. Ralph Ibbott's manuscript does that.

* * *

I have said more than once that women are indeed the workers of Tanzania. In the village women have no holidays and no working hours.[1]

When on the 6th of March, 1957, the British colony of the Gold Coast became independent Ghana, many of us knew that humanity had taken a major step towards liberation. The apparently unbreakable crust of imperialism in Africa had cracked, and we rejoiced.

In our euphoria and our ignorance, few of us saw how fragile was the independence for which people had struggled so fiercely. We had assumed, for example, that once Ghanaians had won political power, nothing could stop them from tackling poverty, ending exploitation, and reclaiming all they had been deprived

---

1 Julius Nyerere speaking to the United Women of Tanzania, Arusha, 1967.

of by colonialism. It took years for us to acknowledge how the new political independence was subverted by the old predators and even used by them to rule more profitably. Tragically, in country after country we have seen the colonialism defeated by massive movements return in new and in some ways more deadly forms. Leaders of such popular movements, like Lumumba of the Congo, and heads of State who would not make a deal, like Kwame Nkrumah of Ghana, were assassinated or overthrown.

The ex-colonial middle class moved up when the colonial flag came down, distancing themselves from the aspirations of the population, which had made a way for them. So-called leaders acquiesced in the corruption they were offered and facilitated the exploitation of the people and resources they now ruled. The new managerial class shielded itself by claiming that to criticize them was to attack Africanization or Indianization, etc., and the movement they themselves were undermining.

By 1967, a decade after Ghana's independence, when Tanzania gave us the *Arusha Declaration*, all the lessons were there to be learnt. But few were ready or able to learn them. The remarkable Julius Nyerere was a stunning exception.

Nyerere, the Mwalimu—the teacher—had seen India become independent in August 1947, giving a mortal blow to European imperialism. "When Gandhi succeeded, I think it made the British lose the will to cling to the Empire."[2] It would not have been lost on him that Gandhi, the Mahatma—the Great Soul—urged that development in India be based not on the cities and industrialization but on the seven million villages where most of the population lived and worked. To many this seemed to accept backwardness. To the Mwalimu and the Mahatma, it was the only chance for their societies to refuse to be crushed by capitalist development. For both, the village was not merely an absence of development but the most appropriate and practical base for it.

Beginning with the refusal of capitalist development, the *Arusha Declaration* is nothing less than an economic, social, and political perspective to enable Tanzanians to develop themselves and their economy in the course of building a "socialist" society.

Nyerere of course begins with Tanzania's poverty. He spells out the obvious which is rarely mentioned, that those in the city benefit most from economic and social development—hospitals, schools, roads, electricity, etc.—and that those in the country finance this development:

> We recognize that we do not have enough money to bring the kind of
> development to each village which would benefit everybody. We also know that
> we cannot establish an industry in each village and through this means erect a
> rise in the real incomes of the people. For these reasons we spend most of our

---

2   This would have been a response to the postwar Labour government in Britain which declared soon after its election that India would be independent.

money in the urban areas and our industries are established in the towns. Yet the greater part of this money that we spend in the towns comes from loans ...To repay the loans we have to use foreign currency which is obtained from the sale of our exports. But...it is likely to be a long time before our industries produce for export... Where, then, shall we get it from? We shall get it from the villages and from agriculture. What does this mean? It means that the people who benefit directly from development which is brought about by borrowed money are not the ones who will repay the loans. The largest proportion of the loans will be spent in, or for, the urban areas, but the largest proportion of the repayment will be made through the efforts of the farmers... All our big hospitals are in towns and they benefit only a small section of the people of Tanzania. Yet if we had built them with loans from outside Tanzania, it is the overseas sale of the peasants' produce which provides the foreign exchanges for repayment. Those who do not get the benefit of the hospital thus carry the major responsibility for paying for them.

The frankness is breathtaking. We have little experience of heads of State telling it like it is with clarity and precision, and taking as their starting point the interests of those with least power. He then spells out exactly whose work in the countryside repays the development debt:

It would be appropriate to ask our farmers, especially the men, how many hours a week and how many weeks a year they work. Many do not even work for half as many hours as the wage-earner does. The truth is that in the villages the women work very hard. At times they work for 12 or 14 hours a day. They even work on Sundays and public holidays. Women who live in the villages work harder than anybody else in Tanzania. But the men who live in villages (and some of the women in towns) are on leave for half of their life.

President Nyerere draws out the economic implications: "The energies of the millions of men in the villages and thousands of women in the towns which are at present wasted in gossip, dancing and drinking, are a great treasure *which could contribute more towards the development of our country than anything we could get from rich nations.*" [our emphasis]

That is, Tanzania would have much less need for foreign loans and "aid" if the men were not "on leave for half their life" while women did most of the work. Equity was a question not only of justice; it was a basic economic necessity.

We can only imagine how the Mwalimu's male colleagues responded when their leader first presented the draft of this basic party document, which exposed the exploitation of women (including of course in their own families). Whatever their reactions, it remained in the final document.

Nyerere's sweeping alternative to the problems he outlined was first and foremost the creation of autonomous socialist villages. This was:

> *a new conception, based on the post–Arusha Declaration understanding* that what
> we need to develop is people, not things, and that people can only develop
> themselves…[our emphasis] *Ujamaa* villages are intended to be socialist
> organizations created by the people, and governed by those who live and work in
> them. They cannot be created from outside, nor governed from outside. No one
> can be forced into an *ujamaa* village, and no official—at any level—can go and
> tell the members of an *ujamaa* village what they should do together, and what
> they should continue to do as individual farmers. No official of the government
> or party can go to an *ujamaa* village and tell the members what they must grow.
> No non-member of the village can go and tell the members to use a tractor, or
> not to use a tractor. For if these things happen—that is, if an outsider gives such
> instructions and enforces them—then it will no longer be an *ujamaa* village![3]

This direction—socialism in action—was gleaned from hard experience of, first, what had been tried and had failed: "All too often…we persuaded people to go into new settlements by promising them that they could quickly grow rich there, or that government would give them services and equipment which they could not hope to receive either in the towns or in their traditional farming places." [4] This had not worked. There were:

> very many cases where heavy capital investment has resulted in no increase in
> output—where the investment has been wasted. And in most of the officially
> sponsored or supported schemes, the majority of people who went to settle lost
> their enthusiasm, and either left the scheme altogether, or failed to carry out the
> orders of the outsiders who were put in charge—and who were not themselves
> involved in the success or failure of the project.[5]

He drew the conclusion: "What we were doing, in fact, was thinking of development in terms of things, and not of people."[6]

The direction was also derived from what was already succeeding. In the Ruvuma area, villages had been created where people were working out what *ujamaa* was in practice: how to live and work collectively, how to overcome the power disparity between women and men, how to decide on and incorporate new agricultural

---

3 *Freedom and Development*, October 16, 1968, circulated shortly after at a meeting of the TANU National Executive Committee. Republished in *Freedom and Development: Uhuru na Maendeleo* (Dar Es Salaam: OUP, 1973), 67.

4 Ibid., 66

5 Ibid., 66–67.

6 Ibid., 66.

information and techniques to raise productivity, how to educate children so they could fully participate in the collective life, how to use expertise from abroad without being dominated by those who provided it…these and other fundamental problems of development were collectively tackled and solved by the whole village population.

Mwalimu used the Ruvuma Development Association's success as an example to others at home and abroad. It was the source of his confidence that his policy of *ujamaa* could succeed—in one area of the country it was visibly succeeding, being taken up by others locally, and being watched throughout the country by people who were considering following the stunning Ruvuma example.[7]

In the months after spelling out the perspective, Mwalimu explained its application to different aspects of social development. With each simple but profound essay or speech, the Teacher gives us clarity—on education, on the struggle against racism, on agriculture, on socialism, on trade unionism. He reformulates and further articulates the perspective. The purpose, he says, is *watu, people* in Swahili—usually translated into English as *man*:

> For in a Tanzania which is implementing the *Arusha Declaration*, the purpose of
> all social, economic and political activity must be people—the citizens, and all
> the citizens, of this country. The creation of wealth is a good thing and something
> which we shall have to increase. But it will cease to be good the moment wealth
> ceases to serve people and begins to be served by people.[8]

Over and over one is reminded of the foundations that Marx laid. Like him, Nyerere's case against capitalism was precisely that people were made to serve production and exchange rather than being served by them. Tanzania would reject the capitalist fetish, that commodities and money have a natural power over people. They would build an economy where freely associated individuals would be in charge of their own production, and consciously and collectively build their own society.

Only now are we discovering that in the last years of his life Marx was working out how, and how much, traditional Indigenous communalism could bypass capitalism and move directly to a communist society; how, under favorable conditions, such societies could be "the fulcrum of social regeneration."[9] This gives new and wider relevance to what the great Tanzanian Teacher found his way to for Tanzania.

---

7   But despite Mwalimu's backing, and at the height of its success, the RDA was destroyed in 1969 by his government.

8   "The Purpose Is Man," speech at the teach-in on the *Arusha Declaration*, Dar es Salaam University College branch of the TANU Youth League, August 5, 1967. In *Freedom and Socialism: Uhuru na Ujamaa* (London: OUP, 1968), 316.

9   Karl Marx, "Letter to Vera Zasulich," in *Late Marx and the Russian Road*, ed. T. Shanin (London: Routledge and Kegan Paul, 1983), 124.

The whole population had to understand what the *Declaration* was proposing, and work out in a collective way if and how they wanted to carry it out. But most people were illiterate—especially of course women who were the main workers—so this had to be explained in person:

> To get *ujamaa* villages established, and to help them to succeed, education and leadership are required. These are the things which TANU [Tanganyika African National Union, the ruling party] has to provide. It is our job to explain what an *ujamaa* village is, and to keep explaining it until the people understand. But the decision to start must be made by the people themselves—and it must be made by each individual.[10]

Thus the first job of leaders was to explain the proposed policy "until the people understand," enabling each individual to decide whether or not they want to act on it.

And thus the *Arusha Declaration* was "a declaration of intent; no more than that."[11] That was all it could be. Only the people could take the deliberate thoughtful action for change. *Ujamaa* would take patience. There were no shortcuts.

Considering how central to development Nyerere declared women to be, we see few references to women *per se* in his writings after the *Declaration*. It may be that some have not been translated from the Swahili, or have not been published at all. There is, however, one notable exception.

"Socialism and Rural Development" was written a few months after *The Arusha Declaration;* he considered it "an integral part" of the *Declaration* itself.[12] In it he gives us a vital historical context to his social and political analysis. Nyerere says there are "two basic factors which prevented traditional society from full flowering":

> The first of these was…an acceptance of one human inequality….women in traditional society were regarded as having a place in the community which was not only different, but was also to some extent inferior….women did, and still do, more than their fair share of the work in the fields and in the homes. By virtue of their sex they suffered from inequalities which had nothing to do with their contribution to the family welfare….within traditional society ill-treatment and enforced subservience could be their lot. This is certainly inconsistent with our socialist conception of the equality of all human beings… If we want our country to make full and quick progress now, it is essential that our women live on terms of full equality with their fellow citizens who are men.

> The other aspect of traditional life which we have to break away from is its poverty.

---

10   *Freedom and Development*, 68.

11   "The Purpose Is Man," 315.

12   "Socialism and Rural Development" in *Freedom and Socialism*, 337–66.

So that inequity and poverty were what *ujamaa* was to overcome. These two weaknesses reinforced each other. "*Full and quick progress*" in overcoming inequality between women and men was central to ending poverty.

Aiming for equity in a country with scarce resources, Nyerere concentrated to the best of his ability on policies giving women the help they needed to undermine traditional subservience.

The most basic change would be the *ujamaa* village itself which by its nature opened the possibility of ending male domination of the rural economy. In an *ujamaa* village women would be collective owners of the land they worked and of its product, participating in all decisions on crops, methods, distribution, etc. Women's workload would become a collective consideration as would men's; each would do an equitable share, raising productivity and accelerating the elimination of poverty. The very nature of *ujamaa* opened the way for women to break from their traditional subservient position and collectively recreate social relationships.

Women were helped in other ways, including with positive discrimination in university education—light years ahead of much richer countries.

But the tradition was heavy against women. That story is still to be told.

We are not able even to list here all that Tanzania accomplished with this truly remarkable political leader. We note only that Dar Es Salaam was a center of the antiapartheid and other liberation movements on the continent. Nyerere's dedication to African unity and thus his support for Kwame Nkrumah's Pan-Africanism was integral to his perspective for Tanzania. With characteristic frankness and clarity, by 1997 he used the occasion of the fortieth anniversary of Ghana's independence to lay bare the "major reason" Pan-Africanism failed:

> Too many of us had a vested interest in keeping Africa divided. Prior to the
> independence of Tanganyika I had been advocating that the East African
> countries should federate and then achieve independence as a single political unit.
> I had said publicly that I was willing to delay Tanganyika's independence in order
> to enable all the three mainland countries to achieve their independence together
> as a single federated State. I made the suggestion because of my fear—proved
> correct by later events—that it would be very difficult to unite our countries if we
> let them achieve independence separately. Once you multiply national anthems,
> national flags and national passports, seats at the United Nations, and individuals
> entitled to a 21-gun salute, not to speak of a host of ministers and envoys, you
> would have a whole army of powerful people with vested interests in keeping
> Africa balkanized.[13]

---

13 Kwame Nkrumah & African Unity (Vigor, Commitment & Sincerity). Speech on 40th anniversary of Ghana independence, Accra, March 6, 1997.

He is describing not only a personal weakness, but a sector which often claims to speak for the anticapitalist movement but whose ambition leads it to work, even to repress and to kill, for our enemies. This managerial sector, government or nongovernmental, undermines every popular movement, yet is not often called to account—hardly ever in such unambiguous terms.

The Venezuelan revolution is daily having to confront not the corruption of a newly independent African State forty years ago, but that pervasive corruption inherited from a century of oil production. President Chávez, the revolution's leader, must constantly guard against the threat not only of subversion and violence from the United States but of subversive ambition at home. The grassroots movement, which drives the revolution forward is subverted also by ever-present corruption which attempts to undermine and demoralize it.[14] Chávez combats this threat first of all by calling it. Addressing the newly elected regional officials on November 12, 2004, he said:

> A public servant cannot be engaged in business... There is a medicine against being corrupt: send personal and material ambitions to hell. He who has this kind of weakness is just a step away from corruption. He who aspires to live in a luxurious great house, who aspires to possess material goods or who already has them and wants more, is a step away. So in this new strategic moment I urge you to struggle hard against the scourge of corruption.

On a visit to China in 1968, Nyerere spoke of sectors whose skills, in short supply in a nonindustrial country, make them vulnerable to ambition and therefore to corruption:

> Chairman Mao has many times called for the "Red Expert"—the skilled man who is devoted to the political creed of China. We in Tanzania search for the "committed expert." Both of us are really trying to find the kind of expert, whether he be skilled in scientific subjects, in administration, or in any of the other many jobs we need, who seeks only to use his knowledge and abilities for the service of the people—and service as the people themselves define it. Such people do exist, but the temptations for anyone in a position of power are very great.[15]

Perhaps the most startling section in the *Declaration* is Part Five, known as the Leadership Code, which sets a standard for both party and government personnel against offers of any form of corruption, from small businessmen to mighty multinationals and predatory imperial powers. To corrupt what cannot be overthrown or defeated in other ways is now known to be integral to international power relations.

---

14 See Statement from Women Housewives Workers in the Home To President Chávez, February 4, 2006, http://www.globalwomenstrike.net/English2006/StatementFromWomenToChavez.htm.

15 The Supremacy of the People, speech during his second State visit, Beijing, China, June 18, 1968. In *Freedom and Socialism*, 37.

Even in a recent Hollywood thriller about the oil industry, a CIA operative proclaims: "Corruption is why we win!"

There was a price Tanzania paid for having taken an independent and truly revolutionary road; for trying to develop while bypassing capitalism, and instead building an economy based on cooperation and the participation of each individual. Every wing of capitalism and imperialism has worked overtime to discredit Mwalimu's policies and label the whole seminal Tanzanian experience as an unrealistic failure. Years later, when no longer in office, Nyerere put his critics in their place—almost in passing:

> I was in Washington last year. At the World Bank the first question they asked me was "How did you fail?" I responded that we took over a country with 85 percent of its adult population illiterate. The British ruled us for forty-three years. When they left, there were two trained engineers and twelve doctors. This is the country we inherited. When I stepped down there was 91 percent literacy and nearly every child was in school. We trained thousands of engineers and doctors and teachers. In 1988 Tanzania's per capita income was U.S.$280. Now, in 1998, it is U.S.$140.
>
> So I asked the World Bank people what went wrong. Because for the last ten years Tanzania has been signing on the dotted line and doing everything the IMF and the World Bank wanted. Enrolment in school has plummeted to 63 percent and conditions in health and other social services have deteriorated. I asked them again: "What went wrong?" These people just sat there looking at me. Then they asked what could they do. I told them: have some humility. Humility. They are so arrogant![16]

Those who have visited Tanzania have seen for themselves that it is the most peaceful country in Africa and perhaps in the world. Considering all the populations, in Africa and elsewhere, which have fallen victim to tribal, ethnic, and other proxy wars fomented to advance the interests of European and North American capital, President Nyerere's Tanzania did remarkably well. Mwalimu must have found Tanzania a peaceful country, but it was he who ensured that it remained that way—so different in so many ways from all the countries it borders.

The *Arusha Declaration* sets standards that are relevant far beyond Tanzania. It lays down principles of leadership that are universally applicable: not to tell people what to do, but to give us the information we need to make informed decisions. It demands that we consider what principles should guide relationships between the individual and the economy, and between women and men. It gives us a redefinition of socialism which begins with those of us at the bottom, not of Tanzania only but

---

16 Interview with Mwalimu Nyerere, December 1998, in *The Monitor* (Kampala, 1999), www.africannews. org and *New Internationalist* 309 (January/February 1999).

of the world. Above all, it starts from the assumption that we must never depend on capitalist relations of exploitation to attack and to defeat poverty, inequity, ignorance.

We have to note that this direction and these principles came from a man who did not leave his village for a school till he was about twelve years old—in a society where by that age you are already an adult. His wisdom therefore was the wisdom of the village—where much if not most of the world still lives and works the land— informed by wide reading and experience.

We are pleased and honored to republish the *Arusha Declaration*. Our aim is to make this great document available to those who have never heard of it, and to remind those who may have forgotten what a remarkable struggle for liberation it expressed and impelled forward. As we renew the movement to transform the nature of politics and the economy so that the purpose is once again *watu*—people—we must educate ourselves and each other about our hidden history, which includes an Africa that gives leadership to our struggle, as women, as men, as workers urban and rural, waged and unwaged, everywhere.

INTERVIEW EXCERPTS (2009)

Organizing Internationally, and with Men

Guaranteed Income vs. Wages for Housework

Crucial aspects of our work—how we organize internally from day to day, and our changing views on major questions—rarely get recorded. How many besides our colleagues and ourselves are interested? The only time we get to spell it out is in interviews, especially by people organizing who come from another country. The first three questions were from a woman and a man from Japan—both academics and both organizers with women for welfare. The fourth was from feminists in Turkey.

What does it mean for a women's group to be part of the Global Women's Strike?

It means that they are in touch with a number of other countries and thus there is a whole set of information available to them. So they work out what they are doing, and want to do, in the context of what other women are doing, and that is very powerful and useful. The existence of that connection enhances your power: your decisions are bolder and more realistic because they reflect the power you have which you aren't usually aware of, and which is hard to be aware of. It means that whatever you are doing, you are not only the ten, twenty, thirty, fifty or a hundred people who are having an event or trying to do something; there is a whole international network that is respectful and supportive, and they will advertise what you do so that it will have more credibility and a wider impact.

We have seen with the Strike that women have got the respect of men, and even of local governments, because they see the power of a connection with other women and men, including in Western countries.

Payday, the men's network, works closely with the Strike. Can you talk about your relationship with them?

I'm one of the women who has worked very closely with Payday. They are men who have accepted first of all that the Global Women's Strike is an organization based on those who do caring work. That doesn't mean that they have to be obeisant, or do what women tell them, but they have to acknowledge the work of carers and the power that is for the entire working class.

In this context the men have been concentrating their activity on *refuseniks*, on those women and men, but mainly men, in most countries of the world, who are saying "No" to the military. Not only no to the Iraq war, no to fighting in Afghanistan, but Israel's refuseniks, America's refusers, people who have been saying, "No More War"—each from his own point of view—and who have fought the governments of their countries for their right to refuse to go. And they've been recalling people who have said "no" in the past: no to the Vietnam War, no even to World War II. No to the kind of person the military tries to make you into: a killer and often also a rapist. Supporting and promoting that refusal is the kind of work that men should be doing; it's so useful.

And Payday has made it clear that it's often women—mothers, partners, sisters, and so on—who have fought for these soldiers, who have supported the ones who refused, and that these women have been the foundation of refusal campaigns. That recognition is an enormous power for women and it's an enormous power for men as well as for the antiwar movement. So we work easily and well and mutually respectfully together.

Their Refusing to Kill initiative has become Refusing to Kill and Be Killed, referring to the right not to have to risk your life for "King and Country," as well as opposition to the death penalty in U.S. prisons and elsewhere. The women and men work together on this and on much else.

Some Payday men are doing anti-Zionist work; others are working for protecting the environment. They consult us on all of it, and women's specific interests are integral to any Payday initiative.

And we also make a way for the men because it is the considered view of the women in the Strike that men are not represented very much. Men may look like they have power, but they don't, except over women. Few say how men are exploited—what their whole case and their whole struggle is. Not just at the so-called point of production, but everywhere in the society. Payday attempts to make that case and make it clear that in order to make change, it's not that you push women down, it's that we all move up together against the war and for the caring.

We all want to be caring human beings. Caring is not a job like any other, or less than any other; quite the opposite. Caring is ultimately the basis of all our most important relationships.

Caring has always been a crucial part of keeping the movement together, but nobody noticed because women did it behind the scenes, so to speak. Payday is ready to acknowledge that work and fight alongside us for it to be prioritized. I mean we all had better care for each other or we'll lose.

How do you make decisions?

Our decision-making process is very simple. We have discussions, first of all in small groups working on particular issues. So that if women are working on the question of racist assault or some aspect of racist assault, or some question of welfare, the women who are engaged in that, and the men often also, will meet to discuss it, and work out what they are doing and should be doing, and how and with whom. People consult others who are not in their issue group or organization, but who have information or experience that may be useful.

Then every six or seven weeks we all take a day to meet together and have a kind of clearing house so that everybody knows what everybody else is doing. We are always running to catch up because we are all involved in so many different things. There is a lot of informal consultation that goes on and we try very hard all to stay on the same wavelength.

What do you think of the demand for a guaranteed income?

I feel differently now from what I felt when the Campaign began because now we have established the importance of unwaged caring work. We always understood that the guaranteed income was saying we have the right to live without working for capitalism. That's a good point of view. But it's not enough.

When we say Wages for Housework, we say first of all that the work that women do must be visible and must be acknowledged not merely as work, but as a political fact, as a struggle: that women refuse to do this work. I want to explain that, because a lot of the work that women do is really the maintenance of the human race. And it's clear this work must be done. And not only that it must be done but that it is clearly the most important work in the world. But we can't do it alone, and we don't want men to "help." That's not enough. That's nothing like what is needed.

We need the whole society to be concerned with this work, and for it to be the central priority of the way we live. Nowadays in industrial countries it is perfectly clear that there is very little need to do much production work. We in the West could have access to everything we need and what others elsewhere need can quickly be produced. We need to produce food: we have the technology, and we have many traditional ways of growing food which have been thrown out because capitalism was not interested in healthy food, it was only interested in money. We can all share that work. So we must reorient society to caring. It's not that women should have help caring; it's that to be civilized is to be concerned about each other, and in a situation where there is not want anywhere in the world, where we all have or can get what we need. Guaranteed income does not address this at all.

It doesn't address the question of caring and it doesn't address the question of the forced labor and the position of power between women and men or between white people and people of color or between Third World and industrial people. Wages for housework does. It says: "Pay attention to what people are doing." What is it we are spending our lives doing? And if we are African women, we are growing food twelve to fourteen hours a day, fetching water, firewood…

Wages for Housework is like a searchlight into our real lives and the real relations among us. So whereas we want a guaranteed income, what we want is a *change*. And the change must come from reorienting the whole society against the divisions among us. But first we must see the divisions, acknowledge them, acknowledge the work, so we can refuse them, and build a movement against them. And that's some of what Wages for Housework is about doing.

SPEAKING AT THE U.S. ASSEMBLY OF JEWS CONFRONTING RACISM AND ISRAELI APARTHEID (2010)

June 19–22, held prior to the 2010 U.S. Social Forum in Detroit

IJAN is not merely uncompromisingly anti-Zionist and committed to taking its leadership from the Palestinian struggle, but is also a new kind of organization which has more to do with the twenty-first century than the twentieth, and I am very happy to be involved with it. And my speech can be curtailed because many of the things I believe are terribly important have already been said. But there are still a few things…[laughter]

First of all, the antiapartheid movement in the twentieth century in South Africa is urgent for us to explore further. That movement had deep, deep mistakes built into it, which we do not want to repeat in the struggle against Israeli apartheid. I will just give an idea here. They said that they were nonracist rather than antiracist, and that way they could avoid confronting the power relations among them, based on the racial divisions, and we have suffered bitterly from that lack of clarity and lack of autonomy for the majority who were Black and other people of color.

Secondly, they made South Africa an exception. Once you treat a struggle as an exception you cut the throat of that struggle. You urge support from others on very narrow and indirect terms: they must participate in the liberation movement through you, with no reference to their own experience. IJAN is not doing that. We are saying: the Zionists claim that the genocide of Jews is exceptional; well in some respects it has to be. But it is fundamentally unexceptional—others have faced genocide too. And Zionism is not exceptional either. *Apartheid* is not new, injustice is not new, occupation is not new, imprisoning and torturing children is not new, bombing and experimenting on civilians is not new... We know all about it. [Applause]

In addition, we are going to do research to show that Israel is not merely doing the bidding of the United States from time to time (and vice versa), but is integral to its military, to its policing of the world, is integral to its spreading its propaganda, its influence and its military control. So that when we confront Israel, we confront world imperialism—they are inseparable. [Applause] That means that we are not going to allow the United States to hide behind the agenda when we are describing the Zionist enemy and especially is this true in the United States. Your work is cut out for you.

You know, when IJAN began, and that wasn't very long ago, people who were against the war in Iraq still thought that they could also be Zionists. Yes. I think that's less possible now.

There is one struggle against racism, there is one struggle against imperialism, and what we are doing is concentrating on one part. I want to read a very brief quote from a letter that IJAN London wrote in support of Palestinian and other Arab young people who were demonstrating during the Gaza onslaught and who months later were arrested in their homes at four and five in the morning and then brought before the courts, and some were given sentences of two and three years for having thrown a plastic bottle. This has to do not only with the rise of Islamophobia. This has to do with curtailing all kinds of protest in Britain—again, they are not separable. Different but inseparable.

The supporters were delighted to receive the letter from IJAN. You know, IJAN is a facilitator. IJAN makes a way for others to protest against Zionism. That's one of the jobs we do. We wrote: "Those of us who concentrate on the liberation of Palestine are well aware of the tragedies unfolding elsewhere in the world, from Congo to Iraq, from Sri Lanka to Colombia. Defending our sisters and brothers in Palestine who resist and who struggle to survive, and taking a lead from their resistance is one with all who struggle to survive against violent repression anywhere." Thus we make clear in our day-to-day work that while we concentrate on Palestine, we are not unaware of the sufferings anywhere, and we feel in struggling for the liberation of Palestine, in supporting the Palestinian liberation struggle, we are supporting liberation struggles everywhere. That's our politics. [Applause]

Now we Jewish people have our own independent case against Zionism. It is terribly important to make clear that we are also struggling for ourselves in the Palestinian solidarity movement. And I think one of the greatest crimes against Jews that Israel has perpetrated—aside from saying that Jews did not fight the Nazis, that we went quietly into the camps; we don't know what they were doing (in fact we do; they were making deals with the Nazis)—aside from that, their crime has been to try to cut us off from our history and tradition of taking part in movements against injustice. [Applause]

That's my background and my training. When my father saw a Zionist he would spit. That was because Zionism was the philosophy and ambitions of the bosses against us. That's what I learned in Brooklyn. [Applause]

Although the movement has been very low, it is coming up everywhere, and the tradition of Jewish opposition to exploitation and racism and imperialism is coming alive again. And I believe it's again alive, among other places, in IJAN. This is the movement—the one that we used to have; that we never quite lost, and it's coming back to life. It's a perennial. [Applause and laughter]

Now I want to go quickly to some points of organizing: We are uncompromisingly anti-Zionist. We cannot lose that clarity. That would be to lose the function that we perform by our very existence. It's fundamental. And then people will come in who may not know better and who are a little afraid of the American State—which of us is not?—and they will say, "Well, could we not say the whole thing now? We could say some now and then we could say some later. And there are some people who are *almost* anti-Zionist who will come with us if we do that, and we will have more people." [Laughter] They exist in every movement. But what we say is: we remain uncompromisingly anti-Zionist and we know, or at least we must learn, that our influence, our effectiveness, are not dependent on our numbers but on our clarity and determination—that's terribly important for us to learn. So if there are twenty of us and they have two hundred—that doesn't mean they are going to be ten times more effective than we are; no, it doesn't. It means that because we are so clear and determined they will have to shift their position closer to ours. But we don't turn our nose up at people who do not want to go all the way; we are happy to be supportive of what they are doing, as long as it doesn't undermine our principles. That balance is vital; to do otherwise is to be sectarian and to undermine the movement, and that is not what we are about. [Applause]

There is no alternative to organizing internationally. You can be antiracist in the United States. And many white people always have been. But being fully antiracist is dependent on international connections, on knowing the various ways in which people live and struggle, and incorporating that into what you stand for and what you must be supporting. So then whatever you are doing, you are accountable also to them. There is no other way to be antiracist except what you do takes into account other people's struggles and ensures that you never do anything that undermines other people's struggles. This is not easy but it's absolutely crucial. [Hear! Hear!]

I wanted to say something about the effectiveness of the Palestinian struggle. You know I don't know a lot about it, I'm dependent on those more informed than I to provide the information I wouldn't ordinarily have because I'm also involved in other sections of the movement. And yet you find things out all the time about how important the Palestinian struggle is in the whole of the Middle East. We have to say how much we owe to that struggle and proclaim its importance. The working-class struggle that has gone on in Egypt—by the way, led by women: they walked out of the textile factories, came together, and said, "Where are the men?" They couldn't find them! Anyway, those struggles were inspired by the Palestinians. That's terribly important to know, it's terribly important that what one set of people, whom we are supporting, are doing is also in support of a whole set of other people. And we have to look at the whole of the Middle East again and at other parts of the world to see how much the anti-Zionist struggle is inspiring the rise of the movement in other places.

OK, what's standing in our way? Well the previous speaker made a good start on the NGOs. There are more NGOs per person in Haiti than anywhere else in the world. It's also the poorest country. There is a connection. Somebody is collecting the money, but it's not poor Haitians. That's what the NGOs have done. The NGOs' role has also been in assisting privatization almost everywhere where there was a welfare State. It is NGOs who do it now, who are not accountable, who do what they like and insist they are helping us, and then they have the nerve to say that they are the movement. Well, we can't allow that. And those of us who are in NGOs—some of them do good work, but we must always be aware of their limitations and we must always be aware because of our own experience in NGOs exactly how they work and how they undermine the movement. That's an important job that people from the movement who work for NGOs have to perform.

The same thing is true—forgive me, I'm so sorry—with academia. [Laughter and applause] You know, they get their views from books, or from the movement, without crediting it. Not acceptable. That is a form of theft. And they talk in a language that I do not understand even when it's in English. Now that's not acceptable either. With rare exceptions, we in the movement have to be understood by anybody who wants to hear. We have to be available, accessible, with words of one syllable that relate to people's real experiences of life and struggle.

Academia has had far too much power for far too long—has often been the base of leaders of left-wing movements. They live in academic departments (that tells you what has happened to the Left). You know, it's really not good enough. And those of you who are academics, there's a lot that we need from you. We need information from you, we need connections from you, sometimes we need photocopying from you—there are a lot of things you can do for us, but you can't expect to lead the movement from academia. You can't. The only thing you can lead is a publishing house, which is useful. But we can't confuse the movement with sectors of people who are in places of management of the society. You see, there's a difference between leadership and management, and we don't want management to be leading or attempting to lead the movement.

An important problem that we face in the movement, a vice we have been encouraged to have, is self-indulgence. Our points of reference are the Palestinians in struggle. It is quite important that we look at our habits and see that they conform to our principles, not the other way around.

And now I'm going to get really unpopular. Very closely connected to this is horizontalism. Horizontalism assumes there are no differences among us. Well, there are. Horizontalism is the view that you don't need leadership and that everybody should be on one level. It's not like that. We have first of all to see what society imposes on us in the way of a hierarchy. And it is a very complicated hierarchy. You know, an Indian member of the Global Women's Strike said, "You don't know what it's like in India. We have four thousand castes." I told her that we have four thousand castes in London, only they are not labeled in that way. Of course there are enormous differences between the two societies, but this is just to underline that we too have to acknowledge the hierarchy among us: it's based on class, on race, on gender, on disability, on age, on wages—on sector of society, on all the ways in which we are divided. And one of the things which I expect my leadership to do is to expose the hierarchy so that we can undermine it, not hide it, not make believe it isn't there, not "raise our consciousness" so we don't notice it.

The point is that we need leadership, but not management. You know, for me leadership is not a privilege we bestow but hard work; because if you're a leader you have to work out all the time why you are thinking such backward thoughts. That's what a good leader is doing twenty-four hours a day. Well, twenty.

So I think we have to continue the discussion among us about what relationships we want in our organization, which are an accurate reflection of our political perspective, so that there is one continuum between what our principles are, and what our practice is, internally and externally. I think that's terribly important.

Another thing. I don't know about armed struggle or not armed struggle. I don't have a view about what the Palestinians should do, and I don't think that we can know from this distance.

I want to say finally, the Israelis have got away with what they've got away with because we have allowed it. There's no other reason, there's only us and them. Who else is there? But they got away with it because the theory that enables them to make an exception of themselves is what we in the movement, at least in the West, and I've seen that also in Third World countries, what we have accepted, and that is: identity politics: I have been exploited and therefore I have a right to exploit her, her, him, and him. That's identity politics. I have ambition and I have a right to fulfill my ambition at her expense, her expense, her expense and her expense, because I have been exploited. And when we finish with Zionism, which indeed we will, then we will also have finished with the most crass form of identity politics, the one which allows those who have suffered—or in this case the descendants of the sufferers—to claim the right to exploit, kill and maim without limit. *We will not have any of it,* not we in IJAN, not we in the movement, not we in the world.

Thank you.

HAITI
(2010-2011)

A ny associate of CLR James would have been aware of Haiti's extraordinary history not only through his book but because he spoke of the Haitian Revolution and revolutions generally. When I prepared *The Black Jacobins* for republication at the end of 1961 in Barbados, I saw what a Caribbean book it was, describing a society in some ways not that different from the one I was living in.[1]

On March 3, 2004, Caribbean women in the Global Women's Strike issued a public statement condemning the U.S. coup in Haiti that had taken place three days before. The coup overthrew the democratically elected government of Jean-Bertrand Aristide that had just celebrated the bicentenary of Haiti's independence. Since then, the Strike in Guyana, the UK, and the United States has been working with the Haiti Action Committee in the U.S. in support of the Haitian grassroots.

The following two letters, published in the *Guardian*, tried to get out to the public the real situation in Haiti, and to protest the shockingly demeaning way in which Haiti has often been treated in the Western media. It is one example of how racism works: what the powerful think of you shapes how the media chooses to speak—or not speak—about you. The second letter was signed with Nina López who has done consistent work on Haiti. Square brackets throughout the text usually indicate what was edited out of the original article.

---

1   CLR James, *The Black Jacobins: Toussaint L'Ouverture and the San Domingo Revolution* (New York: Vintage Books, 1989).

Only Aristide Has the Mandate to Lead Haiti's Recovery (January 18, 2010)

It took a catastrophe [the earthquake of January 12, 2010] to put Haiti back on the political map. Yet its contribution to world civilization is considerable. Having extended the 1789 French revolution to Haiti, Black Jacobins ended slavery, leading the way for abolition in the Americas. Western governments never forgave this impertinence, imposing crippling debt, occupations, and dictatorships.

But Haitians never lost awareness that they could overcome and, if necessary, overthrow. In 1986, a mass movement kicked out the murderous Duvaliers whom the west had backed for decades, and in 1990 elected Jean-Bertrand Aristide, a liberation theologian determined to move the population "from destitution to poverty with dignity." He prioritized food security, health, and education, encouraged [reforestation and] agricultural cooperatives, and raised the minimum wage. Within months a U.S.-backed coup overthrew him. Elected again in 2000 with over 90 percent of the vote, he was again removed in 2004, not by "a bloody rebellion" ("Haiti's Exiled Former President Vows to Return," *Guardian*, January 15) but by bloody U.S. marines.

[Jon Henley's rewriting of history, while omitting Aristide, shows the merit of dictatorship and slavery which ensure order and wealth production: "Haiti...was the Pearl of the Antilles, one of the richest islands in France's empire (though eight hundred thousand–odd African slaves who produced that wealth saw precious little of it)." The Economist Intelligence Unit is quoted: "The Duvaliers may have bankrupted the government, they may have been brutal, but they could keep control of the place." ("Haiti: a long descent to hell," *Guardian*, January 15)]

Haitians continue to call for Aristide's return. Will the only person with a mandate to govern be kept from leading their recovery and reconstruction?

False Picture of Foreign Aid to Haiti (November 19, 2010)
With Nina López

The UN forces came to police the 92 percent of Haitian voters who had elected President Aristide and protested about his overthrow by a U.S. coup. They were never "heroes"—except to the elite "cocooned in luxury and indifference" who backed the coup ("Heroes to zeros," *Guardian*, November 17, 2010).

Before accusations of having brought cholera to Haiti (many believe intentionally), UN troops stood accused of murdering and raping Aristide supporters. According to *The Lancet* (UN peacekeepers in Haiti, September 2, 2006): "In just 22 months—from the departure of President Jean-Bertrand Aristide to the end of 2005—eight thousand people were murdered and thirty-five thousand women sexually assaulted." While "criminals" were blamed, "police, armed forces, paramilitaries and foreign soldiers were also implicated."

You have got some things right: Haiti is a "republic of NGOs"; "aid tourism" does hinder reconstruction; and subsidized U.S. imports were responsible for "destroying home-grown agriculture." (Bill Clinton apologized for the starvation his policies inflicted.) But your claim that U.S. troops are "popular and many people want them back," and the fact that U.S.-financed elections on November 28 exclude Aristide's Fanmi Lavalas party from the ballot, disregard the will of a people who, despite every obstacle, continue to let their will be known.

Twice before, in April and June 2009, 90 percent of the Haitian electorate boycotted U.S.-funded elections that illegally excluded Fanmi Lavalas. In June 2010, Haitians brought to the U.S. Social Forum a petition signed by over twenty thousand female earthquake survivors demanding Aristide's return from forced exile. If Aristide were home, Haitians would not be at the mercy of NGOs and others for whom they are merely a business opportunity.

Black Jacobins, Past and Present

As part of a series of reviews of political classics, the UK bimonthly *Red Pepper* asked me to review *The Black Jacobins*. It was published in June 2010.

It took an earthquake whose destructive power was enhanced by dire poverty to rekindle interest in Haiti. Many who want to know who Haitians are seem to have turned to *The Black Jacobins*, a history of the revolution the slaves made.

Seizing on the revolution in France, they took their freedom and got revolutionary Paris to ratify it. But as the revolution's power in France waned, to prevent slavery's return they had to defeat the armies of Spain and Britain as well as France's Napoleon and, amazingly, they did. In 1804 the independent republic of Haiti was born.

Black Jacobins was published in 1938 as a contribution to the movement for colonial emancipation—for Africa first of all, when few considered this possible. By 1963 it had been out of print for years but the exploding anti-imperialist and anti-racist movements had created a new market for it. Later books updating information on Haiti's revolution have not challenged its classic status. It's worth asking why.

First, James takes sides uncompromisingly with the slaves. While he has all the time in the world for anti-racist whites who loved Toussaint and the revolution, his point of reference is the struggle of those who were wresting themselves back from being the possession of others. The book recounts their courage, imagination and determination. But James doesn't glamorize: "The slaves destroyed tirelessly... And if they destroyed much it was because they had suffered much. They knew that as long as these plantations stood their lot would be to labor on them until they dropped. The only thing was to destroy them."

Nor does he shield us from the terrorism and sadism of the masters. But the way the catalogue of tortures is presented does more than torture the reader; it deepens our appreciation of the former slaves' power to endure and overcome. Despite death and destruction, the slaves are never helpless victims. This may explain why strugglers from the Caribbean and even South Africa told the author that at low points in their movements *Black Jacobins* had helped sustain them. This quality is what makes the book thrilling and inspiring—we are learning from the Haitians' determination to be free what being human is about.

Second, Toussaint L'Ouverture possessed all the skills of leadership that the revolution needed. An uneducated, middle-aged West Indian when it began, he was soon able to handle sophisticated European diplomats and politicians who foolishly thought they could manipulate him because he was Black and had been a slave.

James liked to say that while the official claim is that Lincoln freed the slaves, it was in fact the slaves who had freed Lincoln—from his limitations and the conservative restraints of office. Here, James says that "Toussaint did not make the revolution. It was the revolution that made Toussaint." Then he adds: "And even that is not the whole truth."

In other words, while the movement chooses, creates and develops its leadership, historians are unlikely to pin that process down, whatever they surmise from events. What we can be sure of, however, is that the great leader is never a "self-made man," but a product of his individual talents and skills (and weaknesses) shaped by the movement he leads in the course of great upheavals. The Haitian Jacobins created Toussaint and he led them to where they had the will and determination to go.

This is still groundbreaking today, considering that there are parties and organizations, large and small, which claim that their leadership is crucial for a revolution's success. There are also those who believe leadership is unnecessary and it inevitably holds the movement back. In Haiti the slaves made the revolution, and Toussaint, one of them, played a vital role in their winning.

Third, James tells us who many of these revolutionary slaves were. They were not proletarians, "But working and living together in gangs of hundreds on the huge sugar-factories which covered the North Plain, they were closer to a modern proletariat than any group of workers in existence at the time, and the rising was, therefore, a thoroughly prepared and organized mass movement."

This is relevant to the problem of development that the book poses: what are nonindustrial people to do about development after the revolution? The movement has struggled with this question for generations. Toussaint relied on the plantation system of the former masters who claimed to personify "civilization" and "culture"; they ultimately captured and killed him. The ex-slaves would not have it. They wanted their own plots of land, and the end of the plantation—an early form of forced collectivization.

Lenin finally (1923) proposed that the State encourage cooperatives, which, independent of the party, would dominate the economy. Gandhi insisted that Indians must hold on to the cotton industry and its village way of life against all odds. Nyerere proposed *ujamaa* or African socialism for Tanzanians, and with the momentum of the independence movement, people made extraordinary strides (a story still waiting to be told). China under Mao has more to tell us; and some Indigenous Latin Americans are gaining the power to say what they propose.

We know that Haiti went further than the movements elsewhere: it was decades before others abolished slavery. Haiti, so far ahead, was vulnerable to the imperial powers, which it had infuriated by its revolutionary impertinence.

Now, despite often racist reporting of events there, we are learning how the present Black Jacobins have been organizing and where their continuing struggle has reached. President Aristide, whom they elected by 92 percent of the vote, was twice taken from them by an alliance of the United States and the local elite. They demand his return. The least we can do is support that demand.

With Aristide's Return Comes Hope

In March 2010, Mildred Trouillot, wife and colleague of President Aristide, asked me to be among those welcoming them back to Haiti after seven years of forced exile. An edited version of this article appeared in the *Guardian*, March 21, 2011.

The return of former president Jean-Bertrand Aristide and his family to Haiti ends seven long years of campaigning—the 92 percent of voters who elected him a second time in 2000 had never accepted his overthrow in 2004 by a U.S.-backed military coup. They risked their lives against a UN occupation that killed and brutalized thousands to demand his return. And last Friday South Africa, where he had been living in forced exile, flew him back to a rapturous welcome in Port-au-Prince. Thousands were at the airport to welcome him and celebrate their triumph.

I was one of those waiting to greet him at his modest house, from where he had been kidnapped seven years ago. His captors had trashed the house and refurbishment had not yet finished. Workmen were still sweeping paths and adorning tree trunks with flowers and plants while hens and their chicks continued to scratch the ground. This is the modest home of the man accused—by the rich—of stealing.

Some in the waiting crowd were former political prisoners, others were visiting from exile. Yet others, once disheartened after so many defeats—dictators, coups, hurricanes, earthquake, then cholera—had felt they could now return from Haiti's Diaspora. Some young Haitian doctors who finished their training in Cuba had come to thank Aristide for their health program.

We listened on transistor radios for news of his arrival. Finally Aristide's plane had landed, and he was addressing supporters in a number of languages. He was back on Haitian soil two days before the election from which his party had been fraudulently excluded. (The government had given back his passport, but after the election, the government the United States would put in was sure to rescind that decision. Aristide would be kept out again though according to Haitian law a Haitian national must be let in. Thus he had to land before the election.)

Much later his car was heard in the driveway. As the metal barrier that protected the house began to slide open, mainly young people began to flood the path and climb the walls and trees, until we were surrounded by a torrent of the joyous. Lavalas, meaning "flash flood," was the name of Titid's party, and here it was. In their midst, hidden from our view, was the Aristides' car.

We waited another hour to be escorted inside through the singing and dancing crowd. I was welcomed into the arms of his wife Mildred Trouillot. We had worked together via email, but we had never met. Yet we both felt we were close friends. She was unafraid, elated to be back and part of this historic event.

Mildred was modestly grateful for the support, especially from other women, for this triumphant but uncertain moment. Her girls, fourteen and twelve years old, had to see how their father was greeted, she told me, so that "they understood who he was. Nothing else can explain it." The girls' nonnegotiable demand was that they bring their beloved little dog from South Africa with them.

Later, we were brought to meet their father. We would understand the human flood that had swept invited guests (like us) aside, he said. An explanation, pointedly not an apology.

He embraced me as the living connection with my late husband CLR James's *Black Jacobins*. Thabo Mbeki, the president of South Africa when Titid first arrived there, had told him that when Mbeki read this history of revolutionary slaves triumphant, he knew they would end apartheid. It was not so much a book as a weapon for freedom fighters. CLR had implied in the book that that was his intention. How unfair that he never knew the breadth of his success.

On election day we visited Cité Soleil, an impoverished working-class neighborhood which is an Aristide stronghold. We heard that two days earlier the presidential candidate Michel Martelly, a popular musician associated with the Tonton Macoutes—the Duvalier murder squads that terrorized Haiti for decades—had been driven out by Aristide supporters. UN soldiers from Brazil were all around the polling station, menacing, rifles at the ready.

We asked people about Aristide and the elections: they were happy he was back, but he wasn't on the ballot and they urgently needed to hold a government to account.

Yet the presence of Aristide in Haiti has immediately shifted everyone's situation. When he landed he spoke of "the humiliation of the people under tents" and said that "modern-day slavery will have to end today."

What's clear is that the 1804 revolution never ended. The U.S. and the Haitian elite seem as determined as nineteenth century France to keep Haitians enslaved, though sweatshops have replaced plantations and UN tanks Napoleon's army.

Nobody knows yet how Haitians will deal with the rigged election results. Aristide spoke to us about "learning from the people." He is likely to take his cue from their collective response. Having achieved the victory of his return, the movement has again a powerful, compassionate voice.

Speaking at the Aristide Foundation for Democracy

When I met President Aristide, he suggested that I speak at an event of secondary school students at the Aristide Foundation for Democracy, March 23, 2011.

We are thrilled to be here in Haiti and very grateful to be welcomed at the Aristide Foundation. We know the Foundation by reputation, as the base for many grassroots organizations, the place people naturally turned to for shelter and other help after the earthquake [of January, 12, 2010], and where the community (and especially women) come for Saturday meetings to discuss what to do to protect the community from repression and violence.

Thus it is appropriate that we are celebrating the return of President Aristide and his family in this community space. The Haitian people won that return. We know how people risked everything to get him back, and that many lost their lives demonstrating for his return. It says a great deal about his leadership, as president and as head of your movement, and about why he was taken from you.

We have seen his dedication to the grassroots, his boldness, risking his own safety, and his unwavering determination against the powerful and corrupt, both foreign and native. Many of you are too young to have known that leadership close up; now you will have that chance. We are outraged by the lies that are told about him and by attempts to hide how he is loved by Haitians.

Now we have met him and his wife and partner Mildred Trouillot for the first time. I was embraced by Titid as the widow of CLR James, the man who wrote *The Black Jacobins*. The book is about the great events in Haitian and in world history: the revolution the slaves made. The world knows Haitians defeated British imperial power and even Napoleon's army to end slavery and for the country to be independent.

Titid told us this book had put Haiti—a small country in the Caribbean—on the map. When *Black Jacobins* was written, he said, most people didn't even know where Haiti was. Through this book in English, and then in French, people knew about Haiti's great contribution to world civilization. The barbaric French plantation owners—who had the wealth, the resources, the education, all paid for by slave labor—were taught a lesson about civilization and freedom by their former slaves.

I was able to tell Titid something about CLR the historian from the Caribbean. He had never visited Haiti though he had been invited by the poet Feliks Moriso-Lewa (Félix Morisseau-Leroy) and was about to come when Papa Doc took power, which made the visit impossible.

Titid, the political leader of Haiti, suggested that I speak here about CLR. Titid is a teacher, dedicated to making education and other resources available to young people, fortifying them for the inevitable battles ahead. And as you know, there are major battles ahead.

CLR, also a political organizer, wrote this history of Haiti to help other organizers, and said so in his book. Over the years he had been told by rebels, from the Caribbean to South Africa, that when it seemed their misery, persecution, and gross exploitation would never end, reading how Haitians won with nothing but bravery and determination had sustained them. Thus the book made Haiti's revolution useful to many other strugglers elsewhere.

If he were alive today CLR would appreciate the present vibrant movement of the Haitian grassroots, despite horrendous odds. He would see that you have kept voudou and Kreyòl, the religion and the language of a revolutionary people. They are yours; you created them. And they are the foundations that have helped sustain resistance, keeping people together against every attempt to destroy the movement and Haiti's independence with it.

CLR used to comment on the way the French revolution manifested itself in French attitudes and habits even in the twentieth century. If he were here today, he would no doubt remark that after two centuries Haiti today has the same indomitable spirit of its revolution.

This is what it means to be a historian, or at least a good historian, and this is how he educated the people who struggled alongside him in the working-class movement. His starting point was always what grassroots people were trying to do, and to spell out, whether they succeeded or failed, what they accomplished, which the grassroots everywhere is never given credit for—they rob us even of our victories. A good historian must have an independent mind, independent of the dominant ideas that flatter and glorify the powers that be; never arrogantly passing judgment on whether our movement has the "right" consciousness, but appreciating and celebrating what it achieves.

Writing this history was a way of telling all those who were still under European imperial rule that if the Haitians did it, they could do it too. If you were determined enough, and if you had leadership that would help keep you together despite divisions the imperialists had encouraged, for example, between Black people and Brown people, you could win.

Titid when he was in government had worked hard to improve education, and before coming back home he recently wrote: "I will return to the field that I know best and love: education."[2]

All of you here are in school uniform. You are among the lucky ones who are getting an education. You surely know how hard the movement has worked to build schools under the most difficult conditions. We visited one of those beautiful schools built by the movement—it feeds stomachs as well as minds; it is hard to learn on an empty stomach. But most education is funded by parents, often single mothers, who scrub other people's floors as well as their own, submit to sweatshop labor, or spend long hours growing or cooking food they sell on the street, depriving themselves of everything to pay school fees from the lowest incomes. Most of the time, for most of the world, education, if it exists at all, is paid for in this way. Parents, especially mothers, make these sacrifices because they want their children to escape the poverty they the parents have had to endure.

We—not only the young but all of us—want education to help develop our minds. But the truth is that the aim of secondary schools and universities for working-class children is rarely that; it is usually to enable them to rise out of their class, leaving behind those who couldn't afford education or who had talents which didn't flourish in schools. When working-class children in Britain finally got into university because it was free for the first time, these children were often alienated from their

---

2 "Returning to Education in Haiti," *Guardian*, February 4, 2011.

community, no longer sharing the same concerns or even able to speak with their own parents in any meaningful way. They were educated out of their class.

Those of us who have access to this precious commodity which we call education have a choice about what to aim for. We can use it to rise out of poverty. Or we can use it as Titid has used his: to work to eliminate poverty. Along with many of us in the movement for change, he is fighting for education that equips young people to serve the community, not be cut off from it, and for all of us to rise out of poverty together. Not leaving our community behind. Not becoming like or even joining with the people who manage and exploit our communities. Rather, be a power for the grassroots, able to stand up with them in the struggles for survival and for a better future.

But if we make that choice, to work to eliminate poverty, we have then to look at the kind of education we want. This of course we can safely leave to Titid and other Haitians. I only mention here that Mwalimu Julius Nyerere, the first president of independent Tanzania, had much of value to say about this. Mwalimu means teacher in Swahili, the most commonly spoken African language. Mwalimu said that education "must emphasize co-operative endeavor, not individual advancement"; it must "counteract the temptation to intellectual arrogance" so we refuse to become "the well-educated despising those whose abilities are non-academic."[3]

The author of *The Black Jacobins* used his education to write about the history of the Haitians who had been slaves and who, by winning their freedom, paved the freedom road for the whole of the Americas. No school could or would teach them that. Whether or not you can read or write, you can think, and you can act; you can organize for freedom, and address the enormous problems Haiti faces.

We see how much people are suffering here after the earthquake on top of all that has gone before. We see how much money goes into the occupation—the soldiers, the guns, the elaborate uniforms, the military vehicles, all so costly, and so oppressive—that could be used to feed and house and educate people who are still living in tents. We see the threats you have to live with and the heartbreaking deprivation. But we also see the hope and the potential power. And this hope still exists in Haiti today, as if the revolution never left these shores. We are amazed by it every day.

The Global Women's Strike is part of your support network, in the Caribbean, in England, and in North America. Its points of reference are from the Caribbean, from Argentina, and from Europe. One of our jobs is to ensure that Haiti is not dropped from the international political agenda, that it is not ignored and neglected as it was for many years until the earthquake. We will go back to England tomorrow and begin our campaign to find out what the NGOs have done with the millions that were donated for your benefit but which never reached you.

---

3   Education for Self-Reliance in *Uhuru na Ujamaa/Freedom and Socialism OUP* (1967), 273.

During our stay here, we met with women's organizations, one of them very successfully doing microcredit, and with the human rights organization—mostly women—of the great Lovinsky Pierre-Antoine whom we had worked with and who was disappeared in August 2009. They are determined to get justice for Lovinsky and for all the victims of the 1991 and 2004 coups. We told them of our weekly pickets, demanding Lovinsky's return and protesting the UN occupation—in Guyana, the United States and England, including in front of the Brazilian embassy to protest their scandalous involvement in leading the UN's occupation. So now we are in closer touch with Haitian women and men with whom we will be working more closely.

Haiti was the first to end slavery. When Haiti made the revolution there were no international support networks as we know them now, though there were great anti-colonial and antislavery movements in the Americas and the Caribbean. But Haiti is much less alone today. There are revolutions in the Middle East and North Africa of Arab people, refusing dictatorships that have been funded by the United States and their military ally Israel—both major military powers with occupying armies. And there is resistance to occupation in many countries, from Palestine to Afghanistan. The mass movements and revolutions are every day emerging in a number of countries in South and North America and in Europe and Asia.

Whenever we can, we will advertise to these movements that in Haiti, the Black Jacobins never gave up, are still determined, and now have their leader back among them.

GUARDIAN ARTICLES (2010–2011)

In October 2010, the *Guardian* newspaper in the UK invited me to contribute to their Comment pages. These are some of the articles.

The Tory "Big Society" Relies on Women Replacing Welfare

Families with children will bear the brunt of privatization and cuts—leaving carers with more unwaged work than ever.

The welfare State was a legacy of the Second World War. After the misery of the great depression and the slaughter that followed, people demanded change: the welfare of people, including working-class people, was to be central. Millions demanded socialism—and the welfare State was what we got. From 1951 to 1979 the Tories were cautious, some even embracing the civilizing influence of "entitlement": every human being's right not to starve, at least in the UK.

The cuts announced by [government minister] George Osborne yesterday aim once again to make market forces rather than human beings the absolute social and economic priority, throwing us back to the interwar years of deprivation.

One crucial advance had been that universal family allowance (now child benefit) acknowledged mothers as vital workers who produced the human race. As soon as suffrage was won, feminist Eleanor Rathbone, from a Liverpool antislavery family, had worked tirelessly to establish that mothers and children were entitled to an income independent of what men earned—or didn't earn. It would recognize the needs of children and the work and financial autonomy of their carers. Family allowance would redress the gross injustice of the penniless mother who had been economically "disinherited." Mothers and children, though unwaged, were, after all, most of the population.

Rathbone fought for that income to be universal: a mother of any class was entitled to payment for caring work; it was a right, not a charity. But Rathbone expected that this would guarantee women's financial independence, and was deeply disappointed. As women have had to focus on other routes to financial independence over the years, the basic work of the reproduction of the human race has plunged as a social priority. Some feminists did very well out of competing on the market in a man's world. Housework was what their mothers did; they were above that. Their careers could pay for the help of other (lower-waged) women as nannies and cleaners.

Rathbone, on the other hand, knew that: "a people accustomed to measure values in terms of money will persist, even against the evidence of their own eyes, in thinking meanly of any kind of service on which a low price is set and still more meanly of the kind of service which is given for nothing."

Thatcher's "There is no such thing as society" and her hatred for "the culture of entitlement" has determined social policy since 1979. As soon as New Labour came in, Blair called single mothers "workless," and cut one-parent benefit. The job of raising children, it seems, was a time-waster. This framed the recent Welfare Reform Act, which abolished income support, the benefit that recognized mothers' unwaged work, and in crucial respects frames the present cuts. Harriet Harman[1] presented the one-parent cut; Yvette Cooper welfare reform.[2] With what credibility can they oppose Tory cuts?

It has been noted that families with children will bear the brunt of cuts, while the childless two-income family will not. It is the carer who will carry the heaviest load because she has the greater responsibility. And not only for children who will lose education and other allowances, but for relatives with disabilities and pensioner parents whose local services will either be directly cut or contracted out, to be done by workers paid slave wages not to care, but to meet targets.

Mothers had escaped dependence by taking jobs as teachers, librarians, and other public-sector jobs. At the same time, 60.3 percent of the two million single parents had been forced out to jobs (up from 44.7 percent in 1997)—even breastfeeding mothers are having to submit to work-focused interviews. Indeed the number of stay-at-home

---

1 Minister in Tony Blair's Labour government, 1998.
2 Minister in Gordon Brown's Labour government, 2009.

mothers has reached an all-time low as families struggle to make ends meet. Most of these women will be sent home by the cuts. Now what?

Their fate and that of children is unrealistically disconnected, and in any case children's wellbeing is never a consideration. There is little concern for what children are eating (ask Jamie Oliver[3]); or for how many leave school illiterate; or how many are forced to be carers for disabled parents or for siblings when parents are out at work. Nor is child poverty addressed as a tragic scandal, which is why the looming increased impoverishment is not the shock it should be.

Structural adjustment policies, that is, the privatization and cuts which devastated the Third World in the 1980s and '90s, were based on women taking on even more unwaged work or going without—even when it meant starvation. In much the same way, the "big society" plans to drive women to replace decimated services with unwaged work. Our work as carers is again counted on, but never counted.

The cuts are premised on the absurd assumption that market forces are beyond human control. What happened to the free time that technology, for which we suffered unemployment and displacement, was to enable? We reject the prevailing ethos that parents spending time, and society spending resources, on caring is an unaffordable luxury, but obscene salaries, bonuses, and weapons are not. Will we have to fight this out as they're doing in France?

October 21, 2010

International Women's Day: How Rapidly Things Change

To undermine for good the sexual division of labor, women and men must begin with children.

A century ago, International Women's Day was associated with peace, and women's and girls' sweated labor—both of which votes for women were to deal with. Not a celebration, but a mobilization. And because it was born among factory workers, it had class, real class. Later it came to celebrate women's autonomy, but changed its class base and lost its edge. This centenary must mark a new beginning.

We live in revolutionary times. We don't need to be in North Africa or the Middle East to be infected by the hope of change. Enough to witness on TV the woman who, veiled in black from head to foot, led chants in Cairo's Tahrir Square, routing sexism and Islamophobia in one unexpected blow. She and the millions moving together

---

3   Celebrity chef who campaigns for healthier school meals.

have shaken us from our provincialism, and shown us how rapidly things can change. Women in Egypt have called for a million women to occupy Tahrir Square today. Who would have predicted that a month ago?

Feminism has tended to narrow its concerns to what is unquestionably about women: abortion, childcare, rape, prostitution, pay equity. But that can separate us from a wider and deeper women's movement. In Bahrain, for example, women lead the struggle for "jobs, housing, clean water, peace and justice"—as well as every demand we share.

The revolution is spreading. Scott Walker, the Tea Party's state governor in Wisconsin, aims to destroy state workers' collective bargaining rights. As in Britain, most employees and service users attacked by the cuts are women. A male colleague told demonstrators who had occupied the state capitol: "The administration made a calculation that the men would not support the women. Now they know otherwise." He ended his speech with the phrase on everyone's lips: "Fight like an Egyptian!"

Now we know the Tea Party is after women, what will women's organizations do about it? The only one anywhere near is a long-time fighting network of welfare mothers. Wisconsin in the 1990s led on "welfare reform"—the blueprint for UK cuts. Welfare mothers remember that few stood with them then.

It has not always been easy to pull up women's neglected interests from beneath the "general cause." The best way is to ask the women who often shout unheard: the single mothers, the teachers, the nurses, the sex workers, the care workers, the asylum seekers, the pensioners. But as feminists, our hearing and our focus are corrupted when we concentrate on getting women into the corridors of power. Recently the UK government warned big companies that they must "double the number of women in boardrooms"—while it increases the poverty of women and of children. Will we allow that? Or can we turn this around and demand the money from corporations and banks for women, children and all who need it?

Such a turnaround presumes a return of feminism to class. Not the restricted concepts of the 1970s, but a new definition that begins with women internationally—from Bahrain to Palestine, from Haiti to Pakistan, where women fight for survival and justice after earthquakes, floods, coups, and occupations.

How do we deal with the fact that our biology is an encumbrance for Alan Sugar, who wants to question women job applicants about their parental intentions? It's even an embarrassment for some paid to represent us. When a trade union equality worker was asked to endorse our IWD event, she wrote back: "Is it just me—or [is] the mothers' march banner…disturb[ing]?"

Many feminists have become convinced that we can only escape romanticized visions of maternal slavery by denying we are mothers at all. To be a financially independent individual as well as (or instead of) a mother, we have traded away the social power that comes from recognition of the contribution of motherhood—the making of the human race, the creation of the labor force. Marching as mothers we transform the attitude to that work: from a social liability to the social contribution that it is. In this way, we help put all women in a stronger position to demand wages and working conditions that take account of the caring work most of us are already doing, whether we're mothers or not.

New boldness allows us to face what Marx and Engels called "our real conditions of life and our relations with our kind." Women refusing to be trapped at home, and demanding that men not be trapped out of the home, takes us immediately beyond the market, which only considers work that leads to profit for others, not to equity nor to happiness nor even to survival.

To undermine once and for all the sexual division of labor, we—women and men—must aim to work less. We can then begin where we all began, with children. What do they need? First of all, adults (not just parents) who love them and work to make a relationship with them. That is after all what caring is. We need time for this. Prime time.

We cannot be punished for our involvement in this civilizing life process. Nor can we allow men to be excluded from it. So this International Women's Day, we must at least consider claiming the money from banks and wars to pay for the society of carers that only we together can devise. Taking the lead of the women in Tahrir Square, we can change the world.

March 8, 2011

Slut, Where Is Thy Sting?

Women of all ages, colors and backgrounds came together at the SlutWalk in London—this was the new women's movement.[4]

There was a great feeling that the London SlutWalk represented all kinds of women, not because we were all "welcome" but because we did not really differ in what we wanted. We eagerly absorbed and condemned news of each individual crime of discrimination and violence against any woman. But we didn't think this made us superior, the arrogant bearers of the only real truth.

The largely white crowd welcomed women of color not because it was right and moral and good to be against racism, but because it was too late in the day for

---

4   Antirape protest started in Canada in April 2011 after a Toronto policeman told women that to stay safe they "should avoid dressing like sluts." SlutWalk marches and rallies were held in many cities in a number of countries, including the UK and the United States.

racism—antiracism was what we assumed. I had never seen and heard this kind of confident impatience with injustice in a crowd's reaction. Women of color said they were comfortable there and a few young Black women moved right to the front to help carry the lead banner, happy to identify themselves as leading sluts. That's the end of identifying Black women as sex objects personified; sluts of color strike back.

In the same way, the crowd identified with sex workers. There was such empathy when two women from the English Collective of Prostitutes spoke that my first thought was that this was a sex worker audience. But I then realized that the line between women who turn tricks and women who don't was almost invisible, because for them it was not a moral divide, but one of chance and choice. Besides, one reason we were marching was because it wasn't anyone's business what any of us did with our bodies. That included transgender, lesbian, straight, and bisexual women. We were not merely marching together; we were one, claiming not equality but mutual respect for individuality. Establishing your right establishes and safeguards mine.

Perhaps most expressive of how widely this view was held, and the confidence with which women held it, was the way men were welcome on the march. Some were sex workers, some were antiwar protestors, some had started life as women, others were supporting their partners, mothers, or daughters. There was no sense that this was a problem, or that women were in any way undermined or nervous because of their presence. Who is with us *is* us.

In this sense, the SlutWalk was light years ahead of the 1970 women's liberation march, which made way for it. I was at both. Most of the women forty years ago were a bit older and less grassroots than the SlutWalkers, taking themselves more seriously, more aware of their talents and skills, on their way to higher things. Many who marched then are by now retired from professorships at universities, journalism, company managing—what were once nontraditional professional jobs for women. There were no wheelchair users in 1970. But last weekend, women with disabilities were an integral part of the protest, marching and speaking, for sex and against rape.

Once upon a time, the head of a European-wide multinational told a company wife that money was sexy. He didn't only mean he could buy sex, but that with his money, women would find him attractive and he wouldn't have to pay. That was a long time ago. Now women identify with both sex workers and chambermaids; we can all say yes or no. Indeed, there were a number of "We are all chambermaids" placards, referring to the alleged attempted rape by the head of the IMF.

Women on the march knew that to change anything, we needed each other. The three who organized the day, Elizabeth Head, Caitlin Hayward-Tapp and Anastasia Richardson, made that clear when they spoke in the square:

> Sex assault won't be eradicated until asylum seekers can report crimes to the police without fear of deportation. Until sex workers can report crimes to the police

without fear of being criminalized. Until mothers can report crimes to the police without fear of their children being taken from them by social services. Until transgender women can report rape without their status as real women somehow being called into question. And until Black women can report rape without being disbelieved because of the color of their skin.

The—mainly very young—women went wild with delight. They hate rape and all who protect the rapist, from police to the media. They hate the cuts and how women are going to be pummeled. And they hate being defined and divided by the powers that be. This was the new women's movement, born of student protests and Arab revolutions, tearing up the past before our very eyes. It has a lot of work to do but it is not afraid.

By the way, my placard read "Pensioner Slut" and it got many thumbs up. Slut, where is thy sting?!

June 19, 2011

Moran Doesn't Want to Change Much

"Feminism should be as exciting as rock 'n' roll,"
—Caitlin Moran.

I was one of four writers asked to review Moran's book, *How to Be a Woman.*

The book intrigues potential readers with its description as a rewrite of *The Female Eunuch* ("from a bar stool"). But this sets a standard that can't easily be reached, even in comedy. Germaine Greer gave us a major compilation of outrageous words and acts suffered by women. Some of Moran's best prose describes how terrific it was to read this 1970 book—the female fruit of the 1960s, heralding the birth of an autonomous women's movement for liberation.

But in the twenty-first century, when all women have been touched by that movement, feminists such as Moran seem to be isolated in their (Western) sector, not in any way connected with the rest of us. Having arrived in a man's world, they discover they have not shaken the "problems of being a woman": even "famous and powerful women are constantly pilloried for being too fat or too thin, or badly dressed"—and worse.

In fact Moran is speaking to a widely expressed dissatisfaction among women who have found with consternation and sometimes fury that even at the top they are not free of sexism. Their problem is, they live in the same world as the rest of us, where, for example, there is little progress in pay inequity; where 6.5 percent of reported rapes end in a conviction on the charge of rape (and between 75 and 95 percent are still unreported); and where the only move to equity with men is a rise in the proportion of women prisoners, and in the pension age.

Some women with social power complain about these injustices, especially if directly affected by them, but most have not considered that they have to do anything for other women to save their own position in society, let alone their feminist souls. It is just not possible for any women to be "making their own fate," as Moran claims, while the rest of us are condemned to a never-ending day of waged and unwaged slavery.

Moran says feminism is "the belief that women should be as free as men..." But Greer knew that the "first significant discovery we shall make as we racket along our female road to freedom is that men are not free." Greer concludes with a call for revolution and for women to withdraw our labor. Moran doesn't want to change much. She doesn't seem to know that no one will be free until all of us are. The closest we can get to freedom is fighting for it with whoever is as eager as we are to achieve it. Which feminists are with us?

June 20, 2011

MUMIA ABU-JAMAL, JAILHOUSE LAWYER (2011)

O n our first visit to Mumia Abu-Jamal, who spent most of his thirty years in prison on death row, he happened to mention jailhouse lawyers, prisoners who learn how to defend themselves and others against the legal establishment. Neither Niki Adams of Legal Action for Women in London nor I had ever heard this phrase before. By the time we left that day, I had asked Mumia (as he is known to millions) to write a book about jailhouse lawyers. It would be his sixth book. In the years that followed he wrote on his typewriter and I edited on computer, checking back and forth with an ocean between us. It was an education.

The book was published in the United States in 2009. Just before we published in the UK in 2011, prisoners all over Georgia refused to come out of their cells to do another day's work for free. We were able to publish their demands in a stop press in the UK edition. Since then, thousands of other prisoners have protested, including with hunger strikes, in California and elsewhere. The movement inside kept alive by jailhouse lawyers has now burst out and is challenging every injustice of prison life.

After a great struggle, Mumia is no longer on death row. The international support movement, encouraged by this victory and by the widespread prisoners' protests, is now planning actions to free Mumia.

This is an excerpt from my introduction to the UK edition.

* * *

I knew nothing then of what Mumia had had to consider before agreeing to do this book. He has a heavy schedule. He writes articles and the weekly commentaries, which he then phones in to the Prison Radio Project that broadcasts to about a hundred stations. He sends voice messages to events—leaping prison walls to lend his fame and credibility to movement efforts. He carefully annotates and excerpts what he reads since he's allowed only seven books at a time in his cell which, he says (speaking to Americans), is "as large as your bathroom." Despite repression and restraints, Mumia Abu-Jamal is leading *his* life, not the one he planned for himself but certainly not the one his persecutors planned for him either. At the end of each day he can have the satisfaction of evaluating what he's accomplished and what still needs doing.

As I got to know him, via letters, infrequent overseas visits, manuscripts back and forth, and his rare but always thrilling phone calls, it became clear that Mumia personifies the best of the movement of the 1960s: committed, principled, undeterred by the power of the enemy, and determined to win. He became a Black Panther at age fourteen, when millions of young people in many parts of the world were creating communes and collectives. Panther life was also collective but framed by the struggle: self-defense on the one hand, service on the other—from legal and other defense of the community, to the breakfast program for children, to distributing bags of groceries to Black people who needed that help. Mumia notes that it was mostly women who "provided the bulk of the membership and labor": 60 percent of Panther members were women.[1] I'm not sure anyone had told us that before.

By their late teens, many of these young people were experienced political organizers. Some, like the great Fred Hampton who was shot dead, age twenty-one, by the U.S. government when he was asleep, had become distinguished political leaders.[2] Mumia was still a teenager when he spoke at Brother Hampton's Philadelphia memorial.

Mumia's patience and his commitment to changing the world are rooted in this collective activism, this movement training. His history helps explain why his journalism is among the most uncompromising and illuminating in the United States, a beacon for many, especially during the benighted Bush years. The support movement, which has stayed the hand of the State against his execution, and which reaches far beyond U.S. boundaries, is drawn to the anti-racist, anti-prison, but especially anti–death penalty implications of his case; but it is also drawn to this attractive individual. Bypassing the

---

1   *We Want Freedom: A Life in the Black Panther Party* (Cambridge, MA: South End Press, 2008). See especially chapter 7, "A Woman's Party," 159, 164–65. The book is an honest and riveting account of life in the Panthers.

2   After forty years since his murder (by Cook County, Illinois, State Attorney's Office together with the Chicago Police Department and the FBI), Fred Hampton is increasingly recognized as one of the greatest losses among many losses, victim of the U.S. government assassination policy against Black and other movement activists. The distinguished novelist China Miéville recently referred to him as "one of the outstanding political figures in American history" (*Guardian*, July 31, 2010).

self-indulgence, inflated egos and rampaging personal ambition that invaded the move-ment for change in the 1980s, Mumia retains his 1960s principles and habits. No wonder many young prisoners love the wise and compassionate point of reference they call Papa.

Mumia's determined use of his journalism to tell the truth about the establish-ment made him a marked man. The truth that probably endangered him most was the story of MOVE. A nonviolent multiracial alternative community, MOVE was so hated by the Philadelphia police that in 1985 the city inflicted an unprecedented aerial bombing that killed eleven people; five were children. Up to now the city has got away with it.[3] Mumia had never been a MOVE member, but as a young reporter he was among those publicly warned by the notoriously racist mayor Frank Rizzo that whoever continued to report how the MOVE people were being persecuted would be made to pay. Mumia's refusal to avert his eyes from that persecution singled him out for the death penalty.[4]

These qualities shine through on every page of this book, which was written despite petty and malicious prison restrictions. Telephone charges for prisoners are inflated to dollars per minute even as prices dwindle for the rest of us—long letters and precisely annotated hard copy had to substitute for editing meetings. Prisoners are denied computer access; Mumia has yet to go online or access the Internet. Rather, he must buy typewriter ribbons in-house, again at inflated prices, and so lightly inked that the script can barely be read let alone scanned; each draft had to be retyped. Prisons are havens of profiteering (and exploitation) promoted by those who are in charge of "correcting criminals."

Mumia here delights in describing what extraordinary lives of resistance some prisoners have created out of desperation, determination, and imagination. Drawing on his years inside, and an extensive correspondence with jailhouse lawyers he's met or knows by reputation, he sketches portraits of great jailhouse lawyers determined to beat justice out of the system. The reader is swept up in their passionate and skilled advocacy. Often spurred by the need to repair the damage of lazy, uncaring, and compromised "street lawyers," Mumia describes how jailhouse lawyers learn the law, the precedents, the procedures, the jargon, and mount an often formidable legal defense.

Two of the jailhouse lawyers are women dedicated to justice for the least consid-ered of the prison population. The tragedy of imprisonment is perhaps heaviest for women, 70 percent of whom are mothers.[5] The responsibilities of motherhood are with them wherever they are; having been denied the right to care for and protect

---

3 There was never a criminal prosecution of any perpetrators.

4 He narrowly avoided this sentence being carried out before the trial by police assassination. Having been shot by a policeman, he was then beaten. His recovery was almost miraculous. While recover-ing, he was framed.

5 Yolanda Johnson-Peterkin, *Children of Incarcerated Parents*, May 2003.

their young is a sentence in itself: "it's like a living hell."[6] Mother *and* children are punished by—sometimes permanent—separation.[7] Sister prisoners who are jailhouse lawyers have their work cut out.

The United States has the highest incarceration rate in the world: two million people were in prison in 2008.[8] One in every ninety-nine people, and one in every nine Black men aged twenty to thirty-four, are in prison.[9] Thus millions are or have been prisoners. When we also take account of their families, we must face how accurate is Mumia's description of the United States as "the Prisonhouse of nations"; how much that society and its standards are shaped by prisons, and how pernicious is the unspoken official assumption that society is other than what happens to millions of people because of prisons.[10]

So that, despite the millions of people whose lives have passed through prison, the story of jailhouse lawyers and this crucial aspect of their resistance has not been told before. If it had been, the self-help legal history of this massive segregated population would have been acknowledged before now. Mumia's book speaks to those who are or have been inside. And by reintegrating the part of society behind bars, *Jailhouse Lawyers* conveys the power and breadth of the movement for change. A substantial piece of ourselves, which had been wrenched from us and hidden from view is returned.

There is a growing awareness that the "Prisonhouse of nations" has locked away many of the movement's most dedicated and effective activists;[11] that prisons have

6   "As a mother separated from children, partner and dogs, it's like a living hell. Worrying about what's going on at home, running the home from far away. My partner lost it big time yesterday, he's really struggling. People say let them get on with their lives but I can't. Everything in the home was pivotal around me and they all ask me for advice and guidance on what they should do next. Tell them what to feed the puppies, how to fix the Internet... I've had my youngest girl sobbing down the phone. All I can do is talk them through it. My partner tells me I mustn't cry because it upsets him." See http://www.womenagainstrape.net.

7   Eleven percent of children of incarcerated mothers are in foster care, which "can result in a parent losing the right to their children permanently because federal law requires, with limited exceptions, that a state file a petition to terminate parental rights when a child has been in foster care for fifteen out of twenty-two months (See http://www.wpaonline.org/pdf/2008_BJS_parents_Final.pdf). The timetable is especially problematic given that the average time a mother in state prison is expected to serve is forty-nine months" (See: www.finalcall.com/artman/publish/article_4943.shtml). The fostering and adoption of children is another industry which in this case works hand-in-glove with the prison-industrial complex.

8   World Prison Population List, 8th edition (December 2008), International Centre for Prison Studies, School of Law, King's College London.

9   "U.S. Prison Population Hits New High: 1 in 100 Adults Jailed," *Guardian*, March 1, 2008.

10   "The outpouring [of California's expenditure on prisons] has forced the state's governor...to slash other public services including schools with cuts that education leaders have warned could decimate the state's school system" (Ibid.). And this is true not only in the United States: Abu Ghraib and Guantánamo have deep American roots.

11   One of the most famous of these is Leonard Peltier, member of the American Indian Movement. In 1977, he was convicted of the murder of two FBI agents during a siege of the Pine Ridge Indian

been a key political weapon against the movements of people of color especially. Many thousands of Panthers and other militants are inside for their political activism (a function usually associated with concentration camps).[12] Nobody knows how many.

But most prisoners (whoever they were when they went in, on whatever charge) eventually come out. Recently we have met FIPs—formerly incarcerated persons— for whom, as with Malcolm X, prison was a political and organizing education. On their release some are actively involved with their communities, making available what they have learnt, to great and hopeful effect. When the millions of FIPs get it together, they will enable a lot of change.

Once we know about jailhouse lawyers, we can be more useful, and even consider joint action. [A] jailhouse lawyer…relates how a prisoner's legal action is strengthened by "about seventy-five people on the outside [who] march to the federal court house." They win a support house and other services for families who visit those held in a particularly isolated soul-destroying prison. Why can't what jailhouse lawyers do inside be enhanced and reinforced by what we do outside?

Reservation. In 2003, the 10th Circuit Court of Appeals acknowledged that "Much of the government's behavior at the Pine Ridge Reservation and its prosecution of Mr. Peltier is to be condemned. The government withheld evidence. It intimidated witnesses. These facts are not disputed." Yet Mr. Peltier remains in prison.

12 "The first Nazi concentration camps…were intended to hold political prisoners and opponents of the regime." Prisoners might like also to be reminded that almost every anti-imperialist leader and postindependence head of state, from India's Nehru to Kenya's Kenyatta, spent time in prison, and some went directly from prison to government.

STRIVING FOR CLARITY AND INFLUENCE:

THE POLITICAL LEGACY OF CLR JAMES (2001–2012)

It was in the stillness of a seaside suburb that could be heard most clearly and insistently the booming of Franco's heavy artillery, the rattle of Stalin's firing squads and the fierce shrill turmoil of the revolutionary movement striving for clarity and influence. Such is our age and this book is of it, with something of the fever and the fret. Nor does the writer regret it. The book is the history of a revolution and written under different circumstances it would have been a different but not necessarily a better book.[1]

—CLR James, 1938

In 2001, I was invited to address the conference: CLR James Centennial Anniversary: A Tribute to the Fight for Social Revolution. This was a chance to finally speak about his political legacy as I had known it.

CLR had been involved in Marxist organizations from the mid-1930s to the late 1960s, when the Johnson-Forest Tendency which he had founded was disbanded. Those who now wanted to be associated with or at least cite some of his ideas and insights while not stepping beyond establishment boundaries often found his involvement with "small Marxist organizations" an encumbrance. It was often more convenient in the mushrooming CLR James industry for most of his political history to be dismissed as either a detour in an otherwise brilliant career or the foibles of a genius.

---

1   *The Black Jacobins*, Preface to the 1st edition (New York: Vintage Books, 1963, 1989), xi.

I used this centenary conference, first, to prevent the man who had educated or even introduced many people like me to the Marxist movement, from becoming either a cultural guru or a Pan-Africanist disconnected from class struggle. Secondly, I wanted to begin, only begin, to claim finally what some of us consider his substantial political and organizational contribution to the movement.

The conference was in Detroit, once the great Motown, center of the car industry, the heart of industrial unions, and with a radical tradition. Now it was almost a ghost town, but I knew many of those attending the conference had more than a passing interest in CLR's history in the Marxist Left. The terms and organizations I would mention were not unfamiliar to most of them, so detailed explanations would be unnecessary.

It is worth remembering that those who oppose capitalism and all its ways and works when no crowds are in the street must work hard to maintain and enhance that opposition, and prepare for those crowds to appear, as inevitably they must. That fundamentally is what CLR was doing in Marxist organizations.

Politics, if it is fuelled by a great will to change the world, rather than by personal ambition, offers a chance to know the world, and to be more self-conscious of the actual life you are living, rather than being taken over by what you are told you should feel, about yourself and others: a chance, in other words, to live an authentic life. Such politics are a unique enrichment, not a sacrifice. CLR's decades in the Marxist movement shaped—gave a framework, depth, and breadth to—all he did. Years later his work was praised by academics, the literati, critics of many types. But the connection between this acclaimed body of work and his political engagement was rarely even mentioned.

* * *

I want to thank first of all my dear comrade and friend Nettie Kravitz. She recommended to Martin Glaberman, another dear comrade and friend, that I speak, and he recommended that the organizers invite me.

I have to ask before beginning: what is the use of a conference like this? We work hard (we women work especially hard) and we have to decide what it is we are going to do with our precious hours. Is this conference serving a serious purpose? To examine what CLR James found out about how we can organize against those who rule, exploit and impose genocide upon us must be worthwhile. I think CLR has something to tell young people especially who want to avoid the mistakes of the movement in the past, and I'll try to say some of what that is.

Finally, James became famous for his cultural analyses. But you know, appreciating and understanding Shakespeare by itself does nothing for the revolution; nor does cricket by itself. We do him a great injustice if we consider CLR's extraordinary abilities in literature and the arts (including sport) and even as a historian, in a political and organizational vacuum. We don't see how much his work in the so-called cultural sphere was shaped by his committed, collective political work that for most of his adult life was his central concern. Everything he did aimed to strengthen the anticapitalist movement in its "striving for clarity and influence." Yet his political and organizational life has often been dismissed as a distraction. In fact, from the 1930s his life was centered on politics. So it is worth exploring that history, and what it produced, which some of us believe was a unique and vital contribution.

For me (and at least a few others who knew his work firsthand), CLR created two masterworks—others may think more, but certainly two. One of them was *The Black Jacobins* and I'm gratified to see that you have been honoring that masterpiece in this series of lectures.

The second masterwork was the Johnson-Forest Tendency which aimed to create another kind of Marxist organization.

Political organizations that aim to overthrow capitalism are not usually taken seriously enough to be considered as creations, let alone masterworks. Most of us think of organizations as glittering promises, which turn out to be cons. They betray their members and sometimes millions of others as well. Johnson-Forest was based on a root-and-branch critique of the Left and its role within the working-class movement, and offered an organizational reorientation.

CLR went to England from Trinidad in 1932 and had become politically active there both in the anti-imperialist movement and in Trotskyism, the Marxist movement which was anti-Stalinist. Though naturally sympathetic to each other, these two movements were quite separate. CLR related how in London's Hyde Park Corner, where political debates raged, he would step down from speaking on the Pan African podium and step onto the Trotskyist podium.

In 1938, CLR left England for the United States, a country where the divisions of class leaned much less on ancestry and much more directly on the cash nexus. It was different from, and less hidebound, than Europe at that time. Different too was the fact that race replaced imperialism as the dominant political issue after class per se: London, capital of the British Empire, was also capital of anti-imperialism, the movement on which the sun never set—like the Empire itself. He was naturally sponsored by the Socialist Workers Party, the U.S. wing of international Trotskyism, of which he was a member in England. They had invited him on a speaking tour.

Not long after, in 1940, a rift appeared in U.S. Trotskyism, precipitated by Stalin's nonaggression pact with Hitler.[2] This made a debate on the nature of the Soviet

---

2   And within a month Poland had been invaded by both Germany and the USSR, to be followed shortly after by the Soviets stationing troops in the Baltic countries and invading Finland—as it later turned out, all part of the Hitler-Stalin Pact.

Union unavoidable: could it make deals with Hitler and still be a workers' State, as Trotsky and the Socialist Workers Party claimed; could the international working class still be asked to defend the Soviet Union? Or was it a new formation, some kind of "bureaucratic collectivist" society (neither capitalist nor workers' State), as the minority, which wanted to split from the SWP claimed?

The crisis for CLR was that he agreed with neither of these, a minority of one within Trostkyism. In CLR's view, the Soviet Union was State-capitalist. The working class, which in 1917 had made the revolution, had put this State in power, and it still claimed to represent that class. But though production was nationalized, the Soviet State organized merciless exploitation, imposed forced labor, and murdered millions, beginning with those who had been points of reference in the revolution.

Those who were against defense of the Soviet Union in the war in Europe, a large minority, split from the SWP and Leon Trotsky, leader with Lenin of the revolution. CLR was part of this minority, which split and formed the Workers Party. But those with whom he left were hostile to Marxism; they were in this basic respect more alien to him than those he was leaving behind.

CLR knew that this crisis in Trotskyism and in his own political life required a deeper study of Marxism. (He was still relatively new to the movement, though he had rapidly become an international point of reference in it.) He often said that at that point he considered returning to England, where he had a network of friends and comrades with whom he could work, but there were some dedicated movement people in the United States who agreed with his State-capitalist position, and who offered to work with him if he would stay. Together they would reexamine Marxism: study not only Marx and Lenin but also Hegel whose dialectical method was the indispensable foundation of Marxism.

CLR also had to work out what were the implications of this State-capitalist analysis: what did it mean that the working-class movement got to this point, where the State it had itself created had become a capitalist dictatorship against it? For Trotsky, the fact that the economy was nationalized ensured it was a workers' State. He had become trapped in a previous moment when nationalization had meant workers' power. He could not see the new content in the old word. (Years of debate hardly changed Trotskyist minds, though CLR believed that Trotsky would have changed his position, if he had lived.)

CLR built a core in the course of doing this study of Marxism, and then little by little a distinct tendency—not, as was traditional, a faction, implying endless political debates. The tendency formed quietly but steadily within a party, which was hostile to all it stood for. While Grace Chin Lee (now Boggs) helped with the study of Hegel and Marx, sometimes translating from the original German, Rae (Raya Dunayevskaya), a Russian speaker, did research on the Soviet economy. She demystified the Stalinist claim that workers in the Soviet Union were not exploited, and that the contradictions of capitalism didn't apply there. I remember, for example, that Rae discredited the Soviet claim that unemployment—without which capitalism could not discipline labor—had been eliminated; she worked out how the industrial reserve army was hidden from view (dispersed into the countryside where they were invisible to Soviet economists), but always available to function as a discipline on the employed, and of course on the entire working class—the same as it did in every other part of the capitalist world. This was one instance showing that all the fundamentals of capitalist exploitation were in operation in the Soviet Union, nationalized or not.

For the Johnson-Forest Tendency (CLR's party name was J.R. Johnson and Rae's was Freddy Forest), this State-capitalist analysis of the Soviet Union characterized not merely the Soviet State but the new stage of world capitalism. The Soviet revolution had put the State in charge of production, and it had used its nationalized economic structure to leap ahead in capitalist development on the backs of the working class. But only the Soviet beginnings of the State were exceptional: capitalism in other countries was also moving towards more centralized economic planning by the State.

The workers' State had turned against those who at great cost to themselves had put it in power. And in a similar way trade unions and labor parties, which had been created as class weapons through bitter struggle, were now integral to the management of the working class. Governments expected them to "control their members."

Stalinism, Johnson-Forest claimed, was an extreme form of a general phenomenon: the new way the State organized in response to working-class rebellion. We were faced not merely with capital and its management, but with the capitalist management of our own organizations. This was a new political reality—the struggle against capitalism took the form of a struggle within and against the very organizations we had created to overcome capitalism, as much in the United States as in the USSR. This may be more familiar now, but it was new then; it took years before this was widely accepted—or even considered—by the movement.

That view of the crisis in working-class organization was the angry conclusion of workers in Detroit and other industrial centers. They had won union recognition by sit-in strikes and confrontations with the armed National Guard. They were evaluating their enormous struggle at the same time that Johnson-Forest was working out its independent politics. Johnson-Forest had moved its national center from New York to Detroit to shift its milieu from the hothouse of Left intellectualism to that of those industrial workers and their families—not to raise their consciousness but to raise ours. CLR, a great listener, spent hours hearing what (often Black) workers from the auto plants would tell him about how and what they had won in the great sit-down strikes against Ford and General Motors, and that now their daily struggle was to get the union to defend them against the company and its production speedup which was draining their lives away. Through the contract with the company, its rules, and the growing bureaucracy to enforce them, they were losing whatever control of production their great struggle had won.

The Left had the view imported from Europe that U.S. workers were backward; we had not formed a mass labor party as workers in Europe had done. But Johnson-Forest urged the party to "Americanize Bolshevism": to show how Marxism was relevant to the United States. We were premised on the day-to-day spontaneous rebellion which was persistent but "unorganized," in production as well as in the community. That form of struggle had to be our starting point—even where there were labor parties!

Johnson-Forest explored the U.S. experience of revolution: CLR and one or two others studied the Civil War—the Second American Revolution—as a context for organizing in the United States. This gave Johnsonites a Marxist grounding in anti-racism. At one point CLR gave us a class in slavery and the Civil War (of course in private homes, without the knowledge of the Workers Party). And since the women's suffrage movement (mainly but not exclusively white) had its roots in the Abolitionist movement, some of our women studied abolition and the birth of feminism.

Johnsonism was different in every way from both sides of the split in Trotskyism. In the course of destroying the workers' State, Stalinism had corrupted the working-class movement. The study of Marx and Lenin and of Hegel had led to uncovering a reading of Marx where the revolution was dependent on the self-activity of the working class, not on the leadership of a vanguard party. This was a Marx free of Stalinist influence. The Marxist Left had ceased to base itself on working-class self-activity and had substituted the dependence on the vanguard party for the active, creative participation of all the exploited. This had the widest possible implications politically and organizationally. Johnson-Forest aimed to express in political perspective and in organizational structure the revolutionary impulse and self-activity of working-class people, beginning in the most advanced and most powerful capitalist country. We cannot go into all its implications here. But the immediate question that CLR in his boldness began to address is: what kind of an organization do you build which encourages rather than discourages self-activity?

Having established the principle that working-class self-activity was the heart of the revolution, CLR and his core began with their own members. It was the job of the leadership, as part of maintaining and developing the organization's political focus, to help uncover and develop the talents and autonomy of members. This was never quite stated like this (as far as I know), but it was assumed. And it was new.

In 1947, Johnson-Forest tried to get the two wings of Trotskyism together again. By then, Trotsky was dead, murdered by a Stalinist agent. The differences between the parties, which had caused the 1940 split were more pronounced. But for neither was what had happened in the Soviet Union an illumination of the struggle generally, as it was for us. Neither claimed their position on the Soviet Union had any particular relevance to what we should be doing or saying where we worked and lived, or how we should organize. Like Humpty-Dumpty, they could not be put together again.

Trying not to go it alone, which risked the sectarianism that can come so easily from isolation, Johnson-Forest rejoined the SWP, which at least claimed to be Marxist, and which at that time spoke about "The Coming American Revolution."

By then, there were seventy Johnsonites. Seventy people scattered across a very big country—not a lot. But the leader was a Black man, an immigrant from the West Indies and a historian; his two closest colleagues were women, one a Russian immigrant, the other first generation Chinese-American. Much of the membership worked in industry including those who had begun life in the middle class. We were multiracial. We were confident. We felt we were "going somewhere," individually and collectively; with history rather than against it; building not a vanguard party so we could one day be the State, but a movement; antiracist and also antisexist; respectful of the people we worked and lived with, rather than imagining ourselves an elite amongst the backward. Those of us who were working-class least thought that our neighbors or the people we worked alongside, needed us to lead them as those in Left parties seemed to think. Rather, we saw ourselves as uncovering and helping to articulate the infinite variety of ways grassroots people expressed its rebellion.

Before we reentered the SWP, we took three months of independence and reflection outside of any party, what we called the Interim Period. We republished our key documents, a way of ending debate on political differences while ensuring that our politics wouldn't vanish from sight: if anyone wanted to know, the documents were available. We published a bulletin experimenting with the kinds of articles we might write or get our networks to write for a future working-class newspaper. All this was a terrific training: the Interim Period broke with the Left tradition of endless debate as the major political activity.

The most significant document of the Interim Period was *The Balance Sheet*. On the surface, it breaks only with the Workers Party, which we had just walked away from. In reality, in breaking with the vanguard party on which all of Trotskyism was based, it broke with Trotskyism.

CLR begins by distinguishing Trotskyism from Trotsky whose handling of the 1940 split "represented the climax of his great contributions to the international movement." (The proposals of Trotsky to try to keep the movement together were extraordinarily generous and broadminded.) Trotsky, he says, had called the split "unprincipled" and CLR with hindsight agrees. "The split was the most unprincipled split in the history of Bolshevism." He had split to go with the anti-Marxists. He goes on to say:

> The leaders of the present Johnson-Forest Minority took part in all this, and we therefore are qualified to speak…we have a political responsibility to our own past, to the faction which we lead, to the party and to all at home and abroad who are concerned with our movement. We have that responsibility and here discharge it, not only for the past but for the future. The split was a betrayal of our movement.

This is how a serious organization educates its members: the leadership publicly begs pardon for its mistakes, which are usually big ones, since they tend to have big responsibilities. Reading this now, one can't help but be struck by the standards the best of the movement once had, and must have again.

But the document's most important innovation is to analyze the composition, the social layers in Left organizations, and what this must mean for political and organizational direction.

The Workers Party had claimed that it could not unify because the SWP was undemocratic. CLR lists the shallow and self-indulgent case they make for this, and then gives us a completely different conception of democracy and the enormous barriers to achieving it; it is a class orientation:

> The W.P. leaders…believe that their party is a genuinely democratic party. Everybody can express his views, nobody is "suppressed." In reality…it is politically the most bureaucratic conceivable. The party, apart from the leadership, consists of three layers, a layer of party stalwarts—people who have been in the party for years, cannot think of existence outside of the party, and have the attitude, my party, right or wrong… They maintain the party. It is their party in more senses than they think. Despite their devotion the best negative thing that could happen to the party is that these elements should leave in a body. The second layer consists of a younger grouping with similar political ideas as the above but anxious to build the party… Some of them, misguided as they were, did striking work in the unions in New York, Buffalo, and Los Angeles. They do not know what to do next. Finally there are the men who had some leadership in the labor movement and were looking for help, as they saw it—help in the union struggle; genuine proletarian types, Negroes, the youth, eager for knowledge and enthusiastic for the revolution. A party is a whole, a totality, but the leadership must reflect the vanguard of the party. Now the social vanguard of the party is the third element, the least vocal, the least educated in Marxism, the most diffident in expressing themselves among the fast-talking layers above, but revolutionary, sensitive to the movement of the proletariat, and potentially great recruiters, once they clarify themselves. These represent the mass outside.

While beginning as a description of the Workers Party, he is clearly describing Left parties generally. The party reproduced the class hierarchy within it; and was not conscious of it as the enemy within. Then he returns to the WP: "It is precisely here that the WP shows the most bureaucratic tendencies. It has never understood the third layer, never listened to them, never learnt anything from them… Its conception of the relationship of the leadership to the party is only a purer distillation of what it thinks is the relationship between the party and the masses."

This description of the political organization (including his own) was the analysis of State-capitalism applied to organization. State capitalism was the way capital planned its economic and political domination against the rebellion, the creativity, the energy, of the population. Your organization becomes the vehicle for their plan. Simplistic babble about democracy dissolves into dust once you face this hierarchy of layers, which must be organized against.

There has been little will to explore CLR's charge of conservatism within so-called revolutionary organizations. When we asked him where this concept of layers had come from, he always referred us to Lenin. He never said where exactly, but he did quote one precedent. Trotsky, arguing against the split in 1940, had reported Lenin's view of his own party with which he, Trotsky, clearly agreed: "We underestimate the revolutionary movement in the working masses… At the beginning of 1917 Lenin said that the party is ten times more revolutionary than the CC [central committee] and the masses a hundred times more revolutionary than the ranks of the party."

By presuming that the third layer is the vanguard, this analysis confronts the repression of working-class self-activity even within its own anticapitalist organizations. The instruments of that repression are immediately present. Almost invisibly— because it is so common, so taken for granted—those with more formal education, skills, social power, etc., dominate. This hierarchy is not an act of will but the "objective situation." Johnsonites regularly used this phrase. It was a materialist reading of reality. With the best will in the world, the capitalist hierarchy is reproduced against the grassroots with the whole force of capitalist society behind it. To undermine, let alone defeat it, requires far more than voting or democratic rules.

(It was not until the 1960s and the birth first of the Black movement and then of the women's and other movements attacking the social hierarchy that this subtle and not so subtle domination was noticed, categorized and massively opposed.)

The concept of the three layers was first articulated by CLR in this 1947 document. The definitions were refined as they were applied within Johnson-Forest. Those who had had some official posts, for example in trade unions, were clearly no longer third layer. A pamphlet called *Union Committeemen and Wildcat Strikes* showed how a dedicated militant on the lowest rung of union officialdom, taken from the assembly line to deal with workers' grievances against the company, was rapidly corrupted by this relatively minor (but far from trivial) elevation.[3]

The question was: what was to be done about it? How was this hierarchy, often invisible but real and constant, to be undermined?

At the end of the Interim Period, Johnson-Forest returned to the other wing of Trotskyism to try to keep the movement together. It was not possible then to attempt to build the kind of organization we wanted. We kept our heads down, did our work, and avoided political discussions.

Four years later, in 1951, we left Trotskyism altogether. This time it was a principled split; the political direction towards which we were impelled could no longer submit to an increasingly alien politics.

CLR wrote one last document: *The Balance Sheet Completed—Ten Years of American Trotskyism*. It begins: "'Johnson-Forest' has now made its final and complete break with what the Fourth International [the Trotskyist international] of today stands for." He spells out what was fairly obvious, that the 1947 *Balance Sheet* was a critique not only of the WP, but of Trotskyism as a whole.

We left because we were nonaligned: we veered neither toward the support for Stalinism of the SWP which still considered the Soviet Union a workers' State, and which by then claimed that the Red Army had brought socialism to Eastern Europe; nor toward the WP's anti-Stalinism which by then seemed closer to the State Department than to working-class opposition. (Not many years later, shockingly but not surprisingly, the WP dissolved into the Democratic Party and its leadership supported the Vietnam War.)

The Balance Sheet Completed made the case for this final break with Trotskyism. The most exciting of its four sections is called The Life of the Party. Quoting the passages above about the third layer, it goes on to make the case that the break had to take place because our membership was unable to develop within the SWP. It was not theoretical differences that provoked the break, but the political and organizational consequences of these differences.

In *The Balance Sheet Completed*, CLR takes the sectors one at a time.

First "the rank and file worker…native proletarians, white and Negro, men and women… These are the ones who lead the wildcat strikes, symptomatic of the revolt against the bureaucracy. They are not seeking to build caucuses to win posts in unions. They have not joined the party to substitute a good union apparatus for a bad one. They are seeking primarily a revolutionary socialist organization."

Then "The Negroes":

---

3   Martin Glaberman, *Correspondence* 2, no. 9 (1955).

> All politics in the United States are expressed most sharply in the Negro question... The party is not politically educated on the Negro question. The task of the party leaders was to do for the Negroes in the United States what Marx had done in general for the proletariat—establish its role in the transformation of society. It is on this we live. The party did not get it, the Negroes did not get it. The consequence is many painful and some very shameful conflicts.

Followed by "The Women":

> In Los Angeles, one of our younger comrades, without experience, got interested in the woman question.[4] Trained by Johnson-Forest, she without any guidance, went straight to the heart of the question, the proletarian woman. With help from friends inside and outside the party, she sketched out the elements of a theory... Immediately there is a crisis. The S.W.P. does not know anything else about women in the modern world than to tell them that they will gain personal freedom in the party, that imperialism means war, and that their men will be taken away—as characteristic a piece of male chauvinism as you can find.

And finally "Youth":

> On the youth question as on the Negro question, the S.W.P. is blinded by its fear and impotence before the aspirations of those layers of the revolutionary masses who are seeking in the revolutionary party to fortify their instinctive hostility to bourgeois society, their conceptions of a new society and their readiness to work for it.

Exciting, yes, despite outdated language, but a terrible time to have made that leap to independence. It was 1951, and the cold war and McCarthyism were upon us: phones tapped, mail interfered with, visits from the FBI. Some of us lost our jobs (I lost mine), and some were blacklisted (my sister's husband didn't have steady employment for years). When you are under attack some people rise to the occasion but others begin to waver and are tempted to blame the movement rather than the State for difficulties, related or not. Nevertheless, our leadership helped keep us focused.

How did the theory of the third layer shape our now independent organization? We began by putting out a newspaper which everyone, including in our networks, was involved in writing for, editing or commenting on. It had a Women's page, a Negro page, and a Youth page, which were written and edited not only *for* those sectors but *by* them.

By the 1960s, in the United States and elsewhere, underground newspapers mushroomed; all popular, many of them political, where different sectors spoke their minds.

---

4   I was the "younger comrade." One of the party leaders in Los Angeles was a woman. She believed that sexual liberation was the priority for women. I was silently outraged by this self-indulgent trivializing of the enormity of what women were up against.

In some ways they resembled what we were trying to do a decade before: to express the real lives and struggles of the people we were organizing with as well as our own. There were many things we got wrong and didn't know how to do until the movement burst out in the 1960s, but the attempt trained us to concentrate not on recruiting but on involving the public.

Perhaps the most startling Johnson-Forest innovation was the school for the third layer. The leaders were to sit down and learn from us. If I remember rightly, for two or three hours a day for two weeks, two groups of six or eight of us, mixed by race, gender, age, etc., met to discuss with the leadership (but not CLR—he had just been released from immigration detention on Ellis Island and was far from well) and tell them what we thought. What were the topics? I can't remember, though there are two reports, one from each group, which can be dug out.

Every evening after the school CLR would ask how I had got on. One evening I said I didn't agree with Rae, and had told her so. He said, "Well, tomorrow when you go back you will raise the question again."

Next day I did what he said and made my point, but everybody else in the school was against me. I argued but lost. I didn't know what else to do. That night I had to tell him that I had had to let the school move to the next discussion because I was a minority of one. "Look here," he said, "the Russian workers have guns trained against them; that's why they don't talk. What's your excuse?"

Then I understood what the school was about. It was to train us to stand up to our own leaders. It was to train third layer people who are not used to it to express their point of view to those who are "educated" or in other ways more socially powerful, whether or not other third layer people joined us. I think a number of us found our voice. I certainly did.

My close friend Filomena Daddario, also a factory worker, was in the other group, and we compared notes. Her partner was a brainy intellectual, and she had told the school: "The intellectuals talk about working-class instincts. Intellectuals also have instincts. But they're the wrong ones!"

She was about twenty-four years old when she ran for mayor of Oakland, California, to represent us, and to test our ideas and the way we were articulating them. She went about addressing all kinds of organizations. She said she was for socialism and for the rights of workers and of Negroes and of women and of youth— during McCarthyism. Of five candidates, remarkably, she came third. Filomena was a fine speaker, and Oakland is a special city with a socialist history. But Johnson-Forest was also special.

(Of course the second layer wasn't always happy not to be in front and in charge and there were tensions and confrontations, and resentments. But we had CLR on our side—no small matter—and we had to learn to deal with it. But that is another story.)

A form of Johnson-Forest lasted into the 1960s, but the onslaught of the McCarthy witch-hunt including the loss of CLR (forced to leave the United States in 1953) undermined us. Its experience and its ideas continue to be enormously useful to the younger people who hear of them, more every day.

It has been noted that CLR was an early advocate of Black autonomy. He didn't have a problem with women's autonomy either. In Los Angeles, three of us (all housewives) met informally as a women's group from about 1949. But even before that, a resolution I put forward that all the men had to learn to type, was passed unanimously. (Women used to do all the typing in all kinds of organizations.)

How, when others fought to keep the autonomy of women and of people of color, etc., out of their organization? The theory of the third layer is a key. He assumed that, once we were not promoting separatism—a competition with other sectors—what each sector wanted was what the class needed; we were exposing and confronting previously unacknowledged ways in which capitalism exploits, divides, and represses the working class.

But there were other reasons. First, CLR was not threatened by autonomy because his leadership did not depend on having all the answers; it also depended on eliciting answers from others, third layer members first of all. Second, he was himself part of the Black movement; he had urged the Left to accept "the independent validity of the Negro struggle." How could he be against the autonomy of other sectors?

Bearing in mind that the third layer orientation challenged the capitalist hierarchy from the bottom up, we must look again at the work CLR did with Herman Melville, for example. He set out to wrest great literature from the special preserve of intellectuals. He was determined to demonstrate that third layer people could have in some respects a more profound grasp than intellectuals of what great writers set out to describe. But the work had first to be demystified and made accessible. That was the job of leadership.

CLR's analysis of Melville had another purpose as well: it was a way, he said, of getting out of the "holes and corners" into which the Left in the United States had allowed itself to be pushed. Even while fighting his deportation case in 1952, he was speaking at universities about Melville's portrait of the multiracial, multinational working class on the whaling ship, which was a factory, and of the mad, self-indulgent Ahabs who dominated and manipulated them, ruling most of the world. Melville—and Shakespeare, and Milton, etc.—were vehicles that allowed him to make his politics despite McCarthyism.

Finally, *State Capitalism and World Revolution*, written in 1950, contains this short but stunning paragraph, which blew me away when I first read it:

> The first sentence of [Trotsky's] Transitional Program states that the crisis of the revolution is the crisis of revolutionary leadership. This is the reiterated theme.

Exactly the opposite is the case. It is the crisis of the self-mobilization of the proletariat.

If we have to sum up in a few words the political clarity of CLR James (alias J.R. Johnson), these are as good as any. While the Left since the death of Lenin thought that the revolution's success was up to them, CLR's point was that it was up to us, including where necessary against them. We had not sufficiently mobilized ourselves, as was absolutely necessary, to take our movement into our own hands, to make it impossible for any of us to be once removed from our own revolution.

The organizations in which this work was done were small, but their impact was not. The departure from the norm of Left politics that CLR initiated had wide rippling effects. Even when there was no public recognition, and he wasn't even invited to speak, ideas seemed to have a way of disseminating themselves.[5] We would hear that he was spoken of in intellectual, academic, and political circles. Johnson-Forest entered the bones and muscle of the movement and, updated, has shaped the Wages for Housework corner of the movement.

Answers there have been none to CLR's often-quoted question in *Beyond a Boundary*: "What do they know of cricket who only cricket know?" The question implies the answer: Not a lot. We can in turn ask: What do they know of CLR James who know little or nothing of his extraordinarily productive life in the Marxist movement? That question implies a similar answer.

I am grateful to my son Sam Weinstein who helped me recall some of the history in the rewriting of this speech. He grew up and was politically educated in Johnson-Forest. Sam is referred to in Beyond a Boundary *as "the son of our house"; he and CLR were very close.*

---

5   The Left in the UK rarely wanted this famed orator on their platforms in the 1950s and most of the 1960s. And *Beyond a Boundary* could not at first find a publisher. Some of it of course was racism. How much is anyone's guess.

About the Authors

Selma James is a women's rights and antiracist campaigner and author. From 1958 to 1962, she worked with CLR James in the movement for Caribbean federation and independence. In 1972, she founded the International Wages for Housework Campaign, and in 2000 she helped launch the Global Women's Strike whose strategy for change is Invest in Caring Not Killing. She coined the word "unwaged" to describe the caring work women do, and it has since entered the English language to describe all who work without wages on the land, in the home, in the community... In 1975, she became the first spokeswoman of the English Collective of Prostitutes. She is an international point of reference for the International Jewish Anti-Zionist Network (2008). She coauthored the classic *The Power of Women and the Subversion of the Community* which launched the "domestic labour debate." She has addressed the power relations within the working-class movement, and how to organize across sectors despite divisions of sex, race, age, occupation, nationality, disability, etc., South and North.

Other publications include *A Woman's Place* (1952), *Women, the Unions, and Work, or What Is Not to Be Done* (1972), *Sex, Race, and Class* (1974), *Wageless of the World* (1974), *The Rapist Who Pays the Rent* (1982, coauthor), *The Ladies and the Mammies: Jane Austen and Jean Rhys* (1983), *Marx and Feminism* (1983), *Hookers in the House of the Lord* (1983), *Strangers & Sisters: Women, Race, and Immigration* (1985, ed. & introduction), *The Global Kitchen: The Case for Counting Unwaged Work* (1985 and 1995), *The Milk of Human Kindness: Defending Breastfeeding from the AIDS Industry and the Global Market* (2005, coauthor).

Nina López is the joint coordinator of the Global Women's Strike. Her writings and edited volumes include: *Prostitute Women and AIDS—Resisting the Virus of Repression* (1988), *Some Mother's Daughter: The Hidden Movement of Prostitute Women Against Violence* (1998), *The Milk of Human Kindness* (2002), and *Creating a Caring Economy: Nora Castañeda and the Women's Development Bank of Venezuela* (2006).

Marcus Rediker is a an activist and Distinguished Professor of Atlantic History at the University of Pittsburgh. His books include: *Between the Devil and the Deep Blue Sea: : Merchant Seaman, Pirates, and the Anglo-American Maritime World, 1700-1750* (1987), *The Many-Headed Hydra: Sailors, Slaves, Commoners and the Hidden History of the Revolutionary Atlantic* (2000, coauthor), *Villains of All Nations: Atlantic Pirates in the Golden Age* (2004), *The Slave Ship: A Human History* (2007), and many more.

About
PM Press

PM Press was founded at the end of 2007 by a small collection of folks with decades of publishing, media, and organizing experience. PM Press co-conspirators have published and distributed hundreds of books, pamphlets, CDs, and DVDs. Members of PM have founded enduring book fairs, spearheaded victorious tenant organizing campaigns, and worked closely with bookstores, academic conferences, and even rock bands to deliver political and challenging ideas to all walks of life. We're old enough to know what we're doing and young enough to know what's at stake.

We seek to create radical and stimulating fiction and nonfiction books, pamphlets, t-shirts, visual and audio materials to entertain, educate, and inspire you. We aim to distribute these through every available channel with every available technology, whether that means you are seeing anarchist classics at our bookfair stalls; reading our latest vegan cookbook at the café; downloading geeky fiction e-books; or digging new music and timely videos from our website.

Contact us for direct ordering and questions about all PM Press releases, as well as manuscript submissions, review copy requests, foreign rights sales, author interviews, to book an author for an event, and to have PM Press attend your bookfair:

PM Press • PO Box 23912 • Oakland, CA 94623
510-658-3906 • info@pmpress.org

Buy books and stay on top of what we are doing at:

www.pmpress.org

MONTHLY SUBSCRIPTION PROGRAM

These are indisputably momentous times—the financial system is melting down globally and the Empire is stumbling. Now more than ever there is a vital need for radical ideas.

In the four years since its founding—and on a mere shoestring—PM Press has risen to the formidable challenge of publishing and distributing knowledge and entertainment for the struggles ahead. With over 175 releases to date, we have published an impressive and stimulating array of literature, art, music, politics, and culture. Using every available medium, we've succeeded in connecting those hungry for ideas and information to those putting them into practice.

Friends of PM allows you to directly help impact, amplify, and revitalize the discourse and actions of radical writers, filmmakers, and artists. It provides us with a stable foundation from which we can build upon our early successes and provides a much-needed subsidy for the materials that can't necessarily pay their own way. You can help make that happen—and receive every new title automatically delivered to your door once a month—by joining as a Friend of PM Press. And, we'll throw in a free T-Shirt when you sign up.

Here are your options:

- $25 a month: Get all books and pamphlets plus 50% discount on all webstore purchases

- $40 a month: Get all PM Press releases (including CDs and DVDs) plus 50% discount on all webstore purchases

- $100 a month: Superstar—Everything plus PM merchandise, free downloads, and 50% discount on all webstore purchases

For those who can't afford $25 or more a month, we're introducing Sustainer Rates at $15, $10 and $5. Sustainers get a free PM Press t-shirt and a 50% discount on all purchases from our website.

Your Visa or Mastercard will be billed once a month, until you tell us to stop. Or until our efforts succeed in bringing the revolution around. Or the financial meltdown of Capital makes plastic redundant. Whichever comes first.

A New Notion

Two Works by CLR James:
"Every Cook Can Govern" and
"The Invading Socialist Society"

CLR James • Edited by Noel Ignatiev
$16.95 • ISBN: 978-1-60486-047-4

CLR James was a leading figure in the independence movement in the West Indies, and the Black and working-class movements in both Britain and the United States. As a major contributor to Marxist and revolutionary theory, his project was to discover, document, and elaborate the aspects of working-class activity that constitute the revolution in today's world. In this volume, Noel Ignatiev, author of *How the Irish Became White*, provides an extensive introduction to James's life and thought, before presenting two critical works that together illustrate the tremendous breadth and depth of James's worldview.

"The Invading Socialist Society," for James the fundamental document of his political tendency, shows clearly the power of James's political acumen and its relevance in today's world with a clarity of analysis that anticipated future events to a remarkable extent. "Every Cook Can Govern," is a short and eminently readable piece counterpoising direct with representative democracy, and getting to the heart of how we should relate to one another. Together these two works represent the principal themes that run through James's life: implacable hostility toward all "condescending saviors" of the working class, and undying faith in the power of ordinary people to build a new world.

> "It remains remarkable how far ahead of his time he was on so many issues."
>
> —*New Society*

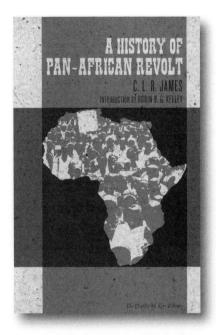

A History of Pan-African Revolt

CLR James • Introduction
by: Robin D.G. Kelley
$16.95 • ISBN: 978-1-60486-095-5

Originally published in England in 1938 (the same year as his magnum opus *The Black Jacobins*), and expanded in 1969, this work remains the classic account of global Black Resistance. Robin D.G. Kelley's substantial introduction contextualizes the work in the history and ferment of the times, and explores it's ongoing relevance today.

"*A History of Pan-African Revolt* is one of those rare books that continues to strike a chord of urgency, even half a century after it was first published. Time and time again, its lessons have proven to be valuable and relevant for understanding liberation movements in Africa and the diaspora. Each generation who has had the opportunity to read this small book finds new insights, new lessons, new visions for their own age… No piece of literature can substitute for a crystal ball, and only religious fundamentalists believe that a book can provide comprehensive answers to all questions. But if nothing else, *A History of Pan-African Revolt* leaves us with two incontrovertible facts. First, as long as Black people are denied freedom, humanity and a decent standard of living, they will continue to revolt. Second, unless these revolts involve the ordinary masses and take place on their own terms, they have no hope of succeeding." —From the Introduction by Robin D.G. Kelley

"I wish my readers to understand the history of Pan-African Revolt. They fought, they suffered—they are still fighting. Once we understand that, we can tackle our problems with the necessary mental equilibrium."

—CLR James

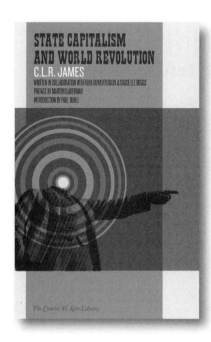

State Capitalism and World Revolution

CLR James, Raya Dunayevskaya, and Grace Lee Boggs •
Introduction by Paul Buhle •
Preface by Martin Glaberman
$16.95 • ISBN: 978-1-60486-092-4

Sixty years ago, CLR James and a small circle of collaborators set forth a revolutionary critique of industrial civilization. Their vision possessed a striking originality. So insular was the political context of their theoretical breakthroughs, however, and so thoroughly did their optimistic expectations for working class activity defy trends away from class and social issues to the so-called 'End of Ideology,' that the documents of the signal effort never reached public view. Happily, times have changed. Readers have discovered much, even after all these years, to challenge Marxist (or any other) orthodoxy. They will never find a more succinct version of James's general conclusions than *State Capitalism and World Revolution*. In this slim volume, James and his comrades successfully predict the future course of Marxism.

Written in collaboration with Raya Dunayevskaya and Grace Lee Boggs, this is another pioneering critique of Lenin and Trotsky, and reclamation of Marx, from the West Indian scholar and activist, CLR James. Originally published in 1950, this edition includes the original preface from Martin Glaberman, and a new introduction from Paul Buhle.

> "When one looks back over the last twenty years to those men who were most far-sighted, who first began to tease out the muddle of ideology in our times, who were at the same time Marxists with a hard theoretical basis, and close students of society, humanists with a tremendous response to and understanding of human culture, Comrade James is one of the first one thinks of."
>
> —E.P. Thompson

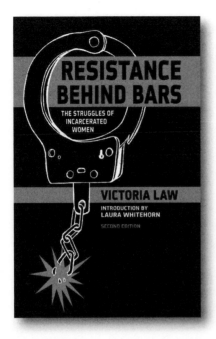

Resistance Behind Bars

The Struggles Of Incarcerated Women, 2nd Edition

Victoria Law • Introduction
by Laura Whitehorn
$20.00 • ISBN: 978-1-60486-583-7

In 1974, women imprisoned at New York's maximum-security prison at Bedford Hills staged what is known as the August Rebellion. Protesting the brutal beating of a fellow prisoner, the women fought off guards, holding seven of them hostage, and took over sections of the prison.

While many have heard of the 1971 Attica prison uprising, the August Rebellion remains relatively unknown even in activist circles. *Resistance Behind Bars* is determined to challenge and change such oversights. As it examines daily struggles against appalling prison conditions and injustices, *Resistance* documents both collective organizing and individual resistance among women incarcerated in the U.S. Emphasizing women's agency in resisting the conditions of their confinement through forming peer education groups, clandestinely arranging ways for children to visit mothers in distant prisons and raising public awareness about their lives, *Resistance* seeks to spark further discussion and research into the lives of incarcerated women and galvanize much-needed outside support for their struggles.

This updated and revised edition of the 2009 PASS Award winning book includes a new chapter about transgender, transsexual, intersex, and gender-variant people in prison.

> "This insightful book calls attention to the power, spirit, and courage of women who find themselves behind bars in the era of mass incarceration. By raising up their voices and stories, and by honoring their struggles, this book makes an important contribution to the growing movement to end prisons as we know them."
>
> —Michelle Alexander, civil rights lawyer, advocate, legal scholar and author
> of *The New Jim Crow: Mass Incarceration in the Age of Colorblindness*

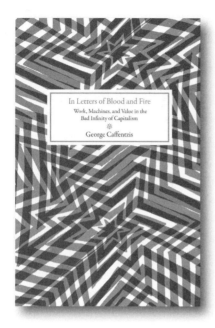

In Letters of Blood and Fire

Work, Machines, and Value in the Bad Infinity of Capitalism

George Caffentzis

In Letters of Blood and Fire

Work, Machines, and Value in the Bad Infinity of Capitalism

George Caffentzis

$19.95 • ISBN: 978-1-60486-335-2

Karl Marx wrote that the only way to write about the origins of capitalism in the sixteenth century is in the letters of blood and fire used to drive workers from the common lands, forests and waters. This collection of essays by autonomist Marxist George Caffentzis argues that the same is true for the annals of 21st century capitalism. Information technology, immaterial production, financialization, and globalization have been trumpeted as inaugurating a new phase of capitalism that put it beyond its violent origins. Instead of being in a period of major social and economic novelty, however, the course of the last decades has been a return to the fire and blood of struggles at the advent of capitalism.

Emphasizing class struggles that have proliferated across the social body of global capitalism, Caffentzis shows how a wide range of conflicts and antagonisms in the labor-capital relation express themselves within and against the work process. These struggles are so central to the dynamic of the system that even the most sophisticated machines cannot liberate capitalism from class struggle and the need for labor. Moreover, the theme of war and crisis permeate the text but are also given singular emphasis, documenting the peculiar way in which capital perpetuates violence and proliferates misery on a world scale. The collection draws upon a careful re-reading of Marx's thought in order to elucidate political concerns of the day. The essays in this collection have been written to contribute to the debates of the anticapitalist movement over the last thirty years. This book is meant to make them more available as tools for the struggle in this period of transition to a common future.

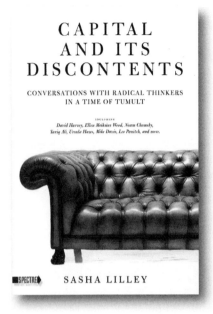

CAPITAL
AND ITS
DISCONTENTS

CONVERSATIONS WITH RADICAL THINKERS
IN A TIME OF TUMULT

INCLUDING
David Harvey, Ellen Meiksins Wood, Noam Chomsky,
Tariq Ali, Ursula Huws, Mike Davis, Leo Panitch, and more.

SASHA LILLEY

Capital and Its Discontents

Conversations with Radical Thinkers in a Time of Tumult

Edited by Sasha Lilley

$20.00 • ISBN: 978-1-60486-334-5

Capitalism is stumbling, empire is faltering, and the planet is thawing. Yet many people are still grasping to understand these multiple crises and to find a way forward to a just future. Into the breach come the essential insights of *Capital and Its Discontents*, which cut through the gristle to get to the heart of the matter about the nature of capitalism and imperialism, capitalism's vulnerabilities at this conjuncture—and what can we do to hasten its demise.

Through a series of incisive conversations with some of the most eminent thinkers and political economists on the Left—including David Harvey, Ellen Meiksins Wood, Mike Davis, Leo Panitch, Tariq Ali, and Noam Chomsky—*Capital and Its Discontents* illuminates the dynamic contradictions undergirding capitalism and the potential for its dethroning. The book challenges conventional wisdom on the Left about the nature of globalization, neoliberalism and imperialism, as well as the agrarian question in the Global South. It probes deeply into the roots of the global economic meltdown, the role of debt and privatization in dampening social revolt, and considers capitalism's dynamic ability to find ever new sources of accumulation—whether through imperial or ecological plunder or the commodification of previously unpaid female labor.

The Left luminaries in *Capital and Its Discontents* look at potential avenues out of the mess—as well as wrong turns and needless detours—drawing lessons from the history of post-colonial states in the Global South, struggles against imperialism past and present, the eternal pendulum swing of radicalism, the corrosive legacy of postmodernism, and the potentialities of the radical humanist tradition. At a moment when capitalism as a system is more reviled than ever, here is an indispensable toolbox of ideas for action by some of the most brilliant thinkers of our times.

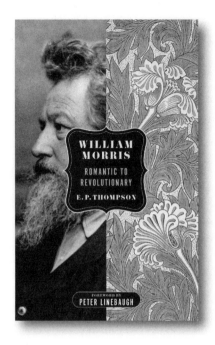

William Morris

Romantic to Revolutionary

E.P. Thompson

$32.95 • ISBN: 978-1-60486-243-0

William Morris—the great nineteenth century craftsman, designer, poet and writer—remains a monumental figure whose influence resonates powerfully today. As an intellectual (and author of the seminal utopian *News From Nowhere*), his concern with artistic and human values led him to cross what he called the 'river of fire' and become a committed socialist—committed not to some theoretical formula but to the day by day struggle of working women and men in Britain and to the evolution of his ideas about art, about work and about how life should be lived.

Many of his ideas accorded none too well with the reforming tendencies dominant in the Labour movement, nor with those of 'orthodox' Marxism, which has looked elsewhere for inspiration. Both sides have been inclined to venerate Morris rather than to pay attention to what he said.

Originally written less than a decade before his groundbreaking *The Making of the English Working Class*, E.P. Thompson brought to this biography his now trademark historical mastery, passion, wit, and essential sympathy. It remains unsurpassed as the definitive work on this remarkable figure, by the major British historian of the twentieth century.

> "Thompson's is the first biography to do justice to Morris's political thought and so assemble the man whole… It is not only the standard biography of Morris; it makes us realize, as no other writer has done, how completely admirable a man this Victorian was—how consistent and honest to himself and others, how incapable of cruelty or jargon and, above all, how free."
>
> —Robert Hughes, *Time Magazine*